BENCHMARK SERIES

Microsoft® EXCEL 2002

EXPERT CERTIFICATION

APPROVED COURSEWARE

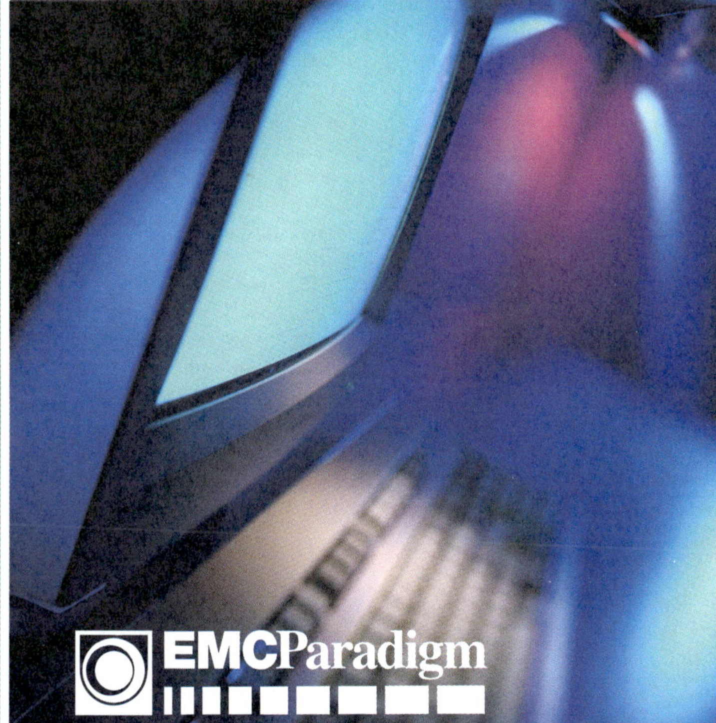

EMCParadigm

MEREDITH FLYNN
Bowling Green University
Bowling Green, Ohio

Senior Developmental Editor	Sonja M. Brown
Developmental Editor	Tom Modl
Special Projects Coordinator	Joan D'Onofrio
Senior Designer	Jennifer Wreisner
Editorial Assistant	Susan Capecchi
Copy Editor	Sharon O'Donnell
Proofreader	Lynn Reichel
Indexer	Donald Glassman

Publishing Team—George Provol, Publisher; Janice Johnson, Director of Product Development; Tony Galvin, Acquisitions Editor; Lori Landwer, Marketing Manager; Shelley Clubb, Electronic Design and Production Manager

Acknowledgments—The author and publisher wish to thank the following reviewers for their technical and academic assistance in testing exercises and assessing instruction:

- Christie Jahn, Lincoln Land Community College, Springfield, Illinois
- David Parker, St. Charles Community College, St. Charles, Missouri

Special thanks to Christie Jahn for preparing Internet Projects and Job Study scenarios as part of the Unit Performance Assessment sections.

Library of Congress Cataloging-in-Publication Data
Flynn, Meredith.
Microsoft Excel 2002: expert certification / Meredith Flynn.
p.cm. – (Benchmark series)
Includes index.
ISBN 0-7638-1447-4 (Text & CD-ROM)
1. Microsoft Excel for Windows. 2. Business—Computer Programs. 3. Electronic spreadsheets. I. Title. II. Benchmark series (Saint Paul, Minn.)

HF5548.4.M523 F552 2002
005.369-dc21 2001040240

Text: ISBN 0-7638-1447-4
Order Number: 05546

Published by **EMC**Paradigm
875 Montreal Way
St. Paul, MN 55102

(800) 535-6865
E-mail: educate@emcp.com
Web site: www.emcp.com

Printed in the United States of America
10 9 8 7 6 5 4 3 2 1

CONTENTS

WELCOME

You are about to begin working with a textbook that is part of the Benchmark Office XP Series. The word *Benchmark* in the title holds a special significance in terms of *what* you will learn and *how* you will learn. *Benchmark*, according to *Webster's Dictionary*, means "something that serves as a standard by which others may be measured or judged." In this text, you will learn the Microsoft Office User Specialist (MOUS) skills required for certification on the Core and/or Expert level of one or more major applications within the Office XP suite. These skills are benchmarks by which you will be evaluated, should you choose to take one or more certification exams.

The design and teaching approach of this textbook also serve as a benchmark for instructional materials on software programs. Features and commands are presented in a clear, straightforward way, and each short section of instruction is followed by an exercise that lets you practice using the new feature. Gradually, as you move through each chapter, you will build your skills to the point of mastery. At the end of a chapter, you are offered the opportunity to demonstrate your newly acquired competencies—to prove you have met the benchmarks for using the Office suite or an individual program. At the completion of the text, you are well on your way to becoming a successful computer user.

EMCParadigm's Office XP Benchmark Series includes textbooks on Office XP, Word 2002, Excel 2002, Access 2002, PowerPoint 2002, Publisher 2002, Outlook 2002, and FrontPage 2002. Note that the programs include the year 2002 in their name, while the suite itself is called Office XP (for "experience"). Each book includes a Student CD, which contains prekeyed documents and files required for completing the exercises. A CD icon and folder name displayed on the opening page of each chapter indicates that you need to copy a folder of files from the CD before beginning the chapter exercises. *(See the inside back cover for instructions on copying a folder.)*

Introducing Microsoft Office XP

Microsoft Office XP, released in May 2001, is a suite of programs designed to improve productivity and efficiency in workplace, school, and home settings. A suite is a group of programs that are sold as a package and are designed to be used together, making it possible to exchange files among the programs. The major applications included in Office are Word, a word processing program; Excel, a spreadsheet program; Access, a database management program; PowerPoint, a slide presentation program; and Outlook, a desktop information management program.

Using the Office suite offers significant advantages over working with individual programs developed by different software vendors. The programs in the Office suite use similar toolbars, buttons, icons, and menus, which means that once you learn the basic features of one program, you can use those same features in the other programs. This easy transfer of knowledge decreases the learning time and allows you to concentrate on the unique commands and options within each program. The compatibility of the programs creates seamless integration of data within and between programs and lets the operator use the program most appropriate for the required tasks.

The number of programs in the Office XP suite varies by the package, or edition. Four editions are available:

- **Standard:** Word, Excel, Outlook, PowerPoint
- **Professional:** Word, Excel, Outlook, PowerPoint, and Access
- **Professional Special Edition:** All Professional package programs plus FrontPage, Publisher, and SharePoint. This edition is available only for a limited time and only to current Office users.
- **Developer:** All Professional package programs (except SharePoint) plus Developer tools

New Features in Office XP

Users of previous editions of Office will find that the essential features that have made Office popular still form the heart of the suite. New enhancements focus on collaboration, or the ability for multiple users to work together on the same document from different locations over the Internet. Another highlight is the Smart Tag feature, which is an icon that when clicked offers a list of commands that are especially useful for the particular job being done. In Excel, for example, a Smart Tag might offer the ability to update a formula or edit an error. A more comprehensive kind of targeted assistance is offered in a new Task Pane, which is a narrow window that appears at the right of the screen to display commands relevant to the current task. Speech recognition technology is available with this edition, offering users the ability to dictate text into any Office program. This feature must be installed separately.

Structure of the Benchmark Textbooks

Users of the Core Certification texts and the complete application textbooks may begin their course with an overview of computer hardware and software, offered in the *Getting Started* section at the beginning of the book. Your instructor may also ask you to complete the *Windows 2000* and the *Internet Explorer* sections so you become familiar with the computer's operating system and the essential tools for using the Internet.

Instruction on the major programs within the Office suite is presented in units of four chapters each. Both the Core and Expert levels contain two units, which culminate with performance assessments to check your knowledge and skills. Each chapter contains the following sections:

- performance objectives that identify specifically what you are expected to learn
- instructional text that introduces and explains new concepts and features
- step-by-step, hands-on exercises following each section of instruction
- a chapter summary
- a knowledge self-check called Concepts Check
- skill assessment exercises called Skills Check

Exercises offered at the end of units provide writing and research opportunities that will strengthen your performance in other college courses as well as on the job. The final activities simulate interesting projects you could encounter in the workplace.

Benchmark Series Ancillaries

The Benchmark Series includes some important resources that will help you succeed in your computer applications courses:

Online Resource Center

Internet Resource Centers hosted by EMC/Paradigm provide additional material for students and teachers using the Benchmark books. Online you will find Web links, updates to textbooks, study tips, quizzes and assignments, and supplementary projects.

Class Connection

Available for both the WebCT and Blackboard e-learning platforms, EMC/Paradigm's Class Connection is a course management tool for traditional and distance learning. The Class Connection allows students to access the course syllabus and assignment schedule online, provides self-quizzes and study aids, and facilitates communication among students and instructors via e-mail and e-discussions.

MOUS CERTIFICATION

APPROVED COURSEWARE

What Does This Logo Mean?

It means this courseware has been approved by the Microsoft® Office User Specialist Program to be among the finest available for learning Microsoft Excel 2002. It also means that upon completion of this courseware, you may be prepared to become a Microsoft Office User Specialist.

What Is a Microsoft Office User Specialist?

A Microsoft Office User Specialist is an individual who has certified his or her skills in one or more of the Microsoft Office desktop applications of Microsoft Word, Microsoft Excel, Microsoft PowerPoint®, Microsoft Outlook® or Microsoft Access, or in Microsoft Project. The Microsoft Office User Specialist Program typically offers certification exams at the "Core" and "Expert" skill levels. * The Microsoft Office User Specialist Program is the only Microsoft approved program in the world for certifying proficiency in Microsoft Office desktop applications and Microsoft Project. This certification can be a valuable asset in any job search or career advancement.

More Information

- To learn more about becoming a Microsoft Office User Specialist, visit www.mous.net.
- To purchase a Microsoft Office User Specialist certification exam, visit www.DesktopIQ.com.
- To learn about other Microsoft Office User Specialist approved courseware from EMC/Paradigm, visit www.emcp.com/college_division/MOUS_ready.php.

EMC/Paradigm Publishing is independent from Microsoft Corporation and not affiliated with Microsoft in any manner. This publication may be used in assisting students to prepare for a Microsoft office User Specialist Exam. Neither Microsoft, its designated review company, nor EMC/Paradigm Publishing warrants that use of this publication will ensure passing the relevant exam.

---

* The availability of Microsoft Office User Specialist certification exams varies by application, application version and language. Visit www.mous.net for exam availability.

EXCEL

EXPERT LEVEL UNIT 1: ADVANCED FORMATTING AND FUNCTIONS

Formatting Excel Worksheets Using Advanced Formatting Techniques

Working with Templates and Workbooks

Using Advanced Functions

Working with Lists

MICROSOFT® EXCEL 2002

EXPERT BENCHMARK MOUS SKILLS-UNIT 1

Reference No.	Skill	Pages
Ex2002e-2	**Managing Workbooks**	
Ex2002e-2-1	Create, edit, and apply templates	
	Creating and editing workbook templates	E43-E47; E47-E50
	Creating a user-defined template and using it to create new workbooks	E47-E50
Ex2002e-2-2	Create workspaces	
	Creating a workspace made up of several workbooks	E50-E52; E54-E55
Ex 2002e-2-3	Use Data Consolidation	
	Consolidating data from several worksheets	E52-E54
Ex2002e-3	**Formatting Numbers**	
Ex2002e-3-1	Create and apply custom number formats	
	Creating and applying a custom number format	E5-E7; E10-E11
Ex2002e-3-2	Use conditional formats	
	Using conditional formats	E20-E22; E23-E25
Ex2002e-4	**Working with Ranges**	
Ex2002e-4-1	Use named ranges in formulas	
	Naming ranges	E84-E85; E87-E88
	Using named range references in formulas	E85-E86; E87-E88
Ex2002e-4-2	Use Lookup and Reference functions	
	Applying HLOOKUP and VLOOKUP	E86-E88
Ex2002e-7	**Summarizing Data**	
Ex2002e-7-1	Use subtotals with lists and ranges	
	Including subtotals in worksheets	E123-E126
Ex2002e-7-2	Define and apply filters	
	Using custom filters	E127-E129
Ex2002e-7-3	Add group and outline criteria to ranges	
	Applying grouping and outlining to structured data	E119-E122
Ex2002e-7-4	Use data validation	
	Including data validation criteria in cells	E105-E111
Ex2002e-9	**Workgroup Collaboration**	
Ex2002e-9-2	Create a shared workbook	
	Creating shared workbooks	E58-E63

CHAPTER 1

FORMATTING EXCEL WORKSHEETS USING ADVANCED FORMATTING TECHNIQUES

PERFORMANCE OBJECTIVES

Upon successful completion of chapter 1, you will be able to:

- **Apply accounting, fraction, and scientific formats**
- **Create and apply custom number formats**
- **Format large labels**
- **Automatically adjust column widths and row heights**
- **Create, apply, and edit styles**
- **Use the Format Painter**
- **Format a worksheet by adding borders and shading**
- **Apply formatting to a worksheet using one of Excel's predesigned AutoFormats**
- **Create and use conditional formatting**
- **Adjust the layout of a worksheet**
- **Use the Paste Special command**
- **Hide and unhide rows, columns, and sheets**
- **Rename sheets**
- **Select colors for worksheet tabs**
- **Format large worksheets**

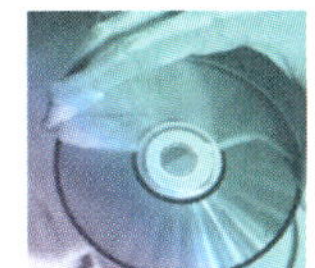

Excel Chapter 01E

Excel includes many formatting features beyond the basic options found on the Formatting toolbar. Although worksheets are commonly used to manipulate financial data, they are also used in many other fields, including science and engineering. Some of these specialized fields use Excel's more advanced formatting features, such as fraction and scientific number formats. In some cases, the numbering format that is needed for a particular worksheet may not be included as one of Excel's preset number formats, in which case a custom format can be created. In other cases, a particular format may be needed only in certain circumstances, in which case a conditional format can be created. An especially large worksheet can also present a formatting challenge as you try to fit the worksheet on as few pages as possible while making it as easy to read and understand as possible.

In this chapter you will learn many advanced formatting techniques that will help you manage not only the most complex or challenging worksheet but also the most basic worksheet. These techniques will help save you time and will help to make your worksheets as readable as possible.

Applying Number Formats

HINT

The three frequently used number formats, Currency, Comma, and Percent, are available as buttons on the Formatting toolbar.

In Excel there are 12 categories by which numbers can be formatted. These categories are found in the Format Cells dialog box, which is accessed either by clicking Format and then Cells or by right-clicking the cell to be formatted and then clicking Format Cells from the shortcut menu. Click the Number tab on the Format Cells dialog box, and all the available categories are displayed in the Category list box, as shown in figure 1.1.

FIGURE 1.1 *Excel's Number Formats*

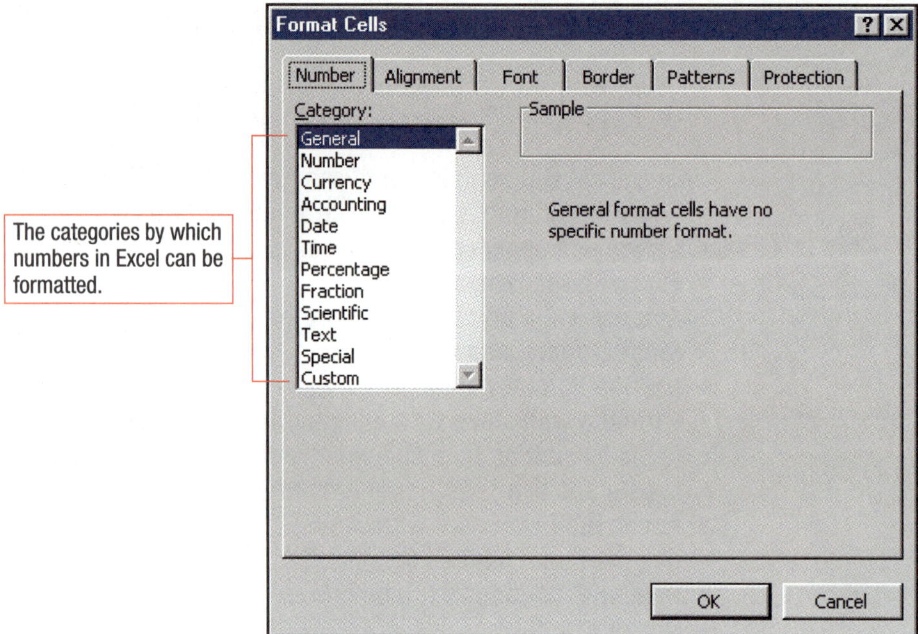

The first three categories listed, General, Number, and Currency, are probably the three most frequently used categories. But some of the more specialized categories, such as Accounting, Fraction, and Scientific, are quite useful as well. The difference between the Currency and Accounting formats is that the Accounting format lines up the currency symbols and the Currency format does not. The Fraction format enables you to display how fractions are displayed in the cells. The Scientific format is used for very large or very small numbers. Engineers and scientists often use the Scientific format, which is also called scientific notation. For example, the Andromeda galaxy (the closest one to our Milky Way galaxy) contains at least 200,000,000,000 stars. Scientists commonly work with such large numbers, so they must use an easier way to write them rather than enter all those zeros. If you entered the number 250,000,000,000, for example, and formatted it as Scientific, it would look like 2.5E+11 on the worksheet. The number after the *E* refers to how many places to the right you have to move the decimal point.

Creating Custom Formats

The last option in the Category list box on the Format Cells dialog box is Custom. This option allows you to create your own format. To create a custom format, first select the cells to which you want the format applied, right-click one of the selected cells, click Format Cells from the shortcut menu, and then click the Number tab. Click *Custom*, the last option in the Category list box. The Type box is displayed, as shown in figure 1.2. The default data that is entered into the Type box depends on the current format of the selected cells.

HINT

A custom numeric format can have up to four parts: a positive number format, a negative number format, a format for zeros, and a format for text. Semicolons are used to separate the parts.

FIGURE 1.2 ***The Custom Option from the Category List Box***

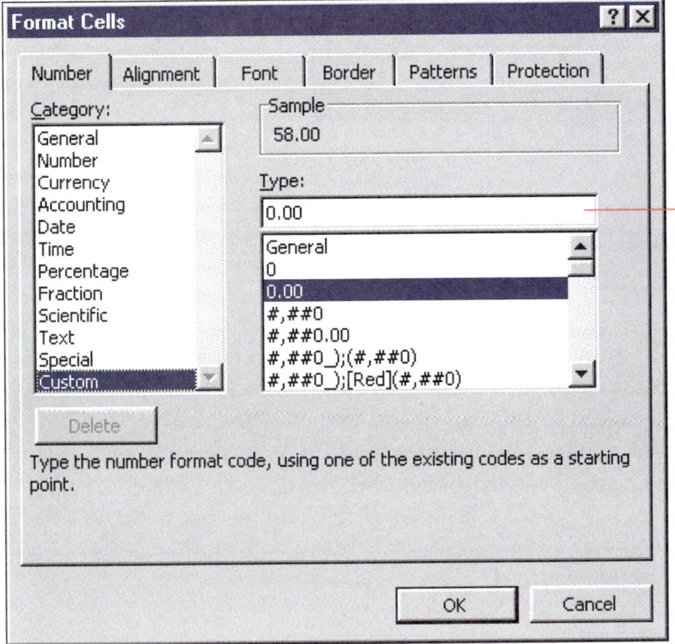

The Type box becomes available when the Custom option from the Category list box is selected.

To create a custom format, enter the desired format in the Type box. If you are entering text that you want to appear, you must enclose the text with quotation marks. For example, you want to create a custom format that uses the text *meters*. You would place the insertion point to the right of the last entry in the Type box, press the spacebar once, and then enter “meters,” as shown in figure 1.3.

FIGURE 1.3 *Creating a Custom Format in the Type Box*

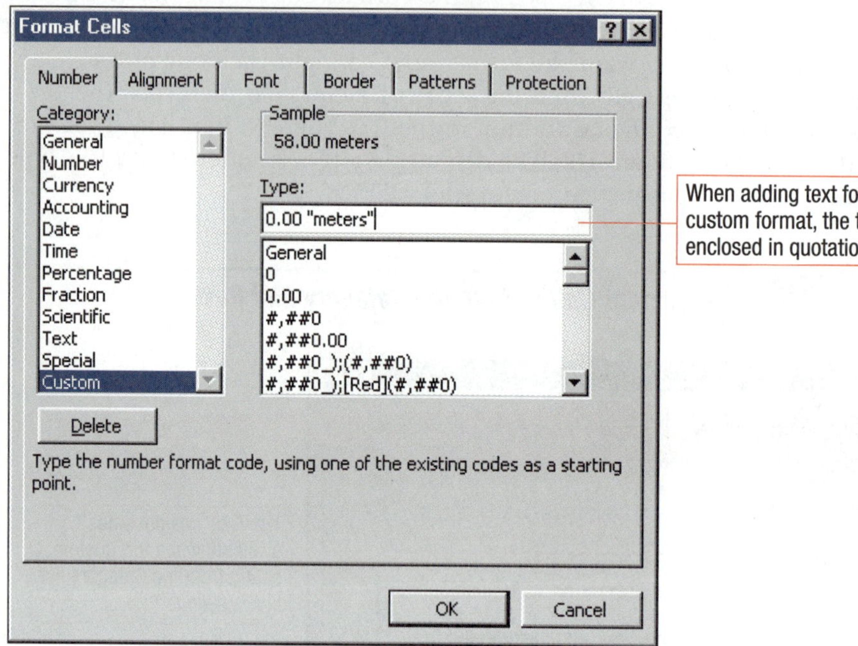

When adding text for a custom format, the text must be enclosed in quotation marks.

Numeric, date, and time formatting codes can be used when creating custom formats. These codes are listed in table 1.1. As is shown in figure 1.4, once you have created a custom format, it is added to the end of the Type list box so that you can use it again. If you want to delete a custom format that you have created, select the format you want to delete from the Type list box and then click the Delete button.

FIGURE 1.4 *Applying and Deleting a Custom Format*

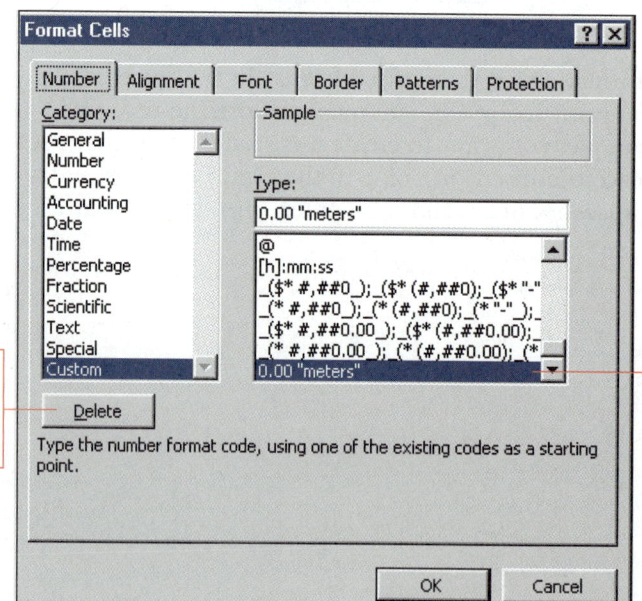

To delete a custom format, select the format to be deleted from the Type list box and press the Delete button.

When you create a custom format, it is added to the end of the Type list. To apply the format elsewhere in the worksheet, simply select the custom format from the Type list box.

TABLE 1.1 Numeric, Date, and Time Formatting Codes

Code	Description
Numeric Formatting Codes	
#	Used to hold the place for a digit. Insignificant zeros are not displayed.
0	Used to hold the place for a digit. Zeros are displayed.
?	Used to hold the place for a digit. Insignificant zeros are represented by a space.
.	Decimal point.
,	Thousands separator.
%	Percentage sign. Entry is multiplied by 100.
;	Used to separate positive number format from negative number format.
_	Used to skip the width of the next character. For example, entering _) skips the width of the right parenthesis character.
/	Used as a separator for fractions.
"text"	Quotation marks are used to insert specified text.
[color]	Braces are used to format entry as specified color.
@	Used to hold the place where user-input text is to appear.
Date Formatting Codes	
m	Displays the month as a number (1, 2, 3, ...10, 11, 12).
mm	Displays the month as a number with a leading zero (01, 02, 03...).
mmm	Displays the month as a three-letter abbreviation (Jan, Feb, Mar...).
mmmm	Displays the month as a complete name (January, February, March...).
d	Displays the day of the month as a number (2, 18, 29).
dd	Displays the day of the month as a number with a leading zero (01, 04, 08).
ddd	Displays the day of the week as a three-letter abbreviation (Mon, Tue, Wed).
dddd	Displays the day of the week as a complete name (Monday, Tuesday, Wednesday).
yy	Displays the year as a two-digit number (92, 94, 98).
yyyy	Displays the year as a complete number (1994, 1998, 2000).
Time Formatting Codes	
h	Displays the hour as a number (1, 8, 10).
hh	Displays the hour as a number with a leading zero (03, 05, 08).
m	Displays the minutes as a number (5, 38, 46).
mm	Displays the minutes as a number with a leading zero (03, 06, 09).
s	Displays the seconds as a number (7, 34, 56).
ss	Displays the seconds as a number with a leading zero (03, 05, 08).
AM/PM	Displays either AM or PM to indicate AM or PM time.
A/P	Displays either A or P to indicate AM or PM time.

Formatting Large Labels

HINT

If at a later time you wish to undo the effects of using the Merge and Center button, right-click the merged cell, click Format cells, click the Alignment tab, click the Merge cells check box so that it is no longer selected, and click OK.

Labels are used as headings to identify the contents of a row or column. If a label on a worksheet is quite large, it may make the worksheet's format look awkward. For example, if the longest entry in a column is only 5 digits, but the label for that column is 50 characters, there will be a lot of wasted space, since the column has to be wide enough to accommodate the label.

Large labels can be handled a couple of different ways in Excel. First, if the label does not have to be confined to one column, the Merge and Center button is useful for centering a label across several columns. To use the Merge and Center button, first enter the label and then select all the cells across which the label is to be centered. Next, click the Merge and Center button. All the cells that were selected are merged into one cell and the label is centered within that one cell. Using the Merge and Center button is useful, for example, for centering a label over an entire worksheet that is made up of many columns.

Merge and Center

Large labels can be handled in several ways, which are found on the Alignment tab of the Format Cells dialog box, shown in figure 1.5. To access these options, right-click the cell containing the label and then click Format Cells on the shortcut menu. On the Format Cells dialog box, click the Alignment tab.

FIGURE 1.5 ***The Format Cells Dialog Box with Alignment Tab Selected***

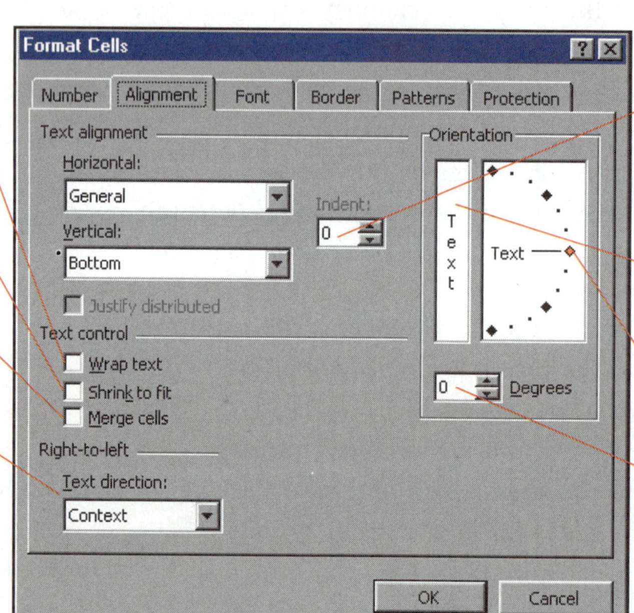

The options under the Text control feature help you manage large labels. Selecting the Wrap text option wraps the label within the cell so that it takes up two or more lines. Selecting the Shrink to fit option reduces the label as necessary to make it all fit within one cell. If two or more cells have been selected, selecting the Merge cells option merges the selected cells into one cell.

The Orientation feature offers another way to handle large labels. By clicking and dragging the red dot, you can angle the label within the cell. As you drag the red dot, the degrees of the angle are displayed in the Degrees box. You can also just enter the degrees of the angle for the label in the Degrees box. If you want the text in the label to be printed vertically, with one character directly underneath another, click the option under Orientation that displays the letters in the word "text" one underneath another.

HINT

Adjust the column to the width you want it to be *before* issuing the command to Wrap Text.

HINT

If under Orientation you choose to have the labels displayed vertically, you should also make a selection from the Vertical drop-down list box, under Text alignment. A vertical label can be placed within a cell at the top, in the center, at the bottom or justified.

Automatically Adjusting Column Widths and Row Heights

The AutoFit option allows you to automatically adjust the width of one or more columns or the height of one or more rows to fit the longest or highest entry. To use this option to adjust the width of columns, first select all the columns to be adjusted. Click Format and then point to Column. Click AutoFit Selection on the Column submenu. The columns are automatically adjusted so that each column is wide enough to display the widest entry in that particular column. To use the AutoFit option to adjust the height of rows, first select all the rows to be adjusted. Click Format and then point to Row. Click Autofit on the Row submenu. The rows are automatically adjusted so that each row is high enough to display the highest entry in that row

You can also automatically adjust the width of columns by double-clicking on the right column heading border. If you want to use this method to automatically adjust the width of several columns at one time, first select the columns and then double-click on the right heading border of any one of the selected columns. Each column is automatically adjusted to display the widest entry in that column. This method also works for automatically adjusting row heights. Simply double-click the bottom row heading border and the row will automatically adjust to display the highest entry in that row. To adjust the height of several rows at a time, select the rows to be adjusted and double-click the bottom row heading border of any one of the selected rows. Each row is automatically adjusted to display the highest entry in that row.

HINT

If you want to specify an exact column width or row height, click either Format, Column, and Width or Format, Row, and Height and key the desired dimension in the dialog box that is displayed.

(Before completing exercise 1, copy to your disk the Chapter 01E *folder from the* Excel 2002 Expert *folder on the CD that accompanies this textbook. Steps on how to copy a folder appear on the inside back cover of this textbook.)*

exercise 1

APPLYING SCIENTIFIC AND CUSTOM FORMATS, ADJUSTING COLUMN WIDTHS, AND FORMATTING LARGE LABELS

1. Open Excel.
2. Open Excel Worksheet E1-01.
3. Save the file using the Save As command and name it Excel E1, Ex 01.
4. Create a custom header by completing the following steps:
   a. Click File and then click Page Setup.
   b. Click the Header/Footer tab.
   c. Click the Custom Header button.
   d. Enter your name in the Left section box.
   e. Click the Right section box to select it. Click the File name button. This will automatically insert the name of the file. Your screen should look like the accompanying illustration.
   f. Click the OK button twice.

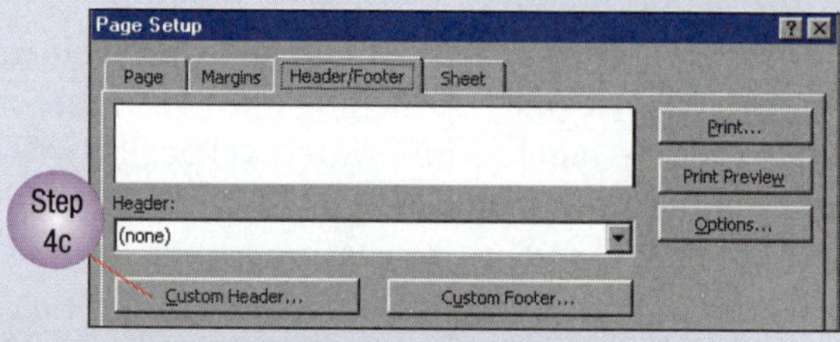

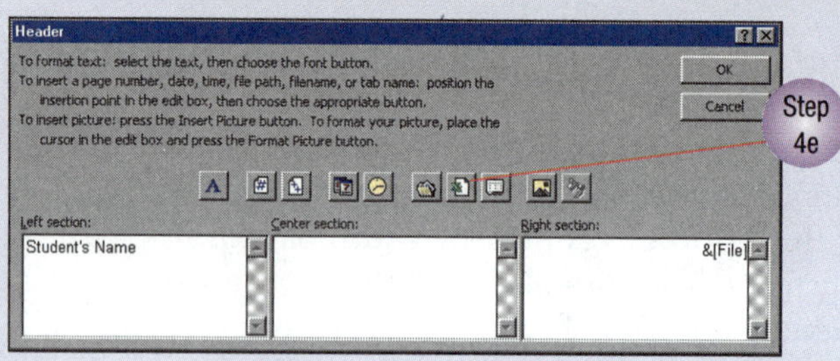

5. An astronomy class at Redwood Community College wants to calculate how far certain stars are from the Sun in miles. To do this they have to convert the distance measured in light-years into miles. The formula to accomplish this is the number of light-years multiplied by the speed of light times seconds in a minute, times minutes in an hour, times hours in a day, times days in a year. Key the following formula in cell C4: **=B4*186000*60*60*24*365.25**
6. The number is too large to be displayed. Widen the column by completing these steps:
   a. Position the mouse pointer on the column boundary between columns C and D until it turns into a double-headed arrow pointing left and right.
   b. Double-click.
7. The number that is displayed is very large and would be more appropriately displayed in scientific notation. Change the format of this number to scientific notation by completing the following steps:
   a. Right-click cell C4.
   b. On the shortcut menu, click Format Cells.
   c. On the Format Cells dialog box, click the Number tab if necessary.
      1) Click *Scientific* in the Category list box.
      2) Click OK.
8. Copy the formula in cell C4 to cells C5 through C16 by completing the following steps.
   a. Select cell C4.
   b. Place the mouse pointer over the AutoFill fill handle in the lower right corner of cell C4. The mouse pointer should look like a plus sign.
   c. Double-click on the AutoFill fill handle in the lower right corner of cell C4.
9. Create the custom format *ly*, which stands for light-years, for the numbers in column B by completing the following steps:

	A	B	C
1	Some Nearby Stars		
2			
3	Star	Distance from the Sun in Light Years	Distance from the Sun in Miles
4	Proxima Centauri	4.2	2.5E+13
5	α Centauri	4.3	

Step 8b

a. Select cells B4 through B16.
b. Right-click on one of the selected cells.
c. On the shortcut menu, click Format Cells.
d. On the Format Cells dialog box, click the Number tab if necessary.
    1) In the Category list box, click *Custom*.
    2) In the Type box, click to the right of the last zero.
    3) Press the spacebar once and enter "**ly**". Be sure to include both sets of quotation marks.
    4) Click OK. The label *ly* now appears in cells B4 through B16.

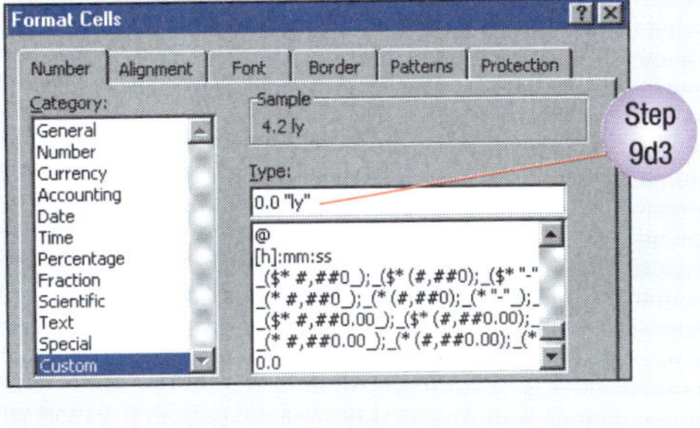

10. Create the custom format *miles* for the numbers in column C by completing the following steps:
    a. Select cells C4 through C16.
    b. Right-click on one of the selected cells.
    c. On the shortcut menu, click Format Cells.
    d. On the Format Cells dialog box, click the Number tab if necessary.
        1) In the Category list box, click *Custom*.
        2) In the Type box, click to the right of the last zero.
        3) Press the spacebar once and enter "**miles**". Be sure to include both sets of quotation marks.
        4) Click OK. The label *miles* now appears in cells C4 through C16.
11. Format the three column labels so that they are at an angle by completing the following steps:
    a. Select cells A3 through C3.
    b. Right-click one of the selected cells.
    c. On the shortcut menu, click Format Cells.
    d. Click the Alignment tab.
        1) Click and drag the red dot in the Orientation box until 45 is displayed in the Degrees box.
        2) Click OK.

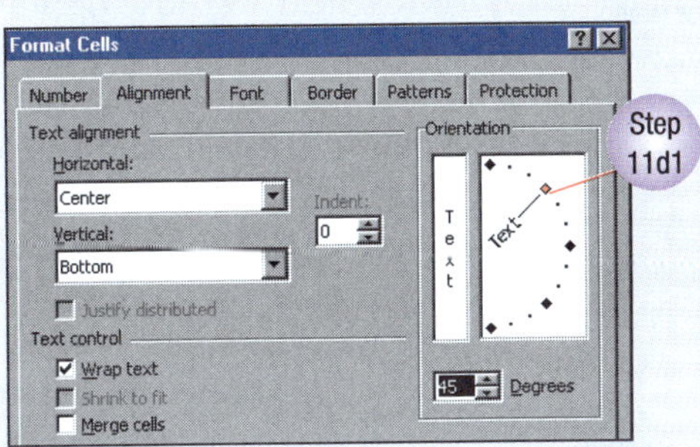

12. Apply the Merge and Center command on cells A1 through D1 by completing the following steps:
    a. Select cells A1 through D1.
    b. Click the Merge and Center button.
13. Change the formatting of the title "Some Nearby Stars" by completing the following steps:
    a. Select cell A1 if necessary.
    b. Click the Bold button.
    c. Change the Font Size to 12.
14. Save the worksheet with the same name (Excel E1, Ex 01).
15. Print and then close Excel E1, Ex 01.

Creating, Applying, and Editing Styles

When working with large worksheets or a workbook that has many worksheets, it is a good idea to apply formatting using styles. A style is a predefined set of formatting attributes, such as font, font size, alignment, color, borders, and so on. In fact, all the options available from the Format Cells dialog box can be defined as part of a particular style. Once a style has been defined, that style can be applied to any cell in a worksheet. Applying formatting using styles has several advantages. First, styles help to assure that the formatting from one worksheet to another is consistent. Second, all the attributes for a particular style have to be defined one time only. If you decide to use the same formatting over and over, you do not have to keep redefining each attribute of the format. Third, if a change needs to be made to the style, you only have to make that change one time in the style's definition, and then that change is automatically reflected in all the cells to which the style has been applied, thus saving a lot of time.

To create a style, select the cells to which the style is to be applied. Click Format and then Style. The Style dialog box, as shown in figure 1.6, is displayed. Each one of the check boxes on the Style dialog box corresponds to one of the tabs on the Format Cells dialog box. To create a new style, enter the name of the style in the Style name box. If any of the options listed on the Style dialog box are not going to be part of the style you are going to create, click in the check boxes next to those options so that they are no longer selected. Click the Modify button and the Format Cells dialog box appears. Make the selections you want for the style from the Format Cells dialog box and then click OK. The Style dialog box is displayed, and the attributes you selected will be listed. Click OK again, and the style will be applied to the selected cells. To apply the style to other cells, simply select those cells, click Format, and then click Style. Click the down-pointing arrow to the right of the Style name box and select the name of the style you want to apply from the drop-down list. Click OK and the style is applied to the selected cells. To delete a style, click the down-pointing arrow to the right of the Style name box, select the name of the style to be deleted, and then click the Delete button.

HINT

The Normal style applies to all unformatted cells in the worksheet. If you modify the Normal style, all the unformatted cells in the worksheet will be changed to reflect whatever modification you make.

FIGURE 1.6 ***The Style Dialog Box***

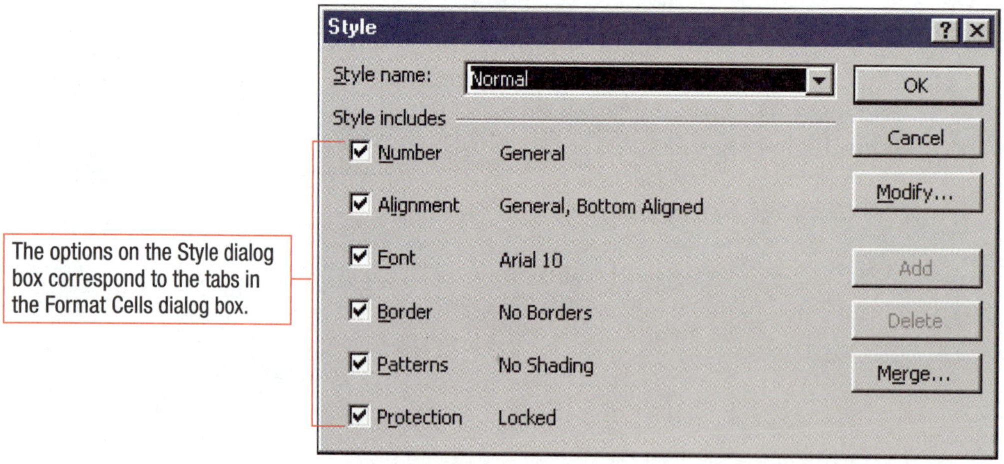

Style

Style name: Normal

Style includes

☑	Number	General
☑	Alignment	General, Bottom Aligned
☑	Font	Arial 10
☑	Border	No Borders
☑	Patterns	No Shading
☑	Protection	Locked

OK | Cancel | Modify... | Add | Delete | Merge...

The options on the Style dialog box correspond to the tabs in the Format Cells dialog box.

Using the Format Painter Button

The Format Painter button allows you to copy the format of one or more cells and apply it to other cells in the worksheet. To use the Format Painter button, select the cell or cells with the formatting you want to copy. Click the Format Painter button on the Standard toolbar. The mouse pointer changes to a paintbrush next to a cross, as shown in figure 1.7. Select the cells to which you want the copied formatting applied. Clicking the Format Painter button one time allows you to apply the copied formatting one time. If you double-click the Format Painter button, you can apply the copied formatting as many times as you want. When you have finished applying the copied formatting, click the Format Painter button again to turn the feature off.

Format Painter

FIGURE 1.7 ***Using the Format Painter Button***

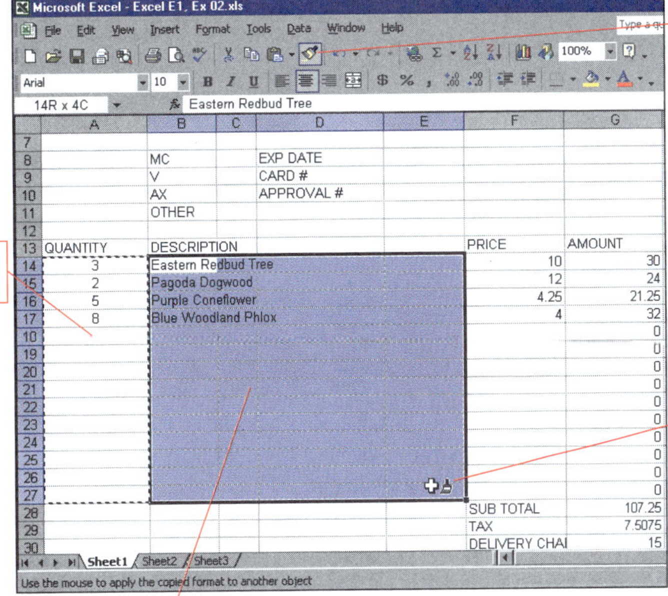

Applying Borders and Shading

Borders and shading can be applied to cells in a worksheet in three ways. You can use either a dialog box or a button on the toolbar, or you can draw them. To apply borders using a dialog box, select the cells to which you want to add borders, right-click one of the selected cells, click Format Cells on the shortcut menu, and then click the Border tab. You can make border selections from the dialog box shown in figure 1.8.

HINT

You must select the line style and line color (found under Line in the dialog box) *before* selecting a border style (the buttons under Presets and Border on the dialog box). Any line style or color you select after selecting the border style will not go into effect.

FIGURE

1.8 Applying Borders and Shading Using the Dialog Box

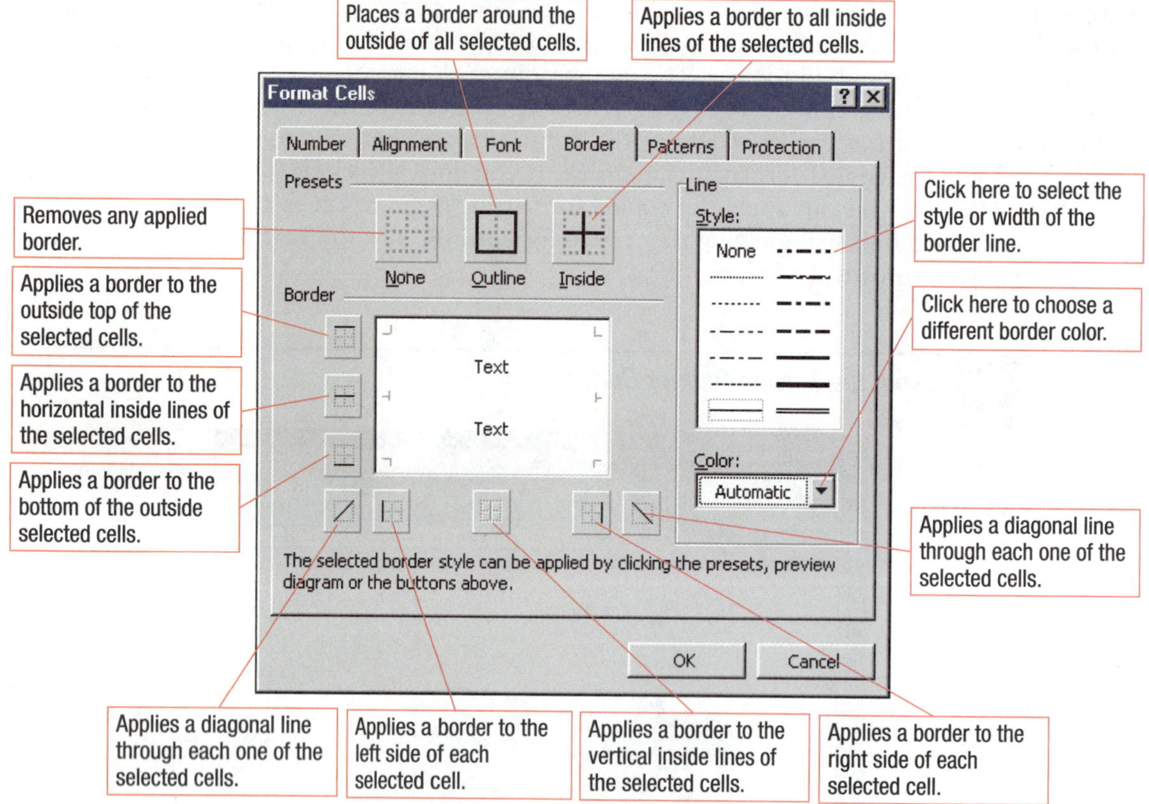

HINT

Border colors other than black are most effective with thicker lines.

To apply borders using the toolbar, click the drop-down arrow to the right of the Borders button on the Formatting toolbar and the border options shown in figure 1.9 are displayed. Click on the button that represents the border style you want. The last selected border style becomes the default for the button on the toolbar. To apply the style that appears on the button on the toolbar, simply click the button. You can click and drag on the menu options blue title bar, and the menu will become a floating palette that you can place anywhere on the worksheet. The palette will be displayed until you click the close box in the upper right corner of the palette.

FIGURE

1.9 Applying Borders Using the Toolbar

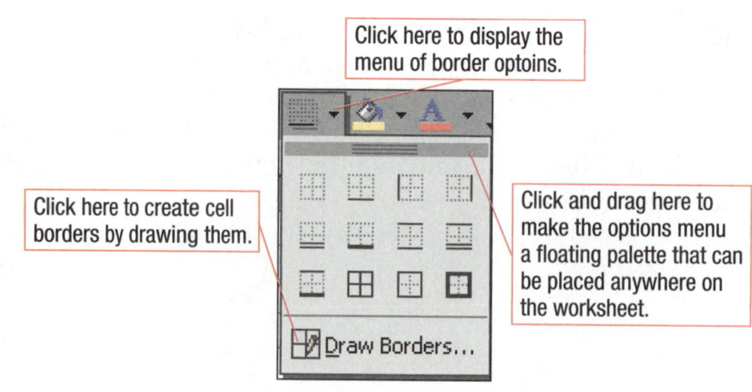

To create a cell border by drawing it, click the Draw Borders option at the bottom of the Borders drop-down menu. The mouse pointer changes to the shape of a pencil. Any cell you "draw" around will have a border.

To apply shading using the Format cells dialog box, click the Patterns tab. Click the option that represents the shading you want to apply. You can apply a pattern to the shading by clicking the down-pointing arrow to the right of the Pattern box and selecting a pattern from the menu that appears. You can also select a color for the pattern from this menu.

To apply shading using the toolbar, click the down arrow to the right of the Fill Color button on the Formatting toolbar and the options shown in figure 1.10 are displayed. Click on the option that represents the shading you want to apply. The last selected color becomes the default for the button on the toolbar. To apply the color that appears on the button on the toolbar, simply click the button. As with the borders menu, you can click and drag on the menu options blue title bar, and the menu will become a floating palette that remains on the worksheet until you click the close button in the upper right corner of the window.

FIGURE 1.10 **Applying Shading Using the Toolbar**

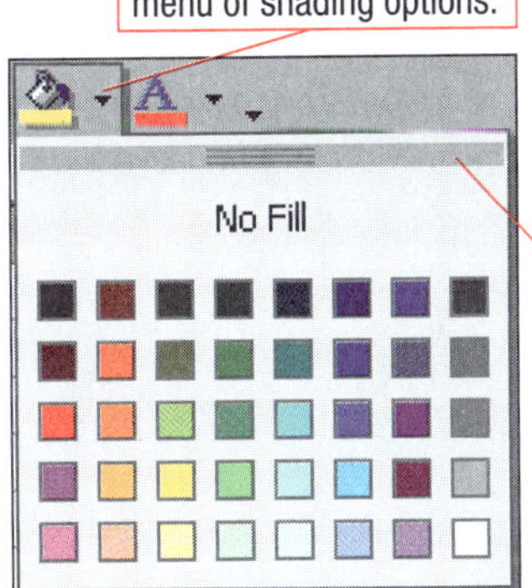

Turning Off Zeros

If a formula is entered into a cell and the cells being referenced by the formula are empty, a zero will be placed in the cell. In some situations, you may not want this zero to be displayed. To turn off zeros in a worksheet, click Tools and then Options. From the Options dialog box that appears, click the View tab. Under Window options, there is a check box for Zero values. If you do not want zeros to be displayed in a worksheet, this check box should be empty. Click the check box so that it is not selected and then click OK.

exercise 2

USING STYLES, THE FORMAT PAINTER BUTTON, CUSTOM FORMATS, BORDERS AND SHADING, AND TURNING OFF ZEROS

1. Open Excel Worksheet E1-02.
2. Save the file using the Save As command and name it Excel E1, Ex 02.
3. Create a custom header that has your name left aligned and the name of the file, Excel E1, Ex 02, right aligned.
4. This worksheet is an invoice used by Greenspace Architects. Greenspace Architects is a nursery that sells plants and flowers and provides landscaping services. The invoice needs to be formatted. Add some lines for filling in the information at the top of the invoice by completing the following steps:
   a. Select cells B3 through E3 and right-click one of the selected cells.
   b. Click Format Cells on the shortcut menu.
   c. Click the Border tab on the Format Cells dialog box.
   d. Click the second option in the first column in the Style list box.
   e. Click the button to apply a border to the bottom of the cell.
   f. Click OK.

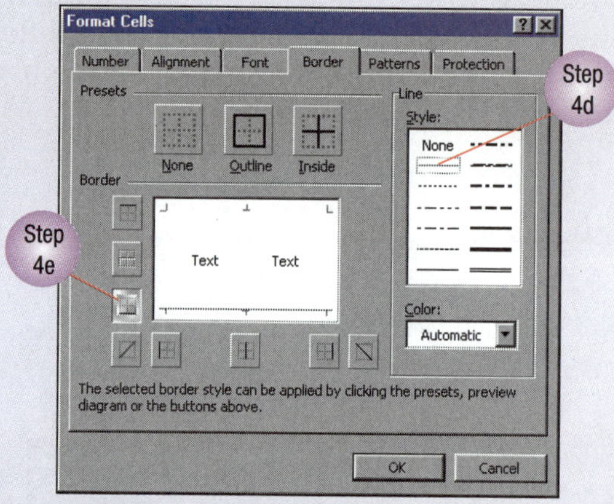

5. Use the Format Painter button to apply the border to the other cells where it is needed at the top of the invoice by completing the following steps:
   a. Select cell B3.
   b. Double-click the Format Painter button.
   c. Select cell G2.
   d. Select cells B4 through E4.
   e. Select cells B5 through C5.
   f. Select cells B6 through C6.
   g. Select cell E5.
   h. Select cells G5 through G6.
   i. Select cells E8 through F10.
   j. Click the Format Painter button to turn it off.
6. The cells next to the labels MC (for Master Card), V (for Visa), and AX (for American Express) are supposed to be check boxes. Place a border around these cells by completing the following steps:
   a. Right-click cell C8.
   b. Click Format Cells on the shortcut menu.
   c. If necessary, click the Border tab on the Format Cells dialog box.
   d. Click the second option in the first column in the Style box.
   e. Under Presets, click the Outline button.
   f. Click OK.
   g. Double-click the Format Painter button.
   h. Select cells C9 through C11.
   i. Click the Format Painter button to turn it off.

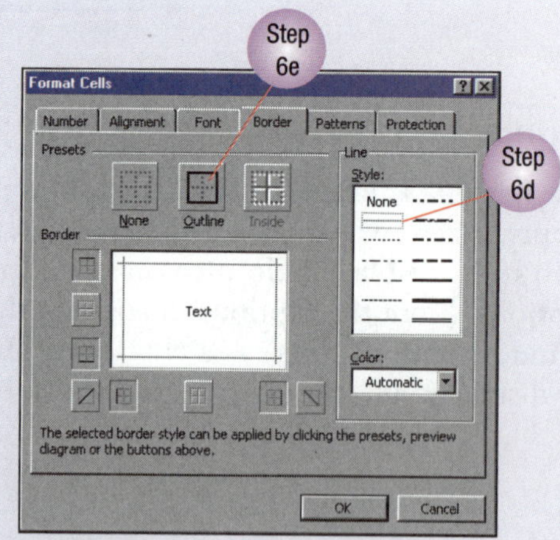

7. Place borders around the ordering information to make it easier to read by completing the following steps:
   a. Select cells A14 through A27.
   b. Click the drop-down arrow to the right of the Borders button.
   c. Click the Outside Borders button, the third button of the last row.
   d. Use the Draw Borders option to draw borders around the remaining cells. Click the drop-down arrow to the right of the Borders button and click Draw Borders. The mouse pointer is now displayed as a pencil. "Draw" borders by selecting cells B14 through E27, F14 through F27, G14 through G27, G28 through G30, and cell G31.
   e. When you have finished drawing borders, click the close button.

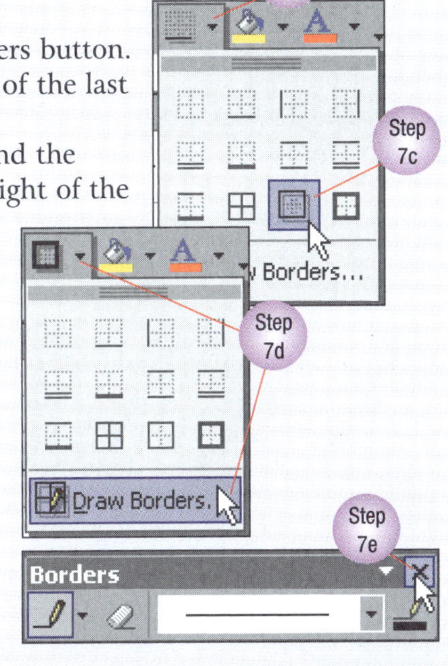

8. Create a style called Label 1 to be used on some of the labels on the invoice by completing the following steps:
   a. Select cell A3.
   b. Click Format and then Style.
   c. Change the name in the Style name box to *Label 1*.
   d. Click the Number check box so that there is no longer a check mark in it.
   e. Click the Modify button.
   f. Click the Alignment tab and from the Horizontal drop-down menu, select *Right (Indent)*.
   g. Click the Font tab and in the Font Style list box click *Bold*.
   h. Click the down-pointing arrow to the right of the Color box and click green, the fourth button in the second row.
   i. Click the OK button twice.
9. Apply the Label 1 style to the invoice by completing the following steps:
   a. Select cells A4 through A6, hold down the Ctrl key, and select the following cells: D5, F5, F6, B8, B9, B10, B11, D8, D9, D10, F28, F29, F30.
   b. Click Format and then Style.
   c. Click the down-pointing arrow to the right of the Style Name box and select *Label 1*.
   d. Click OK.
10. You want to create another style that is similar to the Label 1 style. The easiest way to do this is to start by selecting a cell that uses the Label 1 style. Many of the options you want for the new style will be automatically selected. Create a style called Label 2 by completing the following steps:
   a. Select cell A3.
   b. Click Format and then Style.
   c. Change the name in the Style name box to *Label 2*.
   d. Click the Number check box so that there is no longer a check mark in it.
   e. Click the Modify button.
   f. Click the Alignment tab and from the Horizontal drop-down menu, select *Center*.
   g. Click the OK button twice.
   h. Change the style of cell A3 back to Label 1 by clicking Format and then Style, and then selecting *Label 1* from the Style name list box.
   i. Click OK.

11. Apply the Label 2 style to the invoice by completing the following steps:
   a. Select cells A13 through G13.
   b. Click Format and then Style.
   c. Click the down-pointing arrow to the right of the Style name box and click *Label 2*.
   d. Click OK.
12. Create a style called Label 3 to be used on some of the labels on the invoice by completing the following steps:
   a. Select cell E2.
   b. Click Format and then Style.
   c. Change the name in the Style name box to *Label 3*.
   d. Click the Number check box so that there is no longer a check mark in it.
   e. Click the Modify button.
   f. Click the Alignment tab and from the Horizontal drop-down menu, select *Right (Indent)*.
   g. Click the Font tab.
      1) From the Font style list box, select *Bold*.
      2) From the Size list box, select *12*.
      3) Click the down-pointing arrow to the right of the Color box and select white, the last option in the fifth row.
   h. Click the Patterns tab and select the green that is the fourth option in the second row.
   i. Click the OK button twice.
13. Apply the Label 3 style to cell F31 by selecting cell F31, clicking Format and then Style, and then selecting *Label 3* from the Style name list box.
14. You decide that the font size for the style Label 1 is too large and you want to change it. Edit the Label 1 style by completing the following steps:
   a. Select cell A3.
   b. Click Format and then Style. Make sure that *Label 1* is in the Style name box.
   c. Click the Modify button.
   d. Click the Font tab.
   e. From the Size list box, select *9*.
   f. Click the OK button twice.
15. You are going to format the numbers on the invoice so that they are displayed as prices by creating a custom format for the Number format. You want to include one space to the right of any entry formatted as Number. Complete the following steps:
   a. Select cells F14 through F27.
   b. Right-click one of the selected cells.
   c. Select Format Cells on the shortcut menu.
   d. Click the Number tab.
      1) You want your custom format based on the Number format, so first select *Number* from the Category list box and then select *Custom*.
      2) 0.00 should appear in the Type box. You want to include a space equal to the size of the right parenthesis character to the right of the entry. The symbol for inserting this space is _). Place the insertion point to the right of the last zero in the Type box and press the underline key and then the right parenthesis key.

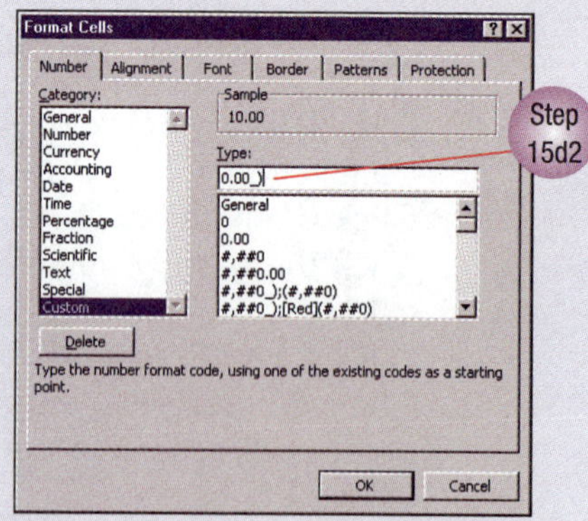

e. Click OK.
f. Cells F14 through F27 should still be selected. Click the Format Painter button.
g. Select cells G14 through G31.

16. You want the first value in a list to be displayed with a dollar sign in front of it. Apply the Accounting format to these cells by completing the following steps:
    a. Select cell F14, hold down the Ctrl key, and select cells G14, G28, and G31.
    b. Right-click one of the selected cells.
    c. Select Format Cells on the shortcut menu.
    d. Click the Number tab and select *Accounting* from the Category list box. Make sure a 2 is displayed in the Decimal places box and a dollar sign is displayed in the Symbol box. If necessary, click the down-pointing arrow to the right of the Symbol box and select the dollar sign.
    e. Click OK.
17. The formulas in some of the cells in column G do not have any corresponding data for making the calculations, so zeros are displayed. Turn off these zeros by completing the following steps:
    a. Click Tools and then Options.
    b. Click the View tab.
    c. Click the Zero values check box so that there is no longer a check mark in it.
    d. Click OK.

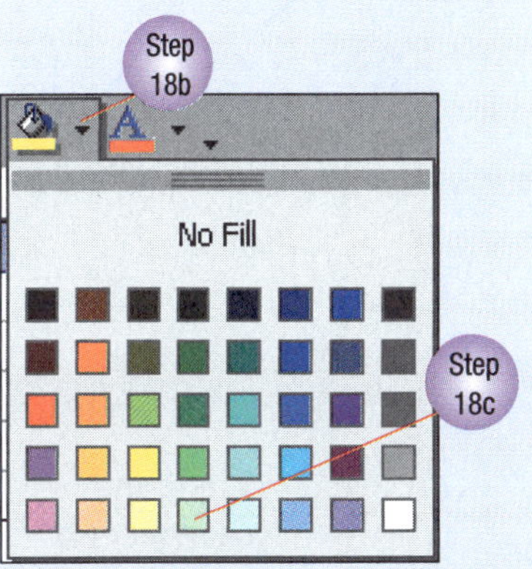

18. You want to make the prices in the Amount column stand out by adding some shading. Complete the following steps:
    a. Select cells G14 through G31.
    b. Click the down-pointing arrow next to the Fill color button on the Formatting toolbar.
    c. Click the palest green color, the fourth option in the last row.
19. Make sure that none of the outside borders you set in step 7 have been lost. There should be an outside border around the following cells: A14:A27, B14:E27, F14:F27, G14:G27, G28:G30, and G31. Reset any missing borders.
20. Save the worksheet with the same name (Excel E1, Ex 02).
21. Print and then close Excel E1, Ex 02.

Using AutoFormat

Excel includes many predesigned formats that can be easily applied to a worksheet. To use a predesigned format, select the cells to which the format is to apply. Click Format and then AutoFormat. The AutoFormat dialog box is shown in figure 1.11. A preview of what each format looks like is displayed. To select a format, click its preview. Seventeen different predesigned formats are available. Use the scroll bar to see more of the formats.

FIGURE 1.11 *The AutoFormat Dialog Box*

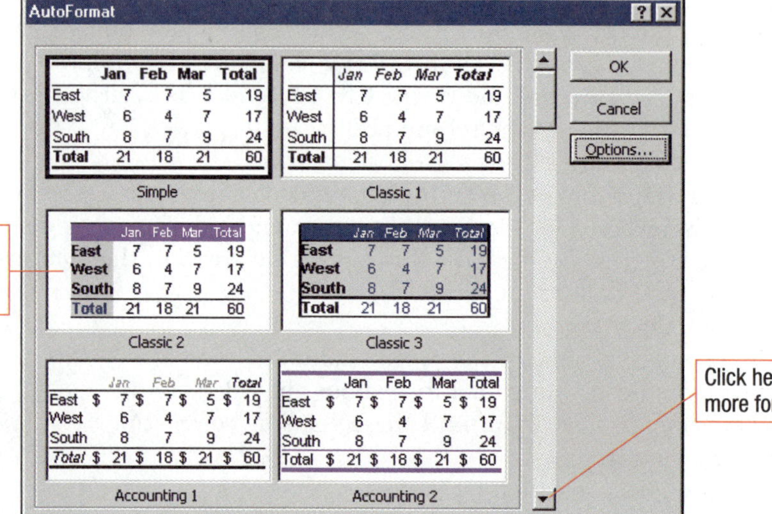

Using Conditional Formatting

There may be times when you want to format cells in a particular way only if they meet a specific condition. For example, you may want to be alerted if sales figures dip below a specific number and therefore want only those entries to be displayed in red. Conditional formatting allows you to specify how cells that meet a specific condition should be formatted. To use conditional formatting, first select the cells to which the formatting should apply. Click Format and then Conditional Formatting. The Conditional Formatting dialog box, as shown in figure 1.12, is displayed.

FIGURE 1.12 *The Conditional Formatting Dialog Box*

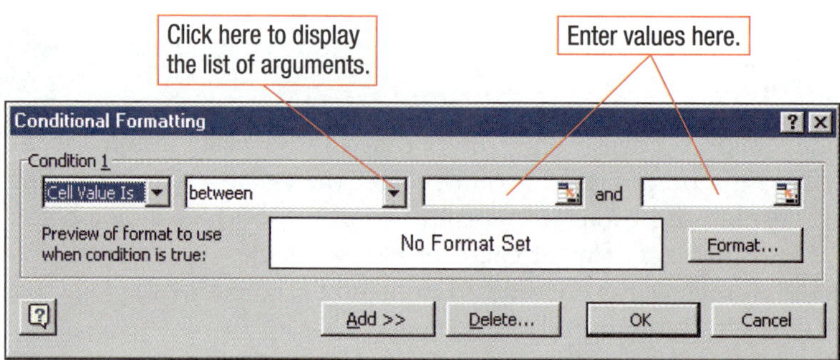

The default entry for the first box is *Cell Value Is*. This is the option you will want in most cases, particularly if the formula in the cell results in a value. If however, the formula in the cell produces a result such as true or false, you would want to click the down-pointing arrow at the right side of the first box and select the *Formula Is* option. The second box enables you to select the argument. Click the down-pointing arrow at the right side of the box to see the list of arguments, which includes *between, not between, equal to, not equal to, greater than, less than, greater than or equal to,* and *less than or equal to*. In the remaining box or boxes you enter a constant value or formula if the *Cell Value Is* option is selected. If a formula is entered, it must begin with an equal sign. If the *Formula Is* option is selected, enter a formula that evaluates to a logical value of true or false.

To set the formatting for the cells that meet the condition you have defined, click the Format button. The Format Cells dialog box appears. Using this dialog box you can set Font style, Underline, Color, Strikethrough, Border, and Patterns. Once you click the OK button on the Format Cells dialog box, the Conditional Formatting dialog box appears again. A preview of what the entries in the cells that meet the condition will look like is displayed in the box called Preview of format to use when condition is true. If you want to set up a second condition, click the Add button. The dialog box expands to include a section for defining the second condition, as shown in figure 1.13. You can define formatting for up to three conditions.

HINT

When using conditional formatting, the Number, Alignment, and Protection tabs are not available on the Format Cells dialog box. The options from these tabs cannot be changed using conditional formatting.

FIGURE 1.13 **Adding a Second Condition for Conditional Formatting**

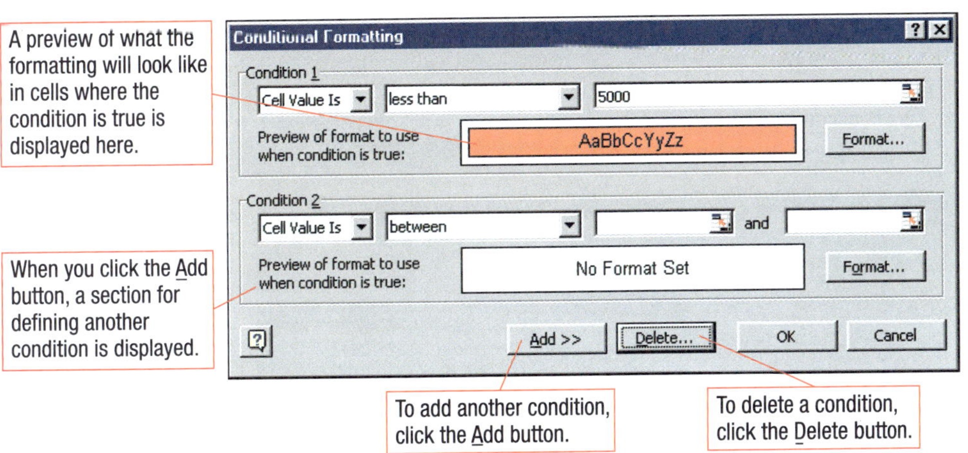

Conditional formatting can also be used for formatting nonnumeric data, such as text strings. Say, for example, the words "Pass" and "Fail" are text strings entered in a worksheet, and you want all the "Pass" text strings to be green and all the "Fail" text strings to be red. To conditionally format these text strings, the *Cell Value Is* option should be selected in the first box on the Conditional Formatting dialog box, the *equal to* option should be selected in the second box, and either **Pass** or **Fail** should be entered in the third box.

To delete a condition, click the Delete button. The Delete Conditional Format dialog box shown in figure 1.14 is displayed. Simply select the condition you want to delete and click OK.

HINT

Use conditional formatting sparingly. If most of the cells in a worksheet use conditional formatting, nothing will really stand out and catch your eye.

FIGURE

1.14 ***The Delete Conditional Format Dialog Box***

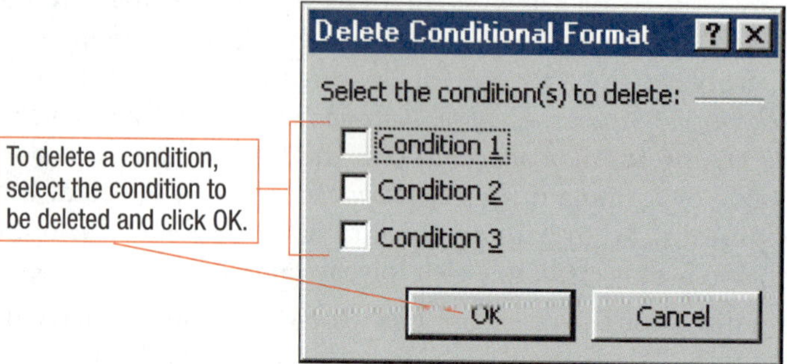

Adjusting the Layout of a Worksheet

HINT

The distance entered in the Header and Footer boxes must be less than the distance entered in the Top and Bottom margin boxes or else the data in the worksheet will overlap the header or footer when the worksheet is printed.

To have a worksheet print on one page, adjustments to the layout of the worksheet are often necessary. You can do several things to adjust the layout of a worksheet to have it print on one page. First, you can make the margins smaller by clicking File and then Page Setup. On the Page Setup dialog box, click the Margins tab. As shown in figure 1.15, there is a box for the Top, Bottom, Left, and Right margins. To change the margins, you can either select the current entry and enter a new margin setting, or click the up or down arrow to the right of the box to make the margin larger or smaller. You can also adjust the distance of the header from the top of the page and the footer from the bottom of the page. In the Center on page section, you can select the Horizontally check box to have the worksheet centered horizontally on the page or the Vertically check box to have the worksheet centered vertically on the page.

FIGURE

1.15 ***The Page Setup Dialog Box with Margins Tab Selected***

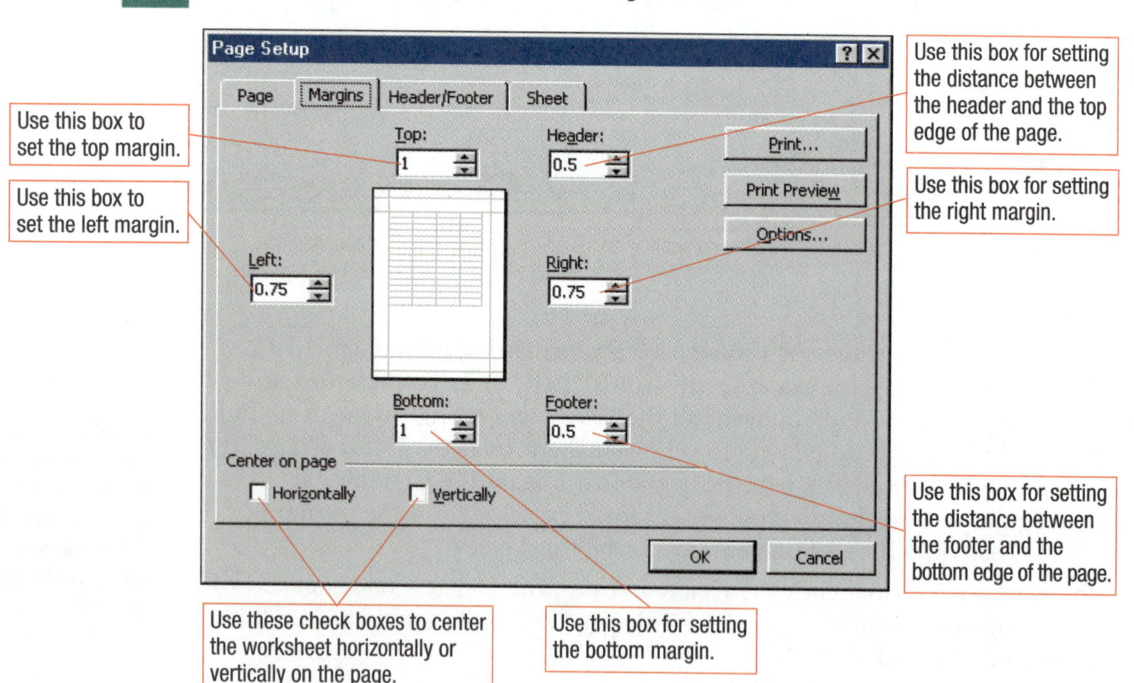

In many cases, worksheets are wider than they are long and would be more appropriately printed in landscape rather than portrait. With portrait orientation, the narrowest edge of the page is at the top. With landscape orientation, the widest edge of the page is at the top. To change the orientation of the page, click File and then Page Setup. On the Page Setup dialog box, click the Page tab. As shown in figure 1.16, the options for Portrait and Landscape orientation are on this tab. You can also scale the size of the worksheet. To reduce the worksheet size by a specific percentage of its full size, either select the current entry in the Adjust to box and enter a new scaling percentage, or click the up or down arrow to the right of the Adjust to box to increase or reduce the scaling percentage. Use the Fit to option to fit the worksheet onto a specified number of pages.

FIGURE 1.16 **The Page Setup Dialog Box with Page Tab Selected**

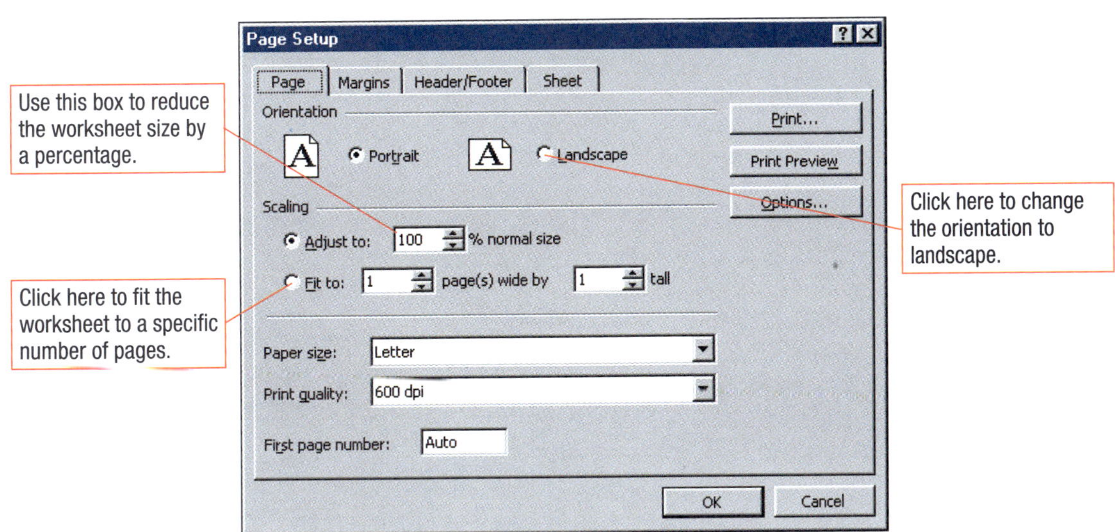

exercise 3 USING AUTOFORMAT, CREATING A CONDITIONAL FORMAT, AND ADJUSTING THE LAYOUT OF THE WORKSHEET

1. Open Excel Worksheet E1-03.
2. Save the file with Save As and name it Excel E1, Ex 03.
3. Create a custom header that has your name left aligned and the name of the file, Excel E1, Ex 03, right aligned.
4. Copper Clad Incorporated is a manufacturing company that designs and manufactures printed circuit boards. The company has a sales force of 12 sales representatives who are responsible for selling their printed circuit boards across the United States. This worksheet records each sales representative's sales for each month in the year 2002. Format the worksheet using AutoFormat by completing the following steps:
   a. Select cells A5 through N18 by completing the following steps:
      1) Click cell A5 to select it.
      2) Move the mouse pointer to the bottom edge of cell A5. The mouse pointer should turn into a four-headed arrow.
      3) Press the Shift key. While holding down the Shift key, double-click the bottom edge of cell A5. Cells A5 through A19 should be selected.

4) Move the mouse pointer to the right edge of the selected cells. The mouse pointer should turn into a four-headed arrow.

5) Press the Shift key. While holding down the Shift key, double-click the right edge of the selected cells. Cells A5 through N18 should now be selected.

b. Click Format and then AutoFormat.

c. Select the Accounting 2 style.

d. Click OK.

5. This worksheet would be more useful if you could tell at a glance when sales figures were over or under a certain amount. If a sales representative's sales figures in a month are over $35,000, you want the entry to be displayed in green. If a sales representative's sales figures in a month are under $8,000, you want the entry to be displayed in red. Format the worksheet using conditional formatting by completing the following steps:

a. Select cells B6 through M17.

b. Click Format and then Conditional Formatting.

c. Click the down-pointing arrow to the right of the second box in the Conditional Formatting dialog box and select *greater than*.

d. Enter **35000** in the third box.

e. Click the Format button.

f. If necessary, click the Font tab.

1) Click *Bold* on the Font style list box.

2) Click the down-pointing arrow at the right side of the Color box.

3) Click the sea green button, the fourth button in the third row.

4) Click OK. In the box called Preview of format to use when condition is true, the letters should be green.

g. Click the Add button. A second condition is added.

h. Under Condition 2, click the down-pointing arrow to the right of the second box in the Conditional Formatting dialog box and select *less than*.

i. Enter **8000** in the third box.

j. Click the Format button for the second condition.

k. If necessary, click the Font tab.

1) Click *Bold* on the Font style list box.

2) Click the down-pointing arrow at the right side of the Color box.

3) Click the red button, the first button in the third row.

4) Click OK. In the box called Preview of format to use when condition is true, the letters should be red.

l. Click OK.

6. As it is currently formatted, the worksheet will not fit on one page. Complete the following steps to adjust the worksheet so that it will fit onto one page.
   a. Click File and then Page Setup.
   b. Click the Page tab if necessary.
   c. Click the Landscape option.
   d. Click the Margins tab.
      1) Select the current setting in the Top box and enter **0.75**.
      2) Select the current setting in the Left box and enter **0.5**.
      3) Select the current setting in the Bottom box and enter **0.5**.
      4) Select the current setting in the Right box and enter **0.5**.
   e. Click the Print Preview button. The worksheet still will not fit on one page.
   f. Click the Close button.
   g. To save room, you do not want any decimal places displayed. Select cells B6 through N18. Click the Decrease Decimal button twice.
   h. You want to automatically adjust the widths of the columns now that the numbers in the cells are not as wide. Cells B6 through N18 should still be selected. Click Format, point to Column, and then click AutoFit Selection.
   i. Click the Print Preview button. The worksheet still does not fit on one page, but it is getting close. Click the Close button.
   j. Click File and then Page Setup.
   k. Click the Page tab if necessary.
   l. Under Scaling, click the Fit to option. The page(s) wide by box and tall box should both display *1*.
   m. Click OK.
7. Save the worksheet with the same name (Excel E1, Ex 03).
8. Print and then close Excel E1, Ex 03.

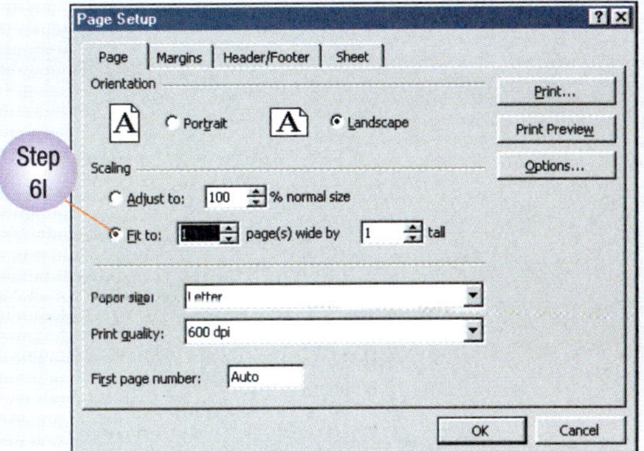

Using the Paste Special Command

When you use the Paste command, the entire contents of the cell or cells, including formulas and formats, are pasted. There may be times when you want to copy the contents of a cell, but you do not want to paste its format or you want to paste just the values and not the formulas. The Paste Special command allows you to do this. To access the Paste Special command, you first have to copy some cells and then click Edit and Paste Special. Or after copying some cells you can click the drop-down arrow next to the Paste button and click Paste Special. The Paste Special dialog box, as shown in figure 1.17, is displayed.

FIGURE 1.17 The Paste Special Dialog Box

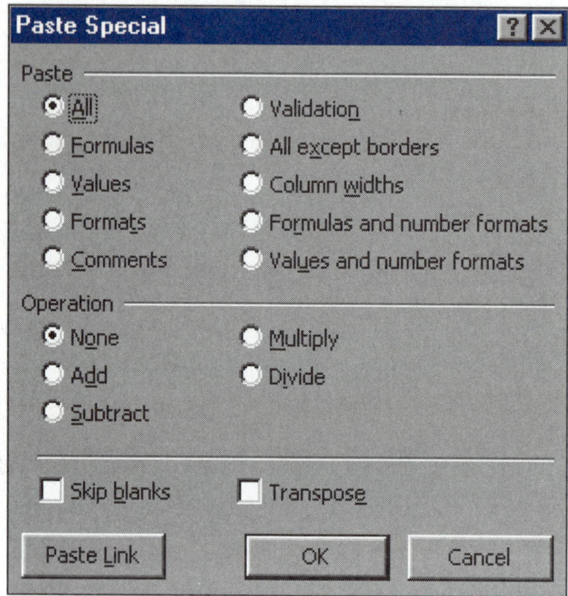

The Paste Special dialog box provides options for many unique pasting situations. Table 1.2 describes all the options on the Paste Special dialog box. All the options under Paste relate to what is going to be pasted. All the options under Operation relate to how the copied cells are to be combined with the cells to which they are being copied. The copied cells could, for example, be added to the cells into which they are pasted. As shown in figure 1.18, some of the options in the Paste Special dialog box are included on the drop-down menu that is displayed when you click the drop-down arrow next to the Paste button.

FIGURE 1.18 The Paste Special Drop-Down Menu

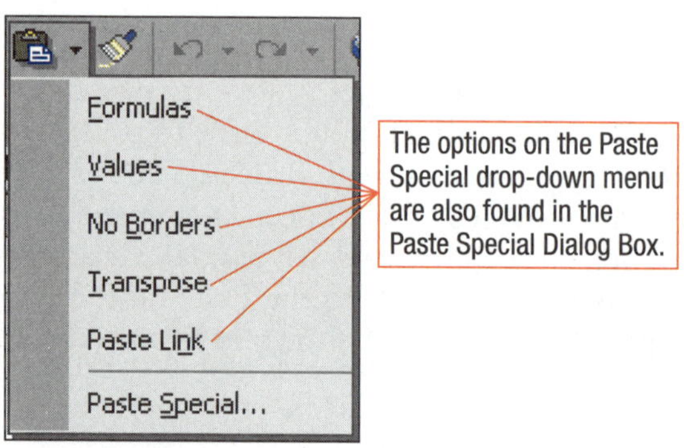

TABLE

1.2 Options from the Paste Special Dialog Box

Option	*Description*
Paste	
All	Pastes the cell's contents and formatting attributes.
Formulas	Pastes only formulas; does not paste formatting attributes.
Values	Pastes values and formula results; does not paste formulas.
Formats	Pastes formats only; does not paste formulas, values, or formatting attributes.
Comments	Pastes comment notes only.
Validation	Pastes data validation criteria only.
All except borders	Pastes the cell's contents and all formatting attributes except borders.
Column widths	Pastes the column widths only; does not paste formulas, values, or formatting attributes.
Formulas and number formats	Pastes only formulas and all number formatting options from the selected cells.
Values and number formats	Pastes only values and all number formatting options from the selected cells.
Operation	
None	The contents of the copied cells replace the contents of the cells into which they are being pasted.
Add	The contents of the copied cells are added to the contents of the cells into which they are being pasted.
Subtract	The contents of the copied cells are subtracted from the contents of the cells into which they are being pasted.
Multiply	The contents of the copied cells are multiplied by the contents of the cells into which they are being pasted.
Divide	The cells into which the copied cells are being pasted are divided by the copied cells.
Skip blanks	Any blank cells that are copied will not replace the contents of the cells into which they are pasted.
Transpose	Places the contents of rows into columns and the contents of columns into rows.

Hiding and Unhiding Rows, Columns, and Sheets

At times you may not want certain columns displayed. Say, for example, you have a worksheet open that contains confidential payroll information. You could hide specific columns so that the confidential information would not be visible to anyone passing by your computer. To hide a column or columns, first select the

HINT
Another way to hide a row is by dragging the bottom border of the row heading to the top border of the row heading. A column can be hidden by dragging the right border of the column heading to the left border of the column heading.

HINT
If a row or column is hidden, it will not print.

columns to be hidden. Click Format, point to Column, and then click Hide. The columns are then hidden. You can tell if a column is hidden because its column header will not be displayed. If you hid column F, the column headers displayed at the top of the worksheet would be D, E, G, H, and so on. To unhide a hidden column, select the column to the left and the column to the right of the hidden column. Click Format, select Column, and then click Unhide.

The process for hiding and unhiding rows is the same as for columns. First select the row or rows to be hidden. Click Format, select Row, and then click Hide. The rows are then hidden. You can tell if a row is hidden because its row header will not be displayed. To unhide a hidden row, select the row above and the row below the hidden row. Click Format, select Row, and then click Unhide.

To hide a sheet, click the tab for that sheet so that it is displayed. Click Format, select Sheet, and then click Hide. The sheet is hidden and its tab is no longer displayed. To unhide a hidden sheet, click Format, select Sheet, and then click Unhide. The Unhide dialog box shown in figure 1.19 is displayed. Select the sheet to be unhidden and click OK.

FIGURE 1.19 ***The Unhide Dialog Box***

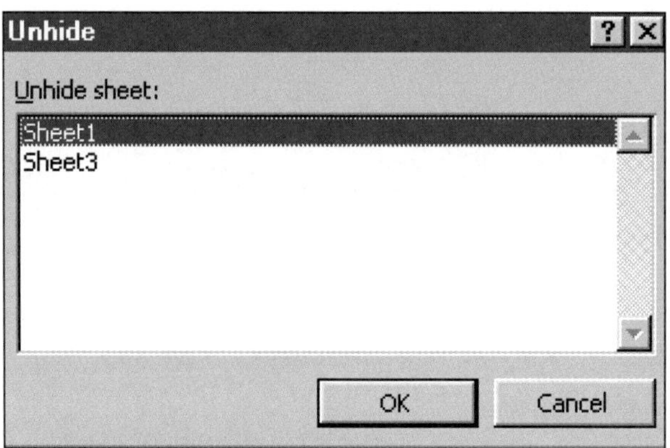

4 USING THE PASTE SPECIAL DIALOG BOX AND HIDING AND UNHIDING COLUMNS

1. Open Excel Worksheet E1-04.
2. Save the file using the Save As command and name it Excel E1, Ex 04.
3. Create a custom header that has your name left aligned and the name of the file, Excel E1, Ex 04, right aligned.
4. This worksheet is for a company called Performance Threads: Theatrical Fabrics, Draperies, and Supplies. Performance Threads is a company that supplies the entertainment industry (theater, film, and television) with a full line of theatrical fabrics, stage draperies, scenic, and production supplies. This worksheet lists some prices for ornate tassels the company sells. Format the numbers in this worksheet by completing the following steps:
   a. Select cells B4 through G4.
   b. Right-click one of the selected cells.
   c. Click on Format Cells from the shortcut menu.
   d. Click the Number tab if necessary.
   e. Click *Fraction* in the Category list box.
   f. Click *Up to one digit (1/4)* in the Type list box if necessary.
   g. Click OK.
   h. Select cells B5 through G5. Hold down the Ctrl key and select cells B7 through G7.
   i. Click the Currency Style button on the Formatting toolbar.
   j. Select cells B6 through G6.
   k. Click the Percent Style button on the Formatting toolbar.
5. Adjust the widths of columns E, F, and G by completing the following steps:
   a. Select columns E, F, and G.
   b. Double-click the column header border between columns E and F.
6. The data is not very easy to read as it is currently arranged on the worksheet. Transposing the columns and rows would make the data easier to understand. Transpose the columns and rows by completing the following steps:
   a. Select cells A3 through G7.
   b. Click the Copy button on the Standard toolbar.
   c. Click cell A9.
   d. Click the drop-down arrow next to the Paste Button and then click Transpose.
   e. Now you need to delete the old data. Select rows 3 through 7, click Edit and then click Delete.
7. Adjust the widths of the columns by completing the following steps:
   a. Select columns A through E.
   b. Double-click on any one of the selected column header borders.
8. You want to delete column D. Select cell E5 and notice that the formula in cell E5 references cell D5. If you delete column D, error messages will appear in column E. To delete column D, you must first change the formulas to values. Complete the following steps to change the formulas to values:
   a. Select cells E5 through E10.
   b. Click the Copy button on the Standard toolbar.

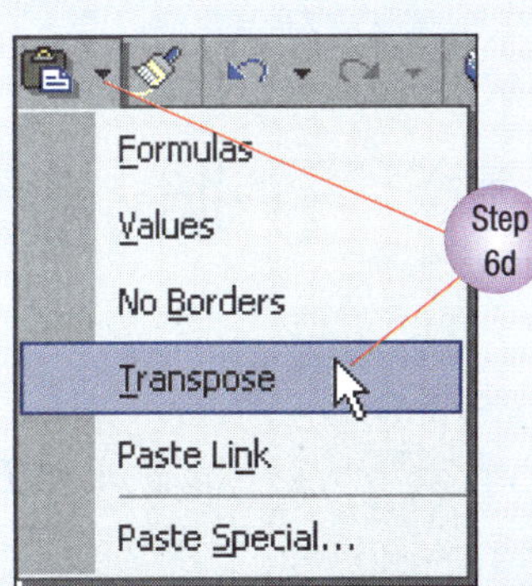

c. Select cell E5.
d. Click the Edit menu and click Paste Special.
e. Under Paste, click the Values option.
f. Click OK. Notice that now there are values, not formulas, in cells E5 through E10.
g. Press Esc to turn off the copy border.

9. Delete column D by completing the following steps:
   a. Select column D.
   b. Click Edit and then click Delete.
10. You want to do some quick calculations. Sales representatives earn 8% commission on sales they make. Complete the following steps to quickly calculate what 8% of the price Per Dozen is.
   a. Enter **8% Commission** in cell E4.
   b. Enter **.08** in cell E5.
   c. Double-click on the AutoFill fill handle in the lower right corner of cell E5.
   d. Select cells D5 through D10.
   e. Click the Copy button on the Standard toolbar.
   f. Select cell E5.
   g. Click Edit and then click Paste Special.
   h. In the Operation section, click the Multiply option.
   i. Click OK.
   j. Press Esc to turn off the copy border.
11. Someone has asked to see the prices for the tassels. You want to hide column E, the sales representatives' commission, before you show them to this person. Hide column E by completing the following steps:
   a. Select column E.
   b. Click Format, point to Column, and then click Hide.
12. Print the worksheet with the column hidden.
13. Unhide the column by completing the following steps:
   a. Select columns D and F.
   b. Click Format, point to Column, and then click Unhide.
14. Save the worksheet with the same name (Excel E1, Ex 04). Close Excel E1, Ex 04.

HINT

Any rows and/or columns you may have defined as print titles to repeat on every page are not displayed in Page Break Preview. They are only displayed in Print Preview.

Print Preview

Using the Page Break Preview Command

The Page Break Preview command enables you to see where page breaks are going to occur. In addition, you can edit where the page breaks are going to appear in this preview mode. If you adjust a page break so that more data is going to appear on a page, Excel automatically scales the data so that it will fit on the page. There are two ways to access the Page Break Preview command. One way is to click View and then click Page Break Preview. The second way is to click the Print Preview button on the Standard toolbar and then click the Page Break Preview button. A display similar to the one shown in figure 1.20 appears. The blue lines indicate the current page breaks. By clicking and dragging on these lines, you can adjust where the page breaks will occur. To return to the Normal view, click the Print Preview button, and then click the Normal View button.

FIGURE 1.20 ***Page Break Preview Mode***

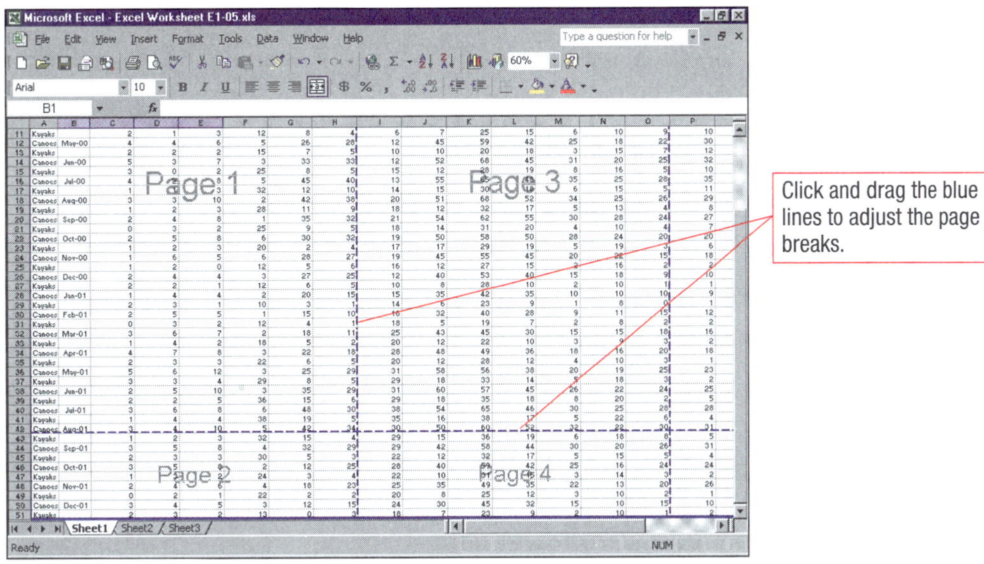

Changing Page Order

As you can see in figure 1.20, a worksheet can be both too wide as well as too long to fit on one page. When this occurs, Excel can either print all the pages going across first and then print the pages going down, or print all the pages going down first and then print the pages going across. In figure 1.20, the pages going down will be printed first (as indicated by the Page 1 and Page 2 labels), and then the pages going across (as indicated by the Page 3 and Page 4 labels). The default setting is to print all the pages going down first and then print all the pages going across. To change this, click File, Page Setup, and then the Sheet tab. As shown in figure 1.21, the options for changing the order in which the pages are printed are found under Page order.

FIGURE 1.21 ***Selecting the Order in Which Worksheet Pages Are Printed***

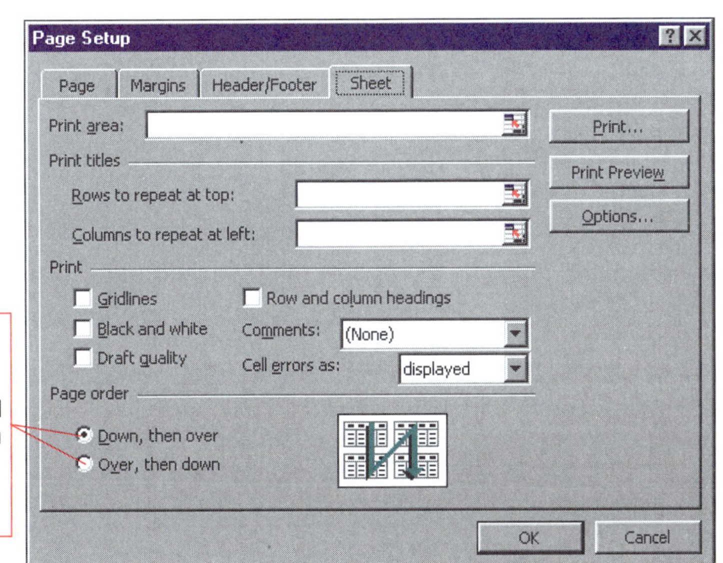

Renaming Sheets and Selecting a Tab Color

The default names on the Sheet tabs are *Sheet1, Sheet2, Sheet3*, and so on. If you want a more descriptive name for your sheets, you can click Format, point to Sheet, and then click Rename. Or you can use the shortcut menu by right-clicking the tab for the sheet and clicking Rename. The name of the currently selected sheet is highlighted. Simply enter the new sheet name and press Enter to rename the sheet.

You can also organize your spreadsheets by assigning colors to the tabs. To assign a color to a tab, either click Format, point to Sheet, and then click Tab Color, or use the shortcut menu by right-clicking the tab for the sheet and clicking Tab Color. The Format Tab Color dialog box shown in figure 1.22 is displayed. Click a color and then click OK. The edge of the tab will change to the selected color.

FIGURE 1.22 ***Selecting a Color for a Worksheet Tab***

exercise 5 TRANSPOSING DATA, CREATING A CUSTOM FORMAT, USING PAGE BREAK PREVIEW, CHANGING PAGE ORDER, RENAMING SHEETS, SELECTING A TAB COLOR, HIDING AND UNHIDING COLUMNS

1. Open Excel Worksheet E1-05.
2. Save the file using the Save As command and name it Excel E1, Ex 05.
3. Create a custom header that has your name left aligned and the name of the file, Excel E1, Ex 05, right aligned.
4. The Whitewater Canoe and Kayak Corporation is a company that makes and sells custom-made canoes and kayaks and related sporting supplies to dealers around the country. This worksheet shows the number of canoes and kayaks Whitewater Canoe and Kayak's resellers ordered each month for the years 2002 and 2003. The data is not very easy to understand the way it is currently formatted. It would be easier to understand if the columns displayed the dates and the rows displayed the resellers. Complete the following steps to transpose the rows and columns:

a. Click cell A3 to select it. Move the mouse pointer to the bottom edge of cell A3. When the mouse pointer turns into a four-headed arrow, hold down the Shift key and double-click. Cells A3 through A51 should be selected. Move the mouse pointer to the right edge of the selected cells. When the mouse pointer turns into a four-headed arrow, hold down the Shift key and double-click. Cells A3 through U51 should be selected.
b. Click the Copy button.
c. Select cell A53.
d. Click Edit and then Paste Special.
e. Click the Transpose check box in the Paste Special dialog box.
f. Click OK.
g. Now you need to delete the old data. Select rows 3 through 51, click Edit, and then click Delete.
h. Select columns A through AW.
i. Click Format, point to Column, and then click AutoFit Selection.
j. Click in any cell so that the columns are no longer selected.
k. Drag the right column heading border to column A until the width of column A is 9.86.
l. Select rows 6 through 24.
m. Click Format, point to Row, and then click AutoFit.

5. You could save a considerable amount of space if all the "Canoes" and "Kayaks" labels were angled. Angle the labels by completing the following steps:
   a. Select row 4.
   b. Right-click on any one of the selected cells and click Format Cells on the shortcut menu.
   c. Click the Alignment tab.
   d. Click the red dot in the Orientation box and drag it until *60* is displayed in the Degrees box.
   e. Click OK.
6. Use the Merge and Center button to merge cells B5 and C5, D5 and E5, F5 and G5, H5 and I5, and so on until the two cells for each date are merged.
7. Adding borders around the two columns that represent one month would make the worksheet easier to understand. Complete the following steps to add the borders:
   a. Select cells B4 through C24.
   b. Right-click on any one of the selected cells and click Format Cells from the shortcut menu.
   c. Click the Border tab.
   d. Under Presets, click the Outline button.
   e. Click OK.
   f. Cells B4 through C24 should still be selected. Double-click the Format Painter button.
   g. Click cell D4. The format is applied. Click cell F4. The format is applied. Continue clicking every other cell until the cells representing each month have a border around them.
   h. Click the Format Painter button to turn it off.
8. You want to create a custom format so that the numbers are indented from the right side of the cell. Complete the following steps to create the custom format:
   a. Select cells B6 through AW24.

b. Right-click on any one of the selected cells and click Format Cells from the shortcut menu.
c. Click the Number tab.
d. Click *Custom* in the Category list box.
e. In the Type box, enter **0_0**.
f. Click OK.

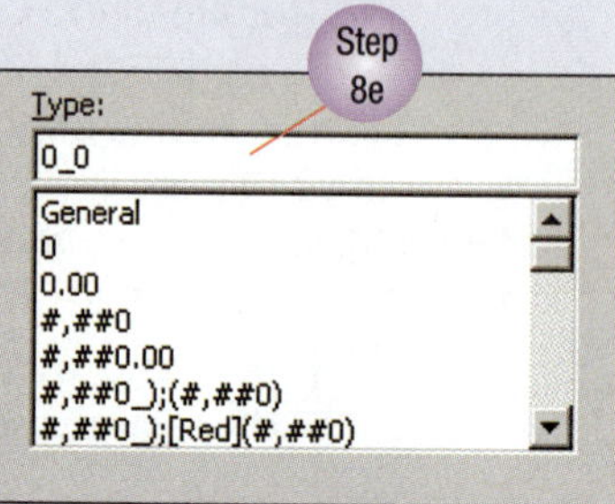

9. Complete the following steps to use the AutoFit command to reduce the widths of the columns:
   a. Select columns B through AW.
   b. Click Format, point to Column, and then click AutoFit Selection.
10. Adding shading to the numbers would also make them easier to read. Complete the following steps to add shading:
    a. Select cells B6 through AW24.
    b. Click the down-pointing arrow to the right of the Fill Color button.
    c. Click the light green button, the fourth button in the last row.
11. Adjust the layout of the worksheet by changing the orientation to landscape and setting the left and right margins to 0.5 inches.
12. You need your labels to appear on each page. Complete the following steps to select rows 4 and 5 to repeat at the top of each page and column A to repeat at the left of each page:
    a. Click File and then click Page Setup.
    b. Click the Sheet tab.
    c. Click the button to the right of the Rows to repeat at top box. 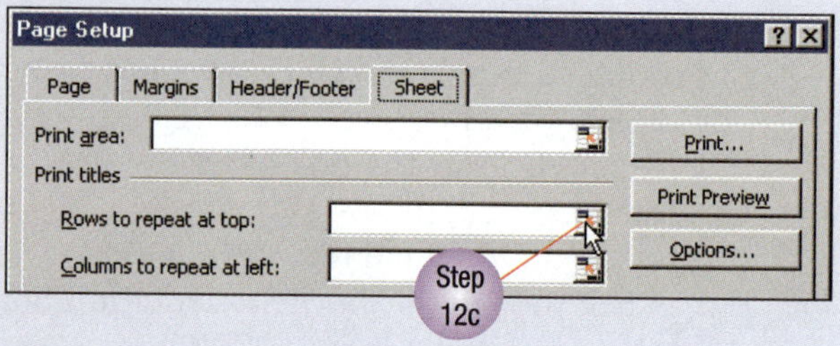
    d. Select rows 4 and 5.
    e. Click the button at the right side of the Page Setup - Rows to repeat at top dialog box that appears.

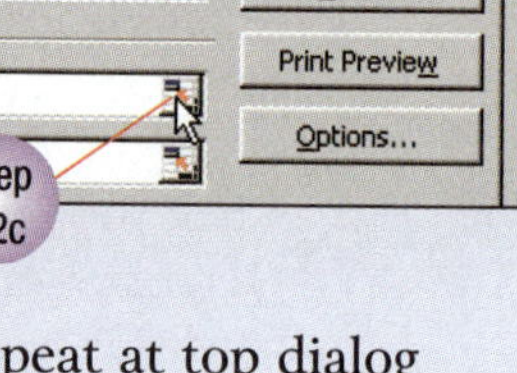

    f. Click the button at the right side of the Columns to repeat at left box.
    g. Select column A.
    h. Click the button at the right side of the Page Setup - Columns to repeat at left dialog box that appears.

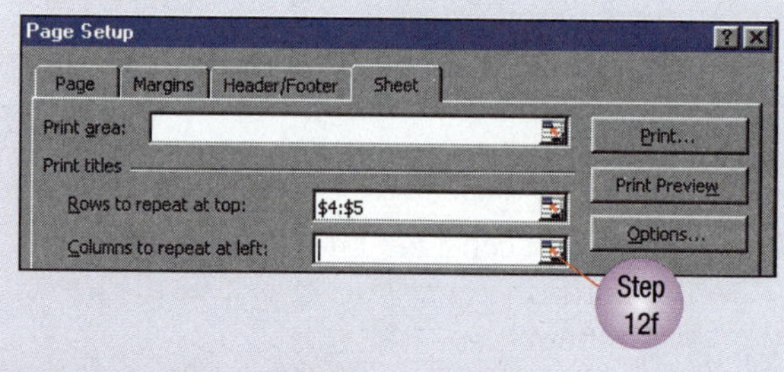

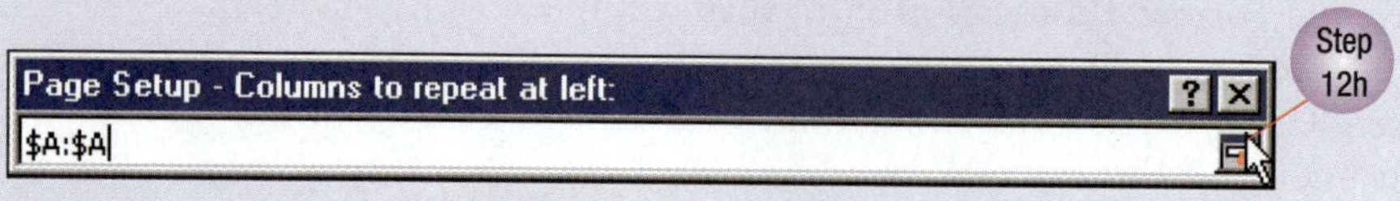

i. Change the Page Order by selecting the Over, then down option under Page order.
j. Click OK.

13. Complete the following steps to use Page Break Preview to change the page breaks.
   a. Click the Print Preview button.
   b. Click the Page Break Preview button. If the Welcome to Page Break Preview dialog box is displayed, click the OK button.
   c. You want the page break between pages 1 and 2 to come after December 2002. Click and drag the vertical blue dotted line until it is on the border between December 2002 and January 2003.
   d. Drag the horizontal blue dotted line until it is between rows 17 and 18.
   e. Click the Print Preview button. Preview the entire worksheet.
   f. Click the Normal View button.

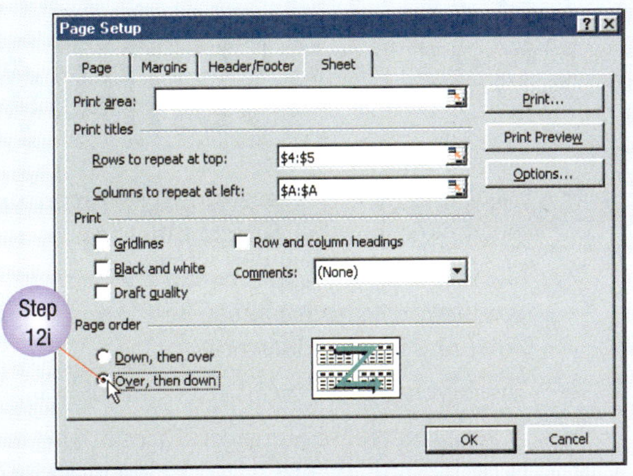

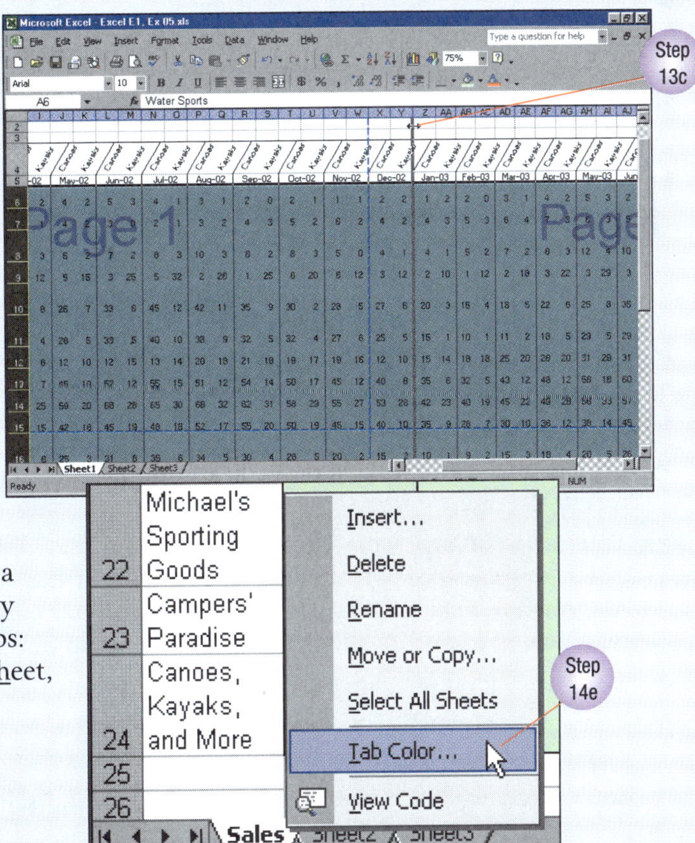

14. Rename the sheet and select a color for the worksheet tab by completing the following steps:
   a. Click Format, point to Sheet, and then click Rename.
   b. Key **Sales**.
   c. Press Enter.
   d. Right-click the Sales worksheet tab.
   e. Click Tab Color.
   f. From the Format Tab Color dialog box, click the red that is the first option in the third row.
   g. Click OK.
15. Save the worksheet with the same name (Excel E1, Ex 05).
16. Print and then close Excel E1, Ex 05.

CHAPTER summary

- Excel includes 12 categories by which numbers can be formatted. Some of Excel's more specialized number formats include Accounting, Fraction, and Scientific.
- The main difference between the Currency and Accounting formats is that the Accounting format aligns the currency symbols at the left side of the cell and the Currency format does not.
- The Scientific format is used for very large or very small numbers.
- When you create a custom format, the format you create is added to the bottom of the Type list box, where it can be selected and used as often as needed.
- Use the Alignment tab of the Format Cells dialog box to manage large labels by wrapping the text within a cell, shrinking the cell's entry to fit within one cell, or rotating the label a specified number of degrees.
- When you automatically adjust the width of a column or the height of a row, the column is displayed at its optimum width or the row is displayed at its optimum height.
- A style is a predefined set of formatting attributes. Each one of the check boxes on the Style dialog box corresponds to one of the tabs on the Format Cells dialog box. There are several advantages to using styles. Using styles helps to assure that the formatting from one worksheet to another is consistent, enables you to define the attributes for a particular style one time only, and simplifies editing.
- The Format Painter button enables you to copy the format of one or more cells in a worksheet and apply it to other cells in the worksheet.
- Excel includes 17 different predesigned formats.
- Conditional formatting allows you to format cells in a specific way only if they meet certain criteria.
- The layout of large worksheets often needs to be adjusted to have the worksheet print on as few pages as possible. Reduce the margins at the Page Setup dialog box with the Margins tab selected. Change the orientation to landscape and reduce the worksheet size by a percentage of its full size at the Page Setup dialog box with the Page tab selected.
- The Paste Special command gives you more control over the results of a paste operation.
- Rows and columns on a worksheet can be hidden so that their contents are neither displayed on the screen nor printed.
- You can change the name on a worksheet tab and select a color for a worksheet tab.

COMMANDS review

Command	Mouse/Keyboard
Apply number format	Click Format, Cells
Create a custom format	Click Format, Cells, and select *Custom*
Format large labels	Click Format, Cells, Alignment tab
Automatically adjust column widths	Click Format, Column, AutoFit Selection
Automatically adjust row height	Click Format, Row, AutoFit
Create a style	Click Format, Style
Apply borders	Click Format, Cells, Border tab
Apply shading	Click Format, Cells, Patterns tab
Turn off zeros	Click Tools, Options, View tab
Apply a predesigned format	Click Format, AutoFormat
Create a conditional format	Click Format, Conditional Formatting
Transpose columns/rows	Click Edit, Paste Special, Transpose check box
Hide columns	Click Format, Column, Hide
Hide rows	Click Format, Row, Hide
Unhide columns	Click Format, Column, Unhide
Unhide rows	Click Format, Row, Unhide
Adjust page breaks	Click View, Page Break Preview
Change order pages are printed	Click File, Page Setup, Sheet tab
Rename sheets	Click Format, Sheet, Rename
Select colors for worksheet tabs	Click Format, Sheet, Tab Color

CONCEPTS check

Completion: On a blank sheet of paper, indicate the correct term, symbol, or command for each item.

1. This numbering format is used to display very large or very small numbers.
2. To create a custom format that uses text, the text must be enclosed by these characters.
3. To center a label across all the columns in a worksheet, click this button on the Formatting toolbar.
4. A label can be formatted so that it prints at an angle at the Format Cells dialog box with this tab selected.
5. Double-click on this location to automatically adjust a column so that the widest entry in the column fits in one cell.
6. These are what each one of the check boxes on the Style dialog box corresponds to.

7. To apply the formatting from one cell to another cell, click this button on the Standard toolbar.
8. Turn off zeros with an option at the Options dialog box with this tab selected.
9. Scale the size of the worksheet by a specific percentage of its full size at the Page Setup dialog box with this tab selected.
10. Use this dialog box to add the values in copied cells to the values in the cells into which they are being pasted.
11. If you are currently viewing a worksheet in the Page Break Preview mode and you want to return to the Normal view, you must click this button on the Standard toolbar.
12. Change the order in which worksheet pages are printed at the Page Setup dialog box with this tab selected.
13. List the advantages of applying formatting using styles.
14. List the steps you would complete to create a conditional format that printed all values greater than 150 as blue and italicized.
15. Column J is currently hidden. List the steps you would take to unhide it.

SKILLS check

Assessment 1

1. Open Excel Worksheet E1-06.
2. Save the worksheet using the Save As command and name it Excel E1, SA 01.
3. Create a custom header that has your name left aligned and the file name right aligned.
4. Center the label in cell A5 across columns A, B, and C.
5. Format the numbers in cells A8 through A12 as fractions, up to one digit.
6. Create a custom format for the numbers in cells A8 through A12. The format should read *inches*.
7. Center and bold each of the labels in row 7.
8. Format the numbers in cells C8 through C12 as Accounting.
9. Add a light yellow shading to cells C8 through C12.
10. Save the worksheet again with the same name (Excel E1, SA 01).
11. Print and then close Excel E1, SA 01.

Assessment 2

1. Open Excel Worksheet E1-07.
2. Save the worksheet using the Save As command and name it Excel E1, SA 02.
3. Create a custom header that has your name left aligned and the file name right aligned.
4. Align the labels in cells B6 through G6 so that they are at a 75 degree angle.
5. Automatically adjust the widths of columns B through G.
6. Center the label in cell A5 across columns A through G.
7. Print the worksheet.
8. Copy cells A7 through A10 to cells A13 through A16.
9. Enter the label **Projections** in cell A12.
10. You want to know how many sections would be offered if the number of sections was increased by 2 for each semester. Enter 2 in cells B13 through G16.

11. Copy cells B7 through G10. Use the Paste Special command to add the values in these cells to the values in cells B13 through G16.
12. Print the worksheet again.
13. Save the worksheet again with the same name (Excel E1, SA 02).
14. Close Excel E1, SA 02.

Assessment 3

1. Open Excel Worksheet E1-08.
2. Save the worksheet using the Save As command and name it Excel E1, SA 03.
3. Create a custom header that has your name left aligned and the file name right aligned.
4. Center the label in A7 across columns A through F.
5. Create a custom format for cells A9 through A14 that does not display the leading zero and adds two single quotation marks to the right of the number to indicate the symbol for inches. *(Hint: You may need to refer to table 1.1. The single quotation marks should be treated like text when creating the format.)*
6. Create a custom format for cells B9 through F14 that displays only one decimal place and adds the capital letter *A*, which is the symbol for amps, to the right of the numbers.
7. Place a border around each cell from cell A7 through cell F14. *(Hint: Use the Borders button on the Formatting toolbar and select the All Borders option, the second button on the last row.)*
8. Add a light green shading to cell A7.
9. Automatically adjust the widths of columns B through F so that they are just wide enough to display the widest entry in each column.
10. Save the worksheet again with the same name (Excel E1, SA 03) and print it.
11. Close Excel E1, SA 03.

Assessment 4

1. Open Excel Worksheet E1-09.
2. Save the worksheet using the Save As command and name it Excel E1, SA 04.
3. Create a custom header that has your name left aligned and the file name right aligned.
4. Format the numbers in column B as fractions, up to one digit.
5. Create a custom format for cells B7 through B10 that adds *lbs* to the right of the numbers. Apply this custom format to cells B14 through B17 and cells B21 through B24.
6. Format the numbers in column C as Accounting with two decimal places and the dollar sign displayed.
7. Select cell A5. Create a style called Header 1. The font for the Header 1 style should be the Century Gothic font (or another sans serif font), the font style should be italic, the size should be 12, and the color should be green.
8. Apply the Header 1 style to cells A12 and A19.
9. Select cell A6. Create a style called Header 2. The horizontal alignment for the Header 2 style should be centered, the font should be Century Gothic (or another sans serif font), the font style should be bold, the size should be 11, and there should be an outside border around the cell.
10. Apply the Header 2 style to cells B6, C6, A13, B13, C13, A20, B20, and C20.
11. Print the worksheet.
12. Edit the Header 1 style so that the font style is bold italic instead of just italic.
13. Edit the Header 2 style so that it includes a light green background.

14. Print the worksheet again.
15. Save the worksheet again with the same name (Excel E1, SA 04).
16. Close Excel E1, SA 04.

Assessment 5

1. Open Excel Worksheet E1-10.
2. Save the worksheet using the Save As command and name it Excel E1, SA 05.
3. Create a custom header that has your name left aligned and the file name right aligned.
4. Apply the AutoFormat style List 1 to cells A7 through B29 as well as to cells D7 through E29.
5. Center the label in cell A6 across columns A and B. Center the label in cell D6 across cells D6 and E6. Center the label in cell A5 across cells A5 through E5.
6. Create a conditional format to apply to the numbers in cells B8 through B29 and cells E8 through E29. If a number is less than 75, it should be displayed in the bold italic font style and the color orange. If a number is greater than 250, it should be displayed in the bold italic font style and the color blue.
7. Save the worksheet again with the same name (Excel E1, SA 05) and print it.
8. Close Excel E1, SA 05.

Assessment 6

1. Open Excel Worksheet E1-11.
2. Save the worksheet using the Save As command and name it Excel E1, SA 06.
3. Create a custom header that has your name left aligned and the file name right aligned.
4. Using the Paste Special command, transpose the entries in cells A4 through K12. *(Hint: You will have to paste the cells to a clear part of the worksheet and then delete the original entries.)*
5. Apply the AutoFormat style Classic 2 to the appropriate cells in the worksheet.
6. Print the worksheet.
7. Hide columns containing the Hourly Rate figures and the Gross Pay figures.
8. Print the worksheet again.
9. Unhide columns that were hidden in step 7.
10. Save the worksheet again with the same name (Excel E1, SA 06).
11. Close Excel E1, SA 06.

Assessment 7

1. Open Excel Worksheet E1-12.
2. Save the worksheet using the Save As command and name it Excel E1, SA 07.
3. Create a custom header that has your name left aligned and the file name right aligned.
4. Angle the labels in row 4 so that they are at a 60 degree angle.
5. Adjust the width of columns B through Y using the AutoFit Selection command.
6. Change the page orientation to landscape. Scale the page so that it fits to 1 page wide by 2 pages tall.
7. Set up the sheet so that rows 2 through 4 print at the top of every page. Set the left and right margins to 0.5 inch.
8. Use the Page Break Preview command to adjust the page breaks so that the temperatures for the state of Montana are printed at the top of page 2.
9. Create a conditional format to apply to all the temperatures. If a temperature is between 70 and 82 degrees, it should display as bold, and the cell should be shaded with pale blue.

10. Save the worksheet again with the same name (Excel E1, SA 07) and print it.
11. Close Excel E1, SA 07.

Assessment 8

1. Open Excel Worksheet E1-13.
2. Save the worksheet using the Save As command and name it Excel E1, SA 08.
3. Create a custom header that has your name left aligned and the file name right aligned.
4. Select cell A4. Create a style named Header 1. The style should use the font Tahoma (or another sans serif font), the font style bold italic, the font size 14, and the color plum.
5. Apply the Header 1 style to cells A14 and A23.
6. Select cells A5 through G5. Create a style named Header 2. The style should use the font Tahoma (or another sans serif font), the font style bold, and the font size 10. In addition, it should have a very light gray background, and the horizontal alignment should be centered.
7. Apply the Header 2 style to cells A15 through G15 and cells A24 through G24.
8. Select cells G6 through G11, G16 through G20, and G25 through G30. Create a conditional format that displays any value greater than 12 as bold and red.
9. Automatically adjust the width of the columns so that all of the labels can be read.
10. Save the worksheet again with the same name (Excel E1, SA 08) and print it.
11. Close Excel E1, SA 08.

Assessment 9

1. Use Excel's Office Assistant to learn how you can remove conditional formats. *(Hint: Click Help and Microsoft Excel Help. Either at the Office Assistant or on the Answer Wizard tab, key the question* ***"How do I remove a conditional format?"*** *and click Search. At the list of topics that displays, click* Delete conditional formats. *Read and then print the information displayed in the Help dialog box.)*
2. Open Excel E1, SA 08. Save the worksheet using the Save As command and name it Excel E1, SA 09.
3. Create a custom header that has your name left aligned and the file name right aligned.
4. Select cells G6 through G11, G16 through G20, and G25 through G30. Using the help information you printed in step 1, remove the conditional formatting from these cells.
5. Print Excel E1, SA 09.
6. Save the worksheet using the same file name (Excel E1, SA 09) and close it.

CHAPTER 2

WORKING WITH TEMPLATES AND WORKBOOKS

PERFORMANCE OBJECTIVES

Upon successful completion of chapter 2, you will be able to:

- **Use an existing Excel template**
- **Create a new template**
- **Create a new workbook based upon a user-defined template**
- **Edit a template**
- **Create and use a workspace file**
- **Open multiple workbooks**
- **Copy several worksheets into a new workbook**
- **Consolidate data into a list**
- **Link workbooks**
- **Share workbooks**

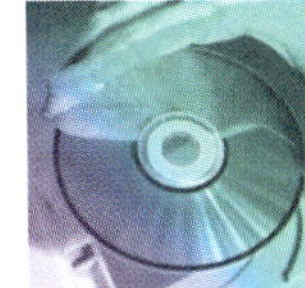

Excel Chapter 02E

Many people in an organization often need to share data and use the same workbooks. Excel includes several features that facilitate the sharing of data and workbooks. A template can be created that anyone in an organization could use as often as desired. A template serves as a pattern for a worksheet. The template includes data that would remain the same every time the worksheet was used. Certain labels and formulas, for example, might never change in a particular worksheet, so they could become a part of the template that anyone in the organization could then use. Being able to work with multiple workbooks at the same time is another feature that makes it easy for people to share workbooks. Several worksheets can be merged into a new workbook. Specific cells in one workbook can be linked to another workbook, making it easy to share data. Two people can even edit the same workbook at the same time. In this chapter you will learn ways to share data using Excel.

Using Excel Templates

Oftentimes worksheets are used over and over again for the same purpose. Calculating a monthly profit and loss statement is a routine task performed in most businesses. Much of the data contained in a monthly profit and loss worksheet, such as the labels and the formulas, would be the same from month to month. The only thing that would change from one month to the next would be the actual numbers. Whenever you have a situation in which the basic format of a worksheet is going to be used repeatedly, using a template is a good idea. A template is like a form that gets filled out over and over again. You retrieve a template that has been created, fill in the relevant data, and save it. When the Save command is given, the Save As box automatically appears so that you can give the file a new name. That way, you always have the original template file to use over again.

The templates for all the Office XP applications are stored in the same folder. The default template folder for all the Office XP applications is:

C:\Windows\Application Data\Microsoft\Templates

For setups with multiple user capacity, the default template folder is:

C:\Documents and Settings*user_name*\Application Data\Microsoft\Templates

Excel comes with a template for a Balance Sheet, an Expense Statement, a Loan Amortization, an Invoice, and a Timecard. These templates are accessed by clicking General Templates under New from template on the New Workbook task pane. If the New Workbook task pane is not displayed, click File and New to display it. Once the Templates dialog box is displayed, click the Spreadsheet Solutions tab. Excel's predesigned templates are shown in figure 2.1.

FIGURE 2.1 **Excel's Predesigned Templates**

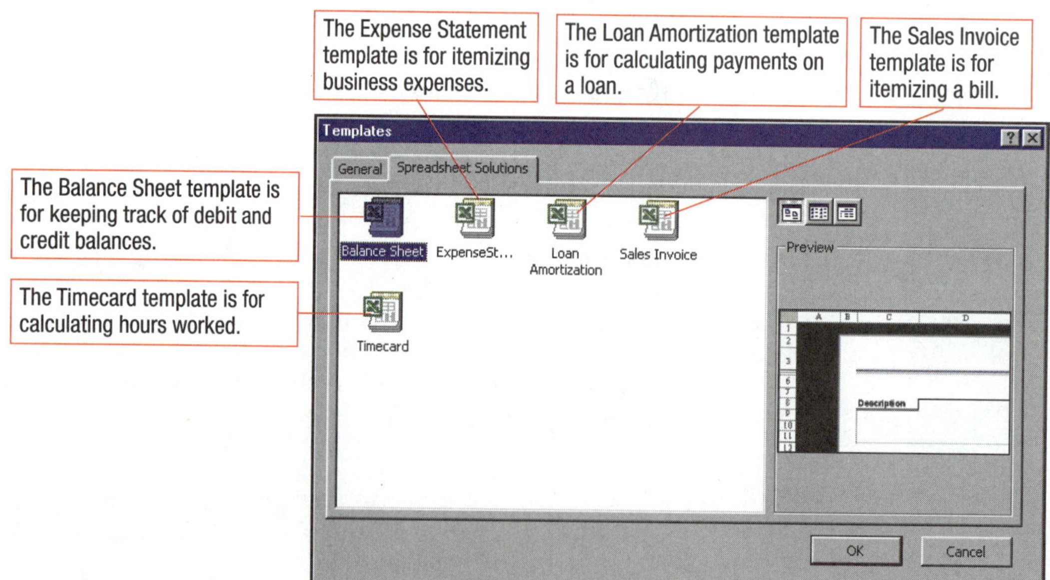

(Before completing exercise 1, delete the Chapter 01E *folder on your disk. Next, copy to your disk the* Chapter 02E *folder from the* Excel 2002 Expert *folder on the CD that accompanies this textbook.)*

1 USING AN EXISTING TEMPLATE

(Note: To complete this exercise, Excel's templates must be installed on your computer system.)

1. Open Excel.
2. If the New Workbook task pane is not displayed, click File and New to display it.
3. Click General Templates.
4. Click the Spreadsheet Solutions tab on the Templates dialog box.
5. Double-click the icon for the *Expense Statement* template.
6. You are ready to use the template. You can move around the Expense Statement using the Tab key. Under the Employee section, key the following data:

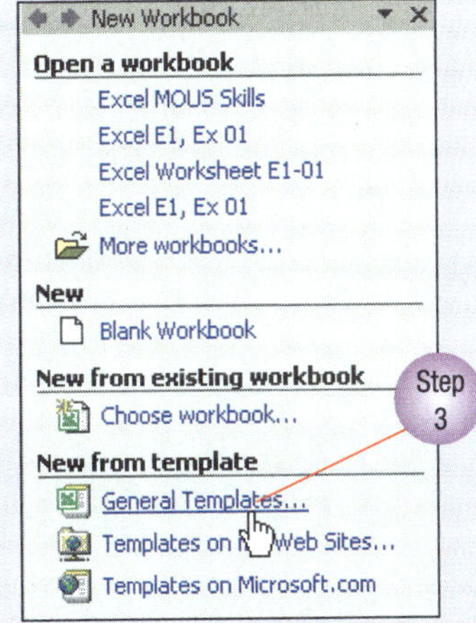

Name:	**Lucinda Getz**
Emp #:	**293**
SSN:	**555-63-1234**
Position:	**Sales Representative**
Department:	**Sales**
Manager:	**Mark Wilcox**
Pay Period From:	**12/6**
Pay Period To:	**12/19**

Key the following data into the expense statement:

Date	*Account*	*Description*	*Lodging*	*Fuel*	*Meals*	*Phone*
12/9	1473-96	Service Call		33.75	15.60	
12/14	2783-92	Update Orders	85.74	126.9	32.40	2.45

Your screen should look like the following illustration:

Employee

Name	Lucinda Getz	Emp #	293
SSN	555-63-1234	Position	Sales Representative
Department	Sales	Manager	Mark Wilcox

Date	Account	Description	Lodging	Transport	Fuel	Meals	Phone
12/9/03	1473-96	Service Call			$ 33.75	$ 15.60	
12/14/03	2783-92	Update Orders	$ 85.74		$ 126.90	$ 34.40	$ 2.45

7. Create a custom header by completing the following steps:
   a. Click File and then click Page Setup.
   b. Click the Header/Footer tab.
   c. Click the Custom Header button.
   d. Key your name in the left section box.
   e. Click in the right section box and click the Insert File Name button.
   f. Click the OK button twice.
8. Save the worksheet by completing the following steps:
   a. Click File and then click Save.
   b. Name the file Excel E2, Ex 01.
   c. Click Save.
9. Print and then close the Excel E2, Ex 01 file.

Creating a New Template

Creating a template is simply a matter of creating a workbook and then saving the workbook as a template. The workbook should contain the standard data that would be used over and over again each time the workbook is used. The two biggest advantages of using templates are they save you time, since much of the data is already entered, and they ensure consistency in the appearance of workbooks.

Since Excel saves workbooks using the extension .xls and it saves templates using the extension .xlt, being able to see the file name extension is quite useful. If you cannot view the extensions, you cannot tell which files are templates and which files are workbooks. If the extensions are not displayed, the option to hide them must be selected. To show file name extensions, use either My Computer or Windows Explorer to find the folder containing the files with the extensions you want to see. Click the folder to select it, and then click View and Folder Options. Click the View tab on the Folder Options dialog box. Under Advanced settings, the check box for the *Hide file extensions for known file types* option will be selected. Click the box so that it is no longer selected and then click OK. The exercises in this book assume that the file extensions are not hidden.

exercise 2 — CREATING A TEMPLATE

1. Open a new Excel workbook.
2. Create a custom header by completing the following steps:
   a. Click File and then click Page Setup.
   b. Click the Header/Footer tab.
   c. Click the Custom Header button.
   d. Key your name in the left section box.
   e. Click the right section box and then click the Insert File Name button.
   f. Click the OK button twice.
3. You are going to create a monthly income statement as a template so that it can be used over again each month. Key the following data in the cells indicated:

Cell	Data
A4	**Whitewater Canoe and Kayak Corporation**
A5	**Income Statement**
A7	**For the Month Ending:**
A9	**Sales**
A10	**Less: cost of goods sold**
A11	**Gross margin**
A13	**Operating expenses:**
A14	**Wages expense**
A15	**Depreciation expense**
A16	**Insurance expense**
A17	**Operating income**
A19	**Other Expenses:**
A20	**Interest expense**
A21	**Net income**

4. Save the file on your student data disk. For now, just save it as a regular workbook file. Name the file Excel E2, Ex 02.

5. Format the worksheet by completing the following steps:
   a. Automatically adjust the width of column A so that the name of the company fits in one cell.
   b. Center the data in A4 across columns A, B, C, and D. Center the data in A5 across columns A, B, C, and D.
   c. Format cells A7, A11, A17, and A21 so that data entered into them will be right-aligned in the cell.
   d. Format the data in cells A4, A5, and A7 so that the font style is bold and the font size is 12.
   e. Format cells C9 through D21 so that numbers entered into those cells are displayed in the Accounting format with zero decimal places and the dollar sign symbol displayed.
   f. Format cell B7 so that data entered in that cell displays as the month (Mar, for example) and year only.
   g. Place a single-line border on the bottom of cells D10, C16, D16, and D20. Place a double-line border on the bottom of cell D21.
6. Enter the following formulas in the cells indicated:

Cell	Formula
D11	**=D9-D10**
D16	**=SUM(C14:C16)**
D17	**=D11-D16**
D21	**=D17-D20**

7. Your screen should now look like the illustration at the right. You are now ready to save the file as a template. Complete the following steps to save the file as a template.
   a. Click File and Save As.
   b. When the Save As dialog box appears, click the down arrow to the right of the Save as type box.
   c. Click Template (*.xlt).
   d. Notice that the file name automatically changed to Excel E2, Ex 02.xlt and that the *Templates* folder is in the Save in box. Click Save.
8. Close the Excel E2, Ex 02.xlt template. You must close the template file before you can make a new worksheet based on it.

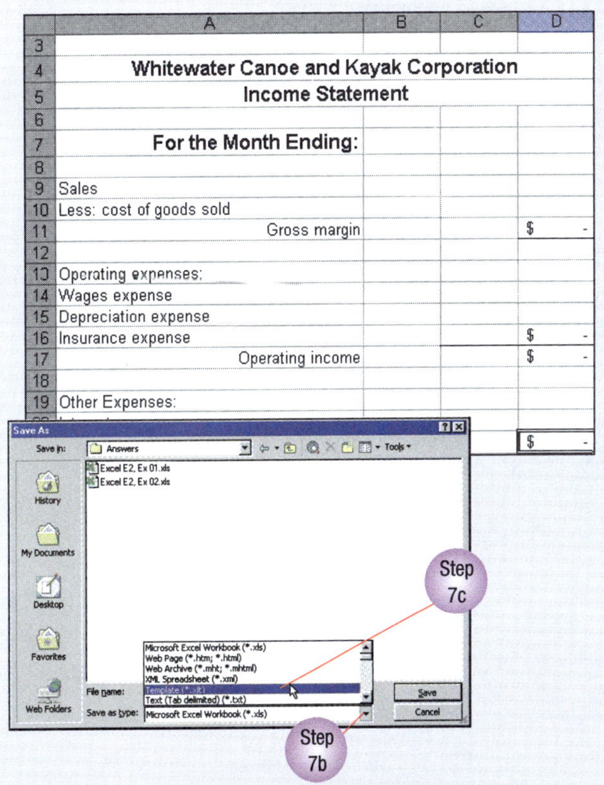

Editing a Template

Once a template has been created, you can easily edit it to make changes that might be needed at a later time. To edit a template, click File and New and then double-click the icon for the template to be edited from the General tab on the New dialog box. Make the necessary changes to the template and then click the Save button. When the Save As dialog box appears, click the down arrow to the right of the Save as type box and then click the Template (*.xlt) option. In the File name box enter the original name of the template and click the Save button. When the warning dialog box appears asking if you want to replace the original template file, click Yes. The edited template will then be saved.

exercise 3

APPLYING AND EDITING TEMPLATES

1. Complete the following steps to open the Excel E2, Ex 02.xlt template.
   a. If necessary, click File and then New to display the New Workbook task pane.
   b. From the New Workbook task pane, click General Templates.
   c. If necessary, click the General tab on the Templates dialog box.
   d. Double-click the *Excel E2, Ex 02.xlt* icon.

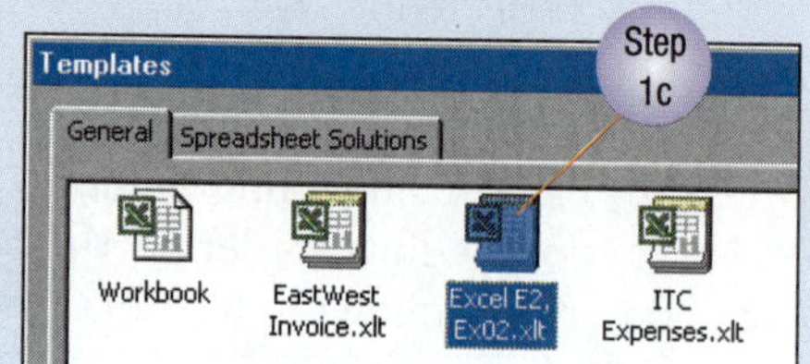

2. Enter the following data in the cells indicated:

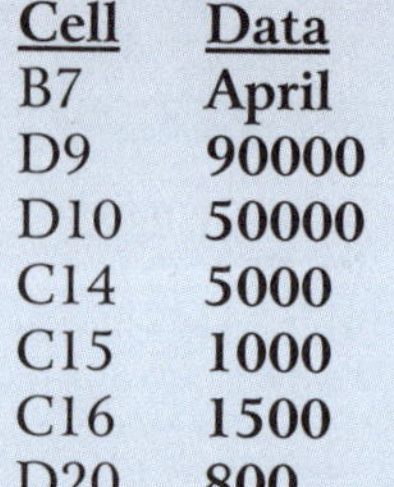

Cell	Data
B7	**April**
D9	**90000**
D10	**50000**
C14	**5000**
C15	**1000**
C16	**1500**
D20	**800**

3. Complete the following steps to save the worksheet.
   a. Click the Save button.
   b. Check the Save in box to make sure that the file is going to be saved on your data disk in drive A.
   c. Currently the name in the File name box is Excel E2, Ex 02.xls. Change the file name to **Excel E2, Ex 02-a.xls**.
   d. Click Save.
4. Print and then close Excel E2, Ex 02-a.xls.
5. You now need to edit the template. Complete the following steps to edit the Excel E2, Ex 02.xlt template.
   a. Click File and then New.
   b. From the New Workbook task pane, click General Templates.
   c. If necessary, click the General tab on the Templates dialog box.
   d. Double-click the *Excel E2, Ex 02.xlt* icon.
   e. Insert a new row 15.
   f. Key **Rent expense** in cell A15.
   g. Click the Save button.
   h. When the Save As dialog box appears, click the down arrow to the right of the Save as type box and click Template (*.xlt).
   i. Change the name in the File name box to **Excel E2, Ex 02.xlt**.
   j. Click Save.
   k. When the warning box appears asking if you want to replace the existing file, click Yes.
6. Close the Excel E2, Ex 02.xlt template. You must close the template file before you can make a new worksheet based on it.
7. Complete the following steps to open the Excel E2, Ex 02.xlt template.

a. Click File and then New.
b. From the New Workbook task pane, click General Templates.
c. If necessary, click the General tab on the New dialog box.
d. Double-click the *Excel E2, Ex 02.xlt* icon. Notice that the new Rent Expense category is now in the template.

8. Enter the following data in the cells indicated:

Cell	Data
B7	**May**
D9	**93000**
D10	**49500**
C14	**5000**
C15	**2200**
C16	**1000**
C17	**1500**
D21	**800**

9. Complete the following steps to save the worksheet.
   a. Click the Save button.
   b. Check the Save in box to make sure that the file is going to be saved on your data disk in drive A.
   c. Currently the name in the File name box is Excel E2, Ex 02.xls. Change the file name to **Excel E2, Ex 02-b.xls**.
   d. Click Save.
10. Print and then close Excel E2, Ex 02-b.xls.
11. You need to delete the template you created from the *Templates* folder. This exercise assumes the default user template folder is:

    C:\Windows\Application Data\Microsoft\Templates

    If this is not the location of the default user template folder on the computer system you are using, you will need to ask your instructor for help.

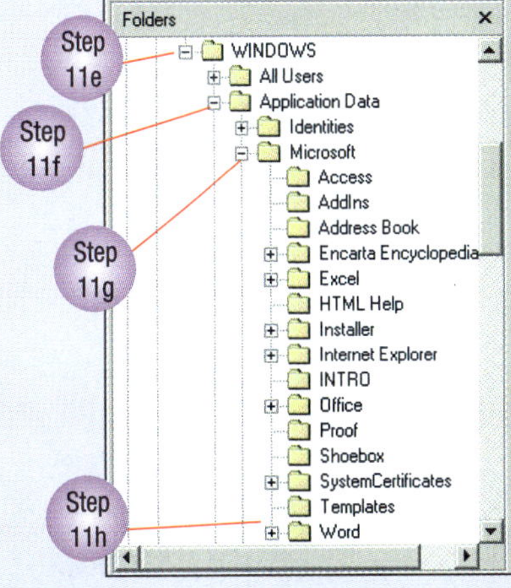

   a. Click the Start button.
   b. Point to Programs and the point to Accessories.
   c. Click Windows Explorer. In the Folders pane, click the plus sign next to My Computer.
   d. Under My Computer, there should be a plus sign next to the Local Disk (C:) directory. If there is, click it. If there is a minus sign next to the Local Disk (C:) directory, skip to the next step.
   e. There should now be a list of folders under the Local Disk (C:) directory. Find the *Windows* folder. If there is a plus sign next to the *Windows* folder, click it. If there is a minus sign next to the *Windows* folder, skip to the next step.
   f. There should now be a list of folders under the *Windows* folder. Find the *Application Data* folder. If there is a plus sign next to the *Application Data* folder, click it. If there is a minus sign next to the *Application Data* folder, skip to the next step.
   g. There should now be a list of folders under the *Application Data* folder. Find the *Microsoft* folder. If there is a plus sign next to the *Microsoft* folder, click it. If there is a minus sign next to the *Microsoft* folder, skip to the next step.
   h. There should now be a list of folders under the *Microsoft* folder. Find the *Templates* folder and click it.

i. Click the icon for the *Excel E2, Ex 02.xlt* template.
j. Click the Delete button. Click the Yes button.
k. Close Windows Explorer.

12. Close Excel.

Using Multiple Workbooks

You can easily work with data from different workbooks at the same time using Excel. By creating a workspace, you can open several workbooks at the same time with just one step. Once several workbooks are open, you can copy all the data from the open workbooks into a new workbook, and consolidate the data from several workbooks into one worksheet.

Arranging Multiple Workbooks in the Desktop

If you want to work with more than one workbook at a time, the workbooks must be arranged so that you can easily read the data contained in each one. To arrange multiple workbooks, click Window and then Arrange. As shown in figure 2.2, there are four options for arranging windows in the desktop: Tiled, Horizontal, Vertical, and Cascade. Select one of these options and then click OK. The open workbooks will be arranged so that the data from each workbook can be viewed at the same time.

FIGURE 2.2 ***The Arrange Windows Dialog Box***

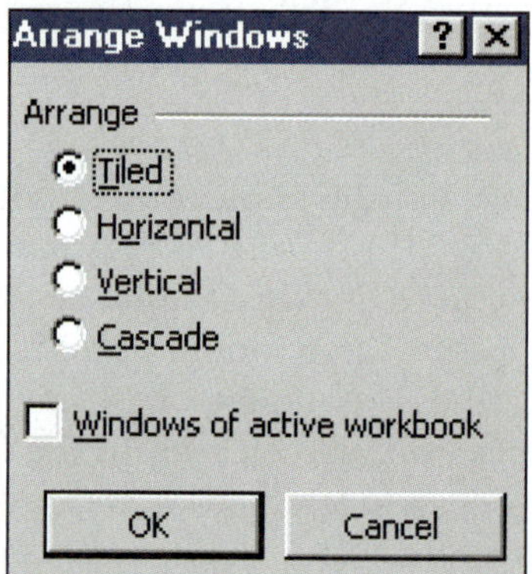

Using a Workspace

If you frequently work with the same group of workbooks, you may want to create a customized workspace. A customized workspace allows you to open a group of workbooks in one step. Information about the open files, such as their locations, window sizes, and screen positions, is stored in a workspace file. Then, instead of opening each individual workbook, all you have to do is open the workspace file, and all the individual workbooks that are a part of the file are opened.

To create a workspace, first open the workbooks you want to be included in the workspace, and then size and position them as you want them to appear each time the workspace file is opened. Click File. You may need to expand the File menu in order to click Save Workspace. Enter a name for the workspace file in the File name box. The extension for a workspace file is .xlw. Whenever you want to open the group of workbooks together, open the workspace file.

Merging Multiple Workbooks into a Single Workbook

Once you have multiple workbooks open at the same time, you can easily copy worksheets from each workbook into a single workbook. To copy a worksheet from one workbook to another, press the Ctrl key and drag the sheet tab of the worksheet you want to copy to the sheet tabs in the workbook where you want to place the copied worksheet.

exercise 4

USING A WORKSPACE AND MERGING WORKSHEETS INTO A WORKBOOK

1. Open Excel.
2. The sales figures for individual sales representatives of Copper Clad Incorporated for the last quarter of 2001 are stored in three separate workbooks. Since these three workbooks are frequently used at the same time, you want to create a workspace for them. Open OctSales.xls, NovSales.xls, and DecSales.xls.
3. All three workbooks are open, but you cannot see them because they are on top of one another. Complete the following steps to adjust how the workbooks are displayed on your desktop:
   a. Click Window and Arrange.
   b. Click the Vertical option on the Arrange Windows dialog box and click OK. The workbooks are now arranged next to each other.
4. Create a workspace by completing the following steps:
   a. Click File. If necessary, expand the menu by clicking the down arrow at the bottom of the menu. Click Save Workspace.
   b. The Save Workspace dialog box appears. Key the following in the File name box: **Last Quarter.xlw**
   c. Click Save.

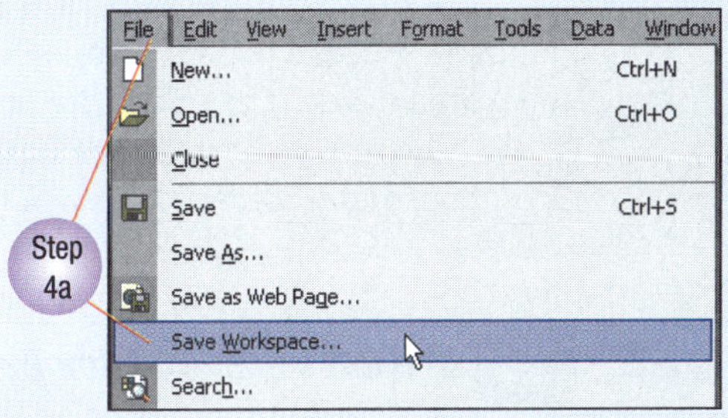

5. Close the OctSales.xls, NovSales.xls, and DecSales.xls workbooks.
6. Open the workspace you just created by completing the following steps:
   a. Click File and Open.
   b. The Open dialog box is displayed. Click *Last Quarter.xlw* to select it.
   c. Click Open. The workspace you created is now open.
7. Open a new workbook and copy the *October 01* worksheet, the *November 01* worksheet, and the *December 01* worksheet into the new workbook by completing the following steps:
   a. Click the New button on the Standard toolbar to open a new workbook.
   b. Click Window and Arrange.
   c. Click the Tiled option on the Arrange Windows dialog box and click OK. Four workbooks should now be displayed: the new blank workbook and Dec Sales.xls, Nov Sales.xls, and Oct Sales.xls.
   d. Click on the Oct Sales.xls sheet to make it active.

e. Press the Ctrl key and drag the October 01 sheet tab to the new workbook, placing it to the left of the *Sheet1* tab.
f. Click on the Nov Sales.xls sheet to make it active.
g. Press the Ctrl key and drag the November 01 sheet tab to the new workbook, placing it between the October 01 tab and the *Sheet1* tab.
h. Click on the Dec Sales.xls sheet to make it active.
i. Press the Ctrl key and drag the December 01 sheet tab to the new workbook, placing it between the November 01 tab and the *Sheet1* tab.

8. The worksheets are now all copied into the new workbook. Close the Dec Sales.xls, Nov Sales.xls, and Oct Sales.xls files. You have to make each workbook active and then close it. Click the Maximize button on the new workbook. Save the new workbook on the data disk using the file name Excel E2, Ex 04.
9. Close Excel E2, Ex 04.

Consolidating Data from Several Worksheets into a List

If you have several worksheets in one workbook or several worksheets from different workbooks, data from each worksheet can be consolidated on a separate worksheet. To consolidate the data, click Data and then Consolidate. The Consolidate dialog box shown in figure 2.3 appears. You first have to decide what function you want performed on the consolidated data. Figure 2.4 shows you the options from the Function drop-down menu. Next you have to select all the references you want consolidated. If you want the consolidated data to include labels, you can select the appropriate check boxes in the Use labels in section. When all the selections have been made, click OK. The data is then all consolidated onto one worksheet.

FIGURE 2.3 ***The Consolidate Dialog Box***

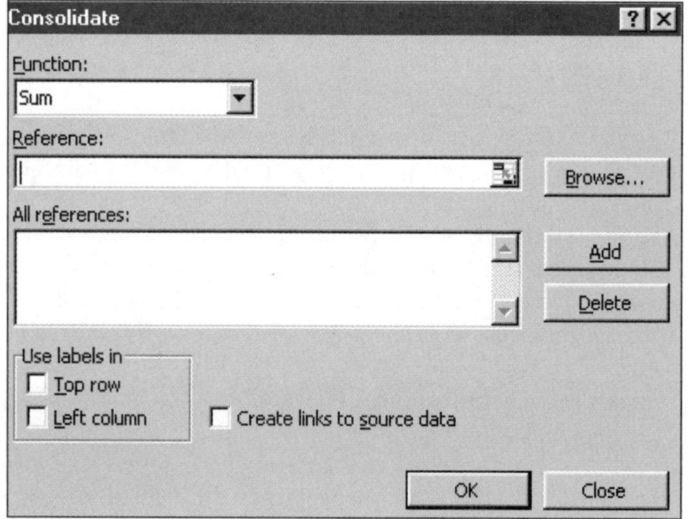

FIGURE 2.4 **_Functions That Can Be Performed on Consolidated Data_**

Sum
Count
Average
Max
Min
Product
Count Nums
StdDev
StdDevp
Var
Varp

CONSOLIDATING DATA INTO A LIST

1. Open Excel E2, Ex 04.
2. Save the workbook with the Save As command and name it Excel E2, Ex 05.
3. You want to consolidate the figures on the three separate worksheets into one worksheet. Complete the following steps to consolidate the data:
   a. Click the *Sheet1* tab.
   b. Click Format, point to Sheet, and then click Rename. Key the following: **Last Qtr 01**
   c. Click cell A1 on the *Last Qtr 01* worksheet.
   d. Click Data and Consolidate.
   e. Check to make sure that Sum is displayed in the Function box.
   f. If necessary, click in the Reference box. The insertion point must be in the Reference box.
   g. Click the October 01 sheet tab. You may have to scroll to the left to see it.
   h. If the Consolidate dialog box is in the way, click on the title bar and drag it to the right. Select cells A1 through B17.
   i. Click the Add button.
   j. Click the November 01 sheet tab.
   k. Cells A1 through B17 should already be selected.
   l. Click the Add button.
   m. Click the December 01 sheet tab.
   n. Cells A1 through B17 should already be selected.
   o. Click the Add button.
   p. In the Use labels in section, click the Top row check box and the Left column check box.

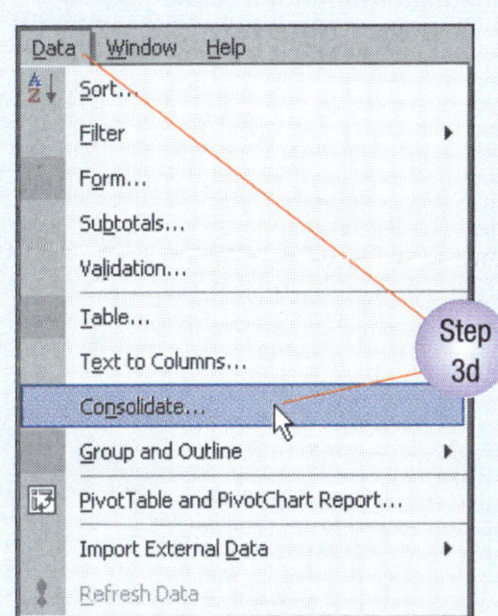

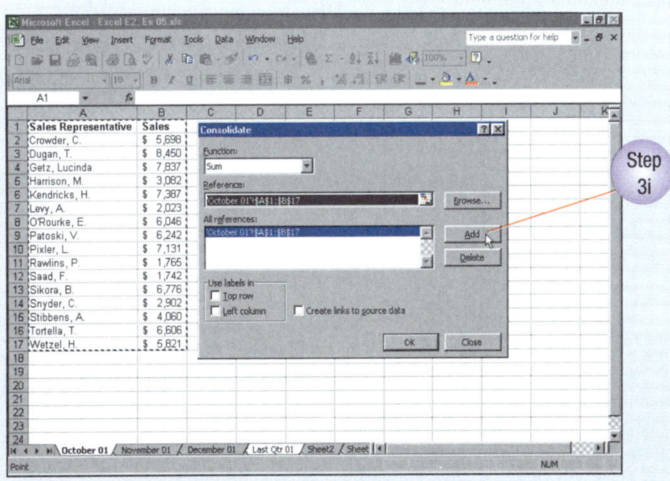

q. Click OK.
4. The data is consolidated in the *Last Qtr 01* worksheet. If necessary, click the Last Qtr 01 sheet tab. Widen column A to display all the names. Add a custom header that displays your name at the left margin and the file name at the right margin. Print the *Last Qtr 01* worksheet.
5. Save the workbook with the same name (Excel E2, Ex 05).
6. Close Excel E2, Ex 05.

Linking Workbooks

In many cases, worksheets utilize data that is already located in another worksheet. For example, someone preparing a quarterly report would need the figures from the monthly reports for each month in the quarter. Instead of reentering all that data into the quarterly report, with Excel you can link the quarterly report worksheet to the monthly reports worksheets. Once a link has been established, if the data in the worksheet to which you have linked is changed, the link will automatically update itself to reflect any changes when the worksheet is opened. A link can be established between worksheets in the same workbook, between worksheets in different workbooks, and even to data found on company intranets or the Internet.

To link worksheets, click the cell where the linked data will be placed and key = to begin the link. Locate the worksheet where the data you want to link to is stored, click the cell to be linked, and then press Enter. The worksheet containing the linked data will appear with the appropriate data displayed in the linked cell. Links can even be used in formulas and functions.

exercise 6 — USING A WORKSPACE AND LINKING WORKBOOKS

1. Before starting this exercise, you need to remove the read-only attribute from the Region Sales Oct, Region Sales Nov, and Region Sales Dec files. To remove the read-only attribute from the Region Sales Oct file, complete the following steps:
   a. Using either Windows Explorer or My Computer, navigate to the Region Sales Oct file on your data disk.
   b. Right-click the Region Sales Oct file.
   c. From the shortcut menu that is displayed, click Properties.
   d. Click the General tab on the File Properties dialog box that is displayed.
   e. In the Attributes section toward the bottom of the dialog box, click the Read-only check box so that it is no longer selected.
   f. Click OK.
2. Repeat step 1 to remove the read-only attribute from the Region Sales Nov and Region Sales Dec files. When you have finished, close either Windows Explorer or My Computer.
3. Open Excel.
4. The quarterly sales figures by regions for the sales representatives of Copper Clad Incorporated for the last quarter of 2001 are stored in three separate workbooks. Create a workspace for these three workbooks by completing the following steps:
   a. Open Region Sales Oct, Region Sales Nov, and Region Sales Dec.

- b. Click Window and Arrange.
- c. Click the Vertical option on the Arrange Windows dialog box and then click OK. You can now see all three workbooks.
- d. Click File. If necessary, expand the menu by clicking the down arrow at the bottom of the menu. Click Save Workspace.
- e. The Save Workspace dialog box appears. Key the following in the File name box: **4th Quarter Sales.xlw**
- f. Click Save.

5. Close the Region Sales Oct, Region Sales Nov, and Region Sales Dec workbooks.
6. Open the workspace you just created by completing the following steps:
   - a. Click File and Open.
   - b. The Open dialog box is displayed. Click *4th Quarter Sales.xlw* to select it.
   - c. Click Open. The workspace you created is now open.
   - d. Open Fourth Qtr Summary.
   - e. Click Window and Arrange.
   - f. Click the Tiled option on the Arrange Windows dialog box and click OK. There are now four worksheets displayed.
7. The Fourth Qtr Summary workbook is going to summarize the data found in the other three workbooks. Click cell B5 in the Fourth Qtr Summary workbook. In this cell, you want the total for the North Region's sales in October, November, and December. Complete the following steps to link the three subtotals for the North Region's sales to the Fourth Qtr Summary workbook (you may need to scroll down in each window in order to select the necessary cell):
   - a. In cell B5 on the Fourth Qtr Summary workbook, key =.
   - b. Click the Region Sales Oct workbook and then click cell C7 in that workbook. Notice that a reference to that cell immediately appears in the Fourth Qtr Summary workbook.
   - c. The insertion point should be back in cell B5 on the Fourth Qtr Summary workbook to the right of the reference to the linked cell. Key +. 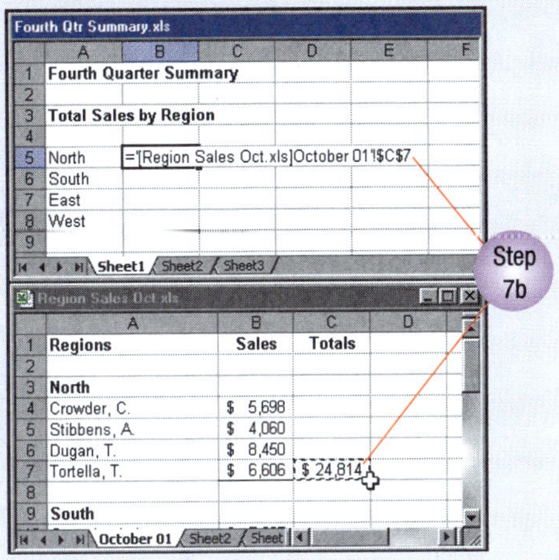
   - d. Click the Region Sales Nov workbook to make it active and then click cell C7 in that workbook.
   - e. Key +.
   - f. Click the Region Sales Dec workbook to make it active and then click cell C7 in that workbook.
   - g. Press Enter. The total for the North Region's sales for the months of October, November, and December appear in cell B5 in the Fourth Quarter Summary workbook.
8. Complete the following steps to link the three subtotals for the South Region's sales to the Fourth Qtr Summary workbook (you may need to scroll down in each window in order to select the necessary cell):
   - a. In cell B6 on the Fourth Qtr Summary workbook, key =.
   - b. Click the Region Sales Oct workbook to make it active and then click cell C13 in that workbook.

c. Key +.
d. Click the Region Sales Nov workbook to make it active and then click cell C13 in that workbook.
e. Key +.
f. Click the Region Sales Dec workbook to make it active and then click cell C13 in that workbook.
g. Press Enter. The total for the South Region's sales for the months of October, November, and December appear in cell B6 in the Fourth Quarter Summary workbook.

9. Complete the following steps to link the three subtotals for the East Region's sales to the Fourth Qtr Summary workbook (you may need to scroll down in each window in order to select the necessary cell):
   a. In cell B7 on the Fourth Qtr Summary workbook, key =.
   b. Click the Region Sales Oct workbook to make it active and then click cell C19 in that workbook.
   c. Key +.
   d. Click the Region Sales Nov workbook to make it active and then click cell C19 in that workbook.
   e. Key +.
   f. Click the Region Sales Dec workbook to make it active and then click cell C19 in that workbook.
   g. Press Enter. The total for the East Region's sales for the months of October, November, and December appear in cell B7 in the Fourth Quarter Summary workbook.
10. Complete the following steps to link the three subtotals for the West Region's sales to the Fourth Qtr Summary workbook (you may need to scroll down in each window in order to select the necessary cell):
   a. In cell B8 on the Fourth Qtr Summary workbook, key =.
   b. Click the Region Sales Oct workbook to make it active and then click cell C25 in that workbook.
   c. Key +.
   d. Click the Region Sales Nov workbook to make it active and then click cell C25 in that workbook.
   e. Key +.
   f. Click the Region Sales Dec workbook to make it active and then click cell C25 in that workbook.
   g. Press Enter. The total for the South Region's sales for the months of October, November, and December appear in cell B8 in the Fourth Quarter Summary workbook.
   h. Enter a function in cell B10 in the Fourth Qtr Summary workbook to add together the sales for the North, South, East, and West regions.
10. Next you want to use a link in an Excel function. In the Fourth Qtr Summary workbook, scroll down until you can see cells A14 through B19. In this area of the worksheet you want to calculate the average sales for each region for the fourth quarter. Complete the following steps to create the necessary links:
   a. On the Fourth Qtr Summary workbook, click cell B16.
   b. Click Insert Function on the formula bar.

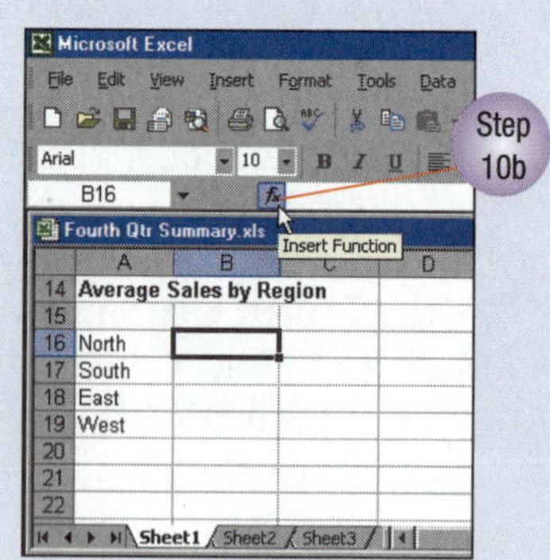

c. In the Or select a category list box, click *Statistical*.
d. In the Select a function list box, click *AVERAGE*.
e. Click OK. The Function Arguments dialog box opens.
f. On the Region Sales Oct workbook, click cell C7. The reference to cell C7 appears in the Formula Palette. If the Function Arguments dialog box gets in the way, you can move it by clicking on it and dragging it to a new location.
g. Key , (a comma).
h. Click the Region Sales Nov workbook to activate it and then click cell C7.
i. Key , (a comma).
j. Click the Region Sales Dec workbook to activate it and then click cell C7.
k. Press Enter.

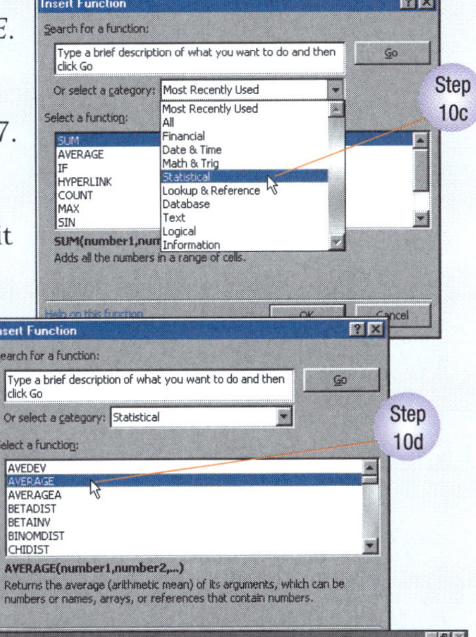

11. Complete steps similar to step 10 to find the average sales for the South Region. Use cell B17 in the Fourth Qtr Summary workbook and cell C13 in the monthly workbooks.
12. Complete steps similar to step 10 to find the average sales for the East Region. Use cell B18 in the Fourth Qtr Summary workbook and cell C19 in the monthly workbooks.
13. Complete steps similar to step 10 to find the average sales for the West Region. Use cell B19 in the Fourth Qtr Summary workbook and cell C25 in the monthly workbooks.

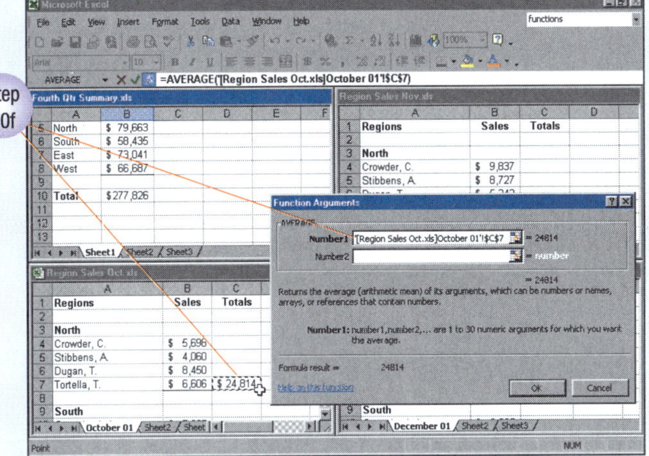

14. Close the Region Sales Oct, Region Sales Nov, and Region Sales Dec workbooks. Save the Fourth Qtr Summary workbook using the file name Excel E2, Ex 06.
15. Create a header for the workbook that displays your name at the left margin and the name of the file at the right margin.
16. Print the Excel E2, Ex 06 workbook and then close it.
17. Someone just discovered there are some mistakes on the Region Sales Dec workbook. Open this workbook and make the following changes:

Cell	**Sales**
B7	**5798**
B10	**3001**
B24	**2609**

Save and close the revised workbook.

Step 18

Microsoft Excel

This workbook contains links to other data sources.
• If you update the links, Excel attempts to retrieve the latest data.
• If you don't update, Excel uses the previous information.

Update | Don't Update | Help

18. Open the Excel E2, Ex 06 workbook. A warning box appears asking if you want to update the links. Click Update.
19. Print the Excel E2, Ex 06 workbook again. Notice how the figures have changed.
20. Save the worksheet with the same name (Excel E2, Ex 06) and close it.

Sharing Workbooks

Excel has many workgroup features—that is, features that make it easy for people to collaborate while using Excel. For example, people can share the same workbook and even use it at the same time. More than one person can make changes to the shared file at the same time. To share a workbook, click Tools and Share Workbook. The Share Workbook dialog box, shown in figure 2.5, appears. On the Editing tab, click the Allow changes by more than one user at the same time option. You can tell that a workbook is shared because the word [Shared] is displayed in the title bar next to the workbook name. Once the option for sharing a workbook has been selected, additional sharing options can be selected from the Advanced Tab on the Share Workbook dialog box, as shown in figure 2.6. Table 2.1 describes the options.

FIGURE 2.5 ***The Share Workbook Dialog Box with Editing Tab Selected***

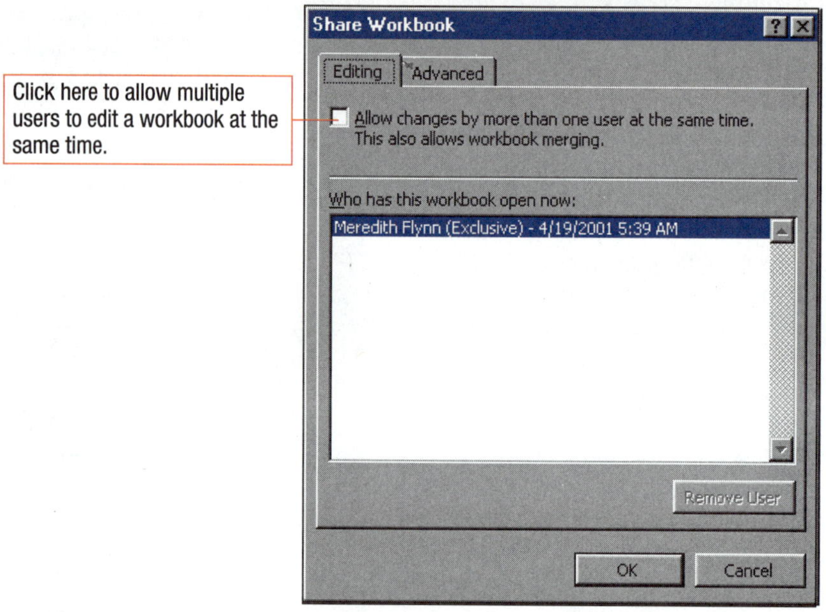

FIGURE

2.6 ***The Share Workbook Dialog Box with Advanced Tab Selected***

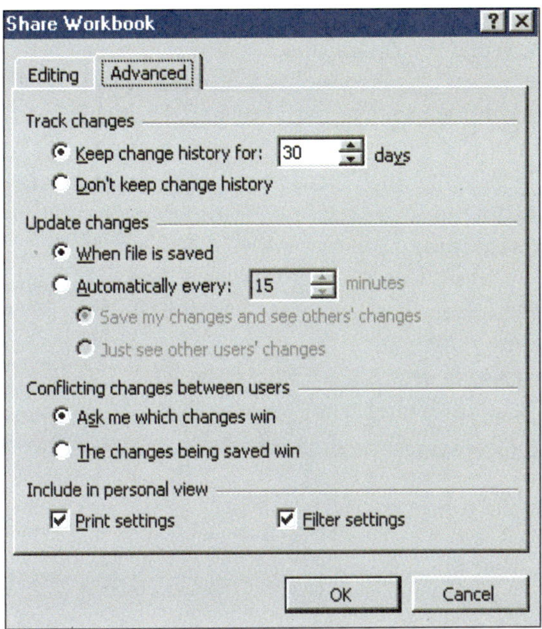

TABLE

2.1 ***Advanced Options for Sharing Workbooks***

Option	Description
Track changes	Sets the time period for how long Excel keeps the change history. The change history keeps track of how conflicting changes to the workbook were resolved.
Update changes	Sets when everyone's changes will be saved. They can be saved when the file is saved or at a regular time interval.
Conflicting changes between users	Sets how to resolve different changes made to the same data. Either your changes are saved over the other users' or Excel can prompt you to choose which change should be saved.

When you no longer want to share a workbook, you can turn the sharing option off by clicking Tools and Share Workbook. Click the Allow changes by more than one user at the same time check box to remove the check mark and then click OK. A warning box will be displayed alerting you that the workbook will no longer be available for shared use. Clicking Yes removes the workbook from shared use.

exercise 7

1. Open Excel Worksheet E2-01 from your data disk.
2. Save the document using the Save As command and name it Excel E2, Ex 07.
3. Create a custom header with your name displayed at the left margin and the file name displayed at the right margin.
4. Assume you are the head of personnel at Whitewater Canoe and Kayak Corporation. Changes need to be made to the employee records. You need to confer with Shirley Aultman, the office manager, regarding these changes. The easiest way to do this is for the two of you to share the worksheet. To tell which person is accessing which worksheet, you have to assign user names to the worksheets. Complete the following steps to change the user name:

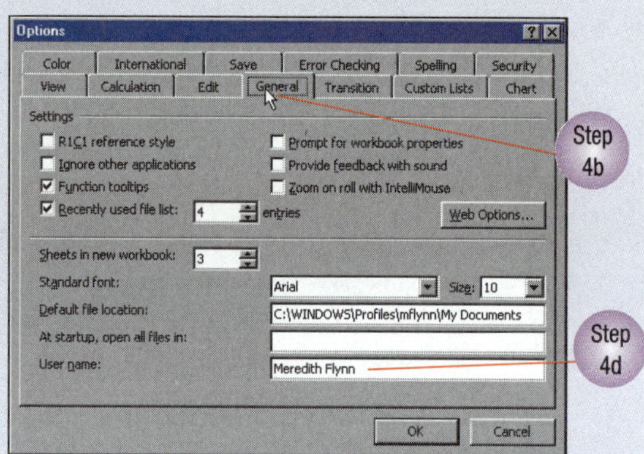

   a. Click Tools and Options.
   b. Click the General tab on the Options dialog box.
   c. Look in the User name box. On a piece of paper, write down the name that is currently entered. When you complete this exercise, you will change the name back.

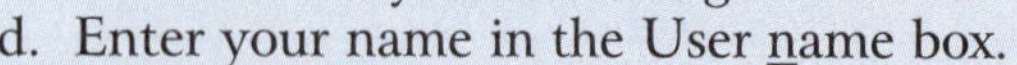

   d. Enter your name in the User name box.
   e. Click OK.
5. Click the Save button on the Standard toolbar.
6. To simulate sharing workbooks, you are going to open another copy of Excel. For the simulation to work, you must open Excel from the Start button. Click the Start button, point to Programs, and then open another copy of Excel.
7. You now have a second copy of Excel running with an unnamed worksheet on the screen. You need to change the user name for this copy of Excel. This will be the copy being run by the office manager. Complete the following steps to change the user name:
   a. Click Tools and Options.
   b. Click the General tab on the Options dialog box.
   c. In the User name box, key **Shirley Aultman**.
   d. Click OK.
   e. Right-click the Windows taskbar and click Tile Windows Horizontally.
   f. Make sure the copy of Excel that currently has the workbook Excel E2, Ex 07 open is on top. If necessary, rearrange the two windows by clicking and dragging on the title bars.

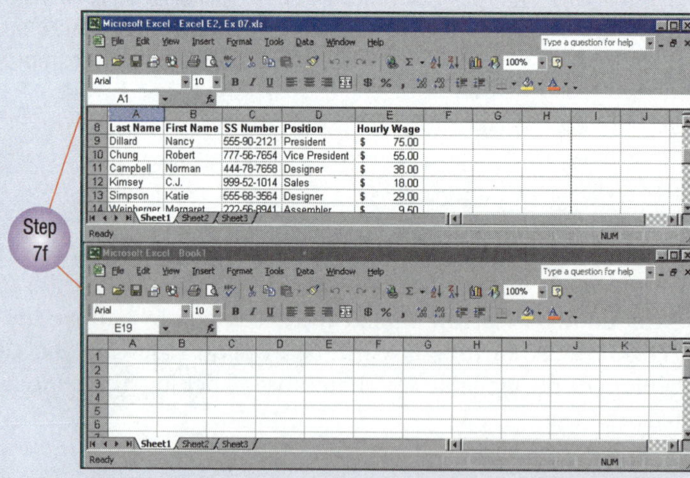

8. You currently have the Excel E2, Ex 07 workbook open. Complete the following steps to see what happens if Shirley tries to open the same workbook.
   a. If necessary, click in Shirley's copy of the program (the one on the bottom) to make sure it is the active program.
   b. Click the Open button on the Standard toolbar of Shirley's program and try to open the Excel E2, Ex 07 file on your data disk.
   c. The File in Use dialog box is displayed. Since Excel E2, Ex 07 has not been designated as a shared workbook, you cannot make any changes to it once it is open.
   d. Click Cancel.
9. Complete the following steps to designate Excel E2, Ex 07 as a shared workbook.
   a. Click in the window for Excel E2, Ex 07 (the top window) to make it active.
   b. On the menu bar of the top window, click Tools and Share Workbook.
   c. Click the Allow changes by more than one user at the same time check box to select it.
   d. Click OK.
   e. A dialog box is displayed notifying you that the workbook will be saved. Click OK.
10. Complete the following steps to open a copy of the shared workbook.
   a. Click in Shirley's copy of the program (the one on the bottom) to select it.
   b. Click the Open button on the Standard toolbar of Shirley's program and open the Excel E2, Ex 07 file on your data disk.

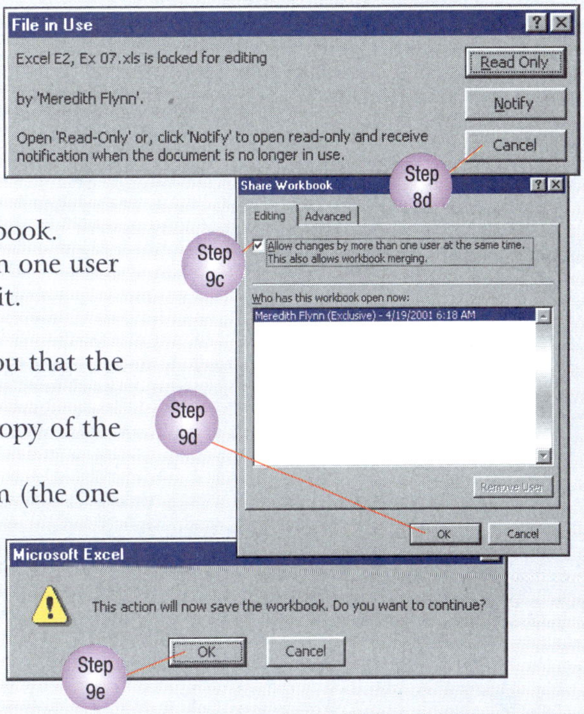

11. The workbook is now open in both program windows. Notice that the word [Shared] appears in the title bar of both windows. Complete the following steps to make changes to the worksheet:
   a. Access Shirley's copy of the workbook (the one on the bottom). Scroll to the bottom of the list and enter the following data for an employee that was just hired:

Cell	**Data**
A27	**Goldman**
B27	**Rona**
C27	**555-30-8311**
D27	**Assistant**
E27	**7.50**

   b. Click the Save button on the Standard toolbar of Shirley's copy of the workbook.
   c. Access your copy of the workbook (the one on top). One of the employees was promoted, and you need to make the necessary changes. Make the following changes to the contents of the cells listed:

Cell	**Data**
D17	**Assistant Manager**
E17	**8.75**

   d. Adjust the width of column D so that the complete position title is displayed.
   e. Click the Save button on the Standard toolbar of your copy of the workbook.

f. If an information box appears notifying you that your workbook was updated with changes made by someone else, click OK. Excel updates the workbook whenever it is saved.

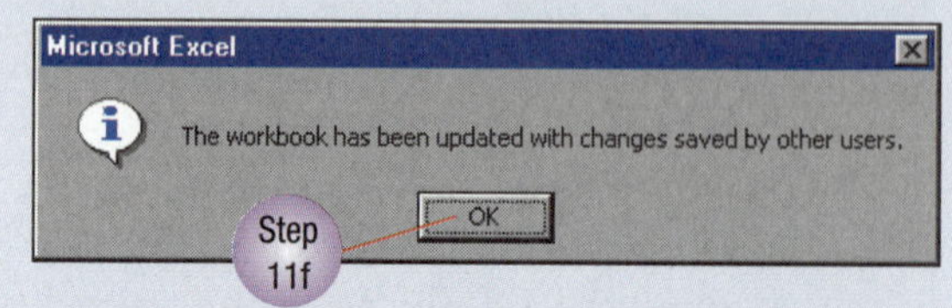

g. On your copy of the workbook, scroll down so that row 27 is displayed. The data on the new employee, entered by Shirley, appears in your worksheet. Notice the small triangles in the upper left corner of each cell. Move the mouse pointer over one of those triangles. Information on the change that Shirley made is displayed.

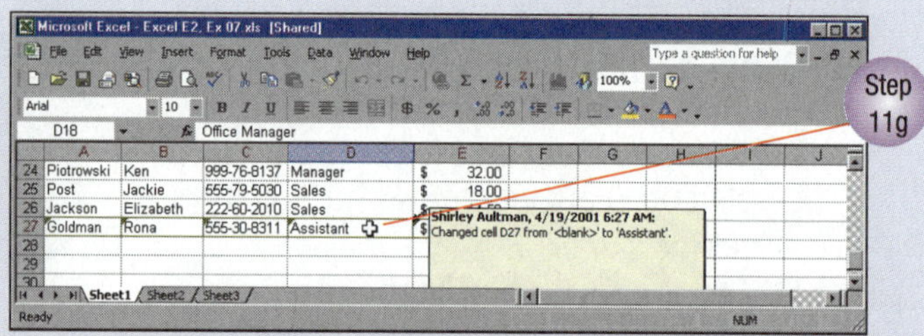

h. Access Shirley's copy of the workbook (the one on the bottom) and save it. When you are notified that the workbook has been updated, click OK. Look at cells D17 and E17 in Shirley's copy of the workbook to see the changes you made in your copy.

12. Complete the following steps to see what happens when users sharing a workbook enter conflicting data into the same cell:
   a. In Shirley's copy of the workbook (the one on the bottom), change the data in cell E14 to 10.75. Save the workbook.
   b. In your copy of the workbook (the one on the top), change the data in cell E14 to 10.25. Save the workbook.
   c. The Resolve Conflicts dialog box appears, notifying you that conflicting changes have been made to the worksheet. The first person who saves the workbook after conflicting changes have been entered is the one who gets to resolve the conflict. Click the Accept Mine button.
   d. Access Shirley's copy of the workbook and save it. When the dialog box appears informing you the workbook has been updated, click OK. Notice that 10.25 is now entered in cell E14 in Shirley's workbook.
   e. Shirley still has an opportunity to reject your changes. On the menu bar in Shirley's copy (the one on the bottom), click Tools and, if necessary, wait a moment for the Track Changes option to display. Point to the Track Changes option and click Accept or Reject Changes.

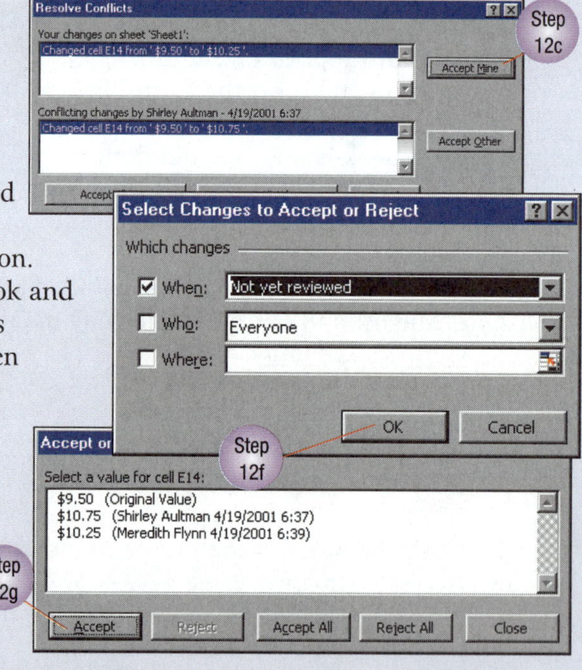

   f. The Select Changes to Accept or Reject dialog box is displayed. You can limit the changes that you review using this dialog box. Click OK to accept the default options.
   g. The Accept or Reject Changes dialog box is displayed. Click the Accept button until your dialog box displays the conflicting numbers entered in cell E14.

h. Shirley is going to reject your change to cell E14. Click the second option in the list, the option originally entered by Shirley, and click Accept. Save the workbook.

i. Access your copy of the workbook (the one on top) and click the Save button. Click OK when the dialog box appears notifying you that changes were made by other users. Now you want to look at a history of the changes that were made. Click Tools on the menu bar of your copy of the workbook, point to Track Changes, and click Highlight Changes.

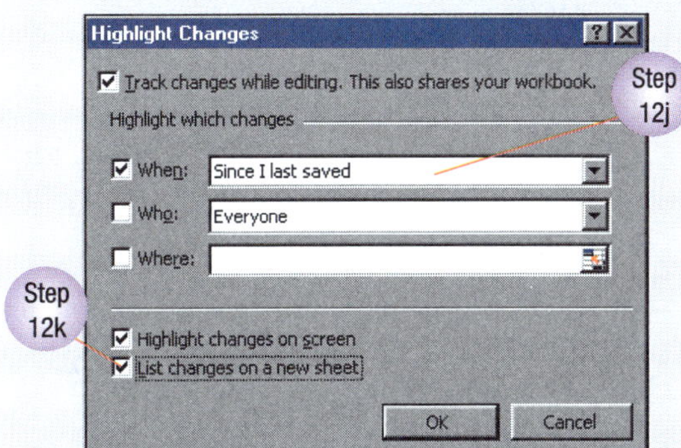

j. The Highlight Changes dialog box is displayed. The *Since I last saved* option should be displayed in the When box.

k. Click the check box to List changes on a new sheet. A check mark should be in the box.

l. Click OK. A new sheet tab is added to the worksheet called *History*. On this worksheet you can see that Shirley rejected your change in cell E14.

m. Save your worksheet (the one on top). Notice that the History sheet tab is no longer displayed. You cannot make any changes to the *History* worksheet, and it is hidden when not needed.

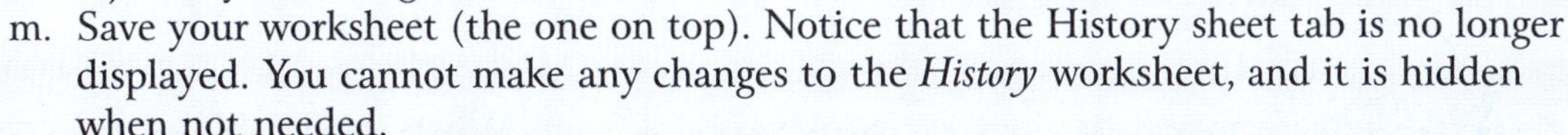

13. Print a copy of your worksheet.

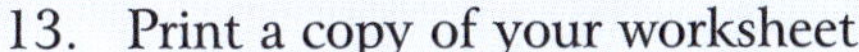

14. Access Shirley's copy of the workbook (the one on the bottom). Change the user name back to the original entry and exit the workbook by completing the following steps:
    a. Click Tools and Options.
    b. Click the General tab.
    c. In the User name box, key the name that was originally displayed when you started the exercise. Click the Save button to save the file.
    d. Click File on the menu bar in Shirley's workbook and click Exit. (You may have to scroll down the menu options in order to display the Exit option.)
15. Access your copy of the workbook. Maximize the window. Complete the following steps to designate that the workbook is no longer to be shared:
    a. Click Tools and Share Workbook.
    b. Click the Allow changes by more than one user at the same time check box so that it is no longer selected.
    c. Click OK.
    d. When the dialog box is displayed asking if you want to remove the workbook from shared use, click Yes.
16. Complete the following steps to change the user name back to the original entry:
    a. Click Tools and Options.
    b. Click the General tab.
    c. In the User name box, key the name that was originally displayed when you started the exercise.
    d. Click OK.
17. Save the worksheet with the same name (Excel E2, Ex 07) and close it.

CHAPTER summary

- If a workbook is used repeatedly for the same purpose, a template should be created for it. A template saves the basic format of a workbook so that labels, formats, formulas—anything that would remain the same each time the workbook is used—do not have to be entered each time. Excel comes with a template for a Balance Sheet, an Expense Statement, a Loan Amortization, an Invoice, and a Timecard.
- The default template folder for all the Office XP applications is:

  C:\Windows\Application Data\Microsoft\Templates

  For setups with multiple user capacity, the default template folder is:

  C:\Documents and Settings*user_name*\Application Data\Microsoft\Templates
- Create a new template by entering the data that will be used repeatedly into the worksheet, clicking File and then Save As. The Save As dialog box is displayed. Save the file as a template by clicking the down arrow to the right of the Save as type box, selecting Template (*.xlt) from the drop-down menu, and then clicking Save.
- Edit a new template by clicking File and New. Open the template to be edited by clicking General Templates on the New Workbook task pane. When the Templates dialog box is displayed, click the General tab and double-click the appropriate icon. Make the changes to the template and click the Save button on the Standard toolbar. When the Save As dialog box is displayed, click the down arrow to the right of the Save as type box, select Template (*.xlt) from the drop-down menu and click Save. Save the file by clicking Yes when the warning dialog box appears asking if you want to replace the original file.
- Creating a workspace allows you to open several workbooks at the same time with just one step. A workspace file uses the extension .xlw.
- Data from one worksheet can be consolidated into another worksheet. For example, data from one worksheet could be consolidated by adding it to the data in another worksheet.
- If a link has been established from cell A5 in *Sheet1* to cell D10 in *Sheet2*, for example, whatever data is entered in cell D10 will automatically appear in cell A5. If the data in cell D10 is changed, then the data in cell A5 will be automatically updated to reflect that change.
- If a workbook is shared, then more than one person can use it and make changes to it at the same time.

COMMANDS review

Command	Mouse/Keyboard
Access Excel's built-in templates	Click File, New, General Templates, Spreadsheet Solutions tab
Display file extensions using Windows Explorer or My Computer	Click View, Folder Options, View tab
Save a template	Click File, Save As, the down arrow to the right of the Save as type box, Template (*.xlt)
Create a workspace	Click File, Save Workspace
Arrange multiple worksheets	Click Window, Arrange
Copy multiple worksheets into a single workbook	Press Ctrl key, drag sheet tab of copied worksheet to sheet tabs in workbook in which copied worksheet is to be placed
Consolidate data	Click Data, Consolidate
Link workbooks	Key =, click the cell to be linked, press Enter
Share workbook	Click Tools, Share Workbook

CONCEPTS check

Completion: For each description, furnish the correct term, command, symbol, or explanation.

1. Click this option on the New Workbook task pane to access the Templates dialog box.
2. This dialog box automatically appears whenever you try to save a template.
3. Click this tab on the Templates dialog box to access Excel's built-in templates.
4. Excel automatically adds this extension to the file name of a template.
5. Click this tab on the Templates dialog box to access the templates that you create.
6. This is the extension given to workspace files.
7. Click this option on the menu bar to arrange multiple windows on the desktop.
8. Press this key while dragging the sheet tab of a worksheet you want to copy to a different workbook.
9. Click this option on the menu bar to consolidate data.
10. This is the first thing you key into a cell that is to contain linked data.
11. This is displayed in the title bar next to the workbook name of a workbook that is currently being shared.
12. To allow two or more people to make changes to a workbook at the same time, you have to access this dialog box.
13. List the advantages of using templates.
14. List the steps you would take to link cell E5 in a workbook named Quarterly Profits to cell F15 in a workbook named January Sales.
15. List the steps you would take to display the file extensions to the file names of the files in a folder called *Quarterly Statements.*

SKILLS check

Assessment 1

1. Open Excel.
2. Open Excel's built-in template named Sales Invoice.
3. Click Insert Company Information Here. Enter the following data. Press Alt + Enter to move the insertion point to the next line.
   Whitewater Canoe & Kayak
   34982 Olympia Blvd
   Seattle, WA 98101
4. At the bottom of the invoice, click where it says "Insert Fine Print Here". Key the following: **Shipping charges included in unit price**
5. At the bottom of the invoice, click where it says "Insert Farewell Statement Here". Key the following: **River Adventure Specialists**
6. Save the file as a template in the default template folder using the file name **Whitewater Invoice**.
7. Close the Whitewater Invoice template.
8. Open the Whitewater Invoice template.
9. Enter the following customer information:

Name:	**Rocky Mountain Outfitters**
Address:	**39853 Highway 50**
City:	**Howard**
State:	**CO**
ZIP:	**81233**
Phone:	**(719) 555-8032**
Order No.	**RT-594**
Rep.	**Jackson**

10. Enter the following information:

Qty	Description	Unit Price
3	**15′ Pathfinder, vinyl trim, forest green**	**1149**
2	**14′ 6″ Trekker, vinyl trim, spruce**	**1199**
4	**12′ Excursion, red**	**679**

11. Toward the bottom of the invoice next to *Payment*, click *Select One*. Click the drop-down list arrow and click the Check option.
12. Create a custom header that prints your name at the left margin and the file name at the right margin.
13. Save the worksheet on your student data disk as an Excel workbook using the file name Excel E2, SA 01.
14. Print the Excel E2, SA 01 file and close it.
15. Delete the Whitewater Invoice.xlt file from the default user template folder.

Assessment 2

1. Open Excel Worksheet E2-02.
2. You are going to create a template. Enter the following data:

Cell	Data
B12	**1st Quarter**
C12	**2nd Quarter**

D12	**3rd Quarter**
E12	**4th Quarter**
F12	**TOTAL**
A13	**Operating Costs**
A14	**Selling Expenses**
A15	**General Administrative**
A16	**Total Costs and Expenses**
B16	**=SUM(B13:B15)**
F13	**=SUM(B13:E13)**

3. Bold and center the labels in row 12.
4. Bold the label in cell A16.
5. Adjust the column widths so that the labels all fit in the columns.
6. Copy the function in cell B16 to cells C16 through F16.
7. Copy the function in cell F13 to cells F14 and F15.
8. Place a single-line border at the bottom of cells B15 through F15. Place a double-line border at the bottom of cells B16 through F16.
9. Save the file as a template in the default user template folder. Name the template Excel Worksheet E2-02.xlt.
10. Close the Excel Worksheet E2-02.xlt template.
11. Open the template Excel Worksheet E2-02.xlt.
12. Enter the following data:

Cell	Data
B13	**21589**
B14	**15733**
B15	**7036**
C13	**23579**
C14	**21627**
C15	**9458**
D13	**26722**
D14	**24691**
D15	**10499**
E13	**31834**
E14	**25637**
E15	**14675**

13. Create a custom header that prints your name at the left margin and the file name at the right margin.
14. Save the worksheet as an Excel workbook on your student data disk using the file name Excel E2, SA 02-A.
15. Print and then close the Excel E2, SA 02-A file.
16. Open the template Excel Worksheet E2-02.xlt.
17. Edit the template by entering the following data:

Cell	Data
G12	**AVERAGE**
G13	**=AVERAGE(B13:E13)**

18. Copy the function in cell G13 to cells G14 and G15. *(Hint: Ignore the Divide by zero error message. This message will go away as soon as data is entered into the worksheet.)*
19. Save the file as a template in the default user template folder. Name the template Excel Worksheet E2-02.xlt. Replace the existing file.
20. Close the Excel Worksheet E2-02.xlt template.
21. Open the template Excel Worksheet E2-02.xlt.

22. Enter the following data:

Cell	Data
B13	20201
B14	14354
B15	6991
C13	24002
C14	20823
C15	9324
D13	25624
D14	23951
D15	11056
E13	30089
E14	24394
E15	13987

23. Create a custom header that prints your name at the left margin and the file name at the right margin.
24. Save the worksheet as an Excel workbook on your student data disk using the file name Excel E2, SA 02-B.
25. Print and then close the Excel E2, SA 02-B file.
26. Delete the Excel Worksheet E2-02.xlt file from the default user template folder.

Assessment 3

1. Open Excel.
2. Open Net Income 1st Qtr, Net Income 2nd Qtr, Net Income 3rd Qtr, and Net Income 4th Qtr. Arrange the workbooks using the Window Arrange command. Select the Tiled option. Save a workspace for the four files. Name the workspace Income.
3. Close the four files. Open Income.xlw.
4. Open a new workbook. Arrange the five workbooks using the Window Arrange command. Use the Tiled option.
5. Copy the *1st Qtr* worksheet, *2nd Qtr* worksheet, *3rd Qtr* worksheet, and *4th Qtr* worksheet into the workbook you opened in step 3.
6. Close the Net Income 1st Qtr, Net Income 2nd Qtr, Net Income 3rd Qtr, and Net Income 4th Qtr workbooks.
7. Maximize the new workbook and save it on the student data disk using the file name Excel E2, SA 03.
8. Rename the *Sheet1* tab to TOTALS.
9. Copy the labels in cells A11 through A22 in the *1st Qtr* worksheet to cells A11 through A22 in the *TOTALS* worksheet. Automatically adjust the width of column A so that the labels all fit in the column.
10. Click cell B10 in the *TOTALS* worksheet. Consolidate the data in cells E10 through E22 on the *1st Qtr, 2nd Qtr, 3rd Qtr,* and *4th Qtr* worksheets so that the totals on each worksheet are added together. Use the labels in the top row. Adjust the width of column B so that the consolidated data is displayed.
11. If necessary, click the TOTALS sheet tab. Add a custom header that displays your name at the left margin and the file name at the right margin. Print the *TOTALS* worksheet.
12. Save the workbook with the same name (Excel E2, SA 03).
13. Close Excel E2, SA 03.

Assessment 4

1. Open Excel.
2. Open Fall Enrollment, Spring Enrollment, and Summer Enrollment. Arrange the workbooks using the Window Arrange command. Select the Vertical option. Save a workspace for the three files. Name the workspace Enrollment.
3. Close the three files. Open Enrollment.xlw.
4. Open a new workbook. Arrange the four workbooks using the Window Arrange command. Use the Tiled option.
5. Copy the *Fall, Spring,* and *Summer* worksheets into the workbook you opened in step 3.
6. Close the Fall Enrollment, Spring Enrollment, and Summer Enrollment workbooks.
7. Maximize the new workbook and save it on the student data disk using the file name Excel E2, SA 04.
8. Rename the *Sheet1* tab to AVERAGE ENROLLMENT. Select a color for the worksheet tab.
9. Copy the labels in cells A13 through A18 in the *Fall* worksheet to cells A13 through A18 in the *AVERAGE ENROLLMENT* worksheet. Automatically adjust the width of column A so that the labels all fit in the column.
10. Click cell B14 in the *AVERAGE ENROLLMENT* worksheet. Consolidate the data in cells D14 through D18 on the *Fall, Spring,* and *Summer* worksheets so that the average of the data is calculated. Do not use any labels.
11. If necessary, click the AVERAGE ENROLLMENT sheet tab. Key the label **Average Enrollment** in cell B13. Bold the label in B13.
12. Adjust the width of column B so that the label fits in the column.
13. Format cells B14 through B18 to the Number format with no decimal places displayed.
14. Add a custom header that displays your name at the left margin and the name of the workbook, Excel E2, SA 04, at the right margin.
15. Print the *AVERAGE ENROLLMENT* worksheet.
16. Save the workbook with the same name (Excel E2, SA 04) and close it.

Assessment 5

1. Before starting this exercise, you need to remove the read-only attribute from the Net Income 1st Qtr, Net Income 2nd Qtr, Net Income 3rd Qtr, and Net Income 4th Qtr files. To remove the read-only attribute from the Net Income 1st Qtr file, complete the following steps:
   a. Using either Windows Explorer or My Computer, navigate to the Net Income 1st Qtr file on your data disk.
   b. Right-click the Net Income 1st Qtr file.
   c. From the shortcut menu that is displayed, click Properties.
   d. Click the General tab on the File Properties dialog box that is displayed.
   e. In the Attributes section toward the bottom of the dialog box, click the Read-only check box so that it is no longer selected.
   f. Click OK.
2. Repeat step 1 to remove the read-only attribute from the Net Income 2nd Qtr, Net Income 3rd Qtr, and Net Income 4th Qtr files. When you have finished, close either Windows Explorer or My Computer.
3. Open Excel Worksheet E2-03. Save it as Excel E2, SA 05.
4. Open the Income.xlw file you created in assessment 3. Use the Windows Arrange command to arrange the windows vertically.

5. Link cell B13 in the Excel E2, SA 05 worksheet to cell E11 in the Net Income 1st Qtr worksheet.
6. Link cell B14 in the Excel E2, SA 05 worksheet to cell E11 in the Net Income 2nd Qtr worksheet.
7. Link cell B15 in the Excel E2, SA 05 worksheet to cell E11 in the Net Income 3rd Qtr worksheet.
8. Link cell B16 in the Excel E2, SA 05 worksheet to cell E11 in the Net Income 4th Qtr worksheet.
9. Close the Net Income 1st Qtr, Net Income 2nd Qtr, Net Income 3rd Qtr, and Net Income 4th Qtr workbooks. Maximize the window for the Excel E2, SA 05 file.
10. Add a custom header to the Excel E2, SA 05 worksheet that displays your name at the left margin and the file name at the right margin.
11. Print the Excel E2, SA 05 worksheet.
12. Open the Net Income 2nd Qtr workbook. Key the following into cell C11: **69302**
13. Save and close the Net Income 2nd Qtr workbook.
14. Notice the updated value in cell B14. Print the Excel E2, SA 05 worksheet again.
15. Save the workbook with the same name (Excel E2, SA 05) and close it.

Assessment 6

1. Open 4th Quarter Sales.xlw. You created this file in exercise 6.
2. Open Excel Worksheet E2-04. Save it as Excel E2, SA 06. Use the Windows Arrange command to arrange the windows vertically.
3. Link cell B14 in the Excel E2, SA 06 worksheet to cell C27 in the Region Sales Oct worksheet.
4. Link cell C14 in the Excel E2, SA 06 worksheet to cell C27 in the Region Sales Nov worksheet.
5. Link cell D14 in the Excel E2, SA 06 worksheet to cell C27 in the Region Sales Dec worksheet.
6. Close the Region Sales Oct, Region Sales Nov, and Region Sales Dec workbooks. Maximize the window for the Excel E2, SA 06 file.
7. Add a custom header to the Excel E2, SA 06 worksheet that displays your name at the left margin and the file name at the right margin.
8. Print the Excel E2, SA 06 worksheet.
9. Open the Region Sales Oct workbook. Key the following into cell B11: **6742**
10. Save and close the Region Sales Oct workbook.
11. Notice the updated value in cell B14. Print the Excel E2, SA 06 worksheet again.
12. Save the workbook with the same name (Excel E2, SA 06) and close it.

Assessment 7

1. Open Excel Worksheet E2-05. Save it as Excel E2, SA 07.
2. Create a custom header with your name displayed at the left margin and the file name at the right margin.
3. The production manager, Ed Snyder, and the vice president of finance, Beverly Peterson, both need to make changes to Copper Clad's budget figures for January and February. They are going to do this by sharing the workbook. Click Tools and Options. Click the General tab on the Options dialog box. Look in the User name box. On a piece of paper, write down the name that is currently entered. When you complete this assessment exercise, you will change the name back to what is currently entered. Assign the user name Ed Snyder to the workbook that is currently open.

4. Click Tools and Share Workbook. Click the Allow changes by more than one user at the same time check box to select it. Click OK. Click OK to save the workbook.
5. Start another copy of the Excel program by clicking the Start button, selecting Programs, and then opening another copy of Excel. Change the user name for this copy of Excel to Beverly Peterson.
6. Right-click the taskbar and click Tile Windows Horizontally.
7. Click in Beverly's copy of Excel to select it, and then open the E2, SA 07 file. Beverly's copy of Excel should be on the top. If it's not, rearrange the windows.
8. The workbook is now open in both program windows. Notice that the word [Shared] appears in the title bar of both windows. Access Beverly's copy of the workbook (on the top) and make the following changes:

Cell	Data
B14	**16309**
C14	**19986**
B17	**8.50**
C17	**8.50**

9. Save the worksheet.
10. Access Ed Snyder's copy of the workbook (on the bottom) and make the following changes:

Cell	Data
B15	.75
C15	.75

11. Save the workbook. When the information box appears telling you the workbook has been updated with changes saved by other users, click OK. Move the mouse pointer over the blue triangles to read about the changes that were made.
12. Access Beverly's copy of the workbook and save it. When the information box appears telling you the workbook has been updated with changes saved by other users, click OK. Move the mouse pointer over the maroon triangles to read about the changes that were made.
13. In Beverly's copy of the workbook, enter 0.5 in cells B15 and C15. Save the workbook. In Ed's copy of the workbook (on the bottom), enter 1 in cells B15 and C15. Save the workbook. The Resolve Conflict dialog box is displayed. Click the Accept All Mine button.
14. Access Beverly's copy of the workbook and save it. When the dialog box appears informing you the workbook has been updated, click OK. Click Tools on the menu bar in Beverly's workbook and point to the Track Changes option. Click Accept or Reject Changes. Click OK to accept the default options. Click the Accept button until the dialog box displays the conflicting values entered in cell B15. Click the second option in the list, Ed Snyder's change to 0.75 and click the Accept button. When the dialog box displays the conflicting values entered for C15, click the second option in the list, Ed Snyder's change to 0.75, and then click the Accept button. Save the workbook.
15. Access Ed Snyder's copy of the workbook (on the bottom) and click the Save button. Click OK when the dialog box appears notifying you that changes were made by other users. Look at a history of the changes that were made by clicking Tools on the menu bar of Ed's copy of the workbook, pointing to Track Changes, and then clicking Highlight Changes. Click the down arrow at the right side of the When box. Select the *Since I last saved* option. Click the check box next to List changes on a new sheet. A check mark should be in the box. Click OK. A new sheet tab is added to the worksheet called *History*. On this worksheet you can see that Beverly rejected your changes in cells B15 and C15.

16. Save Ed's copy of the workbook (on the bottom). Print a copy of the workbook.
17. Access Beverly's copy of the workbook. Change the user name back to the original entry by clicking Tools and Options. Click the General tab. In the User name box, key the name that was originally displayed when you started the exercise. Click OK. Save the workbook. Click File on the menu bar in Beverly's workbook and click Exit.
18. Access Ed's copy of the workbook. Maximize the window. Designate that the workbook should no longer be shared by clicking Tools and Share Workbook. Click the Allow changes by more than one user at the same time check box so that it is no longer selected. Click OK. When the dialog box is displayed asking if you want to remove the workbook from shared use, click Yes.
19. If necessary, change the user name back to the original entry.
20. Save the worksheet with the same name (Excel E2, SA 07) and close it.

Assessment 8

1. When cells that supply data to a link are changed, Excel will not automatically update the link if the workbook containing the link is closed. Use Excel's Office Assistant to learn how you can manually update links. *(Hint: Click Help and Microsoft Excel Help. At the Office Assistant or the Answer Wizard tab, key the question **"How do I update a link manually?"** and click Search. At the list of topics that displays, click* Control When links are Updated *and then* Update only some of the links to other workbooks. *Read and then print the information displayed in the Help dialog box.)*
2. Open the Region Sales Nov workbook. Key the following into cell B17: **6090**. Save the workbook using the same name. Close the workbook.
3. Open Excel E2, SA 06. When the dialog box appears asking if you want to update this workbook with changes made to another workbook, click Don't Update. Save the worksheet using the Save As command and name it Excel E2, SA 08.
4. Using the help information you printed in step 1, update the linked objects in this workbook manually.
5. Print Excel E2, SA 08.
6. Save the worksheet using the same file name (Excel E2, SA 08) and close it.

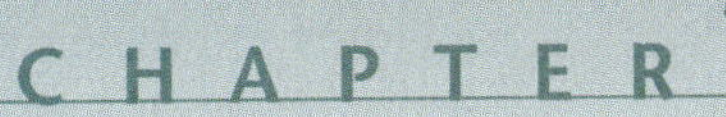

CHAPTER 3

USING ADVANCED FUNCTIONS

PERFORMANCE OBJECTIVES

Upon successful completion of chapter 3, you will be able to:

- **Use the PMT function**
- **Use the PV function**
- **Use the ROUND function**
- **Use the RAND function**
- **Use the SUMIF function**
- **Use the COUNTIF function**
- **Name a range**
- **Use a named range in a formula**
- **Use the VLOOKUP function**
- **Use the IF function**
- **Use array formulas**

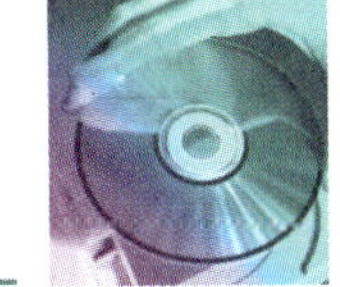

Excel Chapter 03E

Excel includes many functions that make the task of creating a worksheet much easier. A function is a built-in formula. Functions perform complex mathematical, financial, data-manipulation, and logical operations. Excel includes over 200 functions that are divided into the following nine categories:

Financial
Date and Time
Math and Trig
Statistical
Lookup and Reference
Database
Text
Logical
Information

Functions include two parts. The first part is the name of the function, which always immediately follows the equal sign. The second part of the function is the argument. The argument contains the data the function needs to perform the necessary calculations or data manipulations. The argument may contain numbers, formulas, cell references, range names, or other functions, which are called nested functions. In this chapter you will learn how to use some advanced functions as well as how to work with named ranges and use them in formulas and functions.

Entering a Function

Functions can be keyed directly into a cell or entered using the Insert Function button on the formula bar. To enter a function using the Insert Function button, click the Insert Function button on the formula bar, as shown in figure 3.1. The Insert Function dialog box shown in figure 3.2 is displayed. One way to locate a particular function is by entering a query such as "How do I calculate the yearly interest payment for an investment?" in the Search for a function box. Another way is to select a category from the Or select a category list box. All the functions for that particular category are then listed in the Select a function box. Select the particular function you want and then click OK.

FIGURE 3.1 ***The Insert Function Button***

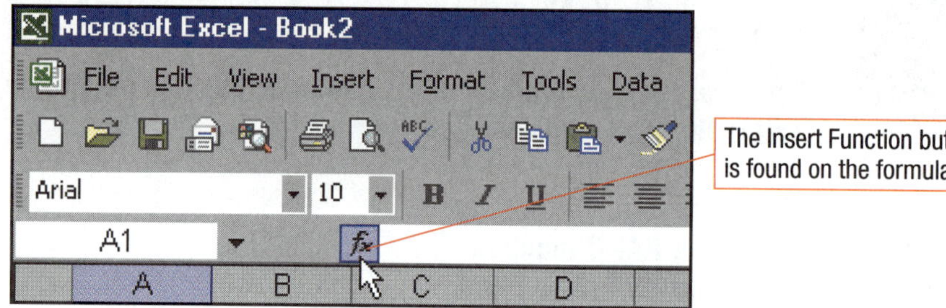

FIGURE 3.2 ***The Insert Function Dialog Box***

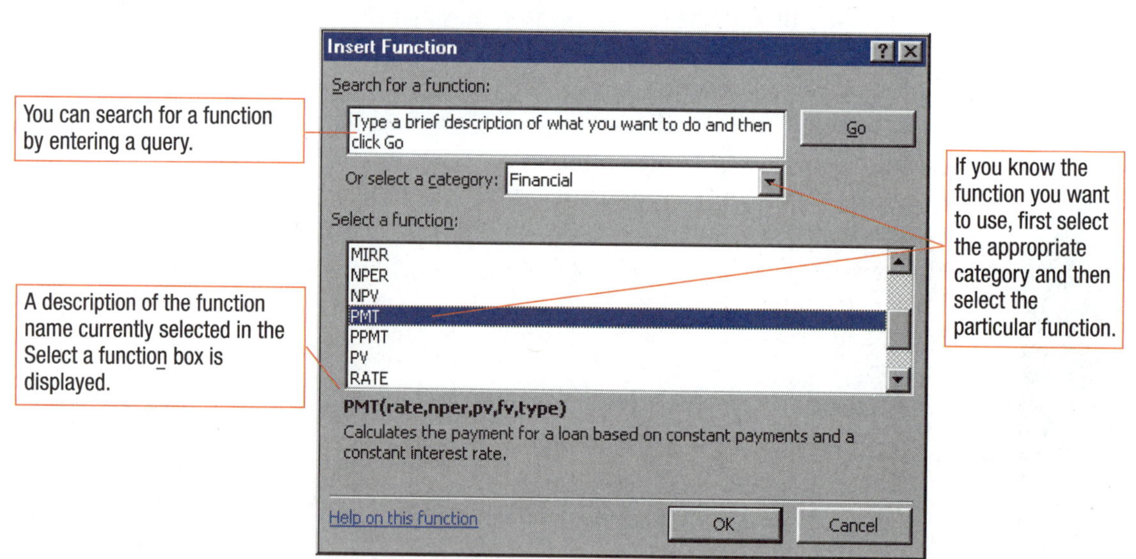

Figure 3.3 shows the Function Arguments dialog box for the PMT function. This is where you enter the data to be used in the formula. Next to each argument name is a box. If the argument name is bold, then that particular argument is required by the function and must have data assigned to it. Cell references, ranges, range names, and formulas may be entered into an argument box. You can either key the data into the argument box or select the appropriate cells from the worksheet to enter them into the argument box. Once the necessary data is entered into the argument boxes, click OK.

FIGURE 3.3 ***The Function Arguments Dialog Box***

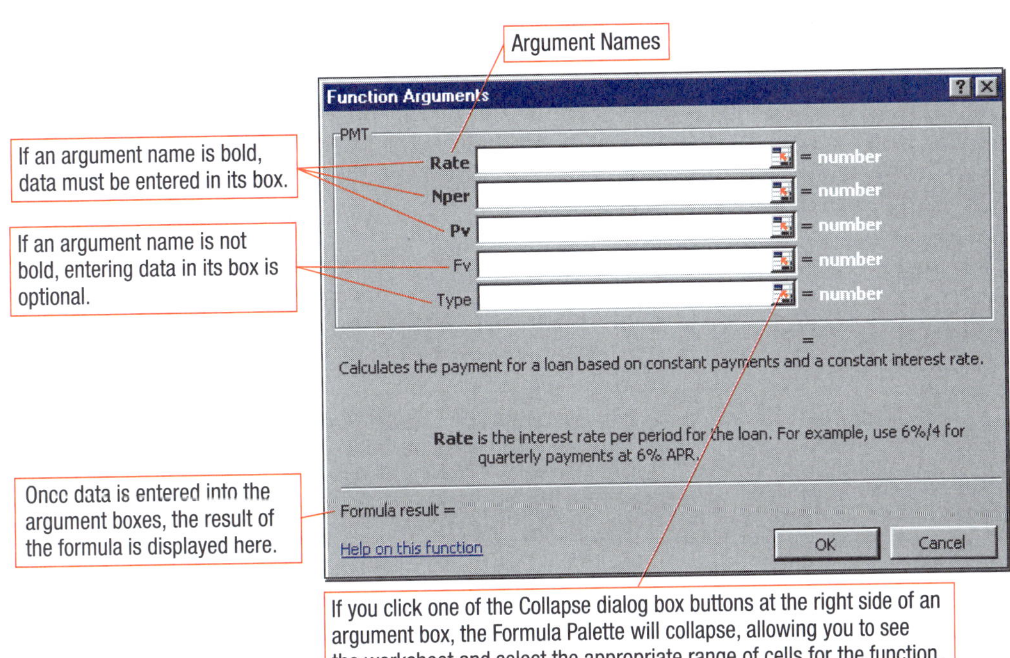

Once an equal sign has been entered into a cell, you can click the drop-down arrow to the right of the Name box to see a list of commonly used functions. The drop-down menu shown in figure 3.4 appears. If you select one of the functions from the list, an expanded Formula Palette for that particular function is displayed. If you select the last option, *More Functions,* the Insert Function dialog box is displayed. From this dialog box you can select any function you want.

Financial Functions

Excel includes many financial functions that are used for calculating loan details, annuities, and investment analyses, for example. An annuity is a periodic series of equal payments. The mortgage on a house is one example of an annuity. A car loan would be another example of an annuity. Table 3.1 describes the common arguments used in Excel's financial functions.

FIGURE 3.4 A Menu of Function Options

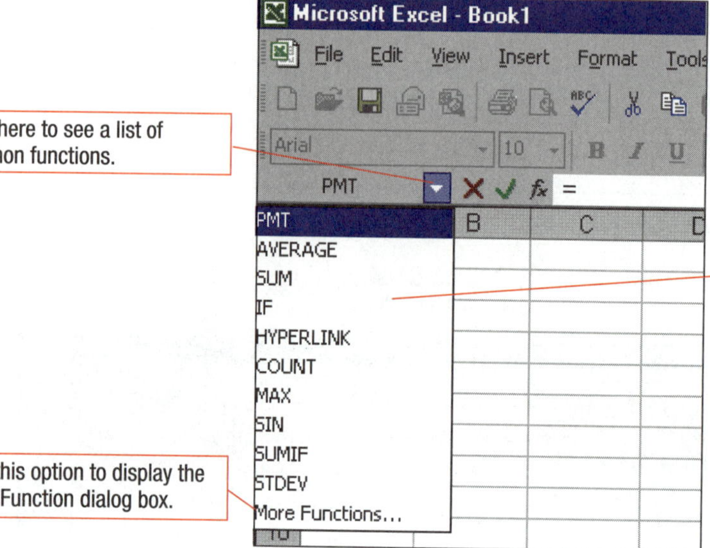

TABLE 3.1 Arguments Used in Excel's Financial Functions

Argument	Argument Name	Description
Present value	Pv	The current value of amounts to be received or paid in the future discounted at some interest rate; the amount that must be invested today at some interest rate to accumulate to some specified future value.
Number of periods	Nper	The number of payments that will be made to an investment or loan. For example, a five-year loan with monthly payments would have 60 periods.
Payment	Pmt	The amount paid or collected for each period.
Future value	Fv	The value of a loan or investment at the end of all the periods.
Rate		The interest rate being charged or paid.
Type		Payments can either be made in arrears (at the end of each period) or in advance (at the beginning of each period). The Type argument determines whether the calculation will be based on payments made in arrears or in advance. Type is the number 0 (payments in arrears) or 1 (payments in advance). If Type is omitted, it is assumed to be 0.

The PMT Function

The PMT function calculates the periodic payment of a loan based on constant payments and a constant interest rate. The format for the PMT function is

=PMT(rate,nper,pv)

Rate is the interest rate per period. Nper is the total number of payments to be made. Pv is the present value of the amount borrowed. Look at the following PMT function:

=PMT(8%/12,60,-13000)

This formula will calculate how much each payment would be if you borrowed $13,000 at 8% interest and were going to repay the loan in 60 installments. Because the payments are made monthly, the interest rate must also be monthly; therefore, the annual rate of interest, or 8%, must be divided by 12. If the loan is for five years, that means there are 60 payments (5 x 12 = 60). The present value of the amount borrowed is -13,000, or minus 13,000, because no payments have yet been made. For all arguments, cash you pay out is represented by a negative number, and cash you receive is represented by a positive number.

(Before completing exercise 1, delete the Chapter 02E *folder on your disk. Next, copy to your disk the* Chapter 03E *folder from the* Excel 2002 Expert *folder on the CD that accompanies this textbook.)*

exercise 1 — USING THE PMT FUNCTION

1. Open Excel Worksheet E3-01.
2. Save the worksheet using the Save As command and name it Excel E3, Ex 01.
3. Create a custom header that displays your name at the left margin and the file name at the right margin.
4. Primrose Decorators is a decorating business owned and operated by Georgia and Paul Sorenson. They have outgrown their current facility and need to relocate. Their plans for relocation must include an approximation of what they can afford to pay for a mortgage. This worksheet is designed to make such an estimate. Look over the worksheet. The interest rate per period is in cell D5. The term of the loan is in row 8, and the amount of money being borrowed is in column B. Complete the following steps to compute the loan payments:
   a. Select cell C9.
   b. Click the Insert Function button on the formula bar.
   c. When the Insert Function dialog box appears, click the drop-down arrow to the right of the Or select a category box. Click *Financial* from the drop-down menu that appears.
   d. Click *PMT* in the Select a function list box.
   e. Click OK.
   f. The Function Arguments dialog box appears. This is where you enter the data needed for the function. Data must be entered for the arguments that are bold. Entering data for the arguments that are not bold is optional. Click the title bar to the dialog box and drag it to the lower right corner of the screen. Make sure the

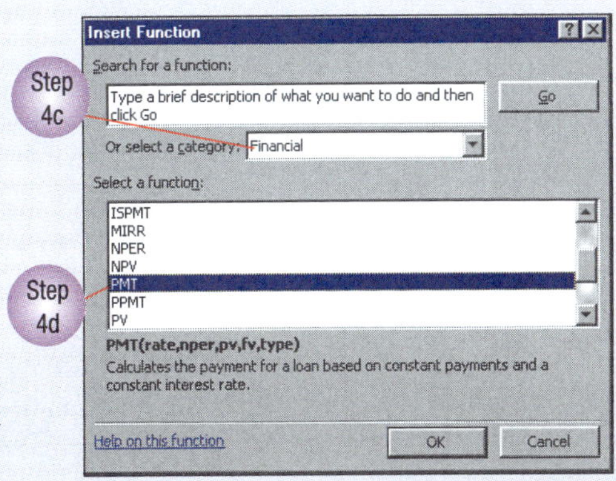

insertion point is in the Rate box. Click cell D5. Press F4 to make the reference to D5 absolute. Key the following: **/12**

g. Place the insertion point in the Nper box. Click cell C8. Press F4 to make the reference to C8 absolute. Key the following: ***12**

h. Place the insertion point in the Pv box. Press the minus sign key (or hyphen) and click cell B9.

i. Click OK.

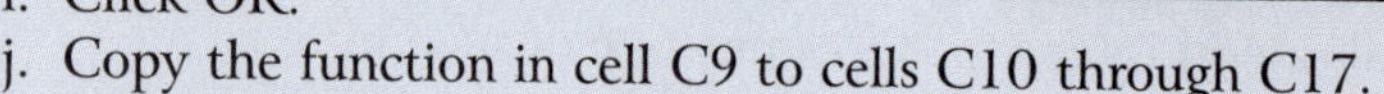

j. Copy the function in cell C9 to cells C10 through C17.

5. Repeat step 4 to enter the appropriate functions into cells D9, E9, F9, and G9. The interest rate and principal for each function remains the same. The total number of payments for the loan will change. Copy the functions as needed. Adjust column widths as needed.
6. The Sorensons do not want to spend more than $3,000 a month on a mortgage. Format cells C9 through G17 so that any value less than or equal to 3,000 is displayed as bold and in the color green.
7. Shade cells B8 through G8 and cells B9 through B17 with a light green color.
8. Print the worksheet.
9. The Sorensons think they may be able to get a better interest rate. Enter **.0675** in cell D5. Print the worksheet again.
10. Save the worksheet with the same name (Excel E3, Ex 01) and close the worksheet.

The PV Function

The PV function calculates the present value that the total amount of a series of future payments is worth right now. The format for the PV function is

=PV(rate,nper,pmt,fv,type)

Rate is the interest rate per period. Nper is the total number of payment periods. Pmt is the payment made each period. Fv is the future value, and type indicates whether the payments are being made in arrears or in advance. Look at the following PV function:

=PV(5%/12,60,150)

This formula will calculate the present value of 60 payments of $150 with a 5% annual percentage rate.

exercise 2

USING THE PV FUNCTION

1. Open Excel Worksheet E3-02.
2. Save the worksheet using the Save As command and name it Excel E3, Ex 02.
3. Create a custom header that displays your name at the left margin and the file name at the right margin.
4. Copper Clad Incorporated is considering purchasing a machine that would generate significant cash savings. The machine costs $35,000. The accountant has to decide whether or not investing $35,000 in the purchase of this machine is a wise investment.

Copper Clad has to make an 18% rate of return on this capital investment in order to make the investment worth it. The company expects to generate a cash savings of $6,500 for the life of the machine, which is estimated to be 15 years. Complete the following steps to use the PV function to make the necessary calculations:

a. Key **18%** in cell B4.
b. Key **15** in cell B5.
c. Key **6500** in cell B6. Format the value in cell B6 as currency with no decimals displayed.
d. Select cell B8. Click the Insert Function button.
   1) Select *Financial* from the Or select a category drop-down list.
   2) Click *PV* in the Select a function list box.
   3) Click OK.
e. The Function Arguments dialog box is displayed. Drag the dialog box to the lower right corner of the screen so you can see cells A4 through B8. The insertion point should be in the Rate box. Click cell B4.
f. Place the insertion point in the Nper box. Click cell B5.
g. Place the insertion point in the Pmt box. Click cell B6.
h. Click OK.

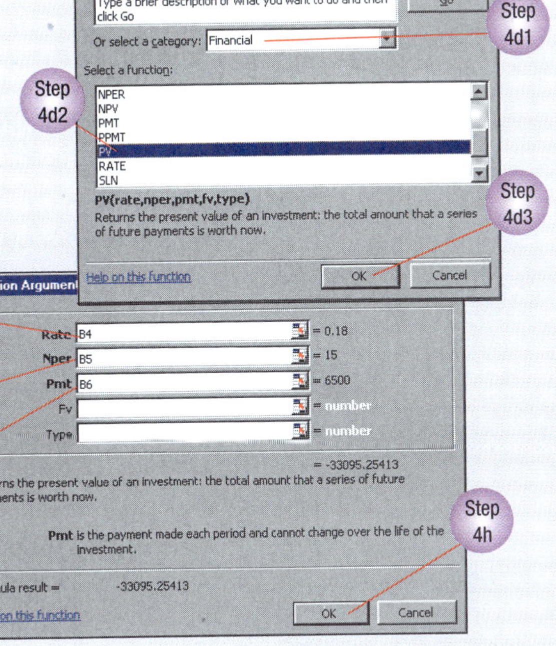

5. The present value of the money is displayed as a negative number because this represents money that would be paid out. The present value of the money is $33,095.25, which is less than the $35,000 cost of the machine. Therefore, this is not a wise investment for the Copper Clad company. The accountant advises the president of Copper Clad that unless the price of the machine can be negotiated down to $33,095, the company should not invest in the machine.
6. Save the worksheet with the same name (Excel E3, Ex 02).
7. Print and close the worksheet.

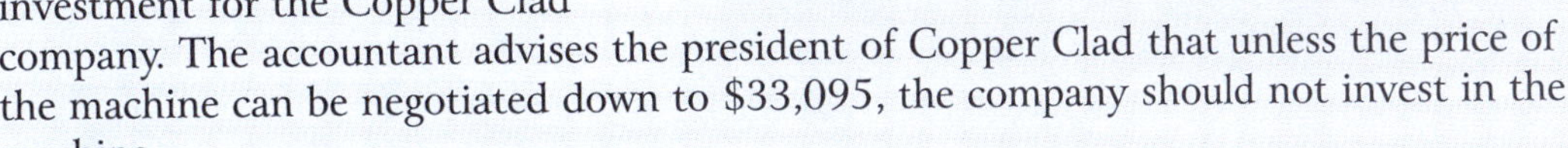

Math and Trig Functions

Excel includes many math and trigonometric functions. These functions perform a wide variety of calculations such as sines, cosines, factorials, exponents, and logs. The following section introduces you to three of Excel's Math and Trig functions.

The ROUND Function

The ROUND function rounds a number to a specified number of digits. The format for the ROUND function is

=ROUND(**number**,**num_digits**)

Number is the number that is to be rounded. Num_digits is the number of decimal places to which the number is to be rounded. If num_digits is 0, then the number is to be rounded to the nearest integer. If num_digits is 1, then the number is to be rounded to one decimal place. If num_digits is a negative number, then the number is to be rounded that many places to the left of the decimal point. For example, if the number is 2345 and num_digits is -2, the number will be rounded to 2300.

The RAND Function

The RAND function is used to calculate random numbers. The function returns a random number greater than or equal to 0 and less than 1. The result of the formula is volatile, which means it will change whenever anything on the worksheet changes. The format for the RAND function is

RAND()

RAND is different from other functions in that it does not have any arguments.

The SUMIF Function

The SUMIF function calculates the total of only those cells that meet a given condition or criteria. The format for the SUMIF function is

SUMIF(**range**,**criteria**,sum_range)

Range is the range of the cells that are to be evaluated by the function. Criteria is the condition or criteria the cell is to match if it is to be included in the sum. The criteria can be a number, an expression, or a text. Sum_range are the actual cells to sum. For example, look at the following worksheet fragment:

	A	B	C
1	**Sales Rep**	**Sales**	**Commission**
2	Hyde, Paul	$25,000	$3,000
3	Snyder, Holly	$36,000	$4,320
4	Jackson, Donna	$13,000	$1,560
5	Carter, Bob	$19,000	$2,280
6	Adamski, Steve	$23,000	$2,760

Using the data from this worksheet fragment, the following SUMIF function would add together only those commissions that were made on sales greater than or equal to $25,000:

SUMIF(B2:B6,">=25000",C2:C6)

The value that would be returned for this function is 7320.

USING THE ROUND, RAND, AND SUMIF FUNCTIONS

1. Open Excel Worksheet E3-03.
2. Save the worksheet using the Save As command and name it Excel E3, Ex 03.
3. Create a custom header that displays your name at the left margin and the file name at the right margin.
4. This is the start of a worksheet that calculates the commissions earned on sales. The sales figures are not yet available, so you need to use the RAND function to generate some figures. Complete the following steps to generate sales figures using the RAND function:
   a. Click cell B5.
   b. Click the Insert Function button.
   c. Click *Math & Trig* from the Or select a category list box.
   d. Click *RAND* from the Select a function list box.
   e. Click OK.
   f. The Function Arguments dialog box is displayed. The RAND function does not take any arguments, so click OK.
   g. The RAND function generates numbers between 0 and 1. You want to generate numbers between 0 and 100,000, so you have to multiply the function by 100,000. Click in the formula bar and key ***100000**.
   h. Click the Enter button.

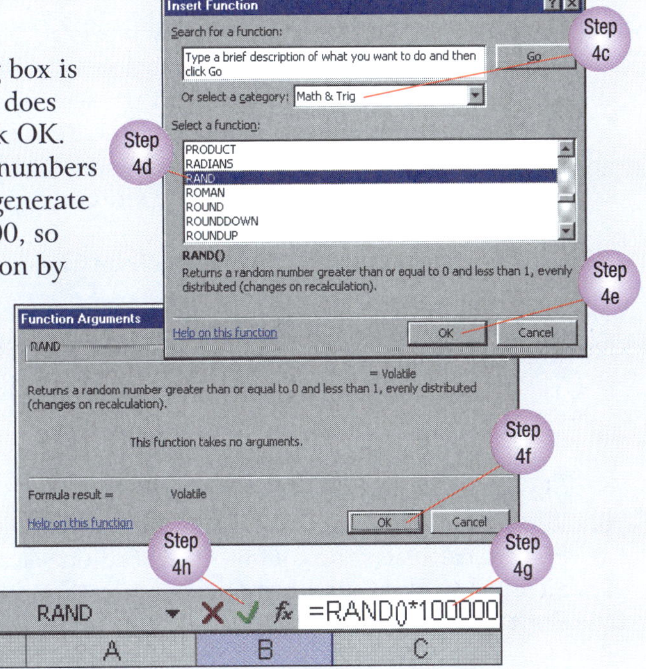

5. The sales figures need to be rounded to the nearest 100. To do this, you will need to create a nested function. Complete the following steps to nest the current RAND function inside a ROUND function:
   a. If necessary, click cell B5 to select it.
   b. In the formula bar, place the insertion point between the equal sign and the letter *R*. Key the following: **ROUND(**
   c. In the formula bar, place the insertion point after the last zero in 100000. Key the following: **, -2)**. When you have finished, the nested function in the formula bar should be:
      =ROUND(RAND()*100000,-2)
   d. Click the Enter button on the formula bar.
   e. Double-click the AutoFill handle in the lower right corner of cell B5 to copy the cell to cells B6 through B16.
6. Copper Clad Incorporated pays its sales representatives a 10% commission. Complete the following steps to calculate the commissions on the sales:
   a. Click cell C5 to select it.
   b. Key the following in cell C5: **=B5*.1**

c. Click the Enter button on the formula bar.
d. Double-click the AutoFill handle in the lower right corner of cell C5 to copy the formula.

7. You may notice that every time you change something on the worksheet, the random numbers change. That is because they are volatile. Next you want to calculate the commissions paid on sales over $40,000. Complete the following steps to use the SUMIF function to make the calculation:
   a. Click cell F3 to select it.
   b. Click the Insert Function button on the formula bar.
   c. Click *Math & Trig* from the Or select a category list box.
   d. Click *SUMIF* from the select a function list box.
   e. Click OK.
   f. The Function Arguments dialog box is displayed. Click and drag the dialog box to the lower right corner of the screen.
   g. The insertion point should be in the Range box. On the worksheet, select cells B5 through B16.
   h. Place the insertion point in the Criteria box.
   i. Key the following: **>40000**
   j. Place the insertion point in the Sum_range box.
   k. On the worksheet, select cells C5 through C16. When you have finished, your screen should look similar to the one at the right. Your values will be different because the RAND function is being used.
   l. Click OK.

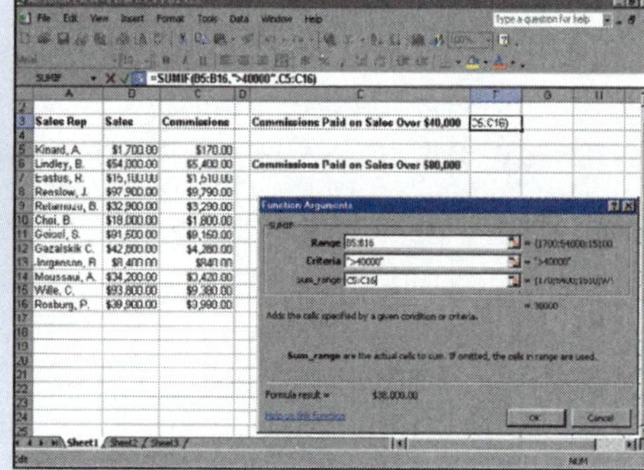

8. Repeat step 7 to enter a SUMIF function in cell F6 that calculates the commissions paid on sales over $80,000.
9. Save the worksheet with the same name (Excel E3, Ex 03).
10. Print and close the worksheet.

Statistical Functions

Excel's statistical functions are used on lists of data. Some of the simpler statistical functions are AVERAGE, MAX, and MIN. Excel also includes very complex statistical functions that can calculate deviations, distributions, correlations, and slopes, for example.

The COUNTIF Function

The COUNTIF function counts the number of cells in a given range that meet a specific condition.The format for the COUNTIF function is

=COUNTIF(**range,criteria**)

The range is the range of cells to be counted. The criteria is the condition that must be met in order for that cell to be counted. The condition can be a number, expression, or text. Suppose, for example, you had a worksheet that kept track of the weather for the past month. Look at the worksheet segment at the right:

Using this worksheet segment, the COUNTIF function =COUNTIF(B2:B32,"Clear") would return 7.

	A	B
1	**Day of the Month**	**Cloud Report**
2	1	Overcast
3	2	Partly Cloudy
4	3	Overcast
5	4	Overcast
6	5	Partly Cloudy
7	6	Partly Cloudy
8	7	Partly Cloudy
9	8	Clear
10	9	Clear
11	10	Partly Cloudy
12	11	Clear
13	12	Overcast
14	13	Overcast
15	14	Overcast
16	15	Partly Cloudy
17	16	Clear
18	17	Clear
19	18	Overcast
20	19	Overcast
21	20	Overcast
22	21	Partly Cloudy
23	22	Clear
24	23	Overcast
25	24	Overcast
26	25	Overcast
27	26	Partly Cloudy
28	27	Partly Cloudy
29	28	Clear
30	29	Overcast
31	30	Overcast
32	31	Overcast

exercise 4 USING THE COUNTIF FUNCTION

1. Open Excel Worksheet E3-04.
2. Save the worksheet using the Save As command and name it Excel E3, Ex 04.
3. Create a custom header that displays your name at the left margin and the file name at the right margin.
4. This worksheet keeps track of grades for a CS100 class at Redwood Community College. The instructor wants to know how many students received A's, how many received B's, how many received C's, and so on. Complete the following steps to use the COUNTIF function to find out how many students received A's:
   a. Select cell O6.
   b. Click the Insert Function button on the format bar.
   c. Click *Statistical* in the Or select a category list box.

d. Click *COUNTIF* in the Select a function list box.
e. Click OK.
f. The Function Arguments dialog box is displayed, and the insertion point is in the Range box. Key the following in the Range box: **m6:m58**
g. Place the insertion point in the Criteria box. Key **"A"** in the Criteria box.
h. Click OK.

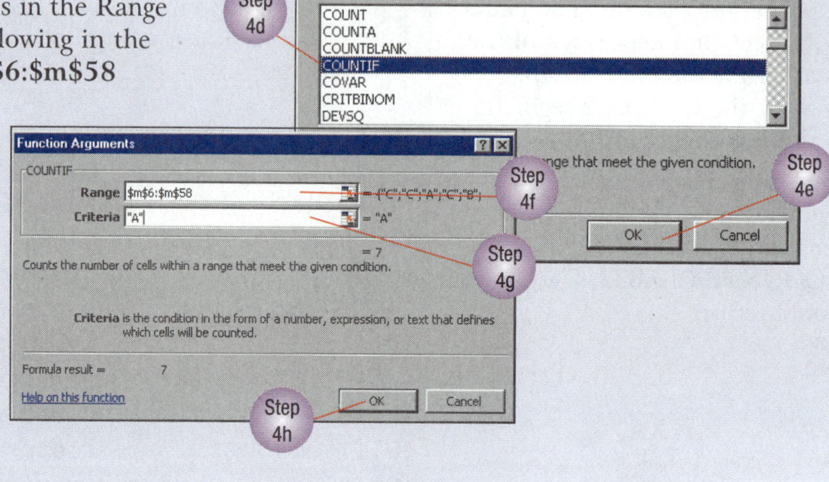

5. Click cell O6 if necessary. Double-click the AutoFill handle to copy the formula. Click cell O7 and edit the function to count the number of B's. Click cell O8 and edit the function to count the number of C's. Click cell O9 and edit the function to count the number of D's. Click cell O10 and edit the function to count the number of F's.
6. Change the orientation of the page to landscape.
7. Select rows 3 through 5 as a print title to repeat at the top of each page.
8. Save the worksheet with the same name (Excel E3, Ex 04).
9. Print and close the worksheet.

Naming a Range

You can define a name that can be used to represent specific cells in a worksheet. The name you create should describe the range of cells. The name *January_Sales*, for example, could be defined for the range of cells containing the January sales figures. When naming a cell or range of cells, the first character of the name must be a letter or an underscore character. The other characters in the name can be letters, numbers, periods, and underscore characters. Spaces are not allowed in names, so use either the underscore character or a period to separate the words used in a name, such as *May_Sales* or *Third.Quarter*. Even though uppercase and lowercase letters can be used in a name, they are not case sensitive. That is, if you created the name *Sales_Tax* and then created a second name *sales_tax*, the second name would simply replace the first.

Any worksheet in a workbook can utilize the names you create. For example, if the name *Freight_Cost* is the name for the range of cells C5 through H25 on *Sheet1*, you can use that name on any other sheet in the workbook to refer to cells C5 through H25 on *Sheet1*.

To create a name for a cell or a range of cells, select the cell or range of cells to be named. Click the Name box at the left side of the formula bar, as shown in figure 3.5. Key the name for the cell or cells and press Enter.

FIGURE

3.5 ***Name Box in Formula Bar***

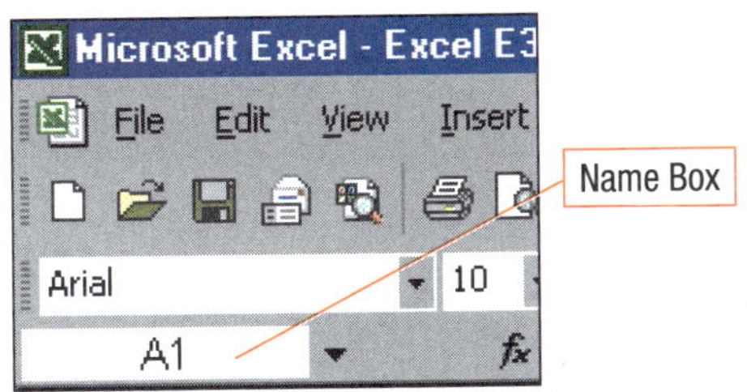

If you want to change a range name, click Insert, point to Name, and then click Define. The Define Name dialog box shown in figure 3.6 is displayed. In the Names in workbook list, click the name you want to change. In the Names in workbook box, select the name to be changed and then key the new name. Click Add. To delete the original name, in the Names in workbook list, click the name to be deleted and then click Delete. Notice in the Refers to box at the bottom of the dialog box the cells to which the name refers are displayed. If you want to change the cells to which the name is to refer, change the cell references in the Refers to box.

FIGURE

3.6 ***Define Name Dialog Box***

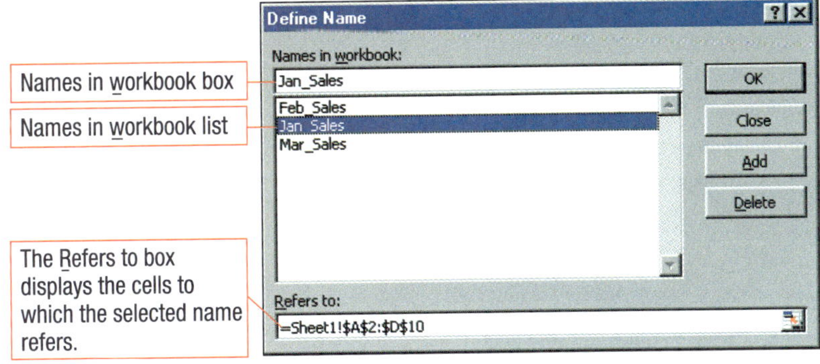

You can select a named range by clicking the down arrow to the right of the Name box and clicking the range to be selected from the drop-down list that appears. If you want to select two or more named ranges, click the first range from the drop-down list, hold down the Ctrl key, and then click the other ranges.

Using a Named Range in a Formula

Range names can be used in formulas in place of the references to the cells. For example, say the sales figures for January are in cells B5 through B30. To find the total of these figures you could use the function =SUM(B5:B30). If you named the range of cells B5 through B30 *Jan_Sales*, you could also use the formula =SUM(Jan_Sales). One of the advantages of using range names in formulas is

that the purpose of the formula is easier to understand. Looking at the formula =SUM(B5:B30) does not provide you with any information about what is being added. But by looking at the formula =SUM(Jan_Sales), you know the sales figures for the month of January are being added.

Lookup and Reference Functions

When worksheets contain long lists of data, you need a way to be able to find specific information within the list. Excel's Lookup and Reference functions provide a way to extract certain information from a list. These functions can return cell references when the information is found, or they can return the actual contents of the found cell.

The VLOOKUP Function

The VLOOKUP function searches for a value in the leftmost column of a table on the worksheet and then enters a value from a specific column, in the same row as the value it found, into a different location in the worksheet. The format for the VLOOKUP function is

=VLOOKUP(**lookup_value**,**table_array**,**col_index_num**)

The lookup_value is the value to be found in the first column of the table that is being searched. The lookup_value can be a value, text, or reference. The table_array is the table, or range, of information in which data is looked up. The col_index_num is the column number in the table from which the matching value should be returned. The first column in the table or range is column 1, the second column is column 2, and so on. For example, look at the table in figure 3.7. This table shows how much various salaries increase year by year if the increase rate is 5%. To look up how much you would be earning in four years if your starting salary was $25,000, you would use the following VLOOKUP function:

=VLOOKUP(25000,B5:G16,5)

FIGURE 3.7 ***A Lookup Table***

Salary.xls

	A	B	C	D	E	F	G
1	**Salary Increases at 5%**						
2							
3			NUMBER OF YEARS WORKED				
4		Starting	1	2	3	4	5
5	SALARY	$ 10,000	$ 10,500	$ 11,025	$ 11,576	$ 12,155	$ 12,763
6		$ 15,000	$ 15,750	$ 16,538	$ 17,364	$ 18,233	$ 19,144
7		$ 20,000	$ 21,000	$ 22,050	$ 23,153	$ 24,310	$ 25,526
8		$ 25,000	$ 26,250	$ 27,563	$ 28,941	$ 30,388	$ 31,907
9		$ 30,000	$ 31,500	$ 33,075	$ 34,729	$ 36,465	$ 38,288
10		$ 35,000	$ 36,750	$ 38,588	$ 40,517	$ 42,543	$ 44,670
11		$ 40,000	$ 42,000	$ 44,100	$ 46,305	$ 48,620	$ 51,051
12		$ 45,000	$ 47,250	$ 49,613	$ 52,093	$ 54,698	$ 57,433
13		$ 50,000	$ 52,500	$ 55,125	$ 57,881	$ 60,775	$ 63,814
14		$ 55,000	$ 57,750	$ 60,638	$ 63,669	$ 66,853	$ 70,195
15		$ 60,000	$ 63,000	$ 66,150	$ 69,458	$ 72,930	$ 76,577
16		$ 65,000	$ 68,250	$ 71,663	$ 75,246	$ 79,008	$ 82,958
17							

Sheet1 / Sheet2 / Sheet3

The VLOOKUP function looks up the look_up value in the first column of the table.

The table_array is the range of cells that make up the entire table. In this case, the table_array is B5:G16.

The returned value is the same row as the look_up value and the same column as the col_index_num.

The col_index_num is the column number in the table in which the returned value should be found-in this case, the fifth column.

The lookup_value is 25,000, or your starting salary. The table_array, or the range of the table, is B5 through G16. The col_index_num is 5 because the fifth column lists the salaries people earn after having worked for four years. This VLOOKUP function would return the value $30,388.

In some cases, the lookup value does not exactly match a value in the first column of the VLOOKUP table. If this happens, the function looks in the first column of the table for the largest value that is less than or equal to the lookup value. Say, for example, your starting salary was $28,000 and you wanted to use the VLOOKUP table in figure 3.7. The VLOOKUP function would look in the first column of the table for the largest value that is less than or equal to $28,000. The value it would find would be $25,000. So, using the VLOOKUP function to look up how much you would be earning in four years if your starting salary was $28,000 would return the same value: $30,388.

exercise 5 USING NAMED RANGES AND THE VLOOKUP FUNCTION

1. Open Excel Worksheet E3-05.
2. Save the worksheet using the Save As command and name it Excel E3, Ex 05.
3. Create a custom header that displays your name at the left margin and the file name at the right margin.
4. This worksheet keeps track of grades for a CS100 class at Redwood Community College. The instructor wants to use the VLOOKUP function to automatically calculate if a student's grade is an A, B, C, D, or F. VLOOKUP tables must always be sorted in ascending order. Key the following into the cells indicated to enter the VLOOKUP table:

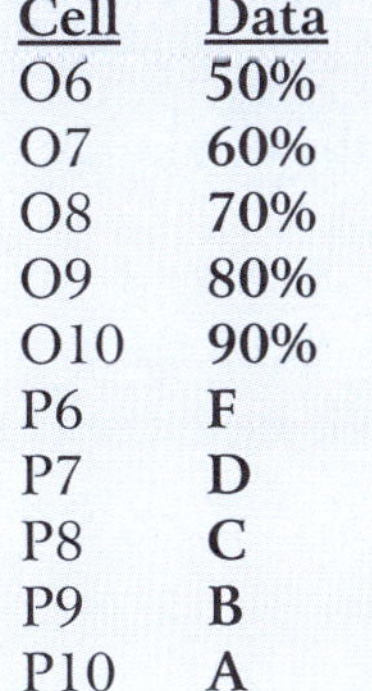

Cell	Data
O6	50%
O7	60%
O8	70%
O9	80%
O10	90%
P6	F
P7	D
P8	C
P9	B
P10	A

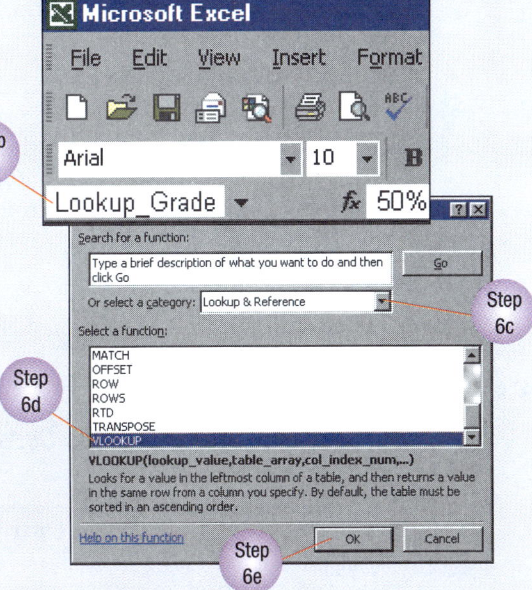

5. Name the table you just entered Lookup_Grade by completing the following steps:
   a. Select cells O6 through P10.
   b. Click the Name box and key **Lookup_Grade**.
   c. Press Enter.
6. Complete the following steps to enter a VLOOKUP function that will look up the appropriate grade for the first student:
   a. Click cell M6 to select it.
   b. Click the Insert Function button on the formula bar.
   c. Click *Lookup & Reference* in the Or select a category list box.
   d. Click *VLOOKUP* in the Select a function list box.
   e. Click OK.

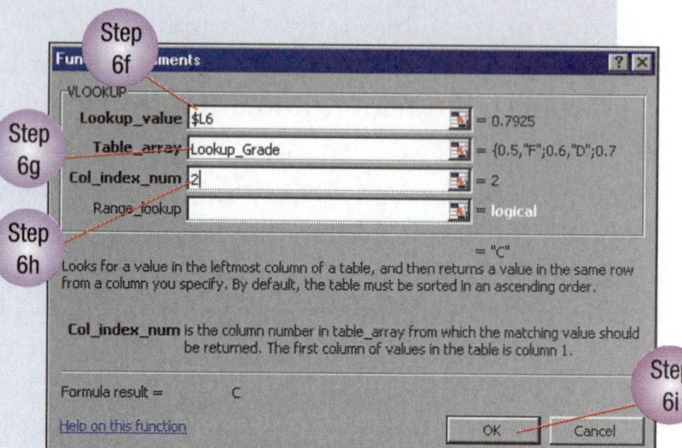

f. The Function Arguments dialog box is displayed, and the insertion point is in the Lookup_value box. Key **$L6** in the Lookup_value box. You are going to be copying the formula, so the reference to column L has to be absolute.
g. Place the insertion point in the Table_array box. You are going to use the range name to refer to the table. Key **Lookup_Grade**.
h. Place the insertion point in the Col_index_num box and key **2**.
i. Click OK.

7. Double-click the AutoFill handle in the lower right corner of cell M6 to copy the function to cells M7 through M58.
8. Change the orientation of the page to landscape.
9. Select rows 3 through 5 as a print title to repeat at the top of each page.
10. Save the worksheet with the same name (Excel E3, Ex 05).
11. Print and close the worksheet.

Logical Functions

Excel's logical functions are used to perform logical tests, which test whether or not a statement is true or false. Depending on the outcome of the logical test, a specific result is returned.

Using the IF Function

An IF function is a logical function that sets up a conditional statement to test data. If the condition is true, one value will be returned. If the condition is false, another value will be returned. The format for an IF statement is

=IF(logical_test,value_if_true,value_if_false)

The logical_test is a condition that can be evaluated as being true or false. The value_if_true is the value that should be returned if the logical_test is true. The value_if_false is the value that should be returned if the logical_test is false. Look at the following IF function:

=IF(B7=1, C7*.10, C7*.12)

If the value in cell B7 is 1, then the contents of cell C7 will be multiplied by .10. If the value entered in cell B7 is not 1, then the contents of cell C7 will be multiplied by .12. Table 3.2 shows the conditions that can be used in an IF function and their operators.

TABLE 3.2 **Operators That Can Be Used in an IF Function**

Comparison	Operator
Less than	<
Greater than	>
Less than or equal to	<=
Greater than or equal to	>=
Equal to	=
Not equal to	<>

exercise 6 THE IF FUNCTION

1. Open Excel Worksheet E3-06. This worksheet is located on your student data disk.
2. Save the worksheet using the Save As command and name it Excel E3, Ex 06.
3. Create a custom header that displays your name at the left margin and the file name at the right margin.
4. Sales representatives for Whitewater Canoe and Kayak Corporation earn a commission on their sales. Sales representatives who are managers earn a 12% commission. If a sales representative earns 10%, the commission code is 1. If a sales representative earns 12%, the commission code is 2. Complete the following steps to use an IF function to calculate the commission amount for C. J. Kimsey:
   a. Click cell D8 to select it.
   b. Click the Insert Function button on the formula bar.
   c. Click *Logical* in the Or select a category list box.
   d. Click *IF* in the Select a function list box.
   e. Click OK.
   f. The Function Arguments dialog box is displayed, and the insertion point is in the Logical_test box. Key **B8=1** in the Logical_test box.
   g. Place the insertion point in the Value_if_true box.
   h. Key **C8*.10** in the Value_if_true box.
   i. Place the insertion point in the Value_if_false box.
   j. Key **C8*.12** in the Value_if_false box.
   k. Click OK.

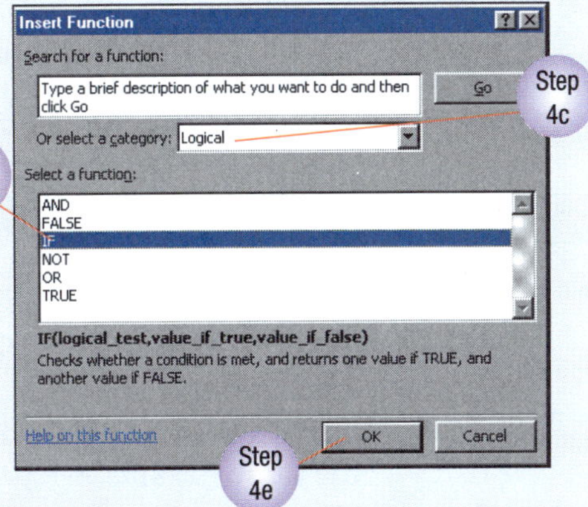

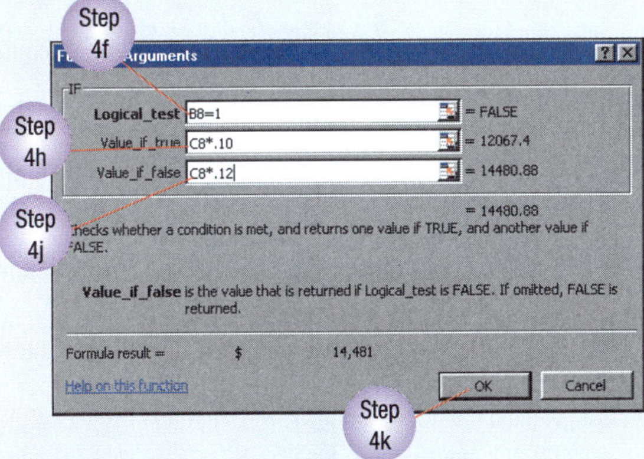

5. Double-click the AutoFill handle in the lower right corner of cell D8 to copy the function to cells D9 through D13.
6. Whitewater Canoe and Kayak Corporation has decided to give a bonus to sales representatives who sell more than $85,000 in merchandise. Sales representatives who sell more than $85,000 in merchandise earn a 2% bonus. Those who sell less than $85,000 in merchandise do not earn a bonus. Complete the following steps to use the IF function to calculate the sales representatives' bonuses:
   a. Click cell E6 and key **Bonus**.
   b. Add a border to the bottom of cell E6 to match the border on the bottom of cell D6.
   c. Click cell E8 to select it.
   d. Click the Insert Function button on the formula bar.
   e. Click *Logical* in the Or select a category list box.
   f. Click *IF* in the Select a function list box.

g. Click OK.
h. The Function Arguments dialog box is displayed, and the insertion point is in the Logical_test box. Key **C8>85000** in the Logical_test box.
i. Place the insertion point in the Value_if_true box.
j. Key **C8*.02** in the Value_if_true box.
k. Place the insertion point in the Value_if_false box.
l. Key **0** in the Value_if_false box.
m. Click OK.

7. Double-click the AutoFill handle in the lower right corner of cell E8 to copy the function to cells E9 through E13.
8. Format the cells from E8 through E18 as currency with zero decimal places.
9. Save the worksheet with the same name (Excel E3, Ex 06).
10. Print and close the worksheet.

Using Array Formulas

An array formula is a formula in which the arguments used in the functions that make up the formula are arrays rather than individual numbers. An array is a group of elements that form a complete unit. Array formulas perform multiple calculations that can produce multiple results. The array formula does this by operating on a range of cells rather than on just one cell. With an array formula, the same formula is repeated for a range of cells.

For example, look at the worksheet fragment in figure 3.8.

FIGURE 3.8 **An Example of an Array Formula**

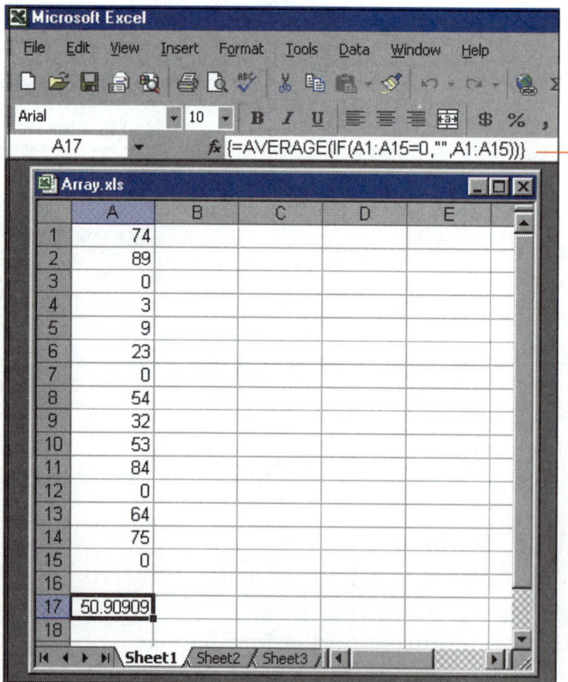

An array formula is always displayed surrounded by braces { }.

Excel's AVERAGE function includes zeros as part of the average. Suppose you wanted to be able to find the average of all non-zero values. An array formula such as the one used in figure 3.8 enables you to do this. By entering the array formula shown in figure 3.8, you are instructing the =AVERAGE function to go through the range A1 to A15 to compare the value in each cell to zero. If the value is zero, it is to be ignored—nothing is assigned to it. If a value is not zero, it is to become a part of the range of cells used in the AVERAGE function. In this case, the array formula operates on the range of cells A1 through A15; it "removes" all the zeros from the range, allowing the AVERAGE function to apply to what is left.

An array formula is created the same way that a regular formula is created. The only difference is that instead of pressing Enter to enter the formula, you press Ctrl+Shift+Enter. Once you press Ctrl+Shift+Enter, Excel automatically surrounds the formula with braces {}.You must press Ctrl+Shift+Enter each time you enter an array formula and each time you edit an array formula. If you try entering an array formula by just pressing Enter, a #VALUE! error is displayed.

If more than one range is used in an array formula, all the ranges must contain the same number of cells. If they do not, an error is returned.

exercise 7 — USING AN ARRAY FORMULA

1. Open Excel Worksheet E3-07.
2. Save the worksheet using the Save As command and name it Excel E3, Ex 07.
3. Create a custom header that displays your name at the left margin and the file name at the right margin.
4. This worksheet keeps track of how many units of each type of canoe or kayak the sales representatives for Whitewater Canoe and Kayak Corporation sold. As sales representatives made sales during the month, those sales were entered into the worksheet. Now the sales manager wants to know the total units of each type of canoe or kayak each sales representative sold. To make this calculation, you need to use an array formula. Complete the following steps to enter an array formula that calculates how many Pathfinders were sold by Claxton:
   a. Click cell G6 to select it.
   b. Key the following in cell G6: **=SUM((A6:A38="Pathfinder") *(B6:B38="Claxton")*C6:C38)**
   c. Press Ctrl+Shift+Enter
   d. Your screen should look similar to the one shown here. Look at the array formula you entered. The formula looks at the data in the three ranges A6 through A38, B6 through B38, and C6 through C38. If the first cell looked at (A6) is Pathfinder, a 1, which represents the value True, is returned. If A6 is not Pathfinder, a 0, which represents the value False, is returned. If B6 is Claxton, a 1 is returned; if it is not, a 0 is

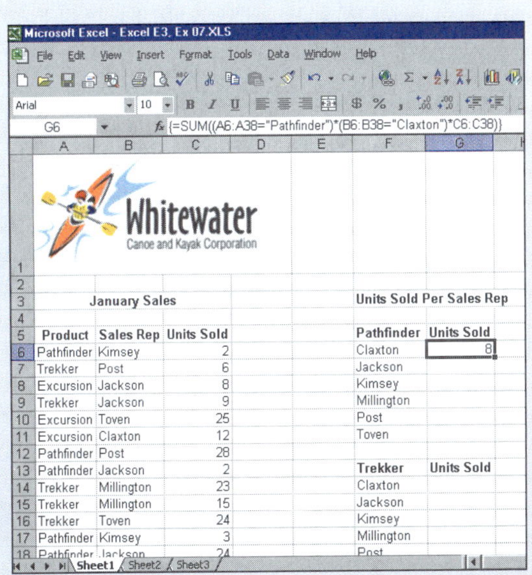

returned. Then C6 is returned and the three values (in this case 1, 0, and 2) are multiplied together. As the array formula loops through all the rows, the results are added together.

5. Complete the following steps to enter an array formula that calculates how many Pathfinders were sold by Jackson:
   a. Click cell G7 to select it.
   b. Key the following in cell G7:
      =SUM((A6:A38="Pathfinder")*(B6:B38="Jackson")*C6:C38)
   c. Press Ctrl+Shift+Enter.
6. Complete the following steps to enter an array formula that calculates how many Pathfinders were sold by Kimsey:
   a. Click cell G8 to select it.
   b. Key the following in cell G8:
      =SUM((A6:A38="Pathfinder")*(B6:B38="Kimsey")*C6:C38)
   c. Press Ctrl+Shift+Enter.
7. Complete the following steps to enter an array formula that calculates how many Pathfinders were sold by Millington:
   a. Click cell G9 to select it.
   b. Key the following in cell G9:
      =SUM((A6:A38="Pathfinder")*(B6:B38="Millington")*C6:C38)
   c. Press Ctrl+Shift+Enter.
8. Complete the following steps to enter an array formula that calculates how many Pathfinders were sold by Post:
   a. Click cell G10 to select it.
   b. Key the following in cell G10:
      =SUM((A6:A38="Pathfinder")*(B6:B38="Post")*C6:C38)
   c. Press Ctrl+Shift+Enter.
9. Complete the following steps to enter an array formula that calculates how many Pathfinders were sold by Toven:
   a. Click cell G11 to select it.
   b. Key the following in cell G11:
      =SUM((A6:A38="Pathfinder")*(B6:B38="Toven")*C6:C38)
   c. Press Ctrl+Shift+Enter.
10. To calculate the units sold for Trekkers, complete the following steps:
   a. Click cell G6.
   b. Place the insertion point between the *A* and the *6* in the formula bar and press F4. The reference to A6 is now absolute ($A$6).
   c. Place the insertion point between the *A* and the *38* in the formula bar and press F4. The reference to A38 is now absolute ($A$38).
   d. Place the insertion point between the *B* and the *6* in the formula bar and press F4. The reference to B6 is now absolute ($B$6).
   e. Place the insertion point between the *B* and the *38* in the formula bar and press F4. The reference to B38 is now absolute ($B$38).
   f. Place the insertion point between the *C* and the *6* in the formula bar and press F4. The reference to C6 is now absolute ($C$6).
   g. Place the insertion point between the *C* and the *38* in the formula bar and press F4. The reference to C38 is now absolute ($C$38).
   h. Press Ctrl+Shift+Enter.
   i. Press the Copy button on the Standard toolbar.
   j. Click cell G14.

k. Press the Paste button on the Standard toolbar.
l. In the Formula bar delete "Pathfinder" and replace it with "Trekker." Be sure to press Ctrl+Shift+Enter to enter the function. The function should look like this: **{=SUM(($A$6:$A$38="Trekker")*($B$6:$B$38="Claxton")*$C$6:$C$38)}**
m. Copy the function in cell G14 to cells G15 through G19.
n. Click cell G15. Delete "Claxton" and replace it with "Jackson." Be sure to press Ctrl+Shift+Enter to enter the function. The function should look like this: **{=SUM(($A$6:$A$38="Trekker")*($B$6:$B$38="Jackson")*$C$6:$C$38)}**
o. Click cell G16. Delete "Claxton" and replace it with "Kimsey." Be sure to press Ctrl+Shift+Enter to enter the function. The function should look like this: **{=SUM(($A$6:$A$38="Trekker")*($B$6:$B$38="Kimsey")*$C$6:$C$38)}**
p. Click cell G17. Delete "Claxton" and replace it with "Millington." Be sure to press Ctrl+Shift+Enter to enter the function. The function should look like this: **{=SUM(($A$6:$A$38="Trekker")*($B$6:$B$38="Millington")*$C$6:$C$38)}**
q. Click cell G18. Delete "Claxton" and replace it with "Post." Be sure to press Ctrl+Shift+Enter to enter the function. The function should look like this: **{=SUM(($A$6:$A$38="Trekker")*($B$6:$B$38="Post")*$C$6:$C$38)}**
r. Click cell G19. Delete "Claxton" and replace it with "Toven." Be sure to press Ctrl+Shift+Enter to enter the function. The function should look like this: **{=SUM(($A$6:$A$38="Trekker")*($B$6:$B$38="Toven")*$C$6:$C$38)}**

11. Repeat step 10 to calculate how many Excursions were sold by each sales representative.
12. Save the worksheet with the same name (Excel E3, Ex 07).
13. Print and close the worksheet.

CHAPTER summary

- A function is a built-in formula. Functions include two parts: the function name and the argument. The argument, which may contain numbers, formulas, cell references, range names, or other functions, provides the data that the function needs to perform the calculation or data manipulation.
- A function can be entered using the Insert Function button on the formula bar.
- Financial functions are used for calculating financial data such as loan details, annuities, and investment analyses.
- An annuity is a periodic series of equal payments.
- The PMT function calculates the periodic payment of a loan based on constant payments and a constant interest rate. The format for the PMT function is =PMT(rate,nper,pv)
- The PV function calculates the present value that the total amount of a series of future payments is worth right now. The format for the PV function is =PV(rate,nper,pmt, fv,type)
- The ROUND function rounds a number to a specified number of digits. The format for the ROUND function is =ROUND(number,num_digits)
- The RAND function calculates random numbers. The format of the RAND function is =RAND()

- The SUMIF function calculates the total of specific cells that meet a given condition or criteria. The format for the SUMIF function is =SUMIF(range,criteria,sum_range)
- The COUNTIF function counts the number of cells in a given range that meet a specific condition. The format for the COUNTIF function is =COUNTIF(range,criteria)
- Names can be assigned to a specific cell or range of cells. The first character in a range name must be an underscore or a letter. The rest of the characters can be letters, numbers, the underscore character, or periods. You cannot use spaces in a range name.
- Range names can be used in formulas in place of the references to the cells. The formula =AVERAGE(Exam1_Grades) would average the values entered in the range of cells named *Exam1_Grades*. Using range names in formulas makes it easier to understand the purpose of the formula.
- Excel's Lookup and Reference functions provide a way to find specific information within a list of data.
- The VLOOKUP function searches for a value in the first column of a table. Upon finding that value, it enters into a different location in the worksheet a value from the table that is in a specific column in the same row as the value that was found in the first column. The format for the VLOOKUP function is =VLOOKUP(lookup_value,table_array,col_index_num)
- Logical functions perform logical tests to see whether or not a statement is true or false. Specific results are returned depending on the outcome of the logical test.
- The IF function sets up a conditional statement to test data. If the condition is true, one value is returned. If the condition is false, a different value is returned. The format for the IF statements is =IF(logical_test,value_if_true,value_if_false)
- Array formulas perform multiple calculations that can produce multiple results. To enter an array formula, press Ctrl+Shift+Enter. Array formulas are always surrounded by braces.

COMMANDS review

Command	Mouse/Keyboard
Enter an array formula	Ctrl+Shift+Enter
Name a range	Click the Name box, key the name, press Enter
Change a range name	Click Insert, point to Name, click Define

CONCEPTS check

Completion: On a blank sheet of paper, indicate the correct term, symbol, or command for each item.

1. This term refers to the second part of a function.
2. This term refers to a periodic series of equal payments, such as the mortgage on a house.
3. A three-year loan with monthly payments would have this many periods.
4. This formula calculates what the monthly payments would be on a five-year, $15,000 loan at a 6% annual interest rate.
5. This formula rounds the number 589.345 to the nearest integer.
6. This formula will generate random numbers between 0 and 100.
7. The result of a RAND function is said to be this term because the result automatically changes whenever anything on the worksheet changes.
8. This function does not have any arguments.
9. This function would add together the values in cells B5:B25 only if the values are greater than zero.
10. This function would count the number of cells in a given range where the values are greater than 250.
11. Click here to create a name for a selected range of cells.
12. This function would look up the value in cell B5 in a table located in cells D20:G35 in the third column of the table.
13. If the value in cell C6 is less than 60, this function will add 5 to it. If the value in cell C6 is greater than 60, the value will not change.
14. Press these keys to enter an array formula.
15. Explain an advantage to using range names in formulas.
16. Explain what is wrong with the following array formula. Edit the formula so that it is correct.

    {=SUM(IF(A5:I5=B5:B10,1,0))}

17. Suppose you correctly edited the array formula from the previous question, but the #VALUE! error is displayed. Explain what you did wrong and what you must do to fix it.

SKILLS check

Assessment 1

1. Open Excel Worksheet E3-08.
2. Save the worksheet using the Save As command and name it Excel E3, SA 01.
3. Create a custom header with your name displayed at the left margin and the file name displayed at the right margin.
4. Georgia and Paul Sorenson, the owners of Primrose Decorators, have made a decision on the building they want to buy to expand their business. Now they want to create a loan amortization table that calculates their payments. Name cell B5 *Rate*. Name cell B6 *Term*. Name cell B7 *Principal*. Name cell B9 *Monthly_Payment*. In cell B9, enter a PMT function that will calculate their monthly payments. Be sure to use the range names in the formula.
5. Enter a formula in cell B11 that will calculate the total amount paid on the loan. This would be the monthly payment times the total number of payments being made. Be sure to use range names in the formula. Use the ROUND function so that the result is rounded to two decimal places. Format the result as currency.
6. Enter a formula in cell B12 that calculates the total interest paid for the loan. This would be the total amount paid minus the principal. Use a range name in the formula.
7. The first entry on the payment schedule, the principal owed at the beginning of the loan is already entered in cell B15. In cell C15, enter a formula that calculates one month's interest on the loan. One month's interest would be the principal times the interest rate. But remember, you have to divide the annual interest rate by 12 to get the interest for one month. Use the cell reference B15 to refer to the principal. Use the range name *Rate* to refer to the interest rate. Use the ROUND function so that the result is rounded to two decimal places. Format the result as currency.
8. In cell D15 enter a formula that will calculate how much of the payment goes toward the principal, which would be the monthly payment minus how much was paid to interest. Be sure to use the *Monthly_Payment* range name in the formula.
9. Enter a formula in cell E15 that calculates the principal owed after the payment is made, which would be the principal minus the amount paid to the principal. Use the cell reference B15 to refer to the principal.
10. Key **=E15** in cell B16 to enter the new principal.
11. Click cell B16 to select it. Double-click the AutoFill handle to copy cell B16 to cells B17 through B180.
12. Click cell C15 to select it. Double-click the AutoFill handle.
13. Click cell D15 to select it. Double-click the AutoFill handle.
14. Click cell E15 to select it. Double-click the AutoFill handle.
15. Select row 14 as a print title to be repeated at the top of each page when the worksheet is printed.
16. Save the workbook with the same name (Excel E3, SA 01).
17. Print and close Excel E3, SA 01.

Assessment 2

1. Open Excel Worksheet E3-09.
2. Save the worksheet using the Save As command and name it Excel E3, SA 02.
3. Create a custom header with your name displayed at the left margin and the file name displayed at the right margin.
4. You recently entered a contest and won the grand prize. You can take this prize in one of two payments. With Option A you will be paid $10,000 now and $3,500 each year for the next five years. With Option B you will not be paid any cash now, but you will be paid $6,000 a year for the next five years. You need to determine which option is the better deal. In cell B3 use the PV function to calculate the present value of $3,500 paid annually for the next five years. Assume the appropriate interest rate is 12%. Remember that the result will be displayed as a negative number because the present value is assumed to be cash that will be paid out.
5. In cell B4, use the PV function to calculate the present value of the one time payment of $10,000. The appropriate interest rate would be 0% because you would be getting the money immediately.
6. In cell B6 enter a formula that adds together the present value of the installment payments and the present value of the cash you would receive now.
7. In cell B11 use the PV function to calculate the present value of $6,000 paid annually for the next five years. Assume the appropriate interest rate is 12%.
8. In terms of the present value, which option is the better deal?
9. Save the workbook with the same name (Excel E3, SA 02).
10. Print and close Excel E3, SA 02.

Assessment 3

1. Open Excel Worksheet E3-10.
2. Save the worksheet using the Save As command and name it Excel E3, SA 03.
3. Create a custom header with your name displayed at the left margin and the file name displayed at the right margin.
4. The EastWest Crossroads Company sells imported and unique gifts through the mail. This worksheet helps the warehouse manager keep track of daily shipping expenses. Shipping expenses depend upon two things: the weight of the package and the zone to which it is being shipped. There are six different shipping zones. Look at cells J6 through P42. This is the table that must be used to look up how much it costs to ship a package. Now look at cells A6 through F54. This is the form the manager used to calculate the shipping expense, together with the total charge for each item shipped.
5. Name the range of cells J8 through P42 *Shipping*.
6. Click cell E7 to select it. Use the VLOOKUP function to enter a formula that finds the shipping expenses for the packages shipped to zone 1. The formula should look up the weight of the package (D7) in the range of cells named *Shipping*. (Be sure to use the range name in the formula.) The costs of shipping packages to zone 1 are found in column 2 of the table.
7. Cell E7 should still be selected. Double-click the AutoFill handle to copy the formula.
8. Enter a formula in F7 that adds together the charge and the shipping expense. Double-click the AutoFill handle to copy the formula.
9. Click cell E15 to select it. Use the VLOOKUP function to enter a formula that finds the shipping expenses for packages shipped to zone 2.

10. Cell E15 should still be selected. Double-click the AutoFill handle to copy the formula.
11. Enter a formula in cell F15 that adds together the charge and the shipping expense. Double-click the AutoFill handle to copy the formula.
12. Enter the appropriate VLOOKUP function in cell E23 to find the shipping expense for zone 3. Copy the formula. Enter the appropriate formula in cell F23 to add together the charge and the shipping expense. Copy the formula.
13. Enter the appropriate VLOOKUP function in cell E31 to find the shipping expense for zone 4. Copy the formula. Enter the appropriate formula in cell F31 to add together the charge and the shipping expense. Copy the formula.
14. Enter the appropriate VLOOKUP function in cell E39 to find the shipping expense for zone 5. Copy the formula. Enter the appropriate formula in cell F39 to add together the charge and the shipping expense. Copy the formula.
15. Enter the appropriate VLOOKUP function in cell E47 to find the shipping expense for zone 6. Copy the formula. Enter the appropriate formula in cell F47 to add together the charge and the shipping expense. Copy the formula.
16. Adjust the width of column F to automatically display the widest entry.
17. Enter today's date in cell B4.
18. Insert a page break so that zones 1, 2, and 3 print on one page and zones 4, 5, and 6 print on a second page.
19. Print the first two pages of the worksheet.
20. Save the workbook with the same name (Excel E3, SA 03).
21. Close Excel E3, SA 03.

Assessment 4

1. Open Excel Worksheet E3-11.
2. Save the worksheet using the Save As command and name it Excel E3, SA 04.
3. Create a custom header with your name displayed at the left margin and the file name displayed at the right margin.
4. This worksheet is used to keep track of Whitewater Canoe and Kayak's weekly payroll. Scroll horizontally and vertically to view the entire worksheet.
5. In cell I9 enter a formula that calculates the total hours that Norman Campbell worked. Copy the formula to cells I10 through I13.
6. In cell K9 use the IF function to enter a formula that calculates the regular pay. If an employee works 40 hours or less during the week, the regular pay would be the hours worked times the wage. If an employee works more than 40 hours a week, the regular pay would be the wage times 40. Enter the appropriate IF function in cell K9. Copy the formula to cells K10 through K13. Format cells K9 through K13 as currency.
7. In cell L9 use the IF function to enter a formula that calculates overtime. If an employee works more than 40 hours during the week, he or she gets paid time-and-a-half on all the hours over 40 that were worked. If the employee does not work more than 40 hours, no overtime pay is earned. *(Hint: Time-and-a-half would be 1.5 times the regular wage. Remember, time-and-a-half is paid only on the hours that are worked over the normal 40 hours.)* Copy the formula to cells L10 through L13. Format cells L9 through L13 as currency.
8. Enter a formula in M9 that calculates the gross pay (regular pay plus overtime). Copy the formula to cells M10 through M13.
9. Use the IF function to enter a formula in cell N9 that calculates the deduction for FICA. Look at the tax table in cells D17 through F21. If the gross pay is less than $600, one set of tax percentages is to be used. If the gross pay is greater than or

equal to $600, a different set of tax percentages is to be used. Click cell N9 to select it and enter the following formula:
=IF(M9<600, M9*$E$18, M9*$F$18)
If the value in M9, which is gross pay, is less than 600, the gross pay will be multiplied by cell E18, which is the FICA tax for gross pay less than $600. If the value in M9 is not less than 600, then the gross pay will be multiplied by cell F18, which is the FICA tax for gross pay that is greater than or equal to $600. Copy the formula to cells N10 through N13. Format cells N9 through N13 as currency.

10. Use the appropriate IF function to enter a formula in cell O9 to calculate the deduction for federal tax. Be sure to reference the cells for federal tax from the tax table. Copy the formula to cells O10 through O13. Format cells O9 through O13 as currency.
11. Use the appropriate IF function to enter a formula in cell P9 to calculate the deduction for state tax. Be sure to reference the cells for state tax from the tax table. Copy the formula to cells P10 through P13. Format cells P9 through P13 as currency.
12. Use the appropriate IF function to enter a formula in cell Q9 to calculate the deduction for local tax. Be sure to reference the cells for local tax from the tax table. Copy the formula to cells Q10 through Q13. Format cells Q9 through Q13 as currency.
13. Enter a formula in cell R9 to calculate the net pay (gross pay minus FICA, federal tax, state tax, and local tax). Copy the formula to cells R10 through R13.
14. Adjust the page setup so that the orientation of the page is landscape, row 7 is printed at the top of every page, and columns A and B repeat at the left of every page. Center the worksheet on the page horizontally.
15. Save the worksheet with the same name (Excel E3, SA 04).
16. Print and close Excel E3, SA 04.

Assessment 5

1. Open Excel Worksheet E3-12.
2. Save the worksheet using the Save As command and name it Excel E3, SA 05.
3. Create a custom header with your name displayed at the left margin and the file name displayed at the right margin.
4. This worksheet is a running tabulation of how many Pathfinders, Trekkers, and Excursions were sold during January by Whitewater Canoe and Kayak's sales representatives. You need to calculate the total units that were sold for each product. Name the range of cells C6 through C38 *Units_Sold*. Name the range of cells A6 through A38 *Product.*
5. Click in cell F5 to select it. Using the SUMIF function, enter a formula that calculates the total number of Pathfinders that were sold in January. Use the range names *Product* and *Units_Sold* in the function.
6. Click in cell F6 to select it. Using the SUMIF function, enter a formula that calculates the total number of Trekkers that were sold in January. Use the range names *Product* and *Units_Sold* in the function.
7. Click in cell F7 to select it. Using the SUMIF function, enter a formula that calculates the total number of Excursions that were sold in January. Use the range names *Product* and *Units_Sold* in the function.
8. Save the worksheet with the same name (Excel E3, SA 05).
9. Print and close Excel E3, SA 05.

Assessment 6

1. Open Excel Worksheet E3-13.
2. Save the worksheet using the Save As command and name it Excel E3, SA 06.
3. Create a custom header with your name displayed at the left margin and the file name displayed at the right margin.
4. This worksheet is used by Performance Threads, a company that supplies the entertainment industry with theatrical fabrics, stage draperies, and scenic and production supplies, to keep track of its inventory of velour fabrics at both its New York and Los Angeles warehouses. You want to add a couple of functions to this worksheet, but the current inventory figures have not yet arrived, so you need to enter some dummy values to make sure your functions are going to work. You want to use the RAND function to generate numbers between 1 and 300. These numbers have to be whole numbers, so you have to use the ROUND function as well. Click cell B8 and key the following formula:
   =ROUND((RAND()*300),0)
   Multiplying the RAND function by 300 produces random numbers between 1 and 300. Copy the formula to cells B9 through B29.
5. Click cell E8. Use the RAND and ROUND functions to generate a whole number between 1 and 300. Copy the formula to cells E9 through E29.
6. Key the following label in both cell A31 and D31:
   # Fabrics with Bolts > 200
   Automatically adjust the widths of columns A and D.
7. Name the range of cells B8 through B29 *NY_Bolts*. Name the range of cells E8 through E29 *LA_Bolts*.
8. Click cell B31. Use the COUNTIF function to count how many cells in the range B8:B29 contain values greater than 200. Use the range name *NY_Bolts* in the formula.
9. Click cell E31. Use the COUNTIF function to count how many cells in the range E8:E29 contain values greater than 200. Use the range name *LA_Bolts* in the formula.
10. Save the workbook with the same name (Excel E3, SA 06).
11. Print and close Excel E3, SA 06.

Assessment 7

1. You can use the PMT function to make payments to annuities other than loans. Say, for example, in five years you want to have saved up $10,000 for the down payment on a house. You can use the PMT function to calculate what you need to save each month to reach your goal. Use Excel's Help feature to figure out how to do this.
2. Enter **How do I determine payments to annuities other than loans?** Press Enter. Click the PMT worksheet function option from the list of recommended functions that is displayed.
3. Scroll through the information that is displayed until you find the example for determining payments to annuities other than loans. Follow the directions to copy the example given to a blank worksheet, and use the example to calculate the amount you would have to save if you were going to save for five years, would earn an annual interest rate of 7%, and wanted to have saved $10,000 in five years.
4. Create a custom header with your name displayed at the left margin and the file name displayed at the right margin.
5. Save the worksheet using the Save As command and name it Excel E3, SA 07.
6. Print and close Excel E3, SA 07.

CHAPTER 4

WORKING WITH LISTS

PERFORMANCE OBJECTIVES

Upon successful completion of chapter 4, you will be able to:

- **Enter data using the Data Form**
- **Use data validation**
- **Sort a list**
- **Perform a multi-level sort on a list**
- **Create a custom list**
- **Find and display records using the Data Form**
- **Edit records using the Data Form**
- **Delete records using the Data Form**
- **Outline a worksheet**
- **Subtotal a list**
- **Filter a list using AutoFilter**
- **Create a custom AutoFilter**
- **Filter a list using advanced filtering**

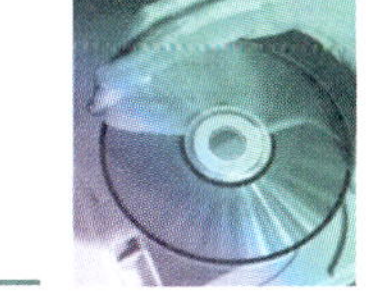

Excel Chapter 04E

In Excel, a list is a series of worksheet rows containing similar sets of data that are identified by labels in the top row. Employee names, addresses, and telephone numbers would be an example of a list. Each column in a list contains similar information based on the label for that column. Column A, for example, might be labeled “Last Name” and contain last names, column B might be labeled “First Name” and contain first names, column C might be labeled “Address” and contain street addresses, and so on. In a list, the labels have to be in the top row; they cannot be in the first column. There are no blank rows in a list.

Excel automatically recognizes a list as a database. A database is used for performing record-keeping tasks such as keeping track of all of a company’s incoming orders or keeping track of inventory. As shown in figure 4.1, each row in the list is a record, and each column in the list is a field. The labels in the first row of the list are the field names. A value found in a single cell is called a field value. The list range is the range of cells that contains all the records, fields, and field names of the list. Once you have your Excel data organized as a list, certain database operations can be performed, such as sorting data, finding specific data, and subtotaling data. The purpose of this chapter is to teach you how to create and use lists in Excel.

FIGURE 4.1 **An Excel List**

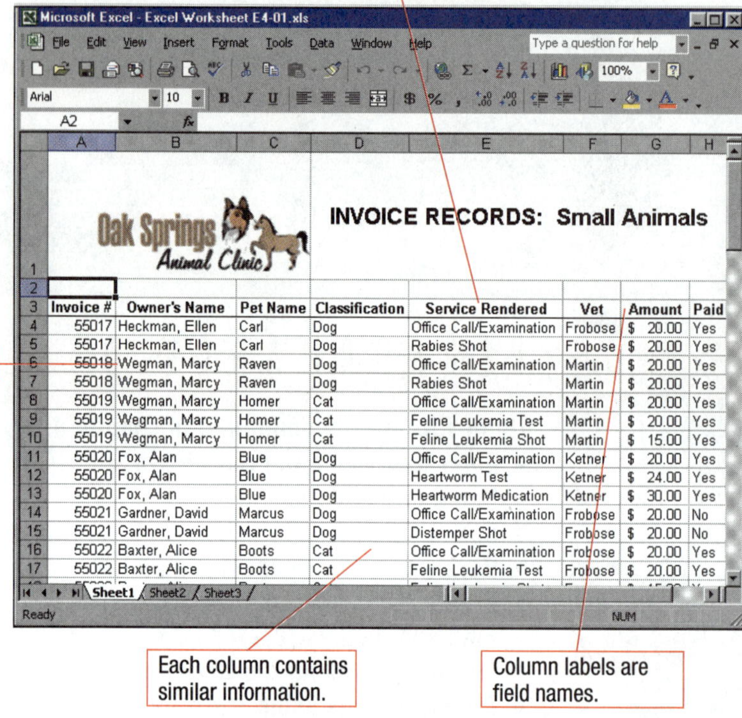

Invoice #	Owner's Name	Pet Name	Classification	Service Rendered	Vet	Amount	Paid
55017	Heckman, Ellen	Carl	Dog	Office Call/Examination	Frobose	$ 20.00	Yes
55017	Heckman, Ellen	Carl	Dog	Rabies Shot	Frobose	$ 20.00	Yes
55018	Wegman, Marcy	Raven	Dog	Office Call/Examination	Martin	$ 20.00	Yes
55018	Wegman, Marcy	Raven	Dog	Rabies Shot	Martin	$ 20.00	Yes
55019	Wegman, Marcy	Homer	Cat	Office Call/Examination	Martin	$ 20.00	Yes
55019	Wegman, Marcy	Homer	Cat	Feline Leukemia Test	Martin	$ 20.00	Yes
55019	Wegman, Marcy	Homer	Cat	Feline Leukemia Shot	Martin	$ 15.00	Yes
55020	Fox, Alan	Blue	Dog	Office Call/Examination	Ketner	$ 20.00	Yes
55020	Fox, Alan	Blue	Dog	Heartworm Test	Ketner	$ 24.00	Yes
55020	Fox, Alan	Blue	Dog	Heartworm Medication	Ketner	$ 30.00	Yes
55021	Gardner, David	Marcus	Dog	Office Call/Examination	Frobose	$ 20.00	No
55021	Gardner, David	Marcus	Dog	Distemper Shot	Frobose	$ 20.00	No
55022	Baxter, Alice	Boots	Cat	Office Call/Examination	Frobose	$ 20.00	Yes
55022	Baxter, Alice	Boots	Cat	Feline Leukemia Test	Frobose	$ 20.00	Yes

Creating a List

Certain rules must be followed when creating a list. The first row of the list must contain the labels or field names. The labels should be formatted differently from the rest of the data in the list. Use bold, italics, or cell borders (or a combination of the three) to differentiate them from the list data. There cannot be any blank rows in the list, which means there cannot be a blank row between the labels and the data.

Only one list should be stored on a worksheet. If you have several related lists, store each one on a separate worksheet. You cannot have any extraneous data stored in columns or rows adjacent to the list, or they might be considered to be a part of the list. It is best not to store any data on the worksheet other than the list itself.

Entering Data Using the Data Form

Data can be entered either by entering it into the individual cells on the worksheet or by using the Data Form. To enter data using the Data Form, select any cell in the list. Click Data. If necessary, expand the menu by clicking the down arrow at the bottom of the list. Click the Form option once it appears. The

Data Form dialog box, as shown in figure 4.2, is displayed. Each field name with a corresponding box is displayed. Click the New button. A new blank record is displayed. The appropriate data can be entered into each box. If more records are to be added, press Enter and another new blank record will be displayed. Once you have completed entering the data, click the Close button to return to the worksheet.

FIGURE 4.2 ***The Data Form Dialog Box***

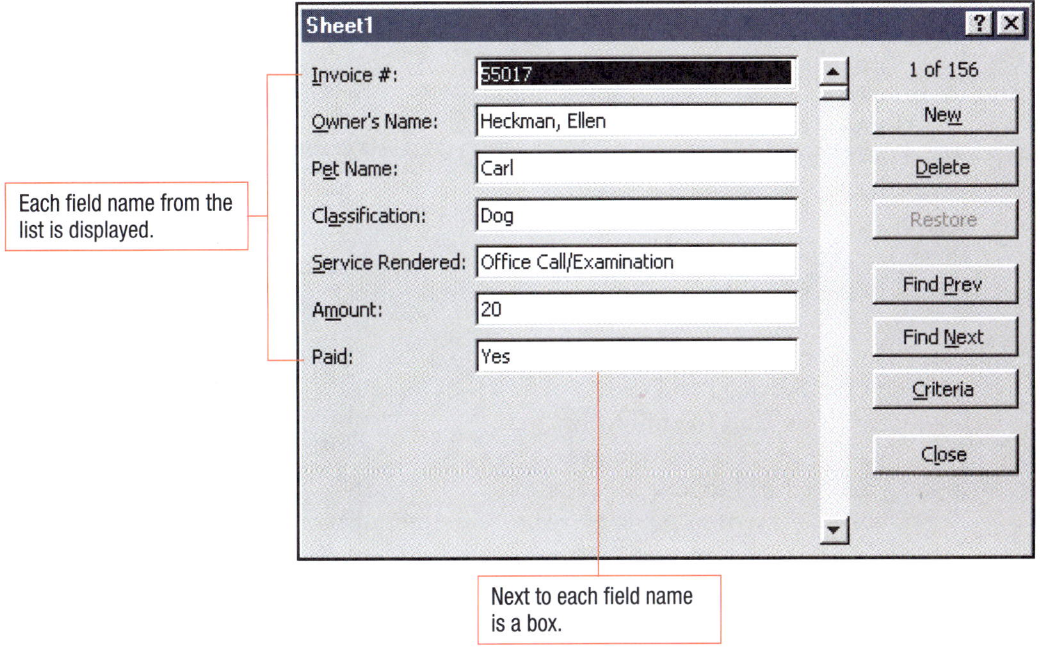

(Before completing exercise 1, delete the Chapter 03E *folder on your disk. Next, copy to your disk the* Chapter 04E *folder from the* Excel 2002 Expert *folder on the CD that accompanies this textbook.)*

exercise 1 ENTERING LIST DATA

1. Open Excel Worksheet E4-01.
2. Save the worksheet using the Save As command and name it Excel E4, Ex 01.
3. Create a custom header that displays your name at the left margin and the file name at the right margin.
4. This worksheet stores a list of invoice records for Oak Springs Animal Clinic. Three veterinarians work at the Oak Springs Animal Clinic, and they specialize in both large and small animals. This worksheet keeps track of the invoices for their small animal business. You want to add three more records to the list. Complete the following steps to add three more records using the Data Form dialog box:

a. Click cell A4.
b. Click Data. If necessary, click the down arrow at the bottom of the menu so that the Form option is displayed. Click Form.
c. The Data Form dialog box is displayed. The record that is displayed in the dialog box is the record from the row that is currently selected. Click the New button.
d. The insertion point is in the Invoice # box. Key the following: **55070**
e. Press Tab. The insertion point moves to the Owner's Name box. Key **Henry, Irene**
f. Press Tab. The insertion point moves to the Pet Name box. Key **Ralph**
g. Press Tab. The insertion point moves to the Classification box. Key **Dog**
h. Press Tab. The insertion point moves to the Service Rendered box. Key **Office Call/Examination**
i. Press Tab. The insertion point moves to the Vet box. Key **Frobose**
j. Press Tab. The insertion point moves to the Amount box. Key **20**
k. Press Tab. The insertion point moves to the Paid box. Key **No**
l. The data for the next record has now all been entered into the Data Form. Press Enter.

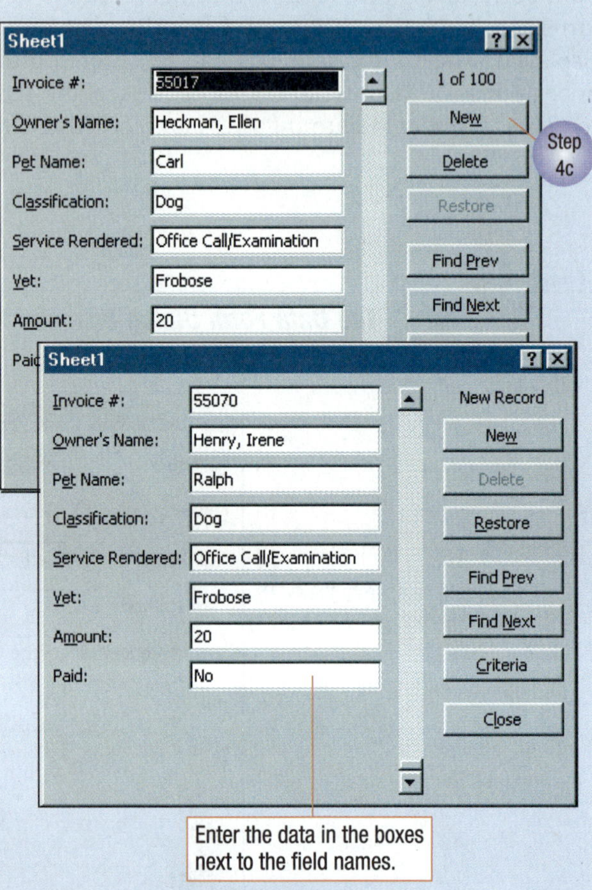

5. The data has been entered into the worksheet, and the boxes are all empty and ready for another record to be entered. By now you should be familiar with entering data using the Data Form. Enter the following two records using the Data Form:

Invoice #: **55070**
Owner's Name: **Henry, Irene**
Pet Name: **Ralph**
Classification: **Dog**
Service Rendered: **Distemper Shot**
Vet: **Frobose**
Amount: **20**
Paid: **No**

Invoice #: **55070**
Owner's Name: **Henry, Irene**
Pet Name: **Ralph**
Classification: **Dog**
Service Rendered: **Rabies Shot**
Vet: **Frobose**
Amount: **20**
Paid: **No**

When you have finished entering the data, click the Close button. If you accidentally press the Enter key instead of the Tab key before you have entered all the data in a record, you can click the Close button, scroll to the bottom of the worksheet, and then enter the data in the appropriate cells on the worksheet.

6. Adjust the page setup so that row 3 repeats as a print title at the top of each page.
7. Save the worksheet with the same name (Excel E4, Ex 01). You are going to use this worksheet in exercise 2.
8. Print and close the worksheet.

Using Data Validation

Excel's data validation feature allows you to specify the exact data that can be entered into a cell. This feature helps to prevent errors from being made when data is entered. Using the data validation feature, entries can be limited to the options on a list. Allowing a user to enter data by selecting it from a list also eliminates having to key in the exact same entry over and over again.

To use the data validation feature, select the cells that have data you want to validate. You can select either an entire column or only specific cells within a column. Click Data and Validation. The Data Validation dialog box, as shown in figure 4.3, is displayed. The entries on the Settings tab allow you to establish the validation criteria. As shown in figure 4.3, clicking the down arrow to the right of the Allow box displays a drop-down menu that lists the options for what can be allowed into the selected cells. The options available on the Settings tab change when something other than Any value is entered in the Allow box.

FIGURE 4.3 ***The Data Validation Dialog Box with the Settings Tab Selected***

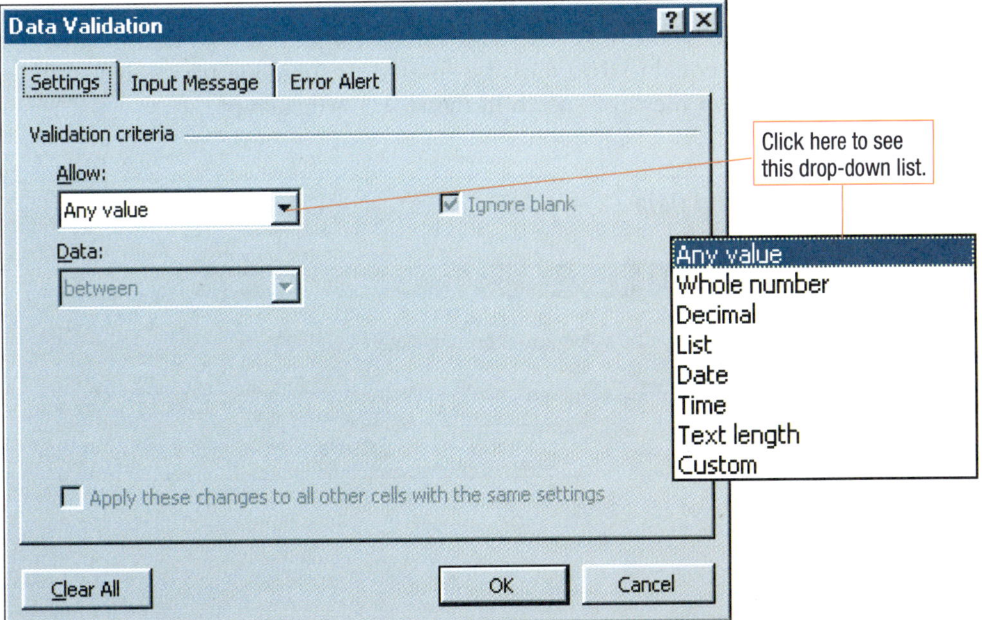

If you select *Whole number, Decimal, Date, Time,* or *Text Length* from the drop-down menu for the Allow box, the Data box is activated, as shown in figure 4.4. Clicking the down arrow to the right of the Data box displays a drop-down list that lists the Data operator options shown in figure 4.4. Select one of the data operators and enter the Minimum and Maximum values.

FIGURE 4.4 **Validating Numeric Data**

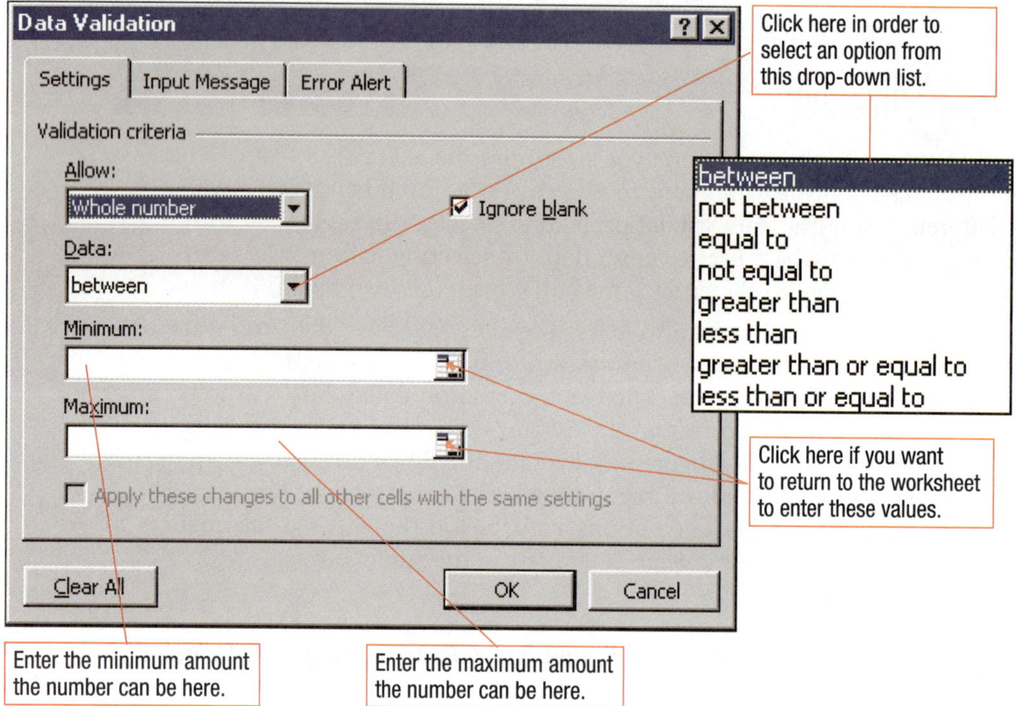

For example, you can set the data validation for a cell so that a whole number greater than or equal to 100 must be entered. If someone tries entering 98 into the cell, the error message shown in figure 4.5 is displayed.

FIGURE 4.5 **Entering Invalid Data**

Validating List Data

In situations in which the same few items are to be entered into a column, you can create a drop-down list containing the options from which the user must choose. First select the entire column to be validated. Click Data and Validation. Click the down arrow to the right of the Allow box and select *List*. Enter the options to be included in the list in the Source box. To select the options from the worksheet, click the Cell Reference button to the right of the Source box, as shown in figure 4.6.

FIGURE 4.6 ***Validating List Data***

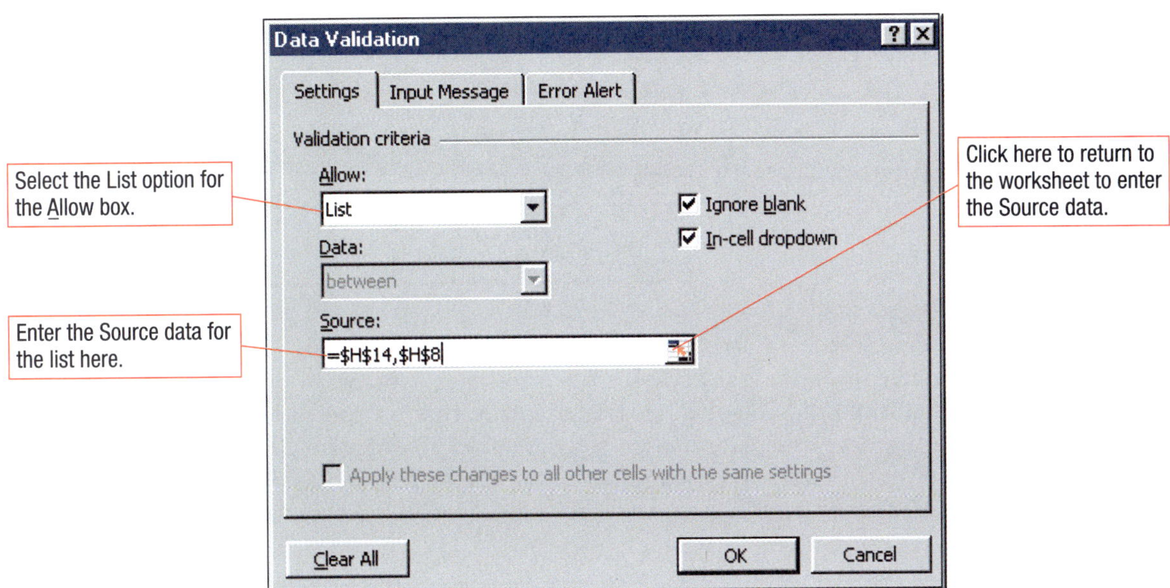

Including Input and Error Messages

You can include messages that will display if a user tries to enter invalid data. To include an input message, click the Input Message tab on the Data Validation dialog box. As shown in figure 4.7, you need to enter the title for the Title bar and the input message. Make sure the Show input message when cell is selected check box is selected. When a user selects the cell, the Input message will be displayed.

FIGURE 4.7 ***Including an Input Message***

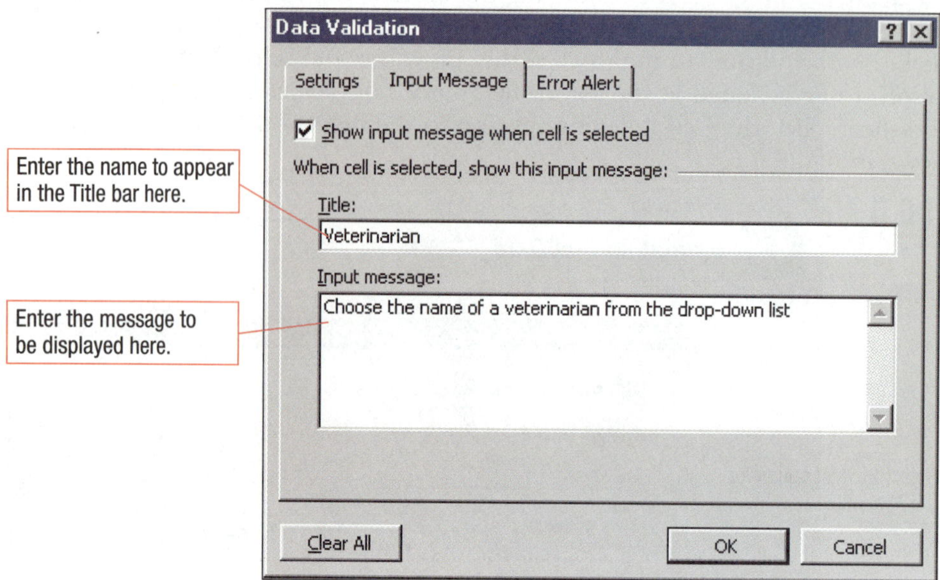

To include an error message, click the Error Alert tab. As shown in figure 4.8, you need to select the style for the error alert, which can be either Stop, Warning, or Information. You also need to enter the title for the Title bar and the error message to be displayed when someone tries to enter invalid data. Make sure the Show error alert after invalid data is entered check box is displayed. When a user tries to enter invalid data, the error message will be displayed.

FIGURE 4.8 ***Including an Error Message***

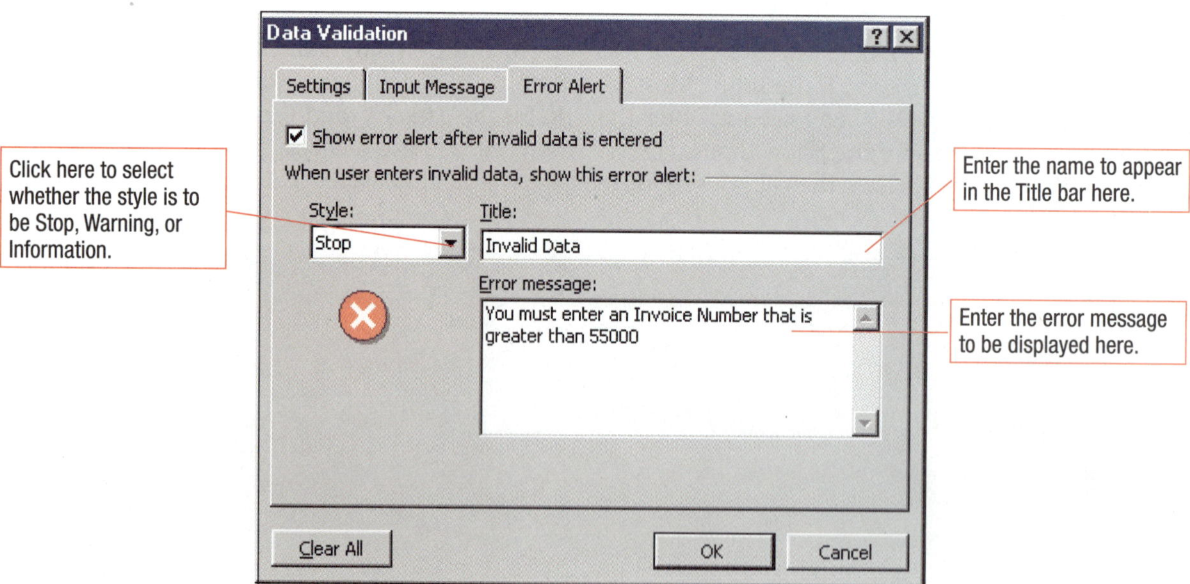

exercise 2 USING DATA VALIDATION

1. Open Excel E4, Ex 01. This is the worksheet that was completed in exercise 1.
2. Save the worksheet using the Save As command and name it Excel E4, Ex 02.
3. Make sure the header displays your name at the left margin and the file name at the right margin.
4. You want to validate some of the data that is entered into this worksheet. Select column A. Complete the following steps to validate data that is entered into column A:
   a. Click Data and then click Validation. If necessary, click the Settings tab.
   b. Click the down-pointing arrow to the right of the Allow box. Select *Whole number*.
   c. Click the down-pointing arrow to the right of the Data box. Select *greater than or equal to*.
   d. Place the insertion point in the Minimum box. Key the following: **55000**
   e. Click the Input Message tab.
   f. Key the following in the Title box: **Invoice Number**
   g. Key the following in the Input message box: **Enter an invoice number. Invoice numbers start at 55000.**
   h. Click the Error Alert tab.
   i. Key the following in the Title box: **Error**
   j. Key the following in the Error message box: **Invoice numbers must be greater than 55000.**
   k. Make sure the *Stop* option is selected in the Style box.
   l. Click OK.

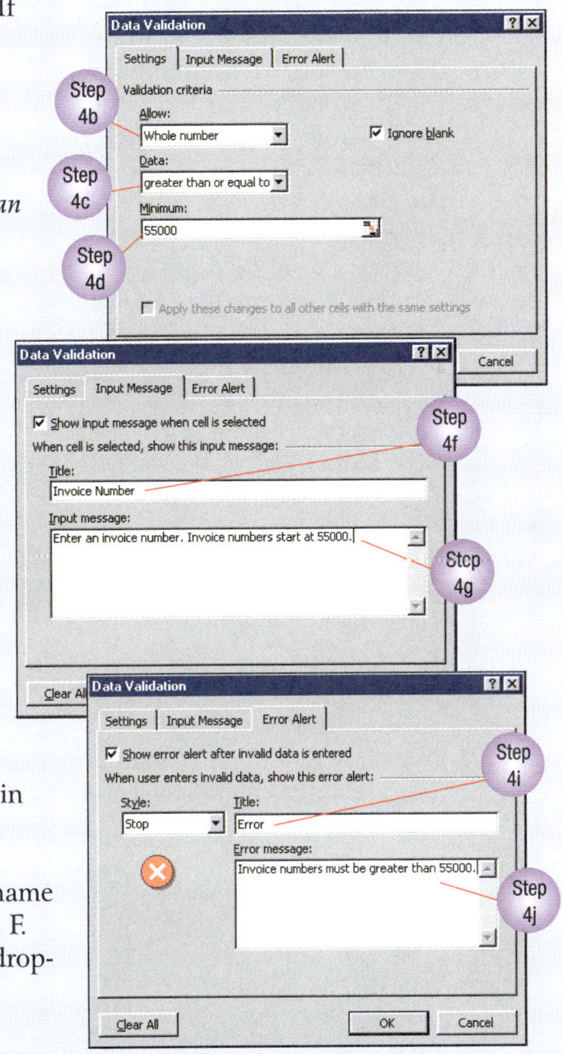

5. The only entry made in column F is the name of one of the veterinarians. Select column F. Complete the following steps to create a drop-down list of options for column F:
   a. Click Data and then click Validation. Click the Settings tab.
   b. Click the down arrow to the right of the Allow box. Select *List*.
   c. Place the insertion point in the Source box. Key **Frobose, Ketner, Martin**
   d. Click the Input Message tab.
   e. Key the following in the Title box: **Veterinarian**
   f. Key the following in the Input message box: **Select one of the veterinarian's names from the drop-down list.**
   g. Click the Error Alert tab.
   h. Key the following in the Title box: **Error**

i. Key the following in the Error message box: **You must select a name from the drop-down list.**
j. Click OK.

6. The only entries made in column H are Yes or No. Select column H. Complete the following steps to create a drop-down list of options for column H:
   a. Click Data and then click Validation. Click the Settings tab.
   b. Click the down arrow to the right of the Allow box. Select *List*.
   c. Place the insertion point in the Source box. Key the following: **Yes, No**
   d. Click the Input Message tab.
   e. Key the following in the Title box: **Paid**
   f. Key the following in the Input message box: **Select either Yes or No from the drop-down list to indicate whether or not the invoice has been paid.**
   g. Click the Error Alert tab.
   h. Key the following in the Title box: **Error**
   i. Key the following in the Error message box: **You must select either Yes or No from the drop-down list.**
   j. Click OK.
7. Use the vertical split bar at the top of the vertical scroll bar to freeze rows 1, 2, and 3 in the window. Complete the following steps to enter a new record:
   a. Select cell A107. This should be the first empty cell at the end of the list. Notice the Invoice Number input message is displayed. 
   b. Key the following in cell A107: **5571**
   c. Press Tab. An error message is displayed informing you that the invoice number you entered is not large enough.
   d. Click the Retry button.
   e. Key the following: **55071**
   f. Press Tab. Key the following: **Mason, Anita**
   g. Press Tab. Key the following: **Snickers**
   h. Press Tab. Key the following: **Dog**
   i. Press Tab. Start to key **Office Call/Examination**. As soon as the first couple of characters are entered, Excel automatically fills in the rest. 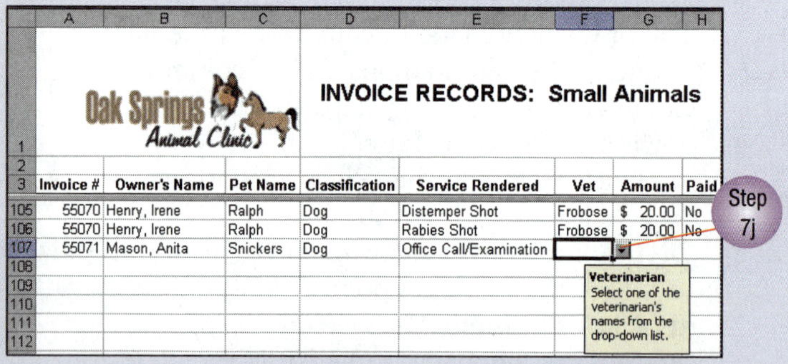
   j. Press Tab. The Veterinarian input message is displayed. A down arrow automatically is displayed to the right of the cell.
   k. Click the down-pointing arrow to the right of the cell and select *Martin* from the drop-down list.
   l. Press Tab. Key the following: **20**
   m. Press Tab. The Paid input message is displayed. A down-pointing arrow automatically is displayed to the right of the cell.

n. Click the down arrow to the right of the cell and select *Yes* from the drop-down list.

8. By now you should be familiar with entering data using data validation. Enter the following records in rows 108 and 109:

Invoice #: **55071**
Owner's Name: ***Mason, Anita***
Pet Name: **Snickers**
Classification: **Dog**
Service Rendered: **Heartworm Test**
Vet: **Martin**
Amount: **24**
Paid: **Yes**

Invoice #: **55071**
Owner's Name: **Mason, Anita**
Pet Name: **Snickers**
Classification: **Dog**
Service Rendered: **Heartworm Medication**
Vet: **Martin**
Amount: **35**
Paid: **Yes**

9. Make any necessary adjustments so that all the columns fit on one page.
10. Save the worksheet with the same name (Excel E4, Ex 02). You are going to use this worksheet in exercise 3.
11. Print and close the worksheet.

Sorting a List

Excel's sort feature helps you organize the data in a list. Column fields can be quickly sorted in ascending or descending order. To sort the data in a column, select any cell in the column by which you want to sort. To sort in ascending order, click the Sort Ascending button on the Standard toolbar. To sort in descending order, click the Sort Descending button on the Standard toolbar.

Sort Ascending

Sort Descending

Performing a Multi-Level Sort

If you want to sort a list by more than one field, you can use the Sort dialog box. Suppose, for example, you wanted to sort first by a last name field and then by a first name field. To perform such a multi-level sort, select any cell in the list to be sorted. Click Data and then click Sort. The Sort dialog box shown in figure 4.9 is displayed.

FIGURE 4.9 *The Sort Dialog Box*

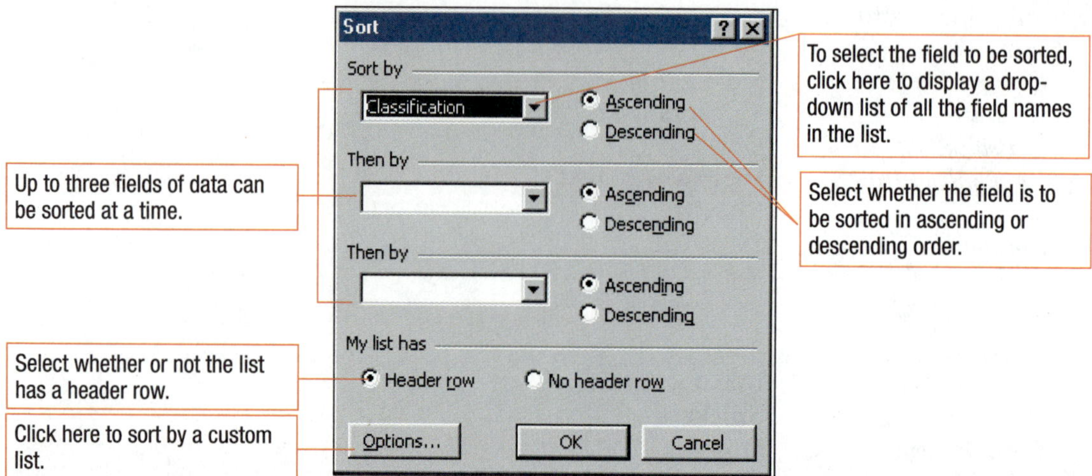

To select the first field to be sorted, click the down arrow to the right of the Sort by box. A list of all the field names is displayed. Select the field name of the column to be sorted first, and select whether the sort should be in ascending or descending order. If you want to sort by a second field, click the down arrow to the right of the first Then by box and select the field name of the column to be sorted next, and so on. At the bottom of the dialog box, select whether or not the list has a header row and then click OK.

Creating a Custom List

At times you may want to sort by an unusual order, that is, not simply ascending or descending. You can do this by creating a custom list. To create a custom list, key the list into a worksheet and select all the cells containing the list. Click Tools and then click Options. Click the Custom Lists tab on the Options dialog box. As shown in figure 4.10, the selected cell range appears in the Import list from cells box. Click the Import button. The list is then displayed in the Custom lists box and the List entries box. Click the OK button.

FIGURE

4.10 *The Options Dialog Box with the Custom Lists Tab Selected*

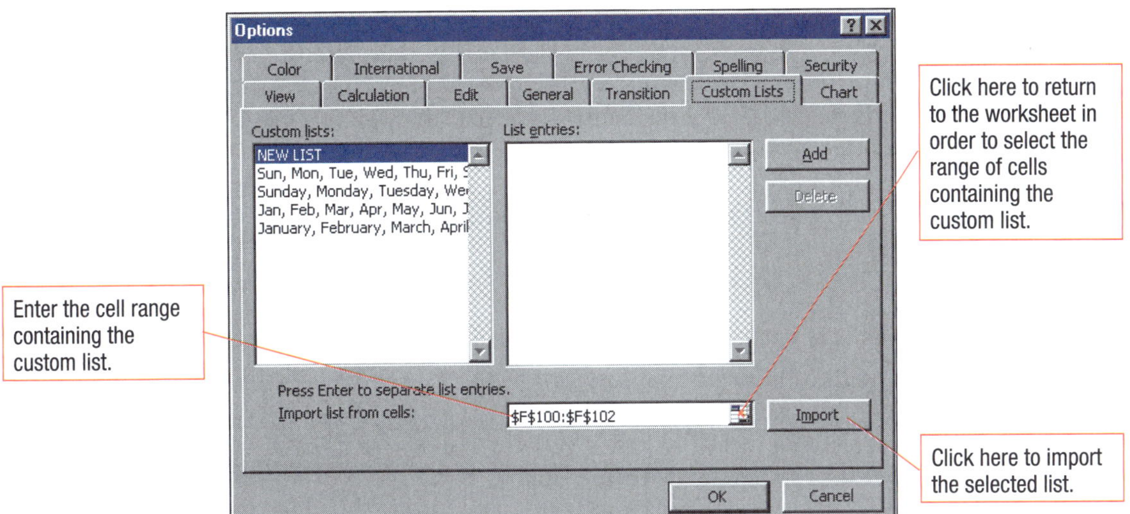

You can use a custom list to sort only the first or top level of the sort. Click the down arrow to the right of the Sort by list box and select the column for which the custom list was created. To sort that column using the custom list, click the Options button at the bottom of the Sort dialog box. The Sort Options dialog box shown in figure 4.11 is displayed. Click the down arrow to the right of the First key sort order box. The custom list will be included in the drop-down menu that appears. Select the custom list and click OK.

FIGURE

4.11 *The Sort Options Dialog Box*

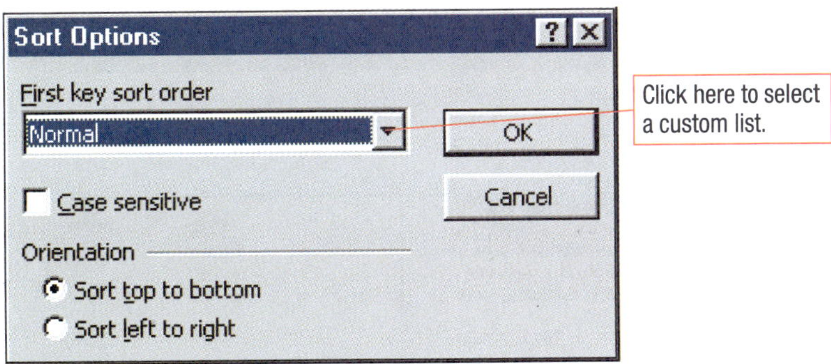

Once a custom list is created, Excel saves it on the computer system so that it is always available. To delete a custom list, Click Tools and then Options. Click the Custom Lists tab on the Options dialog box. Select the custom list to be deleted from the Custom lists box and click the Delete button. Click OK. A box warning you that the list will be permanently deleted is displayed. Click OK.

exercise 3

SORTING A LIST, PERFORMING A MULTI-LEVEL SORT, AND SORTING BY A CUSTOM LIST

1. Open Excel E4, Ex 02. This is the worksheet that was completed in exercise 2.
2. Save the worksheet using the Save As command and name it Excel E4, Ex 03.
3. Make sure the header displays your name at the left margin and the file name at the right margin.
4. Right now the list is sorted by invoice number. You would like to sort it by owner's name. Click cell B4. Click the Sort Ascending button. Scroll through the list to see how it is now sorted.
5. Next try sorting the list by vet. Click cell F4. Click the Sort Ascending button. Scroll through the list to see how it is now sorted.
6. Now you want to sort by the owner's name first, by the classification of animal second, and finally by the pet's name. Select any cell in the list. Complete the following steps to perform the multi-level sort.
   a. Click Data and then Sort.
   b. Click the down-pointing arrow to the right of the Sort by box. Select *Owner's Name*.
   c. Click the down-pointing arrow to the right of the first Then by box. Select *Classification*.
   d. Click the down-pointing arrow to the right of the second Then by box. Select *Pet Name*.
   e. Be sure that Header row is selected at the bottom of the dialog box.
   f. Click OK.
   g. Scroll through the list to see how it is now sorted.

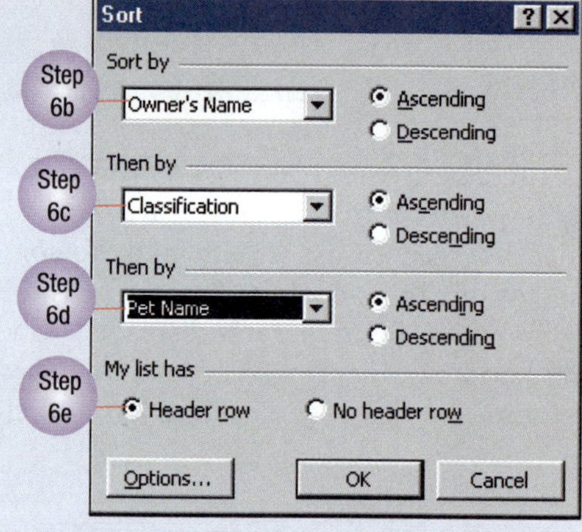

7. Make any necessary adjustments so that the columns all fit on one page. Print the sorted list.
8. The veterinarians want to be able to sort the list in order by who has worked at the clinic the longest. Dr. Ketner has worked there the longest, followed by Dr. Frobose, followed by Dr. Martin. Complete the following steps to create a custom list.
   a. Key **Ketner** in cell I4.
   b. Key **Frobose** in cell I5.
   c. Key **Martin** in cell I6.
   d. Select cells I4 through I6.
   e. Click Tools and then Options.
   f. Click the Custom Lists tab. Check to make sure that the cell range I4:I6 is in the Import list from cells box.
   g. Click the Import button.

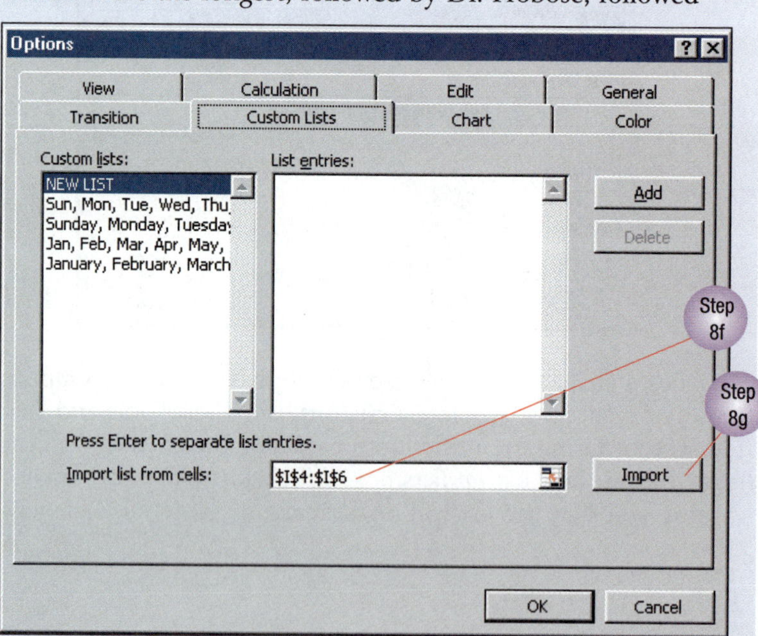

h. Click OK.
i. Delete cells I4:I6.

9. You are ready to sort using the custom list you just created. Complete the following steps to sort by the custom list:
   a. Click any cell in the list.
   b. Click Data and then Sort.
   c. Click the down-pointing arrow to the right of the Sort by box. Select *Vet*.
   d. Click the Options button at the bottom of the dialog box.
   e. Click the down-pointing arrow key next to the First key sort order box. Select *Ketner, Frobose, Martin*.
   f. Click OK.
   g. Click the down-pointing arrow to the right of the first Then by box. Select *Owner's name*.
   h. Click the down-pointing arrow to the right of the second Then by box. Select *Classification*.
   i. Click OK.
   j. Scroll through the list to see how it is now sorted.

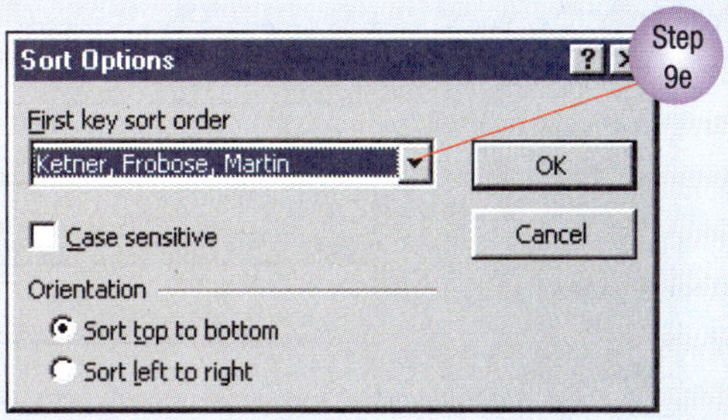

Sort Options
First key sort order
Ketner, Frobose, Martin
OK
Case sensitive
Cancel
Orientation
Sort top to bottom
Sort left to right
Step 9e

10. Make any necessary adjustments so that the columns all fit on one page. Print the sorted list.
11. Complete the following steps to delete the custom list you created:
    a. Click Tools and then Options.
    b. Select *Ketner, Frobose, Martin* in the Custom lists box.
    c. Click the Delete button.
    d. A warning box is displayed letting you know that the list will be permanently deleted. Click OK.
    e. Click OK.

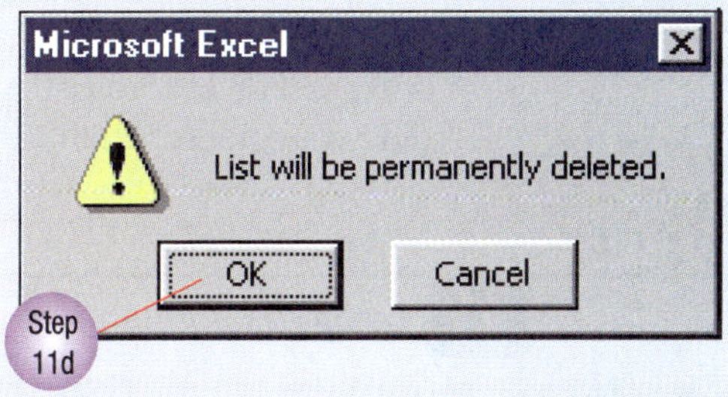

Microsoft Excel
List will be permanently deleted.
OK
Cancel
Step 11d

12. Save the worksheet with the same name (Excel E4, Ex 03). You are going to use this worksheet in exercise 4.
13. Close the worksheet.

Modifying Records

Updates usually have to be made to data lists. Records need to be deleted or edited in some way. In addition to allowing you to enter new records, the Data Form can be used to search for, display, edit, and delete specific records.

Finding Records

To find specific records, select any cell in the data list and click Data and then Form. Clicking the Find Prev button displays the previous record. Clicking the Find Next button displays the next record. Clicking the Criteria button allows you to enter specific criteria Excel will use when searching for the record. A blank record is displayed. You can enter the search criteria in the field name boxes. If you enter criteria in more than one field, the record must contain the criteria in both fields in order to be found. Using the criteria entered in figure 4.12, Excel will find all the records containing "Heckman, Ellen" in the *Owner's Name* field and "Cat" in the *Classification* field.

FIGURE 4.12 *Finding Specific Records*

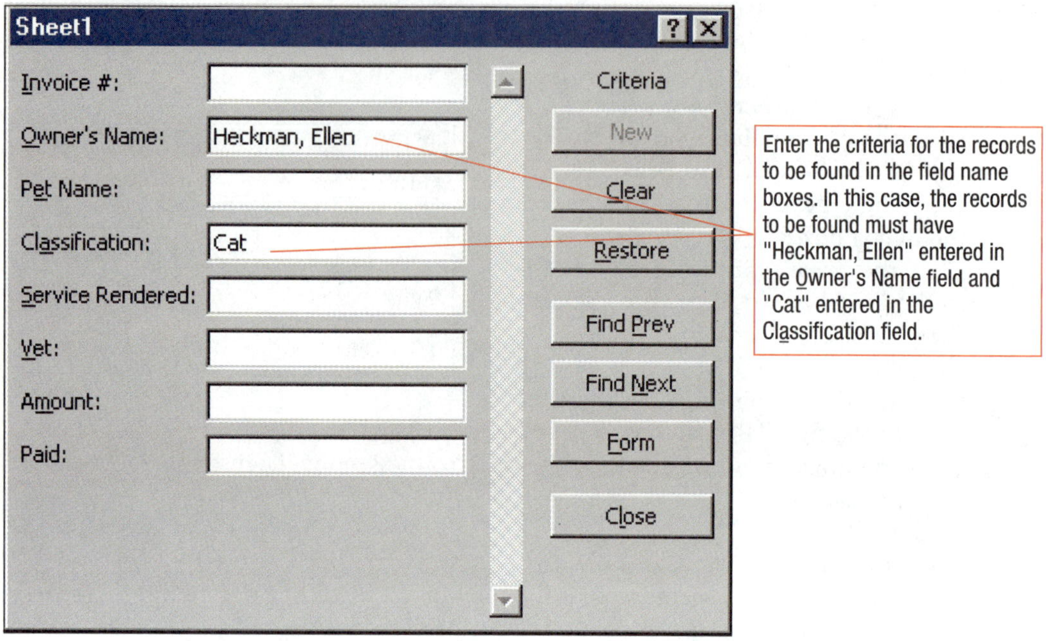

Sheet1

Invoice #:
Owner's Name: Heckman, Ellen
Pet Name:
Classification: Cat
Service Rendered:
Vet:
Amount:
Paid:

Criteria
New
Clear
Restore
Find Prev
Find Next
Form
Close

Enter the criteria for the records to be found in the field name boxes. In this case, the records to be found must have "Heckman, Ellen" entered in the Owner's Name field and "Cat" entered in the Classification field.

The comparison operators listed in table 4.1 can be used as part of the search criteria. For example, if you wanted to find all the records in which the *Amount* field was greater than 20, you would enter **>20** in the Amount box.

TABLE 4.1 *Comparison Operators*

Operators	Description
=	Equals
>	Greater than
<	Less than
>=	Greater than or equal to
<=	Less than or equal to
<>	Not equal to

Once the search criteria have been entered in the boxes, click the Find Next button. The first record Excel finds is displayed. Click the Find Next button until you hear a beep. The beep indicates that Excel could not find any more matches. To return to the worksheet, click the Close button.

Editing Records

Once a specific record has been located using the Data Form, you can make any changes to it right on the Data Form. Key the changes in the appropriate field name boxes. Remember to press Tab to move from field to field and press Enter to move from record to record. Once you click the Close button or move to a different record in the Data Form, whatever changes were made are entered into the worksheet. You can also edit records directly on the worksheet.

Deleting Records

Records can be deleted using the Data Form. Once the record to be deleted has been located using the Data Form, click the Delete button. A warning box is displayed letting you know that the record will be permanently deleted. Click OK to delete the record. You can also delete records by deleting the row containing the record from the worksheet.

4 FINDING, EDITING, AND DELETING RECORDS

1. Open Excel E4, Ex 03. This is the worksheet that was completed in exercise 3.
2. Save the worksheet using the Save As command and name it Excel E4, Ex 04.
3. Make sure a custom header displays your name at the left margin and the file name at the right margin.
4. First you want to find all the records in which Heartworm Medication was the service rendered. Complete the following steps to use the Data Form to conduct the search:
   a. Click any cell in the data list.
   b. Click Data and then Form.
   c. Click the Criteria button.
   d. Key the following in the Service Rendered box: **Heartworm Medication**
   e. Click the Find Next button. The first record found is displayed. Click the Find Next button until no more records are found. How many records were found?
5. Complete the following steps to find all the records where the Heartworm Medication sold cost more than $50.00.
   a. You want to start the search beginning with record 1. To do this, record 1 must be displayed. To display record 1, click the button on the scroll bar and drag it to the top. It should say 1 of 106 in the

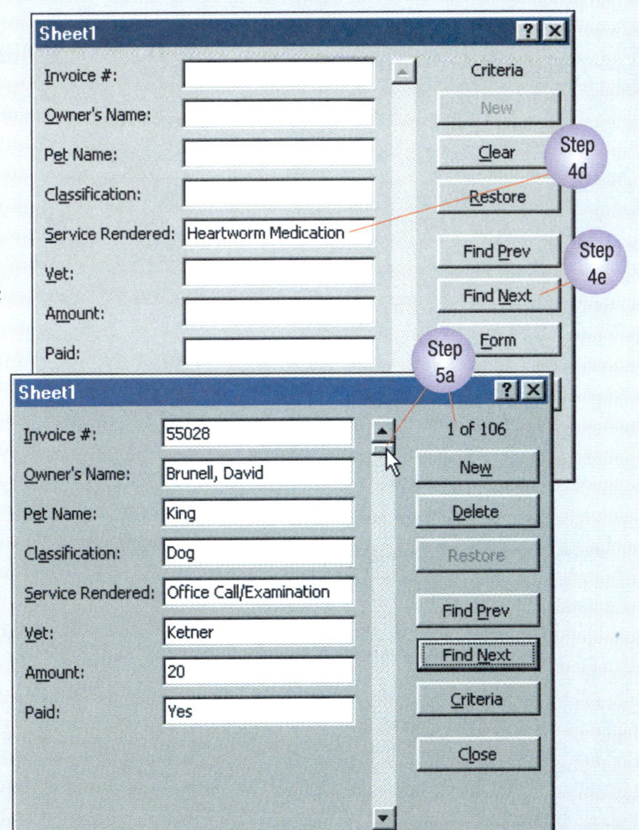

upper right corner of the dialog box. This means the record that is displayed is the first record out of a total of 106 records.

b. Click the Criteria button.
c. "Heartworm Medication" should still be entered in the Service Rendered box. Key **>50** in the Amount box.
d. Click the Find Next button. The first record found is displayed. Click the Find Next button until no more records are found. How many records were found this time?

6. Linda Covington has gotten married and wants her last name changed on all her records. Complete the following steps to make this change:
   a. Use the scroll bar to move to record 1. The first record in the list should be displayed in the Data Form.
   b. Click the Criteria button.
   c. Delete the entries in the Service Rendered box and the Amount box.
   d. Key the following in the Owner's Name box: **Covington, Linda**
   e. Click the Find Next button.
   f. Key the following in the Owner's Name box: **Kale, Linda**
   Be sure to press the Enter key after keying the changes. The editing changes will not be made until the Enter key is pressed. Once the Enter key is pressed, Excel automatically finds the next record with Covington, Linda in the *Owner's Name* field.
   g. Edit the next record that is found so that **Linda Kale** is in the Owner's Name box.
   h. Edit all of Linda Covington's records to reflect her name change.
   i. Click the Find Prev button to make sure there are no more records for Linda Covington. When you have finished, Excel should not be able to find any records for Linda Covington when you press either the Find Next or the Find Prev buttons.

7. A mistake was made on invoice 55070. Irene Henry was charged for a rabies shot, but her dog was not given a rabies shot. Complete the following steps to delete this record.
   a. Use the scroll bar to move to record 1.
   b. Click the Criteria button.
   c. Delete the entry in the Owner's Name box.
   d. Key **55070** in the Invoice # box.
   e. Key **Rabies Shot** in the Service Rendered box.
   f. Click the Find Next button.
   g. Click the Delete button.
   h. A warning box is displayed informing you that the record will be permanently deleted. Click OK.
   i. Click the Close button.

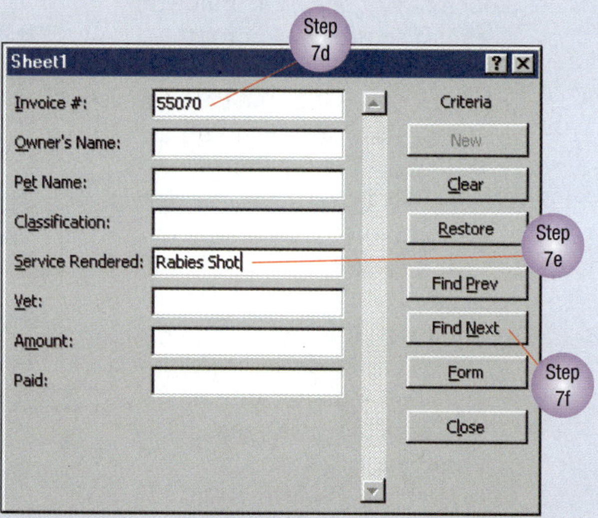

8. Sort the list by Owner's Name first, Classification second, and Pet Name third.
9. Save the worksheet with the same name (Excel E4, Ex 04). You are going to use this worksheet in exercise 7.
10. Print and close the worksheet.

Outlining a Worksheet

When working with long lists of data, quickly finding the specific information you need could be difficult. One way to make locating information in a list easier is by outlining the worksheet. Once you outline a worksheet, a single mouse click will hide or reveal levels of detail within the worksheet. With an outline you can quickly display only the rows or columns that provide summaries. In figure 4.13, for example, the details for the East Central Region's sales are displayed. The details are hidden for the North Central and Northeast Regions' sales. Figure 4.13 has three levels of detail. An outline can have up to eight levels of detail. Each inner level provides details for the preceding outer level. In figure 4.13, level 1 is the row displaying the Grand Total, level 2 comprises the rows displaying the totals for each of the regions, and level 3 comprises the detail rows for all the regions. To see a particular level of the outline, click the outline symbol that represents the number of the level you want to see. These symbols are located in the upper left corner of figure 4.13.

FIGURE

4.13 ***A Worksheet Outline***

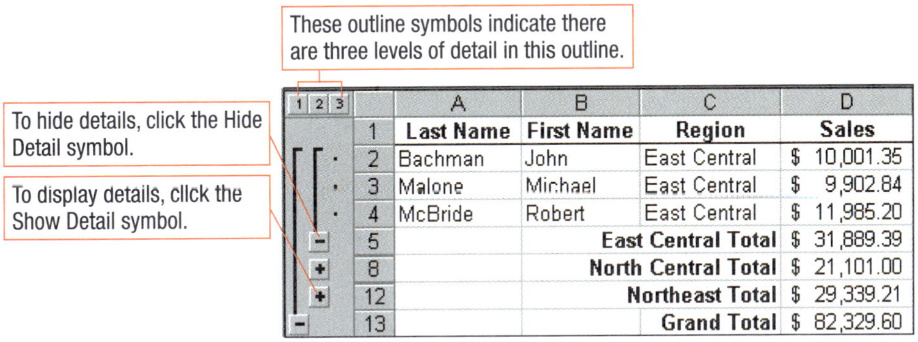

These outline symbols indicate there are three levels of detail in this outline.

To hide details, click the Hide Detail symbol.

To display details, click the Show Detail symbol.

1 2 3		A	B	C	D
	1	**Last Name**	**First Name**	**Region**	**Sales**
·	2	Bachman	John	East Central	$ 10,001.35
·	3	Malone	Michael	East Central	$ 9,902.84
·	4	McBride	Robert	East Central	$ 11,985.20
−	5			**East Central Total**	$ 31,889.39
+	8			**North Central Total**	$ 21,101.00
+	12			**Northeast Total**	$ 29,339.21
−	13			**Grand Total**	$ 82,329.60

If you want to outline a worksheet automatically, it must contain formulas that summarize the data, such as formulas that find subtotals and a grand total. If the summary formulas are in columns, all the columns containing the summary formulas must be either to the right or to the left of the detail data. If the summary formulas are in rows, all the rows containing the summary formulas must be either below or above the detail data. That is, the summary formulas cannot be mixed in with the detail data.

Once you are sure the worksheet is set up correctly, select the range of cells to be outlined. If you want to outline the entire worksheet, click any cell in the worksheet. If you are outlining only a portion of the worksheet, select the range of cells to be outlined. Click Data, point to Group and Outline, and then click Auto Outline. The appropriate outline symbols are displayed. You can then hide and show levels of detail, as explained in table 4.2.

TABLE

4.2 Showing and Hiding Levels of Detail in an Outline

To Show Details	Click
The detail data for a group	The Show Detail symbol [+].
A specific level in an outline	The Row or Column Level symbol [1 2 3].
All detail in an outline	The Row or Column Level symbol for the lowest row or column. If there are three levels, the lowest level would be three.
To Hide Details	**Click**
The detail data for a group	The Hide Detail symbol [-].
A specific level in an outline	The preceding Row or Column Level symbol [1 2 3]. For example, if an outline has three levels, hide the third level by clicking the symbol for level 2.
All detail in an outline	The first level symbol, which would be one.

To remove an outline, click any cell on the worksheet. Click Data, point to Group and Outline, and then click Clear Outline. The outline is removed. None of the data on the worksheet changes when an outline is removed.

Instead of having Excel automatically create an outline for you, you can create an outline manually. To create an outline manually, select the rows or columns that will be hidden when the details are not displayed. One outline area cannot be immediately adjacent to another. If you try, for example, to create one outline level that hides rows 5 through 10 and then try to create a second outline level that hides rows 11 through 15, you will end up with one outline level that hides rows 5 through 15. A row or column has to separate the two areas that you want to outline. In many cases, that row or column will contain the summarization function, such as SUM or AVERAGE.

To create an outline level, select the rows or columns to be outlined. Click Data, point to Group and Outline, and then click Group. The outline is created. To remove an outline, select the rows or columns that make up the outline to be removed. If you want to clear an entire outline, click a single cell in the worksheet. Click Data, point to Group and Outline, and then click Ungroup. The outline is removed.

OUTLINING A WORKSHEET MANUALLY

1. Open Excel Worksheet E4-02.
2. Save the worksheet using the Save As command and name it Excel E4, Ex 05.
3. Create a custom header that displays your name at the left margin and the file name at the right margin.
4. Scroll through the worksheet to look at the information stored in it. The records are sorted by veterinarian, and subtotals for the invoices for each veterinarian are in rows 40, 73, and 111. You would like to be able to easily see just the subtotals. Creating an outline would allow you to do this. Create an outline for the worksheet manually by completing the following steps:
   a. Select row 4. Move the mouse pointer to the bottom of row 4. When the mouse pointer turns into a four-headed arrow, hold down the Shift key and double-click. Rows 4 through 39 should be selected.
   b. Click Data. If necessary, expand the drop-down menu. Point to Group and Outline, and then click Group.
   c. Select row 41. Move the mouse pointer to the bottom of row 41. When the mouse pointer turns into a four-headed arrow, hold down the Shift key and double-click. Rows 41 through 72 should be selected.
   d. Click Data, point to Group and Outline, and then click Group.
   e. Select row 74. Move the mouse pointer to the bottom of row 74. When the mouse pointer turns into a four-headed arrow, hold down the Shift key and double-click. Rows 74 through 110 should be selected.
   f. Click Data, point to Group and Outline, and then click Group. The outline for the worksheet now has two levels.
5. Experiment with displaying different levels of the outline by completing the following steps:
   a. Click the level 1 Column Level symbol. Only the subtotals are displayed.
   b. Print the worksheet.
   c. Click the Show Detail symbol to the left of row 111. The details for Martin's invoices are now displayed. The Show Detail symbol changed to a Hide Detail symbol.
   d. Print the worksheet.
   e. Click the Hide Detail symbol to the left of row 111.

Step 5e

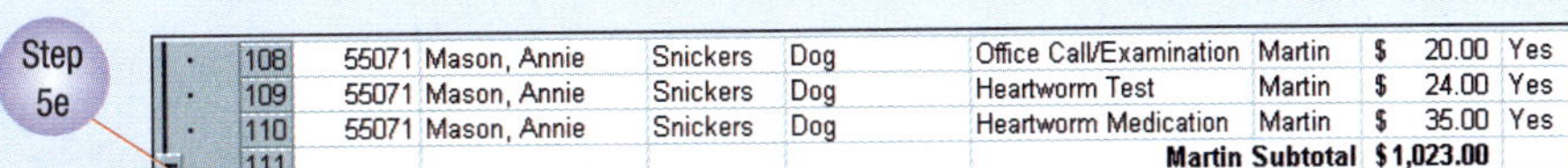

108	55071	Mason, Annie	Snickers	Dog	Office Call/Examination	Martin	$ 20.00	Yes
109	55071	Mason, Annie	Snickers	Dog	Heartworm Test	Martin	$ 24.00	Yes
110	55071	Mason, Annie	Snickers	Dog	Heartworm Medication	Martin	$ 35.00	Yes
111						Martin Subtotal	$1,023.00	

6. Ungroup the records for Frobose by completing the following steps:
   a. Click the Show Detail symbol to the left of row 40. The details for Frobose's invoices are now displayed.
   b. Select row 4. Move the mouse pointer to the bottom of row 4. When the mouse pointer turns into a four-headed arrow, hold down the Shift key and double-click. Rows 4 through 39 should be selected.
   c. Click Data, point to Group and Outline, and then click Ungroup. Frobose's records are no longer grouped.
7. To clear the outline for the rest of the worksheet, click Data, point to Group and Outline, and then click Clear Outline.
8. Save and close Excel E4, Ex 05.

exercise 6

OUTLINING A WORKSHEET AUTOMATICALLY

1. Open Excel Worksheet E4-03.
2. Save the worksheet using the Save As command and name it Excel E4, Ex 06.
3. Create a custom header that displays your name at the left margin and the file name at the right margin.
4. Scroll through the worksheet to look at the information stored in it. The records are sorted by invoice. There is a subtotal for each invoice and a grand total of all the invoices. Outlining this worksheet manually would be a lot of work. Outline the worksheet automatically by completing the following steps:
   a. Click anywhere in the worksheet.
   b. Click Data, point to Group and Outline, and then click Auto Outline. The worksheet is now outlined. The outline has three levels.
5. Experiment with displaying different levels of the outline by completing the following steps:
   a. Click the level 1 Column Level symbol. Only the grand total is displayed.

   b. Print the worksheet.
   c. Click the Show Detail symbol to the left of row 107.
   d. Click the level 2 Column Level symbol. All the invoice totals are displayed.
   e. Click the Show Detail symbol to the left of row 17. The details for invoice 55020 are now displayed.
   f. Print the worksheet.
   g. Click the level 3 Column Level symbol. All the details are displayed.
6. To clear the outline for the worksheet, click Data, point to Group and Outline, and then click Clear Outline.
7. Save and close Excel E4, Ex 06.

Subtotaling a List

Data in a list can be summarized using subtotals. To subtotal a list you must first sort the list by the field on which you want the list subtotaled. For example, suppose you want a subtotal of each veterinarian's invoices. The list would first have to be sorted by veterinarian. Once the list is sorted by the field on which the subtotals are to be based, select any cell in the list. Click Data and then click Subtotals. The Subtotal dialog box, as shown in figure 4.14, is displayed.

FIGURE 4.14 ***The Subtotal Dialog Box***

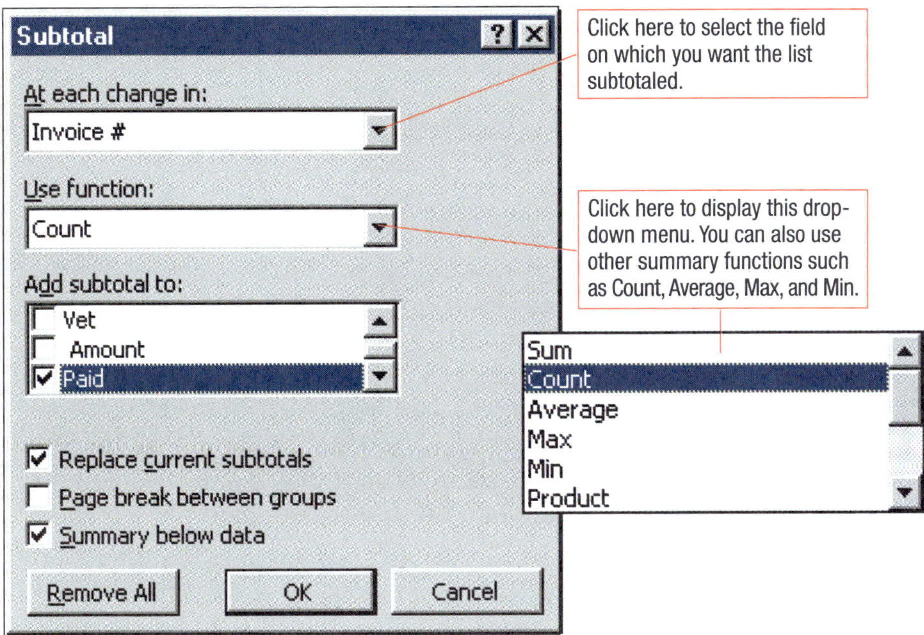

To select the field by which the list is to be subtotaled, click the down arrow to the right of the At each change in box. A list of all the field names is displayed. Click the appropriate field. Click the down arrow to the right of the Use function box. To find subtotals, click *Sum*. Other summary functions, such as Count, Average, Max, and Min, are also available. In the Add subtotal to box, click the check box next to the field containing the values that are to be subtotaled. Click OK. You are returned to the worksheet, and the subtotals along with a grand total are displayed.

Subtotals are displayed in outline view. The Hide Detail Level buttons, as shown in figure 4.15, allow you to display as much or as little of the data as you want. Suppose you want to display only the data subtotal and not all the individual records. Click the Hide Detail Level button for that subtotal, and only that subtotal will be displayed. The Hide Detail Level button changes to a Show Detail Level button. To display the records, click the Show Detail Level button.

FIGURE

4.15 ***Creating Subtotals***

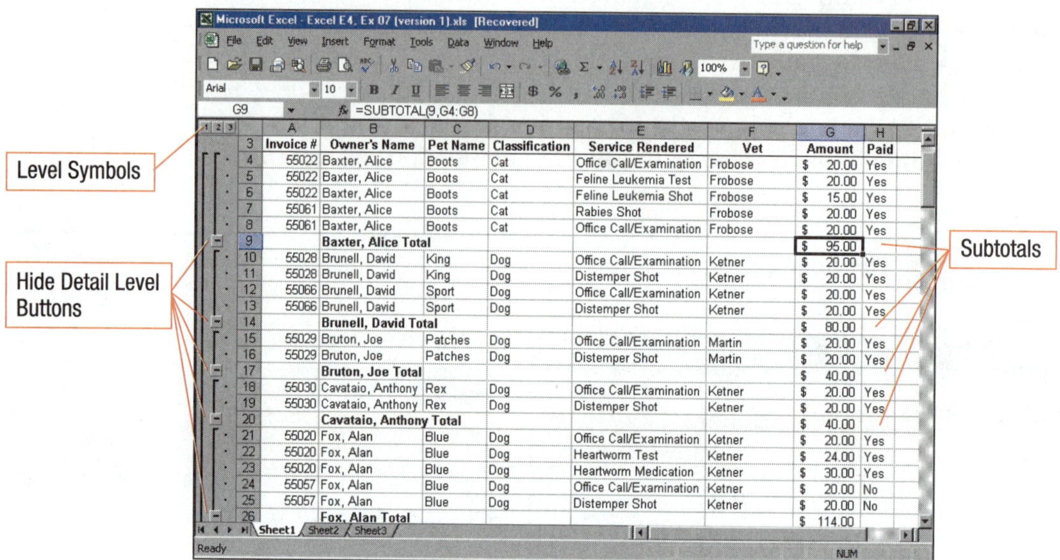

	A	B	C	D	E	F	G	H
3	Invoice #	Owner's Name	Pet Name	Classification	Service Rendered	Vet	Amount	Paid
4	55022	Baxter, Alice	Boots	Cat	Office Call/Examination	Frobose	$ 20.00	Yes
5	55022	Baxter, Alice	Boots	Cat	Feline Leukemia Test	Frobose	$ 20.00	Yes
6	55022	Baxter, Alice	Boots	Cat	Feline Leukemia Shot	Frobose	$ 15.00	Yes
7	55061	Baxter, Alice	Boots	Cat	Rabies Shot	Frobose	$ 20.00	Yes
8	55061	Baxter, Alice	Boots	Cat	Office Call/Examination	Frobose	$ 20.00	Yes
9		Baxter, Alice Total					$ 95.00	
10	55028	Brunell, David	King	Dog	Office Call/Examination	Ketner	$ 20.00	Yes
11	55028	Brunell, David	King	Dog	Distemper Shot	Ketner	$ 20.00	Yes
12	55066	Brunell, David	Sport	Dog	Office Call/Examination	Ketner	$ 20.00	Yes
13	55066	Brunell, David	Sport	Dog	Distemper Shot	Ketner	$ 20.00	Yes
14		Brunell, David Total					$ 80.00	
15	55029	Bruton, Joe	Patches	Dog	Office Call/Examination	Martin	$ 20.00	Yes
16	55029	Bruton, Joe	Patches	Dog	Distemper Shot	Martin	$ 20.00	Yes
17		Bruton, Joe Total					$ 40.00	
18	55030	Cavataio, Anthony	Rex	Dog	Office Call/Examination	Ketner	$ 20.00	Yes
19	55030	Cavataio, Anthony	Rex	Dog	Distemper Shot	Ketner	$ 20.00	Yes
20		Cavataio, Anthony Total					$ 40.00	
21	55020	Fox, Alan	Blue	Dog	Office Call/Examination	Ketner	$ 20.00	Yes
22	55020	Fox, Alan	Blue	Dog	Heartworm Test	Ketner	$ 24.00	Yes
23	55020	Fox, Alan	Blue	Dog	Heartworm Medication	Ketner	$ 30.00	Yes
24	55057	Fox, Alan	Blue	Dog	Office Call/Examination	Ketner	$ 20.00	No
25	55057	Fox, Alan	Blue	Dog	Distemper Shot	Ketner	$ 20.00	No
26		Fox, Alan Total					$ 114.00	

The level symbols, also shown in figure 4.15, allow you to quickly control how much detail is displayed. Clicking the Level 1 button displays the grand total only. Clicking the Level 2 button displays all the subtotals. None of the individual records are displayed. Clicking the Level 3 button displays all the records, subtotals, and the grand total.

When you have finished working with subtotals, they can be removed by selecting any cell in the list and clicking Data and then Subtotals. Click the Remove All button and click OK.

exercise 7

SUBTOTALING A LIST

1. Open Excel E4, Ex 04. This is the worksheet that was completed in exercise 4.
2. Save the worksheet using the Save As command and name it Excel E4, Ex 07.
3. Make sure a custom header displays your name at the left margin and the file name at the right margin.
4. Complete the following steps to subtotal the list by veterinarian:
   a. Sort the list in ascending order on the *Vet* field.
   b. Click Data and then Subtotals.
   c. Click the down-pointing arrow to the right of the At each change in box. Select *Vet*.
   d. Click the down-pointing arrow to the right of the Use function box. Select *Sum*.
   e. Select the Amount check box. Deselect any other check boxes.
   f. Click OK.

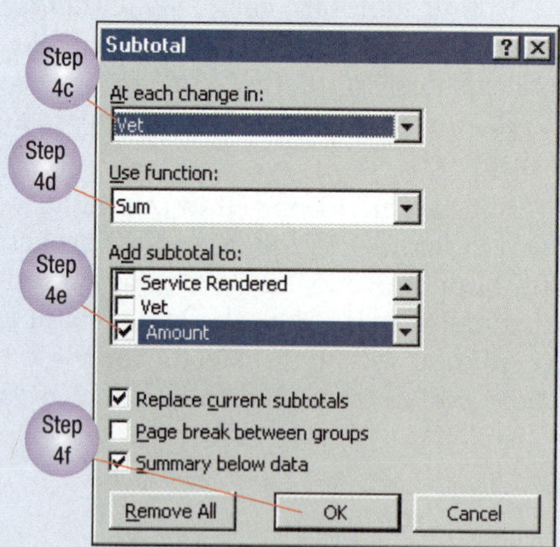

g. The subtotals have been created. Click the Level 2 button.
h. Adjust the width of columns F and G.
i. To see only the records for Dr. Frobose, click the Show Details button to the left of row 40.
j. To see all the individual records, click the Level 3 button. All of the records, subtotals, and the grand total are now displayed.

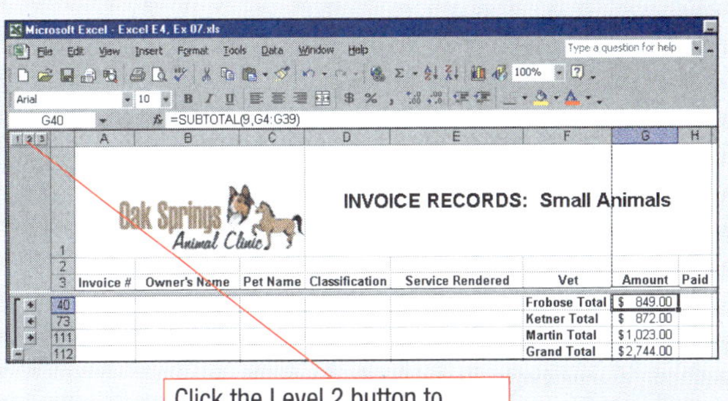

Click the Level 2 button to display only the subtotals and the grand total.

5. Complete the following steps to remove the subtotals:
   a. If necessary, select a cell in the list.
   b. Click Data and then Subtotals.
   c. Click the Remove All button.

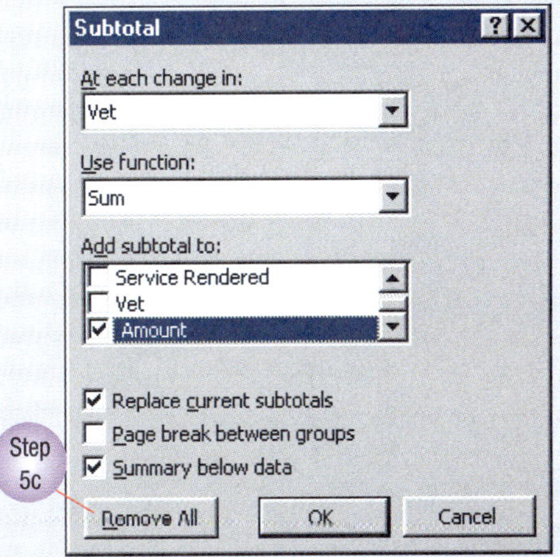

Step 5c

6. Complete the following steps to subtotal the list by invoice number:
   a. Sort the list in ascending order on the *Invoice Number* field.
   b. Click Data and then Subtotals.
   c. Click the down-pointing arrow to the right of the At each change in box. Select *Invoice #*.
   d. If necessary, click the down-pointing arrow to the right of the Use function box and select *Sum*.
   e. Make sure the Amount check box is the only box selected.
   f. Click OK.
   g. The subtotals have been created. Click the Level 2 button.

Select columns B through F and column H.

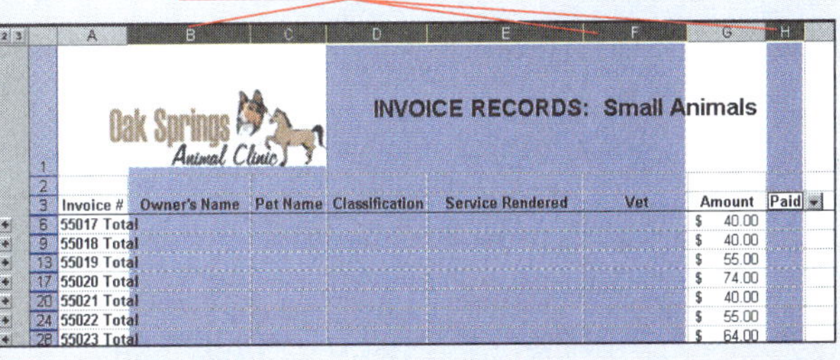

7. You want to print the subtotals, but you want to print only the data in columns A and G. Complete the following steps to print the worksheet:
   a. Select columns B through F. Press the Ctrl key and select column H. Columns B, C, D, E, F, and H should be selected.
   b. Click Format, select Column, and then click Hide.
   c. If necessary, adjust the column widths so that all the data is displayed.
   d. Print the worksheet.
   e. Select columns A through I.
   f. Click Format, select Column, and then click Unhide.
8. Complete the following steps to remove the subtotals:
   a. Click any cell in the list.
   b. Click Data and then Subtotals.
   c. Click the Remove All button.
9. Complete the following steps to subtotal the list by classification:
   a. Sort the list in ascending order on the *Classification* field.

b. Click <u>D</u>ata and then Su<u>b</u>totals.
c. Click the down-pointing arrow to the right of the <u>A</u>t each change in box. Select *Classification*.
d. If necessary, click the down-pointing arrow to the right of the <u>U</u>se function box and select *Sum*.
e. Make sure the Amount check box is the only check box selected.
f. Click OK.
g. The subtotals have been created. Click the Hide Detail Level button to the left of the Cat Total.

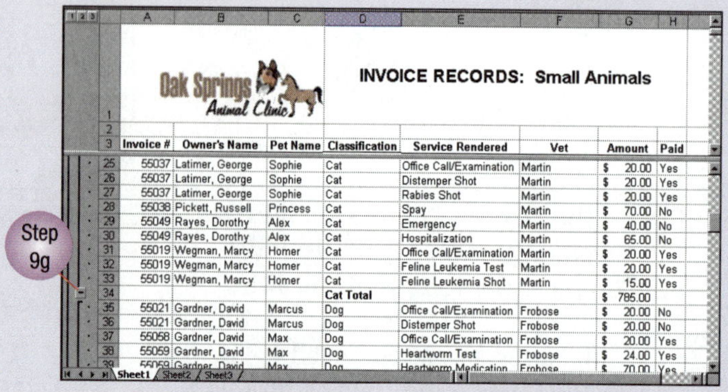

Invoice #	Owner's Name	Pet Name	Classification	Service Rendered	Vet	Amount	Paid
55037	Latimer, George	Sophie	Cat	Office Call/Examination	Martin	$ 20.00	Yes
55037	Latimer, George	Sophie	Cat	Distemper Shot	Martin	$ 20.00	Yes
55037	Latimer, George	Sophie	Cat	Rabies Shot	Martin	$ 20.00	Yes
55038	Pickett, Russell	Princess	Cat	Spay	Martin	$ 70.00	No
55049	Rayes, Dorothy	Alex	Cat	Emergency	Martin	$ 40.00	No
55049	Rayes, Dorothy	Alex	Cat	Hospitalization	Martin	$ 65.00	No
55019	Wegman, Marcy	Homer	Cat	Office Call/Examination	Martin	$ 20.00	Yes
55019	Wegman, Marcy	Homer	Cat	Feline Leukemia Test	Martin	$ 20.00	Yes
55019	Wegman, Marcy	Homer	Cat	Feline Leukemia Shot	Martin	$ 15.00	Yes
			Cat Total			$ 785.00	
55021	Gardner, David	Marcus	Dog	Office Call/Examination	Frobose	$ 20.00	No
55021	Gardner, David	Marcus	Dog	Distemper Shot	Frobose	$ 20.00	No
55058	Gardner, David	Max	Dog	Office Call/Examination	Frobose	$ 20.00	Yes
55059	Gardner, David	Max	Dog	Heartworm Test	Frobose	$ 24.00	Yes
55059	Gardner, David	Max	Dog	Heartworm Medication	Frobose	$ 70.00	Yes

h. Click the Hide Detail Level button to the left of the Dog Total.
i. Hide columns E, F, and H.
j. Adjust the width of column D.
k. Print the worksheet.
l. Select rows C through I.
m. Click F<u>o</u>rmat, select <u>C</u>olumn, and then click <u>U</u>nhide.

10. Complete the following steps to remove the subtotals:
    a. Click any cell in the list.
    b. Click <u>D</u>ata and then Su<u>b</u>totals.
    c. Click the <u>R</u>emove All button.
11. Save the worksheet with the same name (Excel E4, Ex 07). You are going to use this worksheet in exercise 8.
12. Close the worksheet.

Filtering a List

Another way of displaying only certain records in a list is by applying filters to display in the worksheet only those records that meet certain criteria. The records that do not meet the criteria are temporarily hidden from view.

Filtering a List Using AutoFilter

The quickest and easiest way to filter a list is by using the AutoFilter feature. To use AutoFilter, select any cell in the list to be filtered. Click <u>D</u>ata, point to <u>F</u>ilter, and then click Auto<u>F</u>ilter. As shown in figure 4.16, drop-down lists appear next to each column heading. Click the down arrow to the right of the field name you want to filter. The drop-down list that appears allows you to display all the records in the list, display the top 10 records, create a custom filter, or select an entry that appears in one or more records on the list. As you can see in figure 4.16, if you select one of the cell entries, then only those records containing that entry are displayed. To go back to displaying all the records, click the down-pointing arrow to the right of the field name and select *All*.

FIGURE

4.16 ***Using AutoFilter***

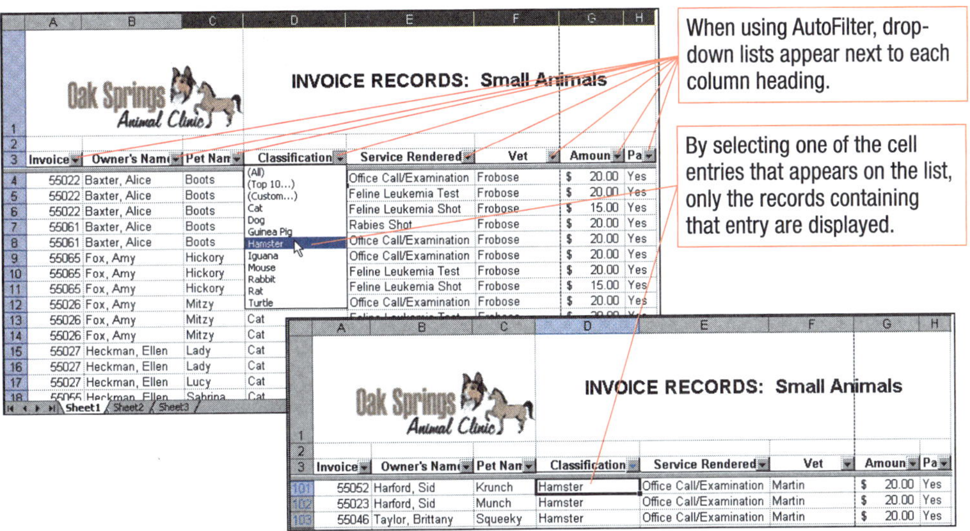

The (Top 10...) option from the drop-down list works only if there are values (rather than text) stored in that column. When you select it, the dialog box shown in figure 4.17 is displayed. You can choose whether you want to display the top or bottom items or percents. You can also indicate how many items (or percents) should be displayed. Click OK and the filtered records are displayed.

FIGURE

4.17 ***The Top 10 AutoFilter Dialog Box***

Creating a Custom AutoFilter

To create a custom AutoFilter, select any cell in the list, click Data, point to Filter, and then click AutoFilter. Click the down-pointing arrow to the right of the field name you want to filter. Select *(Custom...)*. The Custom AutoFilter dialog box is displayed. As shown in figure 4.18, to select a comparison operator, click the down-pointing arrow to the right of the first box under Show rows where. Select one of the comparison operators. Either click the down arrow to the right of the next box to select the data to be compared, or key the data to be compared in the box. A second set of criteria can be entered in the bottom two boxes. If the And option is selected, both sets of criteria must be met by the record. If the Or option is selected, either one or the other set, but not necessarily both, of the criteria must be met by the record. Click OK to display the records that match the criteria. When you have finished with the filter, display all the records by clicking the down-pointing arrow to the right of the field name and selecting *All*.

FIGURE 4.18 **The Custom AutoFilter Dialog Box**

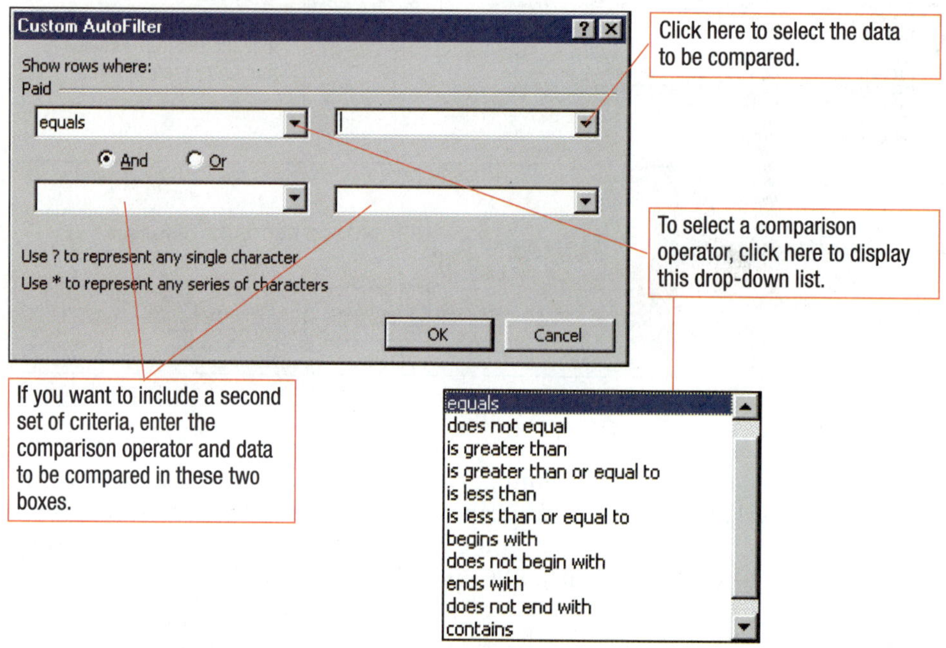

To turn the AutoFilter feature off, click Data, point to Filter, and then click AutoFilter. The AutoFilter feature will then be turned off.

exercise 8 USING AUTOFILTER

1. Open Excel E4, Ex 07. This is the worksheet that was completed in exercise 7.
2. Save the worksheet using the Save As command and name it Excel E4, Ex 08.
3. Make sure a custom header displays your name at the left margin and the file name at the right margin.
4. Sort the list in ascending order on the Invoice column.
5. First you want to see all the records in which the invoices have not been paid. Complete the following steps to filter the records:
   a. Click any cell in the list.
   b. Click Data, point to Filter, and then click AutoFilter. Drop-down lists appear next to all the field names.
   c. Click the down-pointing arrow to the right of the field name *Paid*.
   d. Click *No*.

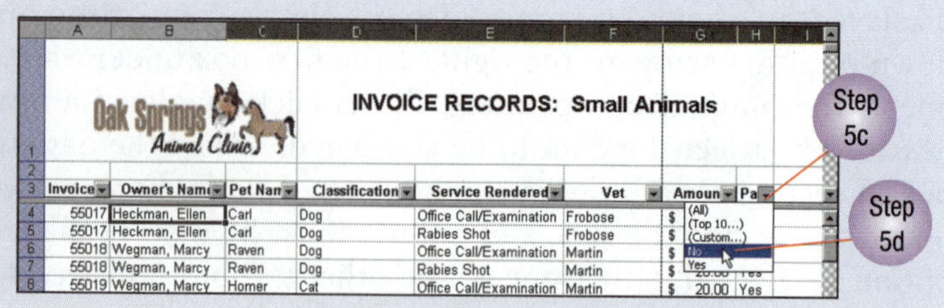

e. Adjust the widths of the columns so that all the columns will fit on one page.
f. Print the worksheet.
g. Click the down-pointing arrow to the right of the field name *Paid.*
h. Click *(All).* All the records are once again displayed.

6. The veterinarians want to know which invoices contributed to the top 5% of their income. Complete the following steps to filter the records:
   a. Click the down-pointing arrow to the right of the field name *Amount.*
   b. Click *(Top 10...).*
   c. In the middle box key **5**.
   d. Click the down-pointing arrow to the right of the last box. Click *Percent.*
   e. Click OK.
   f. Print the worksheet. The worksheet should fit on one page.
   g. Click the down-pointing arrow to the right of the field name *Amount.*
   h. Click *(All).* All the records are once again displayed.

Top 10 AutoFilter
Show
Top | 5 | Percent
OK | Cancel
Step 6c, Step 6d, Step 6e

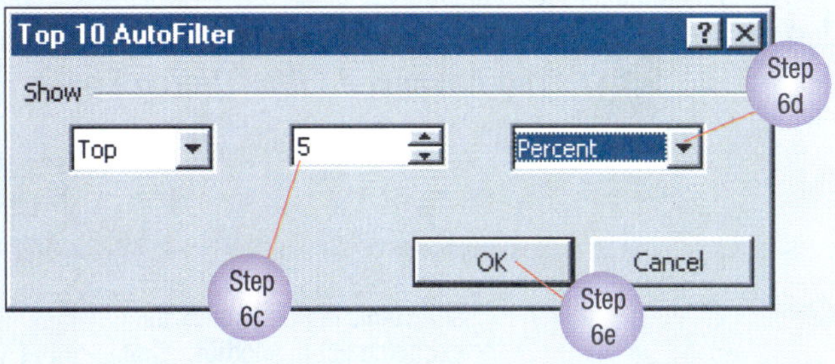

7. The veterinarians want to see the records of all the animals treated that were not dogs or cats. Sort the list in ascending order on the *Classification* field. Complete the following steps to create a custom filter.
   a. Click the down-pointing arrow to the right of the field name *Classification.*
   b. Click *Custom.* The Custom AutoFilter dialog box is displayed.
   c. Click the down-pointing arrow to the right of the first box under Classification. Click *does not equal.*
   d. Click the down-pointing arrow to the right of the second box in the first row. Click *Dog.*
   e. Make sure the And option is selected.
   f. Click the down-pointing arrow to the right of the first box in the second row. Click *does not equal.*
   g. Click the down-pointing arrow to the right of the second box in the second row. Click *Cat.*
   h. Click OK.
   i. Adjust the column widths so that all the data can be seen but still fits on one page.
   j. Print the worksheet.
   k. Click the down arrow to the right of the field name *Classification*.
   l. Click *(All).* All the records are once again displayed.

Custom AutoFilter
Show rows where:
Classification
does not equal | Dog
And | Or
does not equal | Cat
Use ? to represent any single character
Use * to represent any series of characters
OK | Cancel
Step 7c, Step 7d, Step 7e, Step 7f, Step 7g, Step 7h

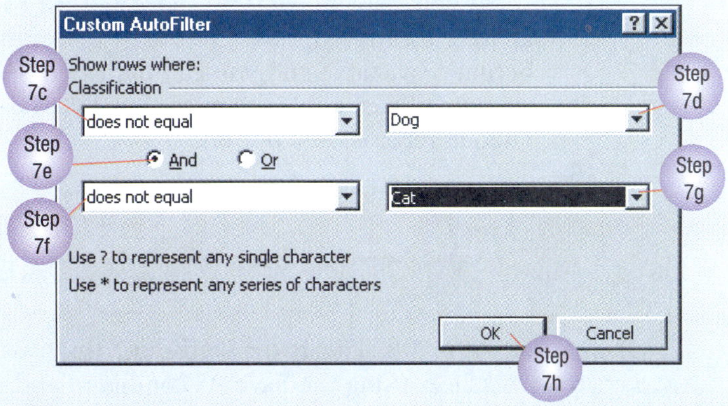

8. Complete the following steps to turn the AutoFilter feature off:
   a. Click any cell in the list.
   b. Click Data, point to Filter, and then click AutoFilter. Drop-down lists should no longer be displayed next to the field names.
9. Save the worksheet with the same name (Excel E4, Ex 08). You are going to use this worksheet in exercise 9.
10. Close the worksheet.

Filtering a List Using Advanced Filters

Using advanced filters allows you to be very precise in searching for specific records. With an advanced filter, you can denote the exact criteria to be found.

Extracting Unique Records

One task for which an advanced filter can be used is to create a list of unique values. To create a list of unique values, select the portion of the list to be extracted from. Click Data, point to Filter, and then click Advanced Filter. The Advanced Filter dialog box shown in figure 4.19 is displayed.

FIGURE 4.19 ***The Advanced Filter Dialog Box***

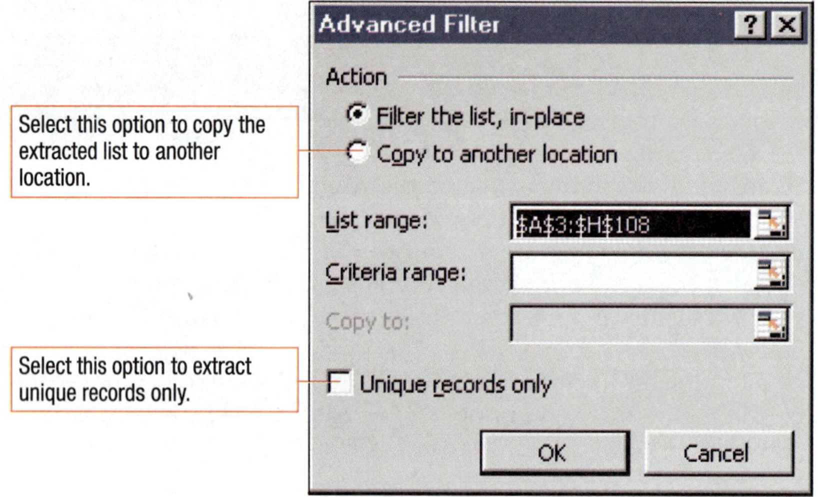

If you want to copy the extracted list to another location, select the Copy to another location option. Once that option is selected, the Copy to option becomes available and you can indicate the cell or cell range to where the the extracted list should be copied. Finally, to extract unique records, select the Unique records only option.

exercise 9

EXTRACTING UNIQUE RECORDS

1. Open Excel E4, Ex 08. This is the worksheet that was completed in exercise 8.
2. Save the worksheet using the Save As command and name it Excel E4, Ex 09.
3. Make sure a custom header displays your name at the left margin and the file name at the right margin.
4. The veterinarians want a list of each client and the names of the clients' pets. Sort the list first by owner's name, then by classification, and then by pet name.
5. You need to select the portion of the list you want to extract from, which would be columns B, C, and D. Complete the following steps to select a portion of the list:
   a. Click cell B3.

b. While holding down the Shift key, double-click the bottom of the cell. Be sure you do not double-click the AutoFill handle. All of the field values in column B should be selected.
c. While holding down the Shift key, press the right arrow key twice. All of the field values in columns B, C, and D should be selected.
d. Click Data, point to Filter, and click Advanced Filter. The Advanced Filter dialog box is displayed.
e. Click the Copy to another location option to select it.
f. Make sure that **$B$3:$D$108** is entered in the List range box.
g. Click the Collapse dialog box button at the right of the Copy to box. Click cell J3. Click the Expand dialog box button
h. Click the Unique records only option to select it.
i. Click OK.

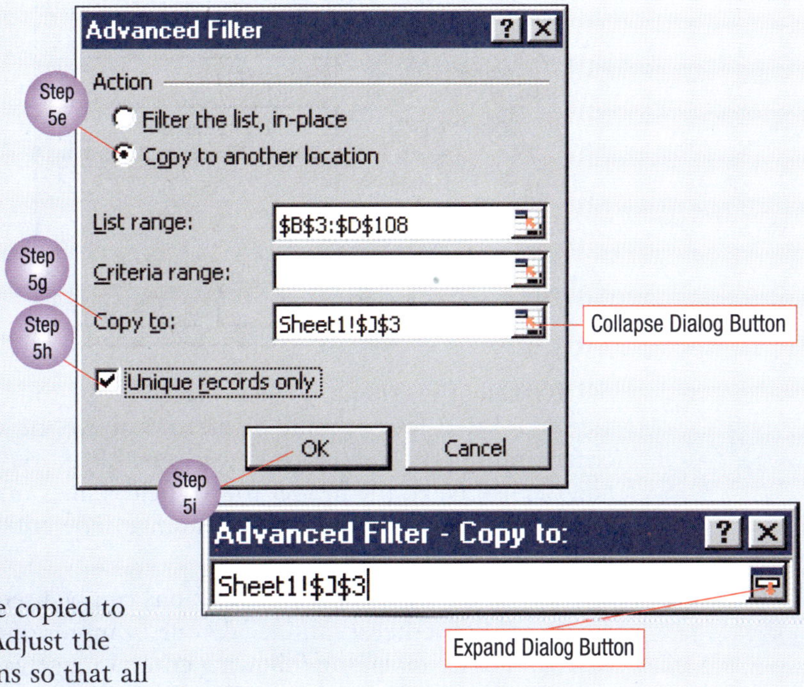

Advanced Filter
Action
Filter the list, in-place
Copy to another location
List range: $B$3:$D$108
Criteria range:
Copy to: Sheet1!$J$3
Unique records only
OK Cancel
Step 5e
Step 5g
Step 5h
Step 5i
Collapse Dialog Button
Advanced Filter - Copy to:
Sheet1!$J$3
Expand Dialog Button

6. The unique records are copied to columns J, K, and L. Adjust the widths of these columns so that all the data can be seen.
7. Complete the following steps to print the unique records:
   a. Click cell J3. While holding down the Shift key, double-click the bottom of the cell. While still holding down the Shift key, press the right arrow key twice. Cells J3 through L51 should be selected.
   b. Click File, point to Print Area, and then click Set Print Area.
   c. Print the records.
8. Click File, point to Print Area, and then click Clear Print Area to clear the print area.
9. Save the worksheet with the same name (Excel E4, Ex 09).
10. Close the worksheet.

Using a Criteria Range

As shown in figure 4.20, the middle box on the Advanced Filter dialog box provides a place to enter a criteria range. Filtering a list using a criteria range is similar to filtering a list using AutoFilter, only instead of selecting the criteria from drop-down lists, the criteria is keyed into the worksheet in the criteria range. The criteria range is a range of cells that is set aside specifically as the place where the search conditions are entered. The criteria range is made up of one header row and one or more rows where the search condition is defined.

FIGURE

4.20 ***The Criteria Range in the Advanced Filter Dialog Box***

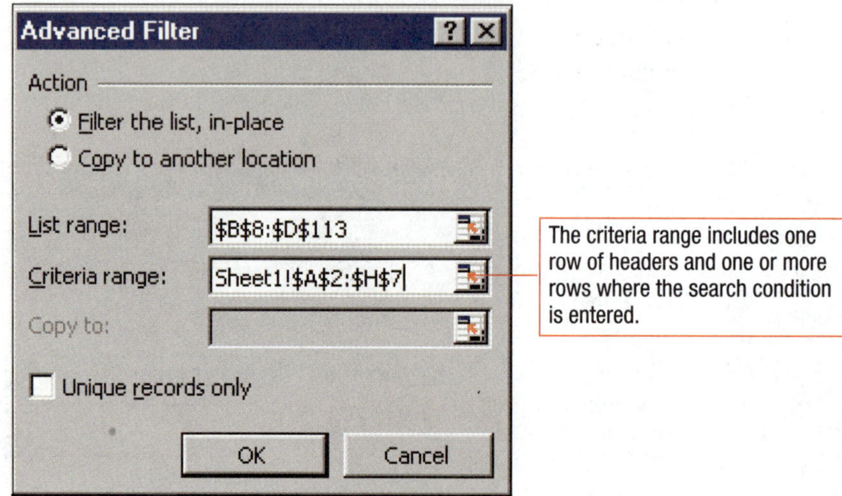

Typically the criteria range is placed in the rows above the list, so the first step is to insert four or more blank rows above the list that can be used for the criteria range. There must be at least one blank row between the criteria range and the list. Next, the header row or field names from the list have to be copied to the first blank row in the criteria range. The criteria is entered into the rows below the header row.

Several different types of conditions can be used with advanced filters. An advanced filter criteria can include one or more conditions applied to a single column. For example, the following criteria range would display rows containing either Frobose or Ketner in the Vet column.

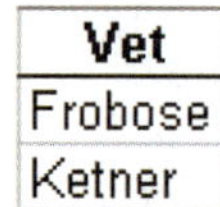

Vet
Frobose
Ketner

You can also have a condition in one column or another. For example, the following criteria range would display rows containing either values greater than 50 in the Amount column or "No" in the Paid column.

Amount	Paid
>50	
	No

When conditions are entered in different rows, either one or the other condition may be met, but not necessarily both. If both conditions must be met, then the criteria must be placed in the same row. For example, the following criteria range would display only those rows containing both values greater than 50 in the Amount column and "No" in the Paid column.

Amount	Paid
>50	No

Once the criteria you want to match have been entered in the criteria range, click any cell in the list. Click Data, point to Filter, and then click Advanced Filter. The Advanced Filter dialog box shown in figure 4.20 is displayed. The range of cells for the criteria range, including the header row, must be entered in the Criteria range box. There must be at least one blank row between the criteria range and the list. Click OK and the records that are found are displayed.

exercise 10 USING A CRITERIA RANGE

1. Open Excel Worksheet E4-04.
2. Save the worksheet using the Save As command and name it Excel E4, Ex 10.
3. Create a custom header that displays your name at the left margin and the file name at the right margin.
4. Complete the following steps to set up a criteria range:
   a. Insert four blank rows above row 2. The header row for the list should now be in row 6.
   b. Copy cells A6 through H6 to cells A1 through H1. The header row should now be in both row 6 and row 1.

	A	B	C	D	E	F	G	H
1	Invoice #	Owner's Name	Pet Name	Classification	Service Rendered	Vet	Amount	Paid
2								
3								
4								
5								
6	Invoice #	Owner's Name	Pet Name	Classification	Service Rendered	Vet	Amount	Paid
7	55017	Heckman, Ellen	Carl	Dog	Office Call/Examination	Frobose	$ 20.00	Yes
8	55017	Heckman, Ellen	Carl	Dog	Rabies Shot	Frobose	$ 20.00	Yes
9	55018	Wegman, Marcy	Raven	Dog	Office Call/Examination	Martin	$ 20.00	Yes
10	55018	Wegman, Marcy	Raven	Dog	Rabies Shot	Martin	$ 20.00	Yes
11	55019	Wegman, Marcy	Homer	Cat	Office Call/Examination	Martin	$ 20.00	Yes

Step 4b

5. You want to find all the records of invoices that were for either feline leukemia shots or feline leukemia tests. Complete the following steps to enter the search criteria in the criteria range:
   a. Click cell E2. Key **Feline Leukemia Shot**.
   b. Click cell E3. Key **Feline Leukemia Test**.

	A	B	C	D	E	F	G	H
1	Invoice #	Owner's Name	Pet Name	Classification	Service Rendered	Vet	Amount	Paid
2					Feline Leukemia Shot			
3					Feline Leukemia Test			
4								
5								
6	Invoice #	Owner's Name	Pet Name	Classification	Service Rendered	Vet	Amount	Paid
7	55017	Heckman, Ellen	Carl	Dog	Office Call/Examination	Frobose	$ 20.00	Yes
8	55017	Heckman, Ellen	Carl	Dog	Rabies Shot	Frobose	$ 20.00	Yes
9	55018	Wegman, Marcy	Raven	Dog	Office Call/Examination	Martin	$ 20.00	Yes
10	55018	Wegman, Marcy	Raven	Dog	Rabies Shot	Martin	$ 20.00	Yes
11	55019	Wegman, Marcy	Homer	Cat	Office Call/Examination	Martin	$ 20.00	Yes

Step 5a

Step 5b

6. If you name the criteria range Criteria, Excel will automatically recognize it as the criteria range. Complete the following steps to name the criteria range Criteria.
   a. Select cells A1 through H3.
   b. Click Insert, point to Name, and click Define.
   c. Key **Criteria**.
   d. Click OK.
7. Complete the following steps to apply the advanced criteria:
   a. Click any cell in the data list (not in the criteria range).

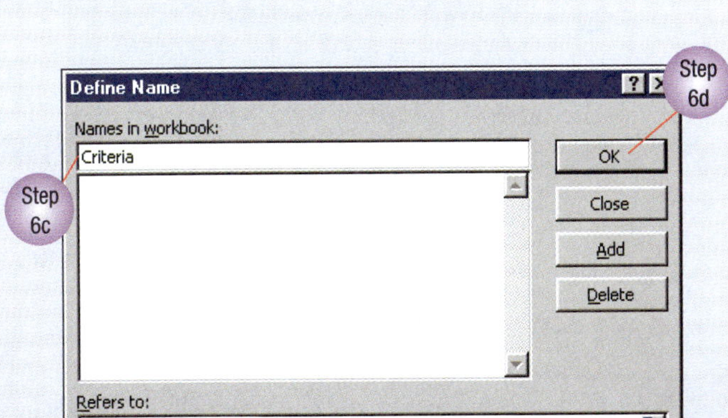

b. Click Data, point to Filter, and then click Advanced Filter. The Advanced Filter dialog box appears. Excel automatically recognizes both the list range and the criteria range.

c. Click OK. Only the records that meet the criteria are displayed.

d. Print the worksheet.

e. Click Data, point to Filter, and then click Show All.

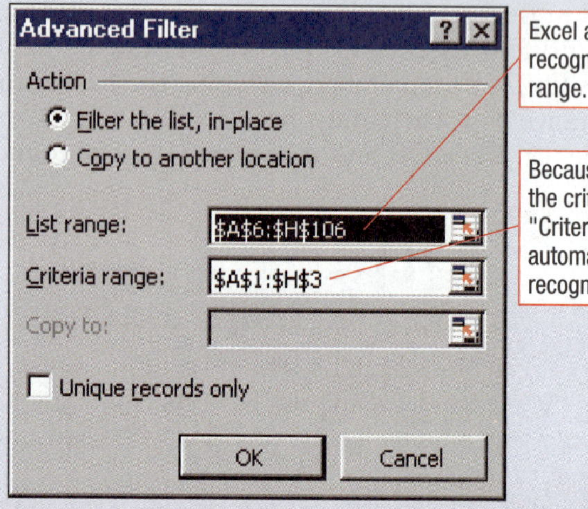

8. Next you want to find invoices that either are over $50.00 or have not been paid. Complete the following steps to apply the advanced criteria:
   a. Clear cells E2 and E3.
   b. Click cell G2. Key **>50**.
   c. Click cell H3. Key **No**.
   d. Click any cell in the data list (not in the criteria range).
   e. Click Data, point to Filter, and then click Advanced Filter. The Advanced Filter dialog box appears. Excel automatically recognizes both the list range and the criteria range.
   f. Click OK. Only the records that meet the criteria are displayed.
   g. Print the worksheet.
   h. Click Data, point to Filter, and then click Show All.
9. Now find the invoices that are both over $50.00 and have not been paid. Complete the following steps to apply the advanced criteria:
   a. Clear cell H3.
   b. Click cell H2. Key **No**. The entries in the criteria range are now both in row 2.
   c. Click any cell in the data list (not in the criteria range).
   d. Click Data, point to Filter, and then click Advanced Filter. The Advanced Filter dialog box appears.
   e. Check to make sure the entry in the List range box is **$A$6:$H$106**.
   f. The criteria range has to be changed because now it is A1 through H2, since the criteria are in row 2. Edit the entry in the Criteria Range box so that it says **$A$1:$H$2**.
   g. Click OK. Only the records that meet the criteria are displayed.
   h. Print the worksheet.
   i. Click Data, point to Filter, and then click Show All.

Advanced Filter
Action
Filter the list, in-place
Copy to another location
List range: $A$6:$H$106 (Step 9e)
Criteria range: $A$1:$H$2 (Step 9f)
Copy to:
Unique records only
OK (Step 9g) Cancel

10. Now find the invoices for when either Frobose, Martin, or Ketner spayed a cat. Complete the following steps to apply the advanced criteria:
   a. Clear cells G2 and H2.
   b. Key the following data in the cells indicated:

Cell	Data
D2	**Cat**

E2	**Spay**
F2	**Frobose**
D3	**Cat**
E3	**Spay**
F3	**Martin**
D4	**Cat**
E4	**Spay**
F4	**Ketner**

c. Click any cell in the data list (not in the criteria range).
d. Click Data, point to Filter, and then click Advanced Filter. The Advanced Filter dialog box appears.
e. Check to make sure the entry in the List range box is **$A$6:$H$106**.
f. The criteria range has to be changed because now it is A1 through H4, since the criteria are in rows 2, 3, and 4. Edit the entry in the Criteria range box so that it says **$A$1:$H$4**.
g. Click OK. Only the records that meet the criteria are displayed.
h. Print the worksheet.
i. Click Data, point to Filter, and then click Show All.

11. Save the worksheet with the same name (Excel E4, Ex 10).
12. Close the worksheet.

CHAPTER summary

- A list is a labeled series of worksheet rows that contain similar sets of data such as student names and addresses. Each row in a list is a record. Each column in a list is a field. The labels in the first row of the list are field names. A value in a cell is a field value. The range of cells containing all the records, fields, and field names is the list range.
- The first row of a list must contain labels or field names. There cannot be any blank rows in the list. There should not be any data in the rows or columns immediately adjacent to the list. Only one list can be stored on a worksheet.
- Records in an Excel list can be entered, edited, and deleted using a Data Form. Data Forms can be used to search for and find only those records that meet specific criteria.
- You can specify the exact data that can be entered into a cell using data validation. You can specify that the data being entered must meet specific criteria or that the data must be selected from a list.
- Sorting helps to organize the data in a list. Sort the data in a column by selecting any cell in the column to be sorted and then clicking the Sort Ascending button to sort in ascending order or the Sort Descending button to sort in descending order.
- To sort in an order other than ascending or descending, a custom list must be created. A custom list can be used to sort the first or top level of a sort only. Once a custom list has been created, it is always available.
- Outlining a worksheet provides a way to quickly find specific information in a long list of data. Levels of detail can be easily displayed or hidden by clicking the Show Detail symbol and the Hide Detail symbol. Rows or columns that provide a summary of the data using functions such as AVERAGE or SUM can be displayed quickly.

- When the data in a list is subtotaled using the subtotal command, it is displayed in outline view. The list must be sorted by the field on which it is to be subtotaled before using the subtotal command. Levels of detail can be hidden or displayed in a list that has been subtotaled using the Show Detail symbol and the Hide Detail symbol.
- Filtering a list using AutoFilter temporarily displays only those records that meet certain criteria. Creating a custom AutoFilter enables the use of comparisons such as equals or is less than. An example of a custom AutoFilter search criterion might be Salary is greater than 50,000.
- An advanced filter extracts the unique records that meet specific criteria. The extracted data can be copied to a new location. With an advanced filter, a list is filtered using a criteria range. The criteria range is usually placed in the rows above the list. The header row (or field names) from the list has to be copied to the first row in the criteria range. The criteria used to filter the list are keyed into the criteria range. If the criteria are keyed into different rows, either one or the other condition may be met, but not necessarily both. If the criteria are keyed into the same row, then both conditions must be met.

COMMANDS review

Command	**Mouse/Keyboard**
Display the Data Form	Click Data, Form
Use data validation	Click Data, Validation
Perform a multi-level sort	Click Data, Sort
Create/Delete a custom list	Click Tools, Options, Custom Lists tab
Outline a worksheet manually	Click Data, Group and Outline, Group
Outline a worksheet automatically	Click Data, Group and Outline, Auto Outline
Subtotal a list	Click Data, Subtotals
Filter a list using AutoFilter	Click Data, Filter, AutoFilter
Filter a list using Advanced Filter	Click Data, Filter, Advanced Filter

CONCEPTS check

Completion: On a blank sheet of paper, indicate the correct term, symbol, or command for each item.

1. This term refers to the individual rows in a list.
2. This term refers to each column in a list.
3. Click this to display the Data Form.
4. Select this option from the drop-down list for the Allow box on the Data Validation dialog box if you want users to be able to enter data by selecting it from a list.
5. Click this tab on the Options dialog box to create a custom list.
6. This is the comparison operator that stands for not equal to.

7. Click this to subtotal a list.
8. Subtotals are displayed in this view.
9. This is what will be displayed if you click the Level 1 button after subtotaling a list.
10. Click this to turn the AutoFilter feature off.
11. Click this option on the Advanced Filters dialog box if you want to extract unique records from a list.
12. This term refers to the range of cells that is set aside as the area where the search conditions are entered when using Advanced Filters.
13. List the rules that must be followed when creating a list.
14. Explain the difference between using the AutoFilter command and the Criteria button on a Data Form.
15. Explain what records are going to be displayed using the following criteria range:

Sales Representative	Sales
Zimmerman	<1000
Robinson	<=1500

SKILLS check

Assessment 1

1. Open Excel Worksheet E4-05.
2. Save the worksheet using the Save As command and name it Excel E4, SA 01.
3. Create a custom header with your name displayed at the left margin and the file name displayed at the right margin.
4. This worksheet keeps track of the profit the EastWest Crossroads Company makes on some of the items in its mail-order catalog. Use the Data Form to add the following three records to the list:

   Item Number **GL-10-1**
   Item **Chinese Nesting Baskets**
   Selling Price **35**
   Unit Cost **18**

   Item Number **GM-39-1**
   Item **Asian Desk Set**
   Selling Price **125**
   Unit Cost **70**

   Item Number **GT-29-1**
   Item **Bird Box**
   Selling Price **85**
   Unit Cost **35**
5. The EastWest Crossroads Company no longer sells the Antler Bookends, Item Number GH-88-2. Use the Data Form to delete this record.

6. The cost of the Stained Glass Lamp, Item Number GH-82-2, has come down. Use the Data Form to edit this record so that the Selling Price is $225.00 and the Unit Cost is $150.00.
7. Adjust the page setup so that row 3 repeats at the top of each page as a print title.
8. Save the workbook with the same name (Excel E4, SA 01).
9. Print and close Excel E4, SA 01.

Assessment 2

1. Open Excel Worksheet E4-06.
2. Save the worksheet using the Save As command and name it Excel E4, SA 02.
3. Create a custom header with your name displayed at the left margin and the file name displayed at the right margin.
4. The Little Music Shop, a music store, sells opera CDs, videos, and laserdiscs. This worksheet is the beginning of a list to keep track of all the opera CDs, videos, and laserdiscs that the store sells. You want to use data validation to make it easier to enter more data into the list. The order numbers are all exactly six characters long. You want to set it up so that an order number that is anything other than six characters cannot be entered. Select column A and display the Data Validation dialog box. From the Allow drop-down list on the Settings tab, select *Text Length*. From the Data list box select *equal to*. Key **6** in the Length box.
5. Include an input message that has Order # for a title. The message should read, "Enter the six-character order number."
6. Include an error message that has Error for a title. The message should read, "The order number must be exactly six characters long."
7. The only three entries that are ever made in the Medium column are Video, CD, or Laserdisc. Create a drop-down list from which the user can select Video, CD, or Laserdisc in order to enter data into column C.
8. Include an input message that has Medium for a title. The message should read, "Select an option from the drop-down list."
9. Include an error message that has Error for a title. The message should read, "The medium must be selected from the drop-down list."
10. The cost for any item in the list will never be over $100.00. Set up data validation so that any decimal entered into column D is less than or equal to $100.00.
11. Include an input message that has Cost for a title. The message should read, "Enter the cost of the video, CD, or laserdisc."
12. Include an error message that has Error for a title. The message should read, "The cost cannot be over $100.00."
13. Starting in row 18, enter the following records into the list:

Order #	Opera	Medium	Cost
COS09V	**Cosi Fan Tutte**	**Video**	**44.95**
COS61C	**Cosi Fan Tutte**	**CD**	**37.95**
DON40V	**Don Carlo**	**Video**	**44.95**
DON40L	**Don Carlo**	**Laserdisc**	**79.95**
DON79C	**Don Carlo**	**CD**	**47.95**

14. Save the workbook with the same name (Excel E4, SA 02).
15. Print and close Excel E4, SA 02.

Assessment 3

1. Open Excel Worksheet E4-07.
2. Save the worksheet using the Save As command and name it Excel E4, SA 03.
3. Create a custom header with your name displayed at the left margin and the file

name displayed at the right margin.

4. Use the Sort Ascending button to sort the list by Order #. Print the worksheet.
5. Use the Sort Descending button to sort the list by Cost. Print the worksheet.
6. Perform a multi-level sort, sorting first by Cost in descending order and then by Opera in ascending order. Print the list.
7. The Little Music Shop wants to be able to sort the list in order of popularity of the medium. Create the following custom list:
   CD
   Video
   Laserdisc
8. Sort the list first by the custom list created in step 7 in ascending order and then by Opera in ascending order. Print the worksheet.
9. Delete the custom list created in step 7.
10. Save the workbook with the same name (Excel E4, SA 03).
11. Close Excel E4, SA 03.

Assessment 4

1. Open Excel Worksheet E4-08.
2. Save the worksheet using the Save As command and name it Excel E4, SA 04.
3. Create a custom header with your name displayed at the left margin and the file name displayed at the right margin.
4. Outline the worksheet manually. Place all the records for CDs in one group, all the records for Videos in another group, and all the records for Laserdiscs in a third group.
5. Display only the average prices for the CDs, Videos, and Laserdiscs. Print the worksheet.
6. Display the details for the Videos. Print the worksheet.
7. Ungroup all the records for Videos.
8. Display the details for CDs and Laserdiscs.
9. Clear the outline for the entire worksheet.
10. Save the workbook with the same name (Excel E4, SA 04).
11. Close Excel E4, SA 04.

Assessment 5

1. Open Excel Worksheet E4-09.
2. Save the worksheet using the Save As command and name it Excel E4, SA 05.
3. Create a custom header with your name displayed at the left margin and the file name displayed at the right margin.
4. This worksheet keeps track of the EastWest Crossroads Company invoices. There is an error in the address of Dennis Davis, which is invoice number 10-6119. Use the Data Form to find the record and change the address for Dennis Davis to P.O. Box 2860.
5. The invoice amount is currently incorrect on invoice 10-6118. Change the invoice amount to 82.58.
6. Sort the list in ascending order first by state, then by last name, and finally by first name.
7. Subtotal the Invoice Totals by State. Adjust the width of column H. Print the worksheet.
8. Collapse the list so that only the subtotals and grand total are displayed. Print the worksheet.
9. Expand the list so that all the details are displayed.

10. Remove the subtotals from the list.
11. Save the workbook with the same name (Excel E4, SA 05).
12. Close Excel E4, SA 05.

Assessment 6

1. Open Excel Worksheet E4-10.
2. Save the worksheet using the Save As command and name it Excel E4, SA 06.
3. Create a custom header with your name displayed at the left margin and the file name displayed at the right margin.
4. Sort the list first by state in ascending order and then by Invoice Total in descending order.
5. Create a custom AutoFilter to find all of the invoices over $1,000. Print the worksheet.
6. Display all the records.
7. Create custom AutoFilters, one for the Invoice Totals and one for State, that will find all the invoices from either California or New York that are under $500. Print the worksheet.
8. Display all the records.
9. Turn the AutoFilter feature off.
10. Save the workbook with the same name (Excel E4, SA 06).
11. Close Excel E4, SA 06.

Assessment 7

1. Open Excel Worksheet E4-11.
2. Save the worksheet using the Save As command and name it Excel E4, SA 07.
3. Create a custom header with your name displayed at the left margin and the file name displayed at the right margin.
4. This worksheet keeps track of the salary and commissions for the sales representatives of Case 'n Crate, a company that manufactures and sells wooden products. Claire Hoag received a raise. Use the Data Form to find her record and change her salary to 1200.
5. The sales figures for Ria Munoz are incorrect. Use the Data Form to find her record and change the sales amount to 12299.76.
6. Sort the list in ascending order first by region, next by percent commission, and finally by last name.
7. Subtotal the Total column by Region. Adjust the width of column H. Print the worksheet.
8. Use the Hide Detail button to hide the details for the East Central region, the South Central region, the Southeast region, and the Southwest region. Print the worksheet.
9. Expand the list so that all the details are displayed.
10. Remove the subtotals from the list.
11. Create a custom AutoFilter command to find all of the sales over $9,000. Print the worksheet.
12. Display all the records.
13. Create custom AutoFilters, one for Region and one for Sales, to find all of the records from either the South Central region or the East Central region that have sales over $10,000. Print the worksheet.
14. Display all the records.
15. Use AutoFilter to find the records of the sales representatives whose sales are in the top 10%. Print the worksheet.
16. Turn the AutoFilter feature off.

17. Save the workbook with the same name (Excel E4, SA 07).
18. Close Excel E4, SA 07.

Assessment 8

1. Open Excel Worksheet E4-12.
2. Save the worksheet using the Save As command and name it Excel E4, SA 08.
3. Create a custom header with your name displayed at the left margin and the file name displayed at the right margin.
4. Sort the list in ascending order by Opera.
5. You want to create a unique list of the opera names. Select cells B3 through B39. Use Advanced Filter to copy the unique records only to cell F3.
6. Adjust the width of column F.
7. Print the worksheet.
8. Save the workbook with the same name (Excel E4, SA 08).
9. Close Excel E4, SA 08.

Assessment 9

1. Open Excel Worksheet E4-13.
2. Save the worksheet using the Save As command and name it Excel E4, SA 09.
3. Create a custom header with your name displayed at the left margin and the file name displayed at the right margin.
4. Sort the list in ascending order by last name.
5. Set up a criteria range for this worksheet. Insert four blank rows above row 2.
6. Copy the labels from row 6 to row 1.
7. Name the range of cells A1 through H3 Criteria.
8. Use Advanced Filter to find the records from either the East Central or the North Central region. Filter the list in place. Print the worksheet.
9. Show all the records.
10. Sort the list in ascending order, first by Region and then by Sales.
11. Use Advanced Filter to find the records that either are from the Northeast region or have sales over $12,000. Filter the list in place. Print the worksheet.
12. Show all the records.
13. Use Advanced Filter to find either the records that are from the East Central region that are over $10,000 or the records from the Southeast region that are over $10,000. Filter the list in place. Print the worksheet.
14. Show all the records.
15. Save the workbook with the same name (Excel E4, SA 09).
16. Close Excel Ch E4, SA 09.

Assessment 10

1. You want to know if wildcard characters can be used when filtering data. Use Microsoft Excel Help to search for the Help topic *Wildcard characters you can use to find text or numbers*. Read and print the Help topic.
2. Open Excel E4, SA 09. You created this file in Assessment 9. Save the worksheet using the Save As command and name it Excel E4, SA 10.
3. Using the information from the Help topic, create an advanced filter using a wildcard character to find any region that ends with *west*. Make sure you use the correct criteria range for the filter. Filter the list in place. Print the worksheet.
4. Show all the records.
5. Save the workbook with the same name (Excel E4, SA 10) and close it.

Advanced Formatting and Functions

ASSESSING proficiency

In this unit, you learned to create, apply, and edit custom formats, styles, conditional formatting, and templates. You also learned how to copy worksheets into a workbook, consolidate data into a list, and link workbooks. You learned how to use the PMT, PV, ROUND RAND, SUMIF, COUNTIF, VLOOKUP, and IF functions. You learned how to enter, edit, and delete data using the Data Form; use data validation; and filter a list.

(Note: Before completing unit assessments, delete the Excel Chapter 04E *folder on your disk. Next, copy to your disk the* Excel Unit 01E *subfolder from the* Excel 2002 Expert *folder on the CD that accompanies this textbook.)*

Assessment 1

1. Open Excel Worksheet 01.
2. Save the workbook using the Save As command and name it Excel, EPA 01.
3. Create a custom header that has your name left aligned and the file name right aligned.
4. This workbook is an invoice used by the EastWest Crossroads Company, which sells imported and unique gifts through the mail. The form is used for taking orders. Add a bottom border for filling in information to the following cells: C4, C5, C6, C7, C8, C9, F7, H7, K8, K9, C12, C13, C14, C15, F15, and H15.
5. Place an outline border around cells K4, K5, and K6.
6. Create a style called Header 1 that includes the following formatting:
   Font: Arial
   Font style: Bold
   Font size: 10
   Color: Brown
7. Apply the Header 1 style to the following cells: A4, A5, A7, A8, A9, E7, G7, A12, A13, A15, E15, and G15.
8. Create a style that is based on Header 1 and name it Header 2. Header 2 should include the following formatting:
   Font: Arial
   Font style: Bold
   Font size: 10
   Color: Brown
   Horizontal alignment: Right

9. Apply the Header 2 style to the following cells: I4, I5, I6, I8, I9, I26, I27, I28, I29, and I30.
10. Create a style that is based on Header 1 and name it Header 3. Header 3 should include the following formatting:

Horizontal alignment:	Center
Font:	Arial
Font style:	Bold
Font size:	10
Color:	White
Cell shading:	Brown

11. Apply the Header 3 style to the following cells: A18 through K18 and I31.
12. Format the worksheet so that zero values are not displayed.
13. Place an outline border around the following ranges of cells: A19:A25, B19:B25, C19:C25, D19:D25, E19:E25, I19:I25, J19:J25, J26:J30, J31.
14. Enter the following data in the cells indicated:

Cell	Data
C4	**Jo Ellen Gammon**
C5	**348 West End Road**
C7	**Arcata**
F7	**CA**
H7	**95521**
K5	**X**
C8	**(707) 555-0922**
K8	**9999 8955 1221 0032**
K9	**09/09/07**

15. Save the worksheet again with the same name (Excel, EPA 01).
16. Print and then close Excel, EPA 01.

Assessment 2

1. Open Excel Worksheet 02.
2. Save the workbook using the Save As command and name it Excel, EPA 02.
3. Create a custom header that has your name left aligned and the file name right aligned.
4. This worksheet keeps track of the number of hours of music lessons given for each instrument. Create a custom number format that will insert the text "hrs" (for *hours*) after a value. Format all the values on the worksheet using the custom format you create.
5. Use conditional formatting to display all the values in cells B4 through M20 that are under 200 in red and all the values that are greater than or equal to 450 as blue.
6. Set the left and right margins to 0.5. Change the orientation of the page to landscape.
7. Use the AutoFit Selection command to automatically adjust the width of all the columns.
8. Format the worksheet using the Classic 2 AutoFormat.

9. Save the worksheet again with the same name (Excel, EPA 02).
10. Print and then close Excel, EPA 02.

Assessment 3

1. Open Excel, EPA 01.
2. Save the workbook using the Save As command and name it Excel, EPA 03.
3. Create a custom header that has your name left aligned and the file name right aligned.
4. Delete the contents of the following cells: C4, C5, C7, C8, F7, H7, K5, K8, K9, A19, A20, B19, B20, C19, C20, E19, E20, I19, and I20.
5. Save the file as a template using the file name EastWest Invoice.xlt.
6. Close the template.
7. Open the EastWest Invoice template.
8. Enter the following data in the cells indicated:

Cell	Data
C4	**Gary Simpson**
C5	**467 Filbert Ave.**
C7	**Chelsea Heights**
F7	**NJ**
H7	**08401**
C8	**(732) 555-0933**
C9	**(732) 555-0805**
K4	**X**
K8	**7777 3471 1144 0008**
K9	**05/01/06**
A19	**35**
B19	**1**
C19	**XD489Z**
E19	**Bamboo Tea Pot**
I19	**32**

9. Save the invoice as an Excel workbook using the file name Excel, EPA 03-a.
10. Print the Excel, EPA 03-a workbook and then close it.
11. Open the EastWest Invoice template.
12. Change the standard delivery charge in cell J27 to $7.50.
13. Save the edited EastWest Invoice template. You want to replace the original template.
14. Close the template.
15. Open the EastWest Invoice template.
16. Enter the following data in the cells indicated:

Cell	Data
C4	**Sue Clanton**
C5	**4402 Feather Sound Dr.**
C7	**Clearwater**
F7	**FL**
H7	**33515**
C8	**(727) 555-6688**

C9	**(732) 555-5832**
K4	**X**
K8	**3333 4562 4578 9977**
K9	**06/01/07**
A19	**28**
B19	**1**
C19	**XD985R**
E19	**Russian Enamel Egg**
I19	**120**

17. Save the invoice as an Excel workbook using the file name Excel, EPA 03-b.
18. Print the Excel, EPA 03-b workbook.
19. Delete the EastWest Invoice template.
20. Close the Excel, EPA 03-b workbook.

Assessment 4

1. Open Excel Worksheet 03.
2. Save the workbook using the Save As command and name it Excel, EPA 04.
3. Create a custom header that has your name left aligned and the file name right aligned.
4. The EastWest Crossroads Company uses this workbook to calculate, in U.S. dollars, the orders they placed in March. Since exchange rates are constantly changing, the exchange rates for the countries with which the EastWest Crossroads Company does business are kept in a separate workbook. You need to link the Excel, EPA 04 workbook with the Exchange Rates workbook. Open the Exchange Rates workbook.
5. Switch back to the Excel, EPA 04 workbook. Enter the following data in the cells indicated:

Cell	Data
C4	**24,568**
C6	**48,952**
C10	**95,670**
C16	**205,678**
C21	**108,952**
C25	**3,467,890**

6. Click cell D4. Enter a formula that multiplies cell C4 on the *March Orders* worksheet in the Excel, EPA 04 workbook by cell C4 on the *Current Exchange Rates* worksheet in the Exchange Rates workbook. The reference to cell C4 in the *Current Exchange Rates* worksheet cannot be absolute. If it is, delete the dollar signs in front of the *C* and in front of the *4*.
7. Copy the formula in cell D4 on the *March Orders* worksheet in the Excel, EPA 04 workbook to cells D5 through D25.
8. Print the *March Orders* worksheet.
9. The exchange rate for Indian rupees has changed. Key **0.02387** in cell C16 on the *Current Exchange Rates* worksheet in the Exchange Rates workbook. Save the workbook using the file name Updated Rates.

10. Switch to the Excel, EPA 04 worksheet and print it again.
11. Save the workbook.
12. Close the Exchange Rates workbook.

Assessment 5

1. Open Excel Worksheet 04.
2. Save the workbook using the Save As command and name it Excel, EPA 05.
3. Create a custom header that has your name left aligned and the file name right aligned.
4. This worksheet contains the instruments sold at the Little Music Shop. The selling price of each instrument is based on a percentage markup. The percentage markup is found in the markup table. For example, if the cost of an instrument is between $0 and $400, the markup is 14%; if the cost of an instrument is between $400 and $500, the markup is 10%; and so on. Enter a formula in cell C4 that uses the VLOOKUP function to calculate the selling price of a bass. The selling price is calculated by multiplying the cost by the markup percentage and then adding that total to the original cost.
5. Copy the formula in cell C4 to cells C5 through C20.
6. Print the *Instruments* worksheet.
7. Save the workbook using the same name (Excel, EPA 05) and print it.
8. Close the Excel, EPA 05 workbook.

Assessment 6

1. Open Excel Worksheet 05.
2. Save the workbook using the Save As command and name it Excel, EPA 06.
3. Create a custom header that has your name left aligned and the file name right aligned.
4. Linda Taylor wants to use this worksheet to calculate what the budget for May expenses should be. Format the worksheet using conditional formatting so that any value that is less than zero is displayed as red.
5. May's budget is going to be based on the differences between what was budgeted in April and what was actually spent. If the difference between the budgeted amount and what was actually spent is greater than or equal to zero, then the budget for May is going to be the same as the budget for April. If the difference between the budgeted amount and what was actually spent is less than zero, then the budgeted amount for May is going to be 8% greater than the budgeted amount for April. Enter an IF function in cell E10 that calculates May's budget for insurance.
6. Copy the IF function in cell E10 to cells E11 through E19.
7. Linda Taylor wants to know the total amount of money that was spent in April that was over the budgeted amounts. Enter a SUMIF function in cell D21 that adds together any number in cells D10 through D19 that is less than zero.
8. Save the workbook using the same name (Excel, EPA 06) and print it.
9. Close the Excel, EPA 06 workbook.

Assessment 7

1. Open Excel Worksheet 06.
2. Save the workbook using the Save As command and name it Excel, EPA 07.
3. Create a custom header that has your name left aligned and the file name right aligned.
4. The Little Music Shop uses this list to keep track of students taking music lessons. Use data validation to make it easier to enter more data into the list. The ID numbers are all exactly seven characters long. Use the Data Validation command to allow a text length equal to seven for column A. Include an input message that has *ID #* for a title. The message should read *Enter seven-character ID number*. Include an error message that has *Error* for a title. The message should read *The ID number must be exactly seven characters long*.
5. Use the Data Validation command to allow a text length equal to two for column F. Include an input message that has *State* for a title. The message should read *Enter the two-letter abbreviation for the state*. Include an error message that has *Error* for a title. The message should read *You must use the two-letter abbreviation for the state*.
6. Create a drop-down list for the data in column I. Create the list from the age groups listed in cells N4 through N8. Include an input message that has *Age Groups* for a title. The message should read *Select the age group from the drop-down list*. Include an error message that has *Error* for a title. The message should read *The age group must be selected from the drop-down list*.
7. Create a drop-down list for the data in column J. Create the list from the instruments listed in cells O4 through O19. Include an input message that has *Instrument* for a title. The message should read *Select the instrument from the drop-down list*. Include an error message that has *Error* for a title. The message should read *Instrument must be selected from the drop-down list*.
8. Use the Data Validation command to allow any whole number between 1 and 12 for column K. Include an input message that has *Level* for a title. The message should read *Enter the student's level, from 1 to 12*. Include an error message that has *Error* for a title. The message should read *The class level must be a whole number between 1 and 12*.
9. Starting in row 7, enter the following records into the list:

ID#	**OA-3698**
Last Name	**O'Neill**
First Name	**Andrew**
Address	**35 Ridgewood Cir.**
City	**Parkfairfax**
State	**VA**
Zip	**22302**
Phone	**(703) 555-0980**
Age	**5–9**
Instrument	**Drums**
Level	**2**

ID#	**FC-3873**
Last Name	**Finn**
First Name	**Carol**
Address	**1909 Park Place Blvd.**
City	**Franconia**
State	**VA**
Zip	**22310**
Phone	**(703) 555-4498**
Age	**Over 25**
Instrument	**Flute**
Level	**9**
ID#	**CB-3698**
Last Name	**Corley**
First Name	**Betsy**
Address	**602 Mitchell St.**
City	**Wellington**
State	**VA**
Zip	**22308**
Phone	**(703) 555-6642**
Age	**15–19**
Instrument	**Oboe**
Level	**10**

10. Change the orientation of the page to landscape.
11. Save the workbook using the same name (Excel, EPA 07) and print it.
12. Close the Excel, EPA 07 workbook.

WRITING activities

The following activities give you the opportunity to practice your writing skills along with demonstrating an understanding of some of the important Word and Excel features you have mastered in this and previous units. Use correct grammar, appropriate word choices, and clear sentence constructions.

Activity 1

The Oak Springs Animal Care Clinic needs a form that will be used to keep the records of each animal seen at the clinic. Create a template that includes spaces for entering the following information:

- Owner's name, address, city, state, Zip Code, and home and work telephone numbers
- Pet's name, birth date, breed, and sex

If you want, insert the clinic's logo onto the form. The Oaksp.tif file contains the logo. In the space below this general information, include a chart that looks similar to the following:

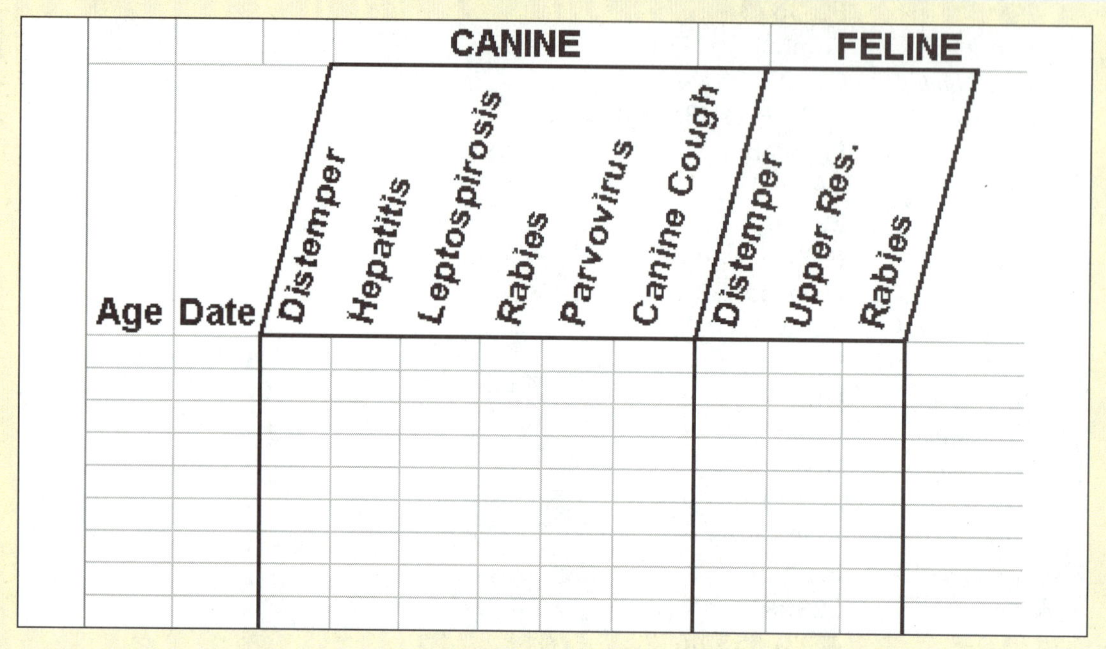

Figure U1.1 • Activity 1

Save the worksheet as a template using the file name Clinic.xlt. Use the template to complete a form for one animal. If you own a pet, use that information for completing the form. If not, use your name and address, but make up information on the pet. After the form has been filled out, save it and name it Excel, Act E1. Print and then close Excel, Act E1.

Activity 2

Georgia and Paul Sorenson, owners of the decorating business Primrose Decorators, offer discounts on large contracts they receive. Rename the *Sheet1* worksheet tab, Contract Discounts. Create a header that prints your name at the left margin and the file name at the right margin. On the Contract Discounts worksheet, include an appropriate title for the worksheet and key the following data:

Contract #	Contract Amount	Discount	Total after Discount
PD-7843	$15,000		
PD-7931	$4,000		
PD-7935	$60,000		
PD-7943	$72,000		
PD-7948	$8,000		
PD-7950	$68,000		
PD-7956	$12,000		
PD-6004	$45,000		
PD-6010	$82,000		
PD-6012	$35,000		

Rename the *Sheet2* worksheet tab, Lookup Table. For contracts under $10,000 there are no discounts, for contracts between $10,000 and $20,000 there is a 1% discount, for contracts between $20,000 and $40,000 there is a 2% discount, for contracts between $40,000 and $80,000 there is a 3% discount, and for contracts over $80,000, there is a 5% discount. On the Lookup Table worksheet, enter a lookup table that reflects these discounts.

Switch to the Contract Discounts worksheet. In the first cell in the Discount column, enter a VLOOKUP function that uses the table on the Lookup Table worksheet to look up the contract amount. The function should return the discount given for that amount. Copy the formula to find the discount for all the contracts.

In the first cell in the Total after Discount column, enter a formula that subtracts the appropriate discount percentage from the contract amount. Copy the formula to find the total after discount for all the contracts.

After the Contract Discounts worksheet is completed, save it and name it Excel, Act E2. Print and then close Excel, Act E2.

INTERNET project

Use Excel Help to read about the existing queries in Excel. Use the Internet to research five companies whose stocks you would like to own. Be sure to write down each company's stock symbol. Use the Data, Get External Data option to run the "Microsoft Investor Stock Quotes" saved query. When asked to enter your stock symbols, separate out each one with a comma and a space (i.e. PFE, MRK, CSCO). If you want the numbers to automatically adjust to the current stock quotes when the file is opened, be sure to check the boxes found in the "Enter Parameter Value" dialog box. Save the file as STOCK and print one copy.

JOB study

The owner of a large furniture company has asked you to create the following worksheet for her.

Thaxton Industries									
Category	Dealer Name	Units Purchased	Retail Price	Cost	Volume Discount	Sell Price	Gross Profit	Commissions	Net Profit/Loss
Wall Unit	SFI Designs	5							
Recliner	CJ Interiors	20							
Desk	Hovey Furnishings	30							
Totals									
Averages									

Insert the following lookup table to determine retail price, cost, and commissions.

Dealer Name	Retail Price	Cost	Commissions
CJ Interiors	1200	600	7%
Hovey Furnishings	2100	945	10%
SFI Designs	3300	1980	5%

Use an =IF statement to specify who receives the volume discount. If a customer purchases 15 or more units, then place "Yes" in the cell; otherwise, place "No." Sell price is 20% off the retail price (retail price x .80). Gross profit is sell price - cost. Net profit/loss is gross profit - commissions.

Be sure to use conditional formatting to find all the net profit/loss greater than or equal to $2,500. Format the worksheet to include borders, shading, fill colors, and other formatting choices. Round your numbers to two decimal places. Copy the information to the next four worksheet tabs within the file. Rename the worksheet tabs as follows:

Worksheet Tab	Rename to
Sheet1	Qtr 1
Sheet2	Qtr 2
Sheet3	Qtr 3
Sheet4	Qtr 4
Sheet5	Year-End

Click the Year-End worksheet tab. Keep the headings and cells containing totals, but delete the cells containing prices. You are going to use Year-End to consolidate the numbers for the Qtr 1–Qtr 4 worksheets. Use the Year-End worksheet to sort the net profit/loss column in descending order. Save the file as FURNITURE and print one copy of each page of the file.

EXCEL

EXPERT LEVEL UNIT 2: INTERPRETING AND INTEGRATING DATA

Using Excel's Analysis Tools

Managing and Auditing Worksheets

Collaborating with Workgroups

Using Data from the Internet and Other Sources

MICROSOFT® EXCEL 2002

EXPERT BENCHMARK MOUS SKILLS-UNIT 2

Reference No.	Skill	Pages
Ex2002e-1	**Importing and Exporting Data**	
Ex2002e-1-1	Import data to Excel	
	Importing data from other applications	E252-E254; E255-E256; E264-E265; E265-E266
	Importing data from the Web	E257; E261-E262; E263-E264
Ex2002e-1-2	Export data from Excel	
	Exporting data to other applications	E256; E257
Ex2002e-1-3	Publish worksheets and workbooks to the Web	
	Publishing Excel worksheets as Web pages	E258; E258-E261
Ex2002e-5	**Customizing Excel**	
Ex2002e-5-1	Customize toolbars and menus	
	Creating custom menus	E211-E214; E214-E217
	Adding and removing toolbar buttons	E211-E214; E214-E217
Ex2002e-5-2	Create, edit, and run macros	
	Creating and running macros	E200-E201; E202-E204; E206-E210; E214-E217
	Using the Visual Basic Editor to edit macros	E205-E206; E206-E210
Ex2002e-6	**Auditing Worksheets**	
Ex2002e-6-1	Audit formulas	
	Tracing dependents and precedents	E219; E219-E220
Ex2002e-6-2	Locate and resolve errors	
	Finding errors in formulas	E217-E218; E219-E220
Ex2002e-6-3	Identify dependencies in formulas	
	Finding dependencies	E217-E218; E219-E220
	Eliminating tracer arrows	E218; E219-E220
Ex2002e-7	**Summarizing Data**	
Ex2002e-7-5	Retrieve external data and create queries	
	Sharing Excel data on the Web using XML	E267
	Querying using XML	E262-E264; E264-E266
Ex2002e-8	**Analyzing Data**	
Ex2002e-8-1	Create PivotTables, PivotCharts, and PivotTable/PivotChart Reports	
	Creating a PivotTable, PivotChart, PivotTable Report, and PivotChart Report	E155-E175
Ex2002e-8-2	Forecast values with *what-if* analysis	
	Forecasting with a trendline	E187-E191
Ex2002e-8-3	Create and display scenarios	
	Making and displaying scenarios	E185-E187
Ex2002e-9	**Workgroup Collaboration**	
Ex2002e-9-1	Modify passwords, protections, and properties	
	Protecting cells	E231-E233; E233-E234
	Adding worksheet and workbook protection	E228-E231; E231-E233
Ex2002e-9-3	Track, accept, and reject changes to workbooks	
	Tracking, accepting, and rejecting changes	E234; E235-E236; E236-E239
Ex2002e-9-4	Merge workbooks	
	Merging multiple versions of the same workbook	E240-E242

CHAPTER 5

USING EXCEL'S ANALYSIS TOOLS

PERFORMANCE OBJECTIVES

Upon successful completion of chapter 5, you will be able to:

- **Create a PivotTable report using the PivotTable Wizard**
- **Format a PivotTable report using AutoFormat**
- **Sort and filter a PivotTable report**
- **Hide and show detail in a PivotTable report**
- **Analyze data using a PivotTable report**
- **Create a PivotChart report**
- **Create an interactive PivotTable for the Web**
- **Analyze data using Goal Seek**
- **Analyze data using Solver**
- **Create scenarios**
- **Create a trendline**

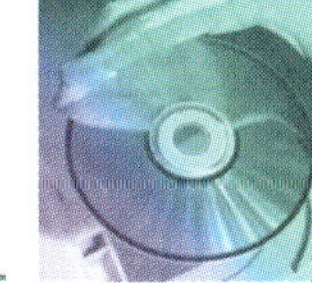

Excel Chapter 05E

When worksheets become large and complex, being able to summarize and analyze the data stored in them becomes increasingly important. Excel includes a number of features to help you analyze data, such as PivotTable reports, PivotChart reports, Goal Seek, Scenario Manager, trendlines, and Solver. The purpose of this chapter is to show you how to analyze data using Excel's analysis tools.

Introduction to PivotTables

Several layers of complexity are involved when analyzing data in an Excel worksheet. Chapter 4 introduced you to some of the simpler ways to analyze data. The Data Form allows you to look up and retrieve specific records one record at a time. AutoFilter allows you to extract particular records from the list based on specific criteria. Advanced Filter allows you to create more complex search criteria for extracting records. PivotTables add another level of complexity for analyzing data. With PivotTables, you can compare several facts about one element in a data list.

A PivotTable is an interactive table that quickly summarizes and analyzes large amounts of data. A PivotTable is interactive because you can easily rotate, or "pivot," its rows and columns to summarize the data in a different way. The interactive PivotTable allows you to easily change the view of the data so that you can see more or less detail. PivotTable reports are useful when you have a long list of figures that you want to summarize in a variety of ways. The PivotTable report summarizes the data in one field by breaking it down according to the data in another field. Figure 5.1 illustrates an example of a PivotTable. The data list in columns A through D lists the first and second quarter sales by sales representative for all the sales regions. This data list is the source data for the PivotTable report in cells F1 through I10. The PivotTable report summarizes the data in the *Sales* field by breaking it down according to the data in the *Region* field and the *Qtr* field. This PivotTable report allows you to easily compare the first and second quarter sales for each sales region. As shown in figure 5.2, you can easily "pivot" the table and have the column field become the row field and vice versa.

> **HINT**
> Creating a PivotTable enables you to have Excel sort, subtotal, and total data for you.

FIGURE 5.1 ***A PivotTable***

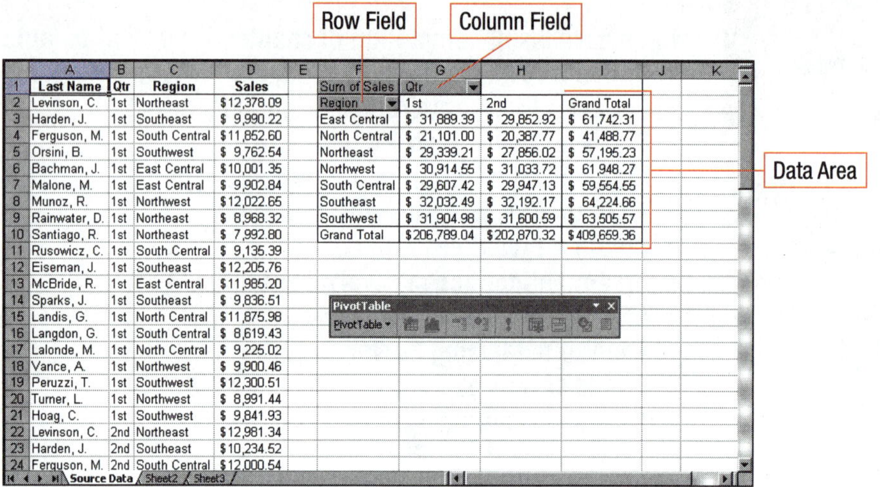

	Last Name	Qtr	Region	Sales
2	Levinson, C.	1st	Northeast	$12,378.09
3	Harden, J.	1st	Southeast	$ 9,990.22
4	Ferguson, M.	1st	South Central	$11,852.60
5	Orsini, B.	1st	Southwest	$ 9,762.54
6	Bachman, J.	1st	East Central	$10,001.35
7	Malone, M.	1st	East Central	$ 9,902.84
8	Munoz, R.	1st	Northwest	$12,022.65
9	Rainwater, D.	1st	Northeast	$ 8,968.32
10	Santiago, R.	1st	Northeast	$ 7,992.80
11	Rusowicz, C.	1st	South Central	$ 9,135.39
12	Eiseman, J.	1st	Southeast	$12,205.76
13	McBride, R.	1st	East Central	$11,985.20
14	Sparks, J.	1st	Southeast	$ 9,836.51
15	Landis, G.	1st	North Central	$11,875.98
16	Langdon, G.	1st	South Central	$ 8,619.43
17	Lalonde, M.	1st	North Central	$ 9,225.02
18	Vance, A.	1st	Northwest	$ 9,900.46
19	Peruzzi, T.	1st	Southwest	$12,300.51
20	Turner, L.	1st	Northwest	$ 8,991.44
21	Hoag, C.	1st	Southwest	$ 9,841.93
22	Levinson, C.	2nd	Northeast	$12,981.34
23	Harden, J.	2nd	Southeast	$10,234.52
24	Ferguson, M.	2nd	South Central	$12,000.54

Sum of Sales	Qtr		
Region	1st	2nd	Grand Total
East Central	$ 31,889.39	$ 29,852.92	$ 61,742.31
North Central	$ 21,101.00	$ 20,387.77	$ 41,488.77
Northeast	$ 29,339.21	$ 27,856.02	$ 57,195.23
Northwest	$ 30,914.55	$ 31,033.72	$ 61,948.27
South Central	$ 29,607.42	$ 29,947.13	$ 59,554.55
Southeast	$ 32,032.49	$ 32,192.17	$ 64,224.66
Southwest	$ 31,904.98	$ 31,600.59	$ 63,505.57
Grand Total	$206,789.04	$202,870.32	$409,659.36

FIGURE 5.2 ***Pivoting a PivotTable***

	Last Name	Qtr	Region	Sales
2	Levinson, C.	1st	Northeast	$12,378.09
3	Harden, J.	1st	Southeast	$ 9,990.22
4	Ferguson, M.	1st	South Central	$11,852.60
5	Orsini, B.	1st	Southwest	$ 9,762.54
6	Bachman, J.	1st	East Central	$10,001.35
7	Malone, M.	1st	East Central	$ 9,902.84
8	Munoz, R.	1st	Northwest	$12,022.65
9	Rainwater, D.	1st	Northeast	$ 8,968.32
10	Santiago, R.	1st	Northeast	$ 7,992.80
11	Rusowicz, C.	1st	South Central	$ 9,135.39
12	Eiseman, J.	1st	Southeast	$12,205.76
13	McBride, R.	1st	East Central	$11,985.20
14	Sparks, J.	1st	Southeast	$ 9,836.51
15	Landis, G.	1st	North Central	$11,875.98
16	Langdon, G.	1st	South Central	$ 8,619.43
17	Lalonde, M.	1st	North Central	$ 9,225.02
18	Vance, A.	1st	Northwest	$ 9,900.46
19	Peruzzi, T.	1st	Southwest	$12,300.51
20	Turner, L.	1st	Northwest	$ 8,991.44
21	Hoag, C.	1st	Southwest	$ 9,841.93
22	Levinson, C.	2nd	Northeast	$12,981.34
23	Harden, J.	2nd	Southeast	$10,234.52
24	Ferguson, M.	2nd	South Central	$12,000.54

Sum of Sales	Region				
Qtr	East Central	North Central	Northeast	Northwest	Sc
1st	$ 31,889.39	$ 21,101.00	$ 29,339.21	$ 30,914.55	$
2nd	$ 29,852.92	$ 20,387.77	$ 27,856.02	$ 31,033.72	$
Grand Total	$ 61,742.31	$ 41,488.77	$ 57,195.23	$ 61,948.27	$

The *Region* field is now the column field.

The *Qtr* field is now the row field.

Creating a PivotTable

A PivotTable report is based on its source data. The source data for a PivotTable can be created from a list, a database, multiple Excel worksheets, or another PivotTable. Chapter 4 covered how to set up a list in Excel. The rules for setting up a list in Excel that were covered in chapter 4 must be followed when using a list as the source data for a PivotTable report.

Instead of working with columns and rows, a PivotTable report works with fields and items. Each field in a PivotTable report corresponds to a column in the source data. The name of the field in the PivotTable report is the column header for that column in the list. Look at figure 5.3, for example. *Region* is a field in the PivotTable report, and it corresponds to the Region column in the source data. An item in a PivotTable report is a unique value in a field. In figure 5.3, *1st* and *2nd* are items. The *Qtr* field contains the items 1st and 2nd. *Sum of Sales* is a data field. A data field is a field from the source list that contains data that is summarized in a PivotTable report. Data field values can be summarized in the PivotTable report using summary functions such as Sum, Count, or Average.

HINT

If you do not see the PivotTable and PivotChart Report button on the Standard toolbar, click the down arrow at the right edge of the toolbar, point to Add or Remove button, and then point to Standard. Click PivotTable and PivotChart Report.

FIGURE 5.3 *How Data Is Organized in a PivotTable Report*

"Qtr" is a field in this PivotTable report. It corresponds to the Qtr column in the source data.

"1st" and 2nd" are items. The Qtr field contains the items 1st and 2nd.

"Sum of Sales" is a data field. The data that is summarized comes from the data field.

"Region" is a field in this PivotTable report. It corresponds to the Region column in the source data.

Sum of Sales	Qtr		
Region	1st	2nd	Grand Total
East Central	$31,889.39	$29,852.92	$61,742.31
North Central	$21,101.00	$20,387.77	$41,488.77
Northeast	$29,339.21	$27,856.02	$57,195.23
Northwest	$30,914.55	$31,033.72	$61,948.27
South Central	$29,607.42	$29,947.13	$59,554.55
Southeast	$32,032.49	$32,192.17	$64,224.66
Southwest	$31,904.98	$31,600.59	$63,505.57
Grand Total	$206,789.04	$202,870.32	$409,659.36

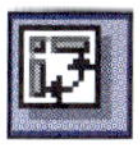

PivotTable and PivotChart Report

When you are creating a PivotTable from an Excel list, the first step is to name the range of cells that make up the list *Database*. Excel will then automatically recognize the list as the data source. Excel's PivotTable Wizard takes you step-by-step through the process of creating a PivotTable. Figure 5.4 illustrates the three dialog boxes that make up the PivotTable Wizard. Once you have named your list *Database*, click Data and then click PivotTable and PivotChart Report. Step 1 of the PivotTable and PivotChart Wizard is displayed. You can also access the PivotTable Wizard by clicking the PivotTable and PivotChart Report button on the Standard toolbar. As shown in figure 5.4, you first have to identify where the data source to be used is located and whether you want to create a PivotTable or a PivotChart. In step 2 you have to identify the range of cells that make up the data source. If you named the list *Database*, then Excel will automatically enter the correct range. In step 3 you have to identify whether you want the PivotTable placed on a new worksheet or on the same worksheet as the list. When you have made all the necessary selections, click the Finish button.

HINT

If you do not name the list to be used as a data source Database, another way to have Excel automatically recognize the list as the data source is to position the cell pointer in the list before activating the PivotTable Wizard.

FIGURE

5.4 The PivotTable and PivotChart Wizard

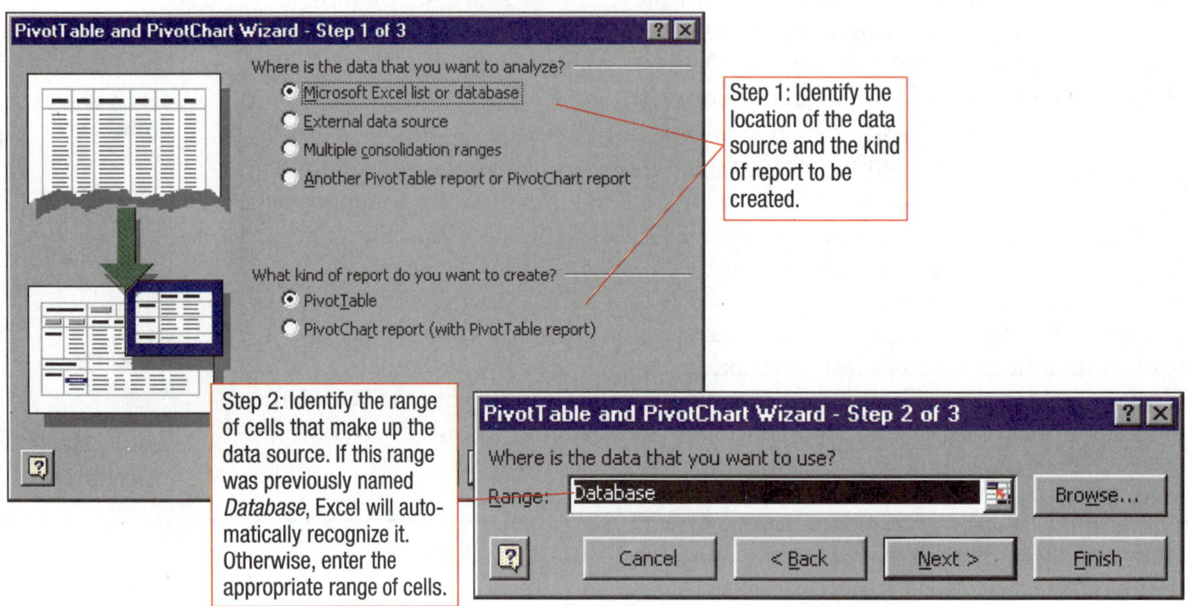

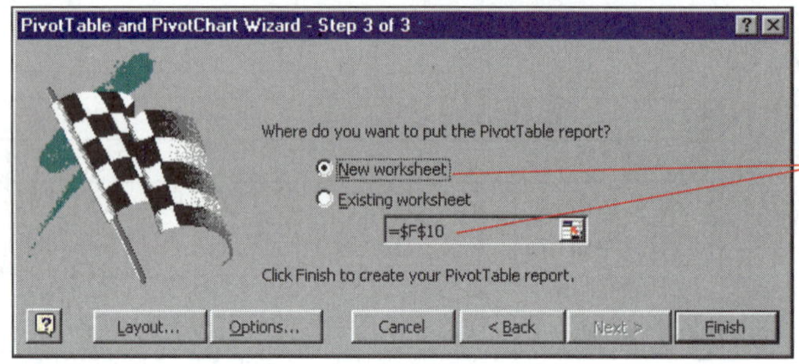

HINT
If the Pivot Table Toolbar is not displayed, click View, point to Toolbars, and then click PivotTable.

HINT
In order for the PivotTable Field List to be displayed, the Show Field List button on the PivotTable toolbar must be selected.

HINT
The order in which you should drag fields to the PivotTable diagram is fields in the row, column, and page areas first. Drag fields to the data area last. Using this order helps prevent delays when dropping fields from the PivotTable toolbar to the PivotTable diagram.

Once you click the Finish button, the PivotTable diagram, PivotTable toolbar, and PivotTable Field List are displayed, as shown in figure 5.5. In the PivotTable Field List is a group of field buttons. Drag the fields with data to be displayed in rows from the PivotTable Field List to the Drop Row Fields Here area of the diagram. Drag the fields with data to be displayed in columns from the PivotTable Field List to the Drop Column Fields Here area of the diagram. More than one field can be dragged to each area. Drag fields to be used as page fields from the PivotTable Field List to the Drop Page Fields Here area. To remove a field from the PivotTable, simply drag it off the diagram. To rearrange the fields in the PivotTable, simply drag them from one area to another.

FIGURE

5.5 The PivotTable Diagram and PivotTable Toolbar

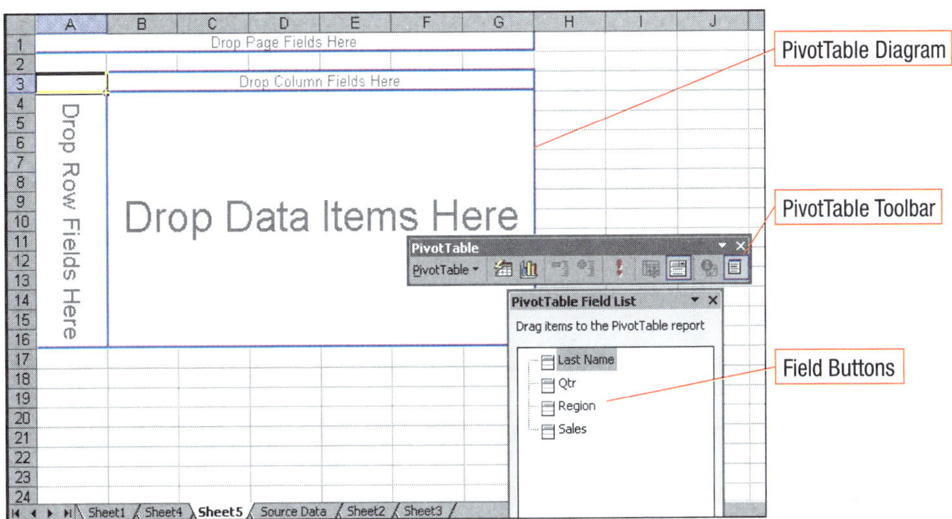

1 CREATING A PIVOTTABLE AND FILTERING A PIVOTTABLE REPORT

1. Open Excel Worksheet E5-01.
2. Save the worksheet using the Save As command and name it Excel E5, Ex 01.
3. This worksheet contains a list of orders made to the Whitewater Canoe and Kayak Corporation by various stores. You are going to use this list to create a PivotTable. Complete the following steps to name the range of cells that make up the list:
   a. Select cells A3 through F68.
   b. Click in the name box at the left side of the formula bar and then key **Database**.
   c. Press Enter.
4. Complete the following steps to create the PivotTable:
   a. Click Data and then click PivotTable and PivotChart Report.
   b. The PivotTable and PivotChart Wizard - Step 1 of 3 dialog box is displayed. You want the default selections to analyze the data in a Microsoft Excel list or database and to create a PivotTable. Click Next.
   c. The PivotTable and PivotChart Wizard - Step 2 of 3 is displayed. Database should already be entered in the range box. Click Next.
   d. The PivotTable and PivotChart Wizard - Step 3 of 3 dialog box is displayed. The default option is to put the PivotTable on a new worksheet, which is fine. Click Finish.
   e. The PivotTable diagram and PivotTable toolbar are displayed. Double-click the *Sheet1* tab and then key **PivotTable**. Press Enter.
   f. Create a custom header for the PivotTable worksheet that displays your name at the left margin and the file name at the right margin.

g. Drag the Store field button from the PivotTable Field List to the Drop Row Fields Here area of the PivotTable diagram.
h. Drag the Model field button from the PivotTable Field List to the Drop Column Fields Here area of the PivotTable diagram.
i. Drag the Units field button from the PivotTable Field List to the Drop Data Items Here area of the PivotTable diagram.

5. The PivotTable is displayed on the worksheet. The PivotTable summarizes how many units of each model were ordered by each store. Grand totals for the total number of units that were ordered by each store and the total number units that were sold of each model are also displayed. Print the worksheet.
6. You want to rearrange the PivotTable so that you see the data as a summarized list. Complete the following steps to rearrange the PivotTable:
    a. Move the mouse pointer over the Model field button in the PivotTable diagram. Notice that the mouse pointer changes to a four-headed arrow shape.
    b. Click and drag the Model field button until it is under the Store field button. The models are summarized in the first column, the stores in the second, and the totals in the third. Print the worksheet.
    c. Click the Store field button on the PivotTable diagram and drag it over the Model field button on the PivotTable diagram. Now the stores are summarized in the first column and the models in the second. Print the worksheet.
    d. Now you want to display only the units sold of the Excursion. Click the down arrow to the right of the Model field button.
    e. Click the Pathfinder and Trekker check boxes so that they are no longer selected.
    f. Click OK. The only figure displayed now represents the units sold of the Excursions.

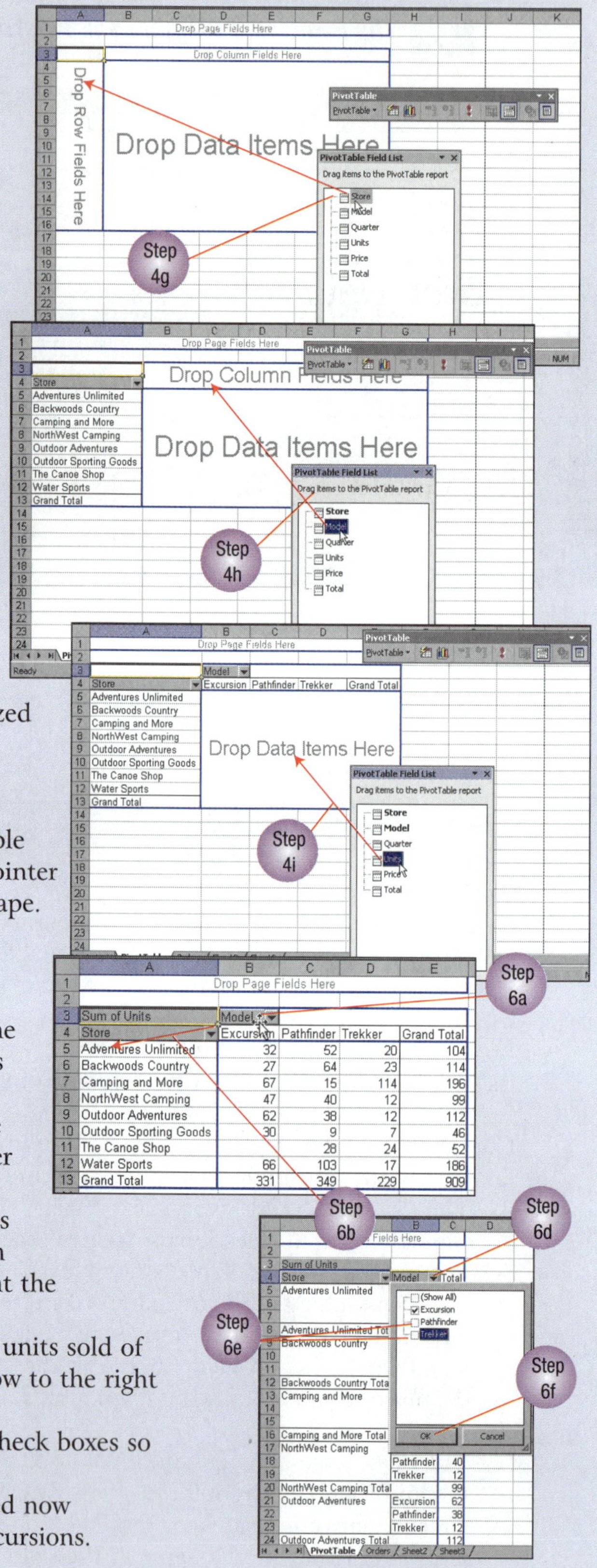

g. Click the down arrow to the right of the Model field button.
h. Click the Pathfinder check box and the Trekker check box so that they are selected. Click OK.

7. You can filter data in the PivotTable by dragging a field button to the Drop Page Fields Here area of the PivotTable diagram. Using a page field allows you to display the data for a single item at a time. Complete the following steps to use a page field:
   a. Drag the Model button from the PivotTable diagram to the Drop Page Fields Here area of the PivotTable diagram.
   b. Now the PivotTable is displaying the total for all the models. Click the down arrow to the right of the cell that has (All) entered in it. Click *Pathfinder.*
   c. Click OK. Now the PivotTable is displaying the total number of Pathfinders ordered by each store.
   d. Click the down arrow to the right of the cell that now has Pathfinder entered in it and select *Excursion*. Click OK. Now the PivotTable is displaying the total number of Excursions ordered by each store.
   e. Click the down arrow to the right of the cell that now has Excursion entered in it and select *All*. Click OK. 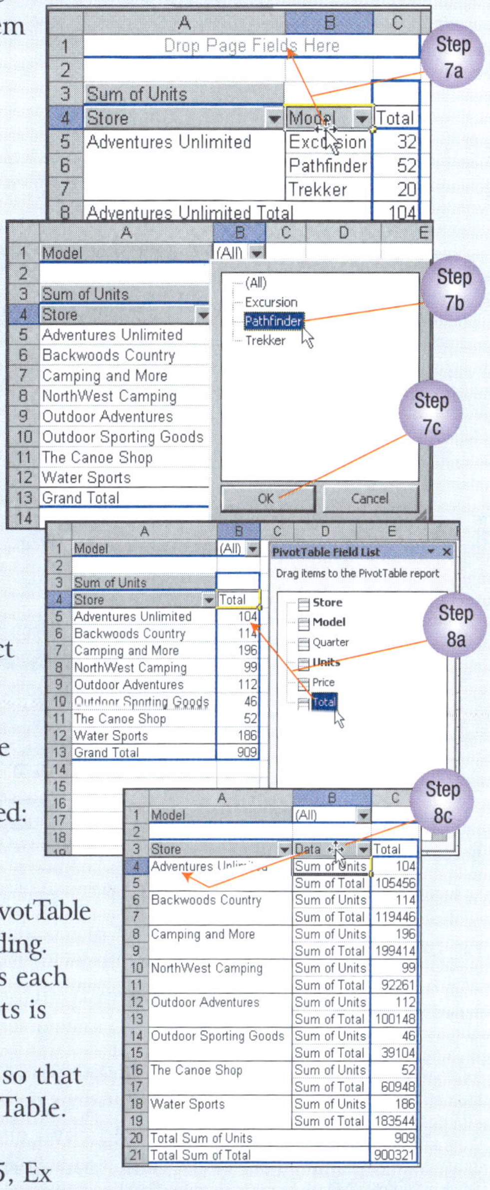
8. The PivotTable you have worked with so far has summarized the number of units sold. More than one field can be summarized at a time. Complete the following steps to add a second field to be summarized:
   a. The Data Items area of the PivotTable now lists the total number of units ordered by each store. Click and drag the Total field button from the PivotTable Field List to the cell under the Total column heading.
   b. A summary for both the total number of units each store ordered and the total cost for all the units is now displayed. Print the worksheet.
   c. Drag the Data field button on the PivotTable so that it is under the Store field button on the PivotTable.
   d. Print the worksheet.
9. Save the worksheet with the same name (Excel E5, Ex 01). You are going to use this worksheet in exercise 2.
10. Close the worksheet.

Formatting and Sorting a PivotTable

A PivotTable report can be formatted much the same way as the cells on a worksheet can be formatted. If the data is in columns, you can select all the cells belonging to a field by moving the mouse pointer to the top of the data field label. The pointer turns into a down arrow. If the data is in rows, move the mouse

pointer to the left of the data field label, and the mouse pointer turns into an arrow pointing to the right. Once the mouse pointer turns into an arrow, click. All the items related to the particular data field are selected. When the items are selected, they can be formatted as you would format any other cell on the worksheet. You can also select and format a single data item.

The entire report can be formatted using the Format Report button on the PivotTable toolbar. When you click the Format Report button, the AutoFormat dialog box shown in figure 5.6 is displayed. Click one of the report styles and click OK.

FIGURE 5.6 *The AutoFormat Dialog Box*

> **HINT** You can use conditional formatting in a PivotTable Report, but you cannot use data validation.

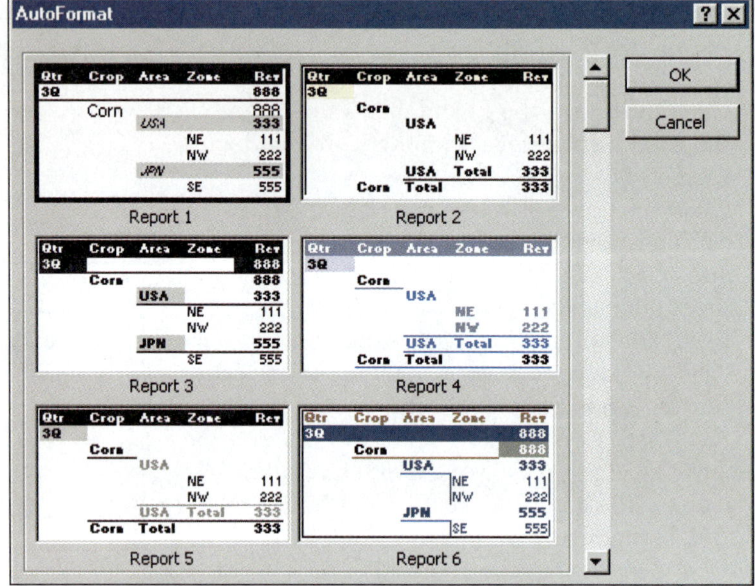

> **HINT** If the Sort and Top 10 option is not displayed on the PivotTable toolbar, click the Toolbar Options drop-down list button at the right end of the toolbar, click Add or Remove Buttons and then point to PivotTable. Click Sort and Top 10.

If you need to sort or change the order of items, you can manually move them. To move an item, drag the border of the item. As you drag, an I-shaped marker shows you the location of the item you are dragging. When you reach the location you want, release the mouse button and the item will appear in its new location.

You can also control how the items in a field are sorted. To sort items in a field in ascending or descending order, first click the field on the PivotTable report to be sorted and then click the Sort and Top 10 option on the PivotTable toolbar. The PivotTable Sort and Top 10 dialog box, shown in figure 5.7, is displayed. When Manual is selected under the AutoSort options, you can manually move the items to the desired order. The Ascending option sorts the items in ascending order, and the Descending option sorts the items in descending order.

FIGURE 5.7 PivotTable Sort and Top 10 Dialog Box

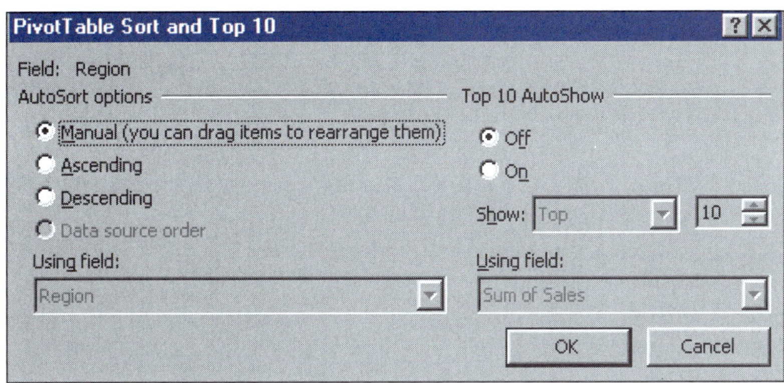

exercise 2 FORMATTING A PIVOTTABLE REPORT

1. Open Excel E5, Ex 01. You created this worksheet in exercise 1.
2. Save the worksheet using the Save As command and name it Excel E5, Ex 02. If necessary, edit the custom header so that the file name is displayed at the right margin.
3. If necessary, click the PivotTable worksheet tab.
4. Numbers from the *Total* field need to be formatted as currency. First you want to arrange the PivotTable report so that those numbers are displayed in columns by themselves. Complete the following steps to arrange the layout of the PivotTable report so the numbers that need to be formatted as currency are displayed in individual columns:
   a. Drag the Data field button in cell A3 to cell C3.
   b. Drag the Model page field button in cell A1 to the Data field button in cell B3.
5. Complete the following steps to format the numbers from the *Total* field as currency:
   a. Click the *Sum of Total* field in cell C5.
   b. Click the Field Settings button on the PivotTable toolbar.
   c. The PivotTable Field dialog box is displayed. Click Number.
   d. The Format Cells dialog box is displayed. Click Currency in the Category list.
   e. Enter **0** in the Decimal places box.
   f. Click OK twice.
6. Since the Camping and More store has placed the most orders, you would like to keep track of this one particular store in your PivotTable. Complete the following steps to format the entries for Camping and More:

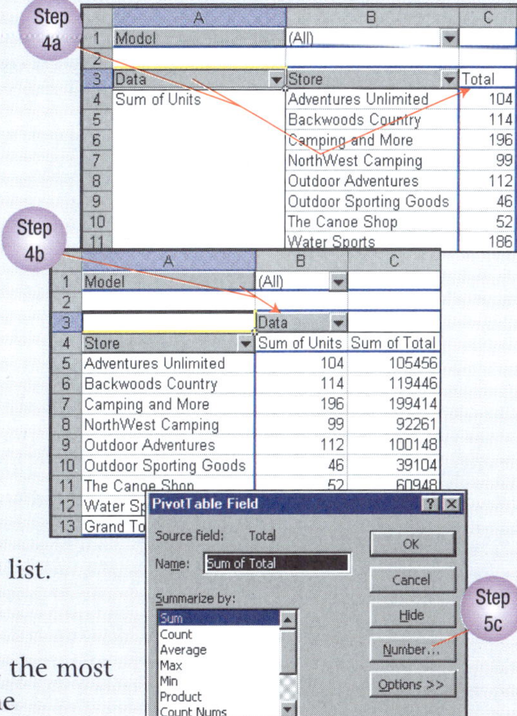

a. Place the mouse pointer to the left of row 8 (at the left side of cell A8). It should turn into an arrow pointing to the right. Once the pointer turns into an arrow pointing to the right, click. Row 8 in the PivotTable report should be selected.

Place the mouse pointer to the left of row 8 so that it turns into an arrow pointing to the right and click . . .

. . . to select row 8 in the PivotTable report.

b. Click the down arrow to the right of the Fill Color button. Click the pale blue option, the sixth option in the fifth row.

c. Drag the Data field button in cell C3 to the Store field button in cell A5. The gray I-shaped pointer showing where the field will be inserted should be to the left of column A. Notice that each instance of Camping and More is highlighted in blue and that all the dollar amounts are still formatted as currency.

Drag the Data field button to the Store field button.

The I-shaped pointer should be to the left of column A.

d. Print the PivotTable worksheet.

7. Save the worksheet with the same name (Excel E5, Ex 02). You are going to use this worksheet in exercise 3.
8. Close the worksheet.

exercise 3

SORTING A PIVOTTABLE REPORT AND FILTERING A PIVOTTABLE REPORT

1. Open Excel E5, Ex 02. You created this worksheet in exercise 2.
2. Save the worksheet using the Save As command and name it Excel E5, Ex 03. If necessary, edit the custom header so that the file name is displayed at the right margin.
3. If necessary, click the PivotTable worksheet tab.
4. You want the models displayed in order from the model that sold the most number of units to the model that sold the least number of units. That order would be Pathfinder, Excursion, and Trekker. Complete the following steps to change the order in which the models are displayed:
   a. Click cell C4.
   b. Drag the right border of cell C4 until the gray I-shaped pointer is between the Pathfinder and Trekker columns.

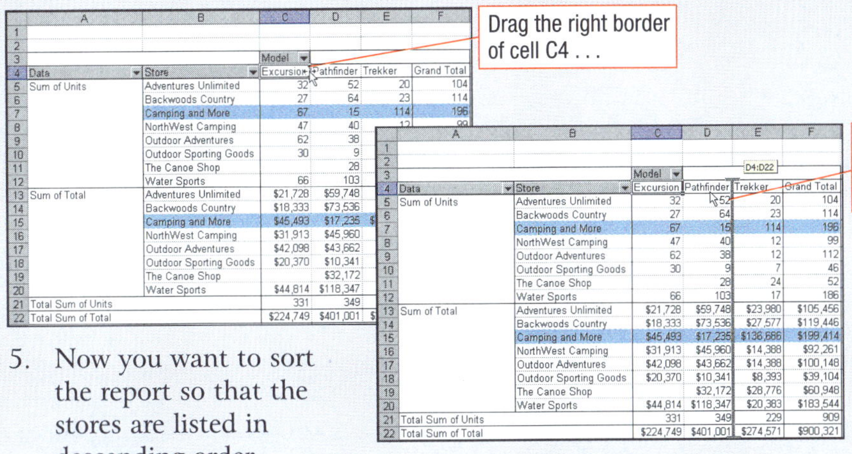

	A	B	C	D	E	F
1						
2						
3			Model			
4	Data	Store	Excursion	Pathfinder	Trekker	Grand Total
5	Sum of Units	Adventures Unlimited	32	52	20	104
6		Backwoods Country	27	64	23	114
7		Camping and More	67	15	114	196
8		NorthWest Camping	47	40	12	99
9		Outdoor Adventures	62	38	12	112
10		Outdoor Sporting Goods	30	9	7	46
11		The Canoe Shop		28	24	52
12		Water Sports	66	103	17	186
13	Sum of Total	Adventures Unlimited	$21,728	$59,748	$23,980	$105,456
14		Backwoods Country	$18,333	$73,536	$27,577	$119,446
15		Camping and More	$45,493	$17,235	$136,686	$199,414
16		NorthWest Camping	$31,913	$45,960	$14,388	$92,261
17		Outdoor Adventures	$42,098	$43,662	$14,388	$100,148
18		Outdoor Sporting Goods	$20,370	$10,341	$8,393	$39,104
19		The Canoe Shop		$32,172	$28,776	$60,948
20		Water Sports	$44,814	$118,347	$20,383	$183,544
21	Total Sum of Units		331	349	229	909
22	Total Sum of Total		$224,749	$401,001	$274,571	$900,321

. . . until the I-shaped pointer is between the Pathfinder and Trekker columns.

5. Now you want to sort the report so that the stores are listed in descending order according to their grand totals. Your screen should look like the above figure with *Data* in cell A4 and *Store* in cell B4. If necessary, drag the *Store* field to cell B4. Complete the following steps to sort the entire table:
   a. Click cell B4, the Store field button.
   b. Click the Field Settings button on the PivotTable toolbar and then click Advanced.
   c. The PivotTable Field Advanced Options dialog box appears. Under AutoSort options, click Descending.
   d. Click the down-pointing arrow to the right of the Using field box. Click *Sum of Total.*
   e. Click OK.
   f. Click OK again.

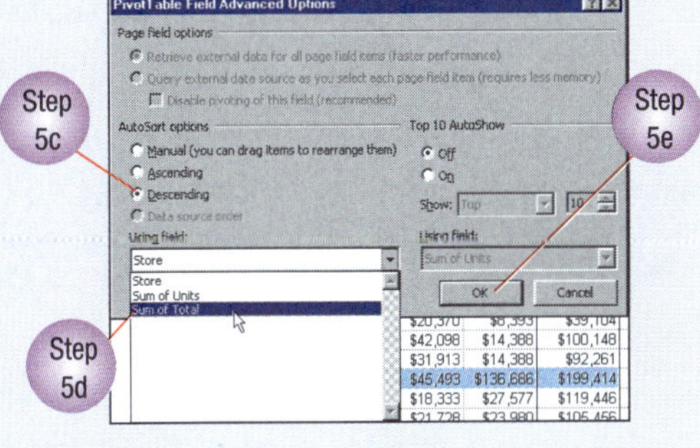

6. Now you want to display the top four stores according to the units ordered. Complete the following steps to filter the report:
   a. Click cell B4, the Store field button.
   b. Click the Field Settings button on the PivotTable toolbar and then click Advanced.
   c. The PivotTable Field Advanced Options dialog box appears. Under Top 10 AutoShow options, click On.
   d. Make sure Top is selected in the first Show box. In the second Show box, enter **4**.
   e. Make sure Sum of Units is selected in the Using field box.
   f. Click OK.
   g. Click OK again. Only the top four stores are displayed. Notice that the Total Sum of Units, Total Sum of Total, and Grand Total reflect only the orders from these top four stores.
7. Print the PivotTable worksheet.
8. Turn the filter off by double-clicking cell B4, the Store field button, clicking Advanced, and under AutoSort options, clicking Manual. Under Top 10 AutoShow, click Off. Click OK twice.
9. Save the worksheet with the same name (Excel E5, Ex 03). You are going to use this worksheet in exercise 4.
10. Close the worksheet.

Managing a PivotTable Report

If PivotTable reports contain long lists of items, reading the information in them may become difficult. On the PivotTable toolbar there is a Hide Detail button and a Show Detail button. Hiding details for items in a PivotTable report can make the report easier to read. To hide details, click the appropriate field button on the PivotTable report and then click the Hide Detail button on the PivotTable toolbar. To show the detail, click the field button again and then click the Show Detail button on the PivotTable toolbar.

HINT

If the Hide Detail button or the Show Detail button is not displayed on the PivotTable toolbar, click the Toolbar Options drop-down list button at the right end of the toolbar, click Add or Remove Buttons, and then point to PivotTable. Click Hide Detail or Show Detail.

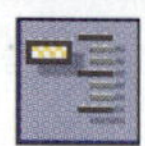

Hide Detail

Show Detail

Hiding details for items is not the same as filtering items. There are two ways to filter items: by clicking the down-pointing arrow to the right of the field button on the PivotTable report and selecting the fields to be displayed, and by using a page field. When a list is filtered, the report assumes the items that are not displayed are not a part of the report. Therefore, they are not included in any of the totals. When you hide details, the report assumes the items that are hidden are still a part of the report, so even though the individual items are not displayed in the report, their numbers are still included in the totals.

At times it may be useful to see exactly which cells from the original list went into making a particular value in the report. To see the cells from the list that go into making a value in the report, double-click the cell containing the value you want to check. The appropriate rows from the original list are displayed.

HINT

A cell on the PivotTable Report must be selected in order for the PivotTable toolbar to be active.

You can remove subtotals and grand totals from a PivotTable report. To remove a subtotal, double-click the appropriate field button. The PivotTable Field dialog box shown in figure 5.8 is displayed. Select None if the subtotals are not to be displayed. To remove grand totals from a report, right-click on any cell in the PivotTable report and then click Table Options on the shortcut menu. The PivotTable Options dialog box shown in figure 5.9 is displayed. On this dialog box there is a selection for Grand totals for columns and one for Grand totals for rows. If the grand totals are displayed in columns, make sure the check box for the Grand totals for columns option is not selected. If the grand totals are displayed in rows, make sure the check box for the Grand totals for rows option is not selected. Click OK.

FIGURE 5.8 *The PivotTable Field Dialog Box*

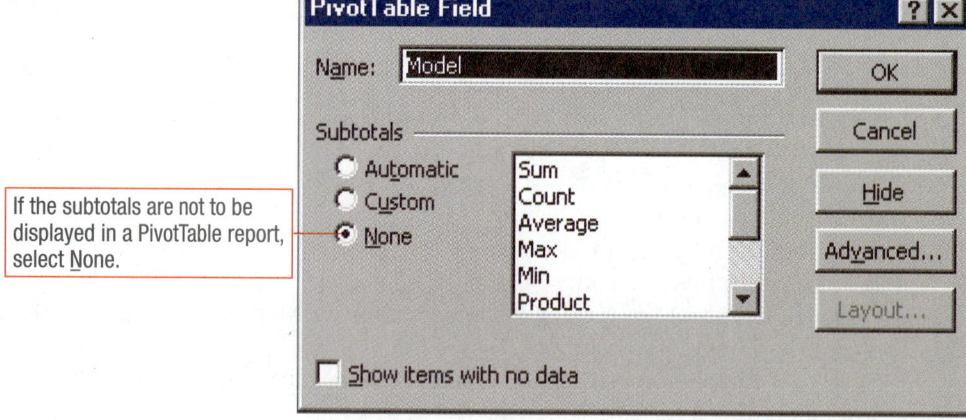

FIGURE

5.9 *The PivotTable Options Dialog Box*

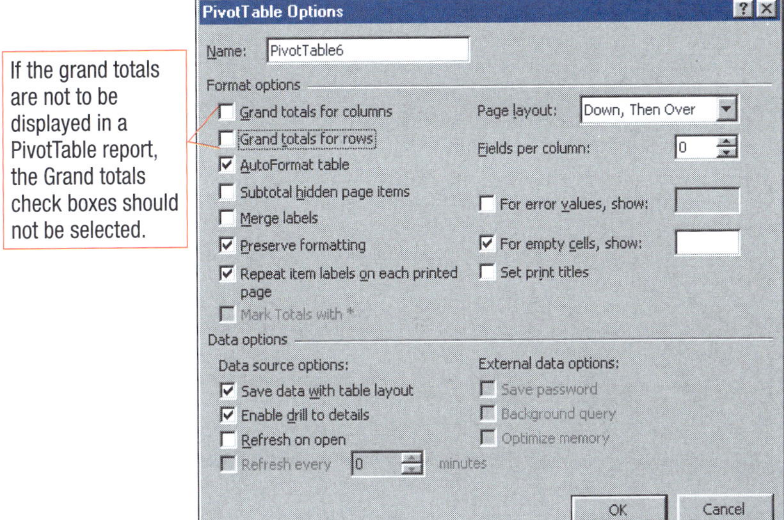

HINT

If formatting is lost when you change the layout of a PivotTable report, right-click any cell in the report and then click Table Options from the shortcut menu. Make sure the Preserve formatting check box is selected. Changes to cell borders are not retained when you change the layout of a PivotTable report.

You can manage the layout of the PivotTable report using the PivotTable Wizard. To do so, click the PivotTable and PivotChart Report button on the PivotTable toolbar. The PivotTable and PivotChart Wizard - Step 3 of 3 dialog box is displayed, as in figure 5.4. Click the Layout button. The PivotTable and PivotChart Wizard - Layout dialog box as shown in figure 5.10 is displayed. You can rearrange the layout of the PivotTable report by dragging the field buttons on the right side of the dialog box to the PivotTable diagram in the middle of the dialog box. To remove a field from the PivotTable, drag the field button off the PivotTable diagram. When you have finished rearranging the report, click OK. The PivotTable and PivotChart Wizard - Step 3 of 3 dialog box is displayed again. Click Finish.

PivotTable and PivotChart Report

FIGURE

5.10 *The PivotTable and Pivot Chart Wizard – Layout Dialog Box*

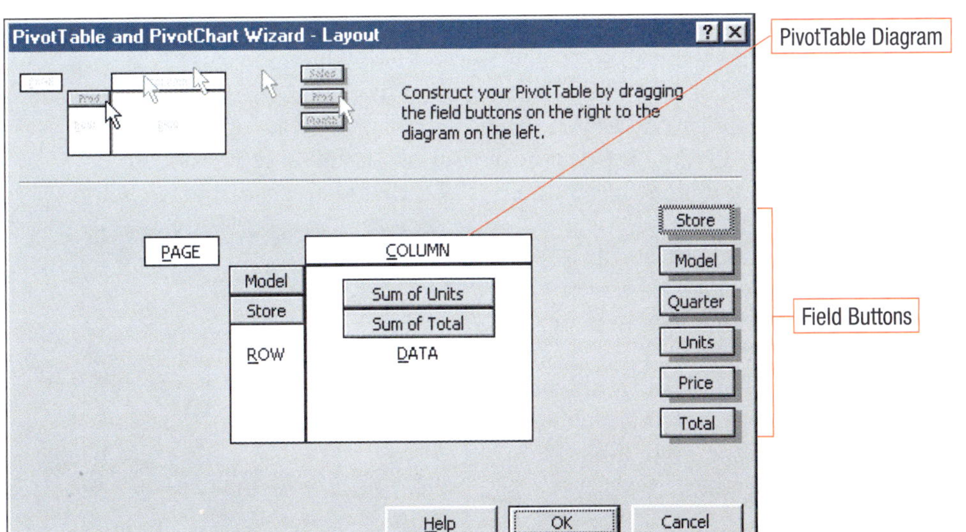

HINT

If the PivotTable and PivotChart Report button is not displayed on the PivotTable toolbar, click the Toolbar Options drop-down list button at the right end of the toolbar, click Add or Remove Buttons, and then point to PivotTable. Click PivotTable and PivotChart Report.

exercise 4

HIDING DETAIL IN A PIVOTTABLE REPORT, CHANGING THE LAYOUT OF A REPORT USING THE PIVOTTABLE WIZARD, REMOVING SUBTOTALS AND GRAND TOTALS FROM A PIVOTTABLE REPORT

1. Open Excel E5, Ex 03. You created this worksheet in exercise 3.
2. Save the worksheet using the Save As command and name it Excel E5, Ex 04.
3. If necessary, click the PivotTable worksheet tab.
4. If necessary, edit the custom header so that the file name is displayed at the right margin.
5. Rearrange the layout of the PivotTable report by dragging the Model field button in cell C3 to the Data field button in cell A4. The I-shaped pointer should be to the left of column A.

Drag the Model field button to the Data field button.

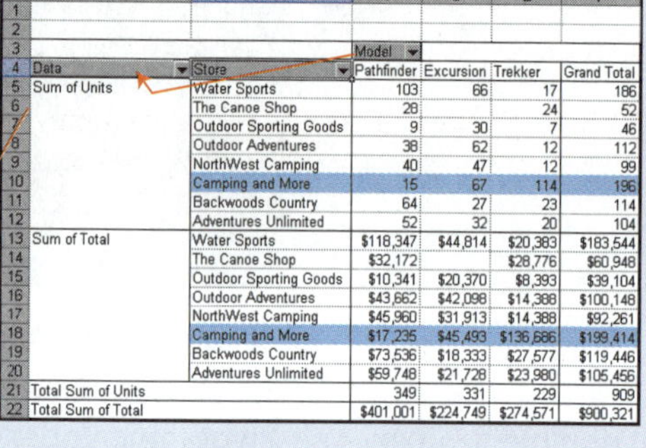

	A	B	C	D	E	F
1						
2						
3			Model			
4	Data	Store	Pathfinder	Excursion	Trekker	Grand Total
5	Sum of Units	Water Sports	103	66	17	186
6		The Canoe Shop	28		24	52
7		Outdoor Sporting Goods	9	30	7	46
8		Outdoor Adventures	38	62	12	112
9		NorthWest Camping	40	47	12	99
10		Camping and More	15	67	114	196
11		Backwoods Country	64	27	23	114
12		Adventures Unlimited	52	32	20	104
13	Sum of Total	Water Sports	$118,347	$44,814	$20,383	$183,544
14		The Canoe Shop	$32,172		$28,776	$60,948
15		Outdoor Sporting Goods	$10,341	$20,370	$8,393	$39,104
16		Outdoor Adventures	$43,662	$42,098	$14,388	$100,148
17		NorthWest Camping	$45,960	$31,913	$14,388	$92,261
18		Camping and More	$17,235	$45,493	$136,686	$199,414
19		Backwoods Country	$73,536	$18,333	$27,577	$119,446
20		Adventures Unlimited	$59,748	$21,728	$23,980	$105,456
21	Total Sum of Units		349	331	229	909
22	Total Sum of Total		$401,001	$224,749	$274,571	$900,321

The I-shaped pointer should be to the left of column A.

6. You want to compare the orders for each model, but it is difficult to do that with all the stores listed. Complete the following steps to hide the detail:
   a. Click the Model field button in cell A3.
   b. Click the Hide Detail button on the PivotTable toolbar. Only the figures for the three models are displayed.
   c. Print the PivotTable worksheet.
   d. Next you want to show the details for the Excursion model only. Click cell A6.
   e. Click the Show Detail button on the PivotTable toolbar. The details for the Excursion model only are displayed.
   f. Display all the detail by clicking the Model field button in cell A3 and then clicking the Show Detail button on the PivotTable toolbar.
7. Find the cell that displays the total number of units of the Trekker model ordered by the store Camping and More. The number is considerably higher than all the other orders, and you want to see the cells in the source data that make up this value. Complete the following steps to see the values from the source data that this number summarizes:
   a. Double-click the cell showing the units of Trekkers ordered by Camping and More. The values from the data source are displayed.
   b. Click the PivotTable worksheet tab to return to the PivotTable report.
8. You want to rearrange the layout of the report using the PivotTable Wizard. Complete the following steps to use the PivotTable Wizard to change the layout of the report:
   a. Click the PivotTable and PivotChart Report button on the PivotTable toolbar.
   b. The PivotTable and PivotChart Wizard - Step 3 of 3 dialog box is displayed. Click Layout.
   c. The PivotTable and PivotChart Wizard - Layout dialog box is displayed. Drag the Quarter button to the COLUMN area on the PivotTable diagram.
   d. Drag the Sum of Units field button off the PivotTable. The only button that should be in the DATA area on the PivotTable diagram is Sum of Total.
   e. Click OK.

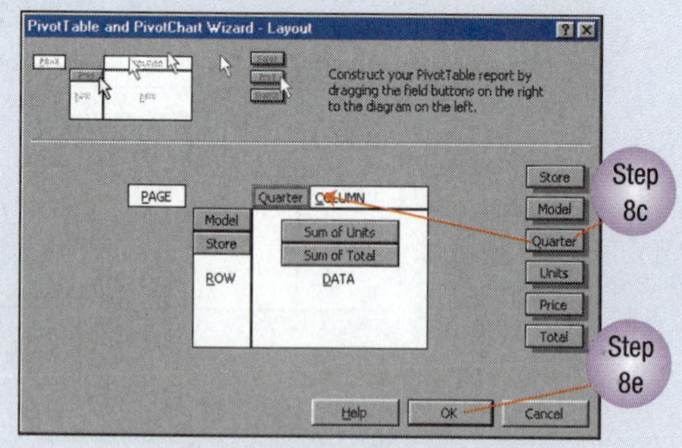

f. Click Finish.

9. Complete the following steps to remove the subtotals and the grand totals from the report:
   a. Double-click the Model field button in cell A4.
   b. Under Subtotals, click the None option.
   c. Click OK.
   d. Right-click any cell in the PivotTable report.
   e. Click Table Options on the shortcut menu.
   f. Click the check box next to Grand totals for columns and the check box next to Grand totals for rows so that they are not selected.
   g. Click OK.
10. Print the PivotTable worksheet.

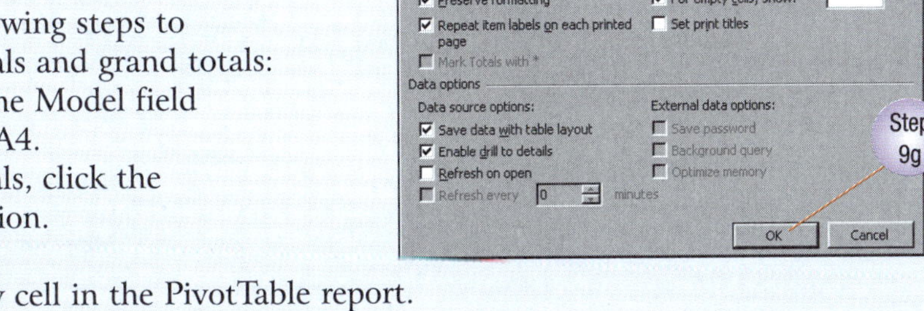

11. Complete the following steps to display the subtotals and grand totals:
    a. Double-click the Model field button in cell A4.
    b. Under Subtotals, click the Automatic option.
    c. Click OK.
    d. Right-click any cell in the PivotTable report.
    e. Click Table Options on the shortcut menu.
    f. Click the check box next to Grand totals for columns and the check box next to Grand totals for rows so that they are selected.
    g. Click OK.
12. Save the worksheet with the same name (Excel E5, Ex 04). You are going to use this worksheet in exercise 5.
13. Close the worksheet.

exercise 5 FORMATTING A PIVOTTABLE REPORT USING AUTOFORMAT

1. Open Excel E5, Ex 04. You created this worksheet in exercise 4.
2. Save the worksheet using the Save As command and name it Excel E5, Ex 05. If necessary, edit the custom header so that the file name is displayed at the right margin.
3. If necessary, click the PivotTable worksheet tab.
4. To format the entire PivotTable report using AutoFormat, complete the following steps:
   a. Click the Format Report button on the PivotTable toolbar.

b. The AutoFormat dialog box is displayed. Click the option for Report 4.
c. Click OK.
d. Use the Page Break Preview command to adjust the layout so that the first and second quarter figures print on the first page and the third quarter figures, fourth quarter figures, and grand totals print on the second page. If necessary, refer to chapter 1 for directions on how to use the Page Break Preview command.
e. Return to Normal view.

5. Print the PivotTable worksheet.
6. Complete the following steps to change the layout of the PivotTable report and to select a different formatting style:
   a. Click the PivotTable and PivotChart Report button on the PivotTable toolbar.
   b. Click Layout.
   c. Drag the Model field button from the ROW area of the PivotTable diagram to the COLUMN area of the PivotTable diagram.
   d. Click OK.
   e. Click Finish.
   f. Click the Format Report button on the PivotTable toolbar.
   g. Scroll down to find the Table 6 option. Click the Table 6 option.
   h. Click OK.
7. Print the PivotTable worksheet.
8. Save the worksheet with the same name (Excel E5, Ex 05).
9. Close the worksheet.

Creating PivotChart Reports

Chart Wizard

A PivotChart report is created from a PivotTable report. You can create the PivotChart report from scratch using the PivotTable and PivotChart Report Wizard. A PivotTable report will be created when you create the PivotChart report. Or you can create a PivotChart report based on an existing PivotTable report by clicking the Chart Wizard button on the Standard toolbar. Row fields in the PivotTable report become category fields in the PivotChart report. Column fields in the PivotTable report become series fields in the PivotChart report. Since a PivotChart report is associated with a PivotTable report, changes made to the PivotTable report are reflected in the PivotChart report and vice versa.

To create a PivotChart report from scratch, name the Excel list that is going to be used as the data source, Database. Click Data and then click PivotTable and PivotChart Report. The PivotTable and PivotChart Wizard - Step 1 of 3 dialog box is displayed. As shown in figure 5.11, you need to select PivotChart report (with PivotTable report) to create a PivotChart report. Click Next. The PivotTable and PivotChart Wizard - Step 2 of 3 dialog box will be displayed. Excel will automatically enter the Database range as the data source. Click Next. The PivotTable and PivotChart Wizard - Step 3 of 3 dialog box is displayed. Since PivotCharts must be linked to a PivotTable, Excel is going to automatically create a PivotTable. Specify whether you want the PivotTable on a new worksheet or on the existing worksheet. The PivotChart will be created on a new worksheet. Click Finish.

FIGURE 5.11 *Creating a PivotChart Report Using the PivotTable and PivotChart Wizard*

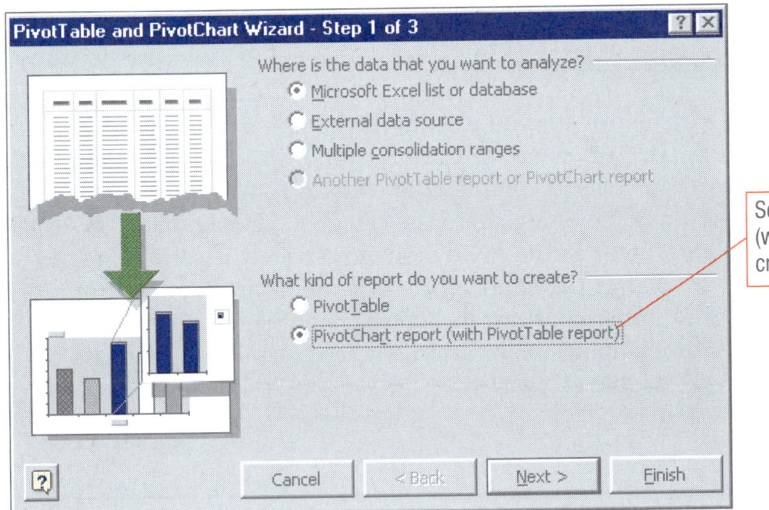

Select PivotChart report (with PivotTable report) to create a PivotChart report.

The PivotChart diagram shown in figure 5.12 is displayed. From the PivotTable toolbar, drag the field buttons for the fields you want to display in categories to the Drop Category Fields Here area of the diagram. From the PivotTable toolbar, drag the fields to be displayed in series to the Drop Series Fields Here area of the PivotChart diagram. From the PivotTable toolbar, drag the fields containing the data to be compared or measured to the Drop Data Items Here area of the PivotTable diagram. You can rearrange the fields by dragging them from one area to another. Remove a field by dragging it off the PivotTable diagram.

HINT

The order in which you should drag fields to the PivotChart diagram is fields in the series, category and page areas first. Drag fields to the data area last. Using this order helps to prevent delays when dropping fields from the PivotTable toolbar to the PivotChart diagram.

FIGURE

5.12 ***PivotChart Diagram***

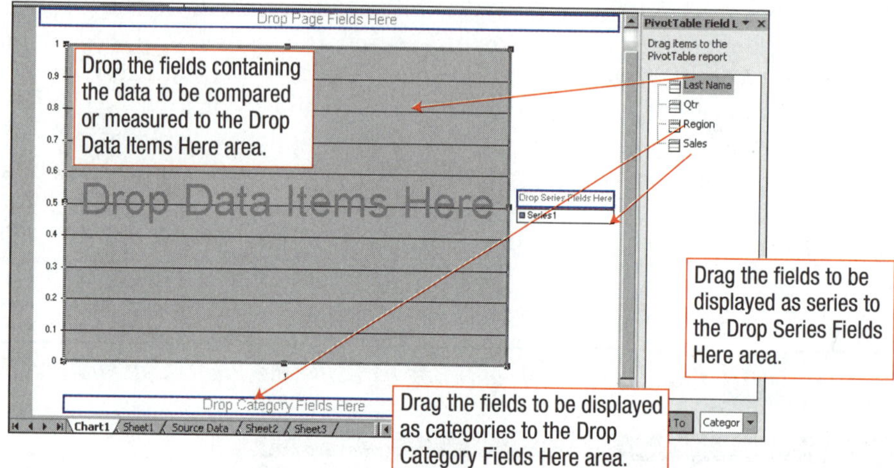

Chart Type

HINT

The type of chart that is depicted on the Chart Type button varies depending on the last chart type that was selected.

To create a PivotChart report from an existing PivotTable report, click any cell in the PivotTable report. Click the Chart Wizard button on the Standard toolbar. Excel automatically creates a stacked column chart on a new worksheet named Chart. Row fields in the PivotTable report are the category fields in the PivotChart report. Column fields in the PivotTable report are the series fields in the PivotChart report. To change the chart type, click the Chart Type button on the Chart toolbar. To make other changes, including changing the chart type, adding or editing titles, or changing the location of the chart, click the Chart Wizard button on the PivotTable toolbar.

exercise 6

CREATING A PIVOTCHART REPORT FOR AN EXISTING PIVOTTABLE REPORT

1. Open Excel Worksheet E5-02.
2. Save the worksheet using the Save As command and name it Excel E5, Ex 06. If necessary, edit the custom header so that the file name is displayed at the right margin.
3. Click the PivotTable worksheet tab, if necessary.
4. You want to make a chart representing the total sales amount of each model of canoe for all the stores in each quarter. Complete the following steps to create a chart from this PivotTable report:
   a. Click any cell in the PivotTable report.
   b. Click the Chart Wizard button on the PivotTable toolbar. Excel automatically creates a stacked column chart on a chart sheet.
   c. Double-click the Chart1 worksheet tab.
   d. Key **PivotChart**.
   e. Press Enter.
5. Create a custom header for the PivotChart worksheet that displays your name at the left margin and the file name at the right margin.

6. You want to make some changes to the PivotChart report. Complete the following steps to edit the chart:
   a. Click the Chart Wizard button on the PivotTable toolbar. The Chart Wizard - Step 1 of 4 - Chart Type dialog box is displayed.
   b. Under Chart type, click Line.
   c. Under Chart sub-type, click the second option in the second row.
   d. Click Next.
   e. Click in the Chart title box. Key **Sales by Quarter**.
   f. Click in the Category (X) axis box. Key **Quarter**.
   g. Click in the Value (Y) axis. Key **Sales**.
   h. Click Next.
   i. Accept the default entries for the Chart Wizard - Step 4 of 4 - Chart Location dialog box. Click Finish.
7. Print the PivotChart worksheet.
8. The PivotChart worksheet should still be displayed. Now you want to create a PivotChart report that shows the figures for the Camping and More store only. Complete the following steps to change the PivotChart report:
   a. Click the down-pointing arrow to the right of the Store field button.
   b. Click the *Camping and More* option.
   c. Click OK.
9. Now only the figures for the store Camping and More are displayed. Print the PivotChart worksheet.
10. Display all the stores by clicking the down arrow to the right of the Store field button, clicking the *All* option, and then clicking OK.
11. Save the worksheet with the same name (Excel E5, Ex 06).
12. Close the worksheet.

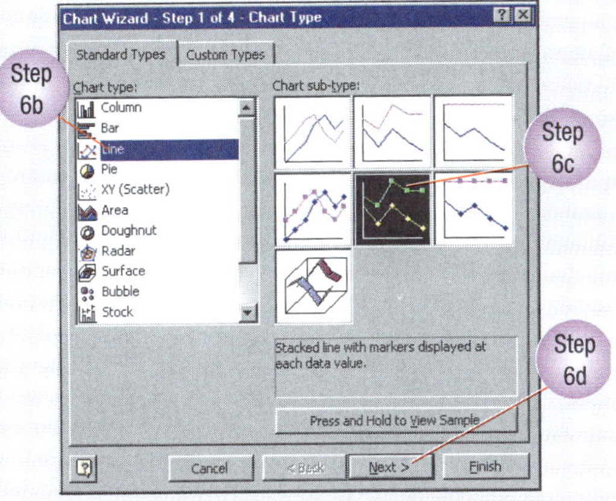

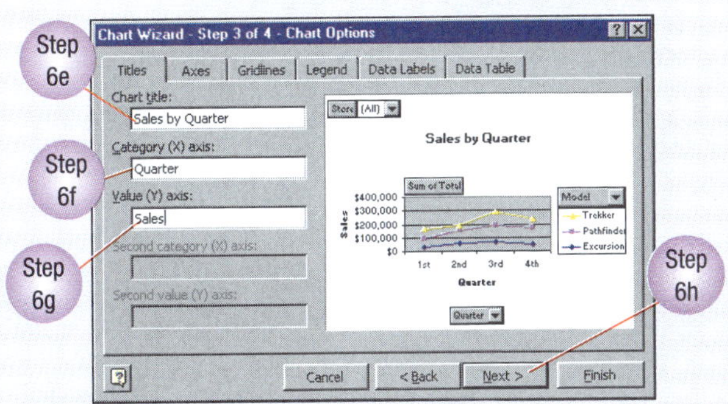

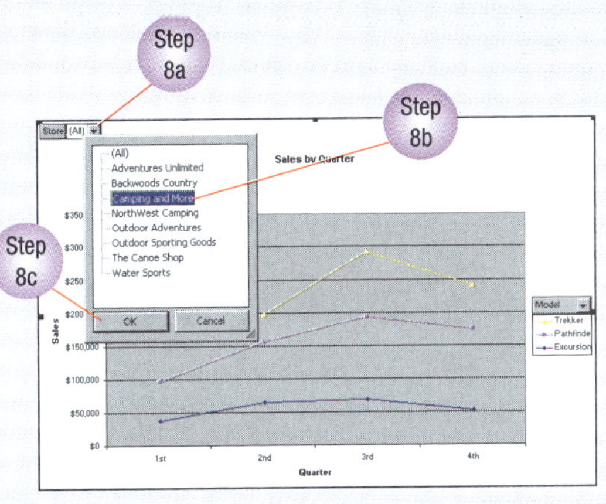

exercise 7

CREATING A PIVOTCHART REPORT FROM SCRATCH

1. Open Excel Worksheet E5-03.
2. Save the worksheet using the Save As command and name it Excel E5, Ex 07. Create a custom header that displays your name at the left margin and the name of the file at the right margin.
3. Complete the following steps to name the data source Database:
   a. If necessary, click the Source Data worksheet tab.
   b. Click cell A1.
   c. Hold the Shift key and double-click the right border of cell A1.
   d. Hold the Shift key and double-click the bottom border of cell A1. The entire list (A3:D81) should be selected.
   e. Click the name box.
   f. Key **Database**.
   g. Press Enter.
4. Complete the following steps to create a PivotChart report from scratch:
   a. Click Data and then click PivotTable and PivotChart Report.
   b. The PivotTable and PivotChart Wizard - Step 1 of 3 is displayed. Under What kind of report do you want to create? click the PivotChart report (with PivotTable report) option.

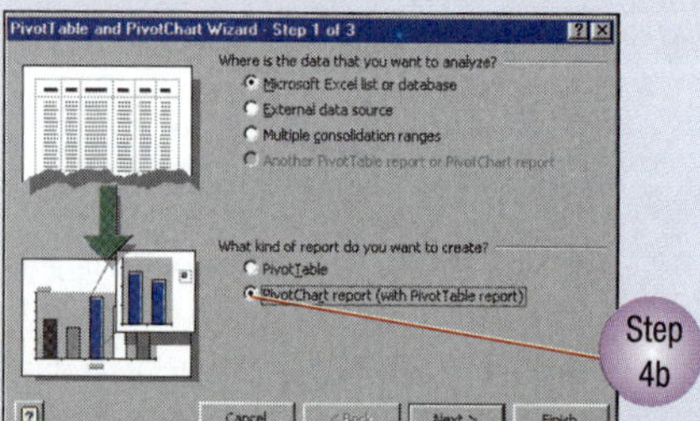

   c. Click Next.
   d. Excel should automatically recognize the Database range. Click Next.
   e. Click Finish.
   f. Double-click the Chart1 sheet tab and key **PivotChart**.
   g. Press Enter.
   h. Drag the Last Name button from the PivotTable Field List to the Drop Page Fields Here area of the PivotChart diagram.
   i. Drag the Qtr button from the PivotTable Field List to the Drop Series Fields Here area of the PivotChart diagram.
   j. Drag the Region button on the PivotTable Field List to the Drop Category Fields Here area of the PivotChart diagram.

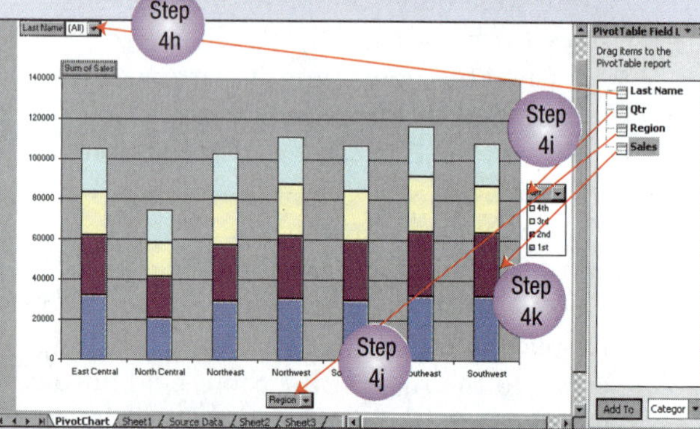

   k. Drag the Sales button on the PivotTable Field List to the Drop Data Items Here area of the PivotChart diagram.
   l. Create a custom header for the PivotChart worksheet that displays your name at the left margin and the file name at the right margin.
5. Complete the following steps to edit the PivotChart report:
   a. Click the Chart Wizard button on the PivotTable toolbar.

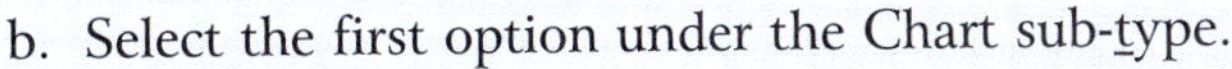

b. Select the first option under the Chart sub-type.
c. Click Next.
d. Click in the Chart title box. Key **Sales by Region**.
e. Click in the Category (X) axis box. Key **Region**.
f. Click in the Value (Y) axis. Key **Sales**.
g. Click Next.
h. Accept the default entries on the Chart Wizard - Step 4 of 4 Chart Location dialog box by clicking Finish.

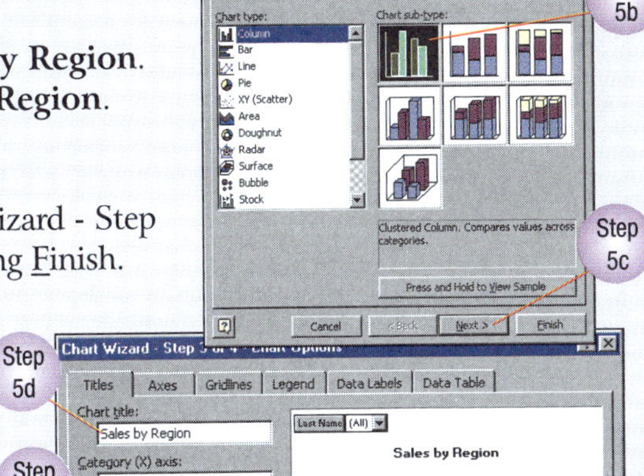

6. The Chart toolbar should be displayed. If it is not, click View, Point to Toolbars, and click Chart to display it.Complete the following steps to format the PivotChart report:
   a. Click the down-pointing arrow to the right of the Chart Objects box, the first box on the Chart toolbar.
   b. Click *Value Axis*.
   c. The value axis is now selected. You want to format the numbers on the value axis as currency.
   d. Click the Format Axis button on the Chart toolbar.
   e. The Format Axis dialog box is displayed. Click the Number tab.
   f. In the Category list box, click *Currency*.
   g. Enter **0** in the Decimal places box.
   h. Click OK.
   i. Click the down-pointing arrow to the right of the first box on the Chart toolbar.
   j. Click *Category Axis*.
   k. Click the Angle Counterclockwise button on the Chart toolbar.

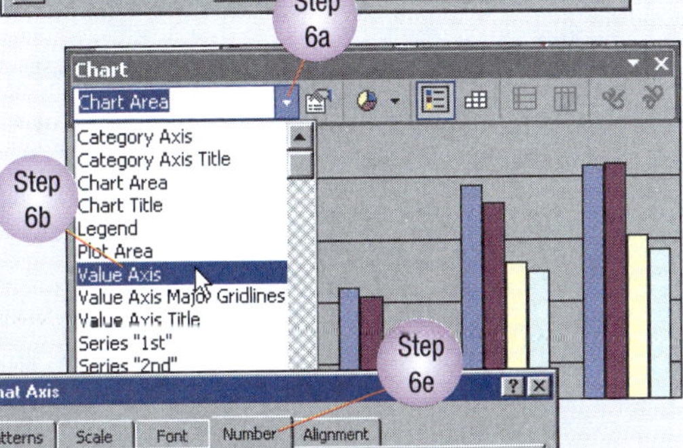

7. Print the PivotChart worksheet.
8. Now you want to see just the sales figures for Levinson. Complete the following steps to display the sales figures for one sales representative:
   a. Click the down-pointing arrow to the right of the Last Name field button.
   b. Click *Levinson, C.*
   c. Click OK.
   d. Print the PivotChart worksheet.
   e. Display all the sales representatives by clicking the down-pointing arrow to the right of the Last Name field button, clicking *(All)*, and clicking OK.
9. Complete the following steps to create a pie chart that illustrates the sales for the fourth quarter:

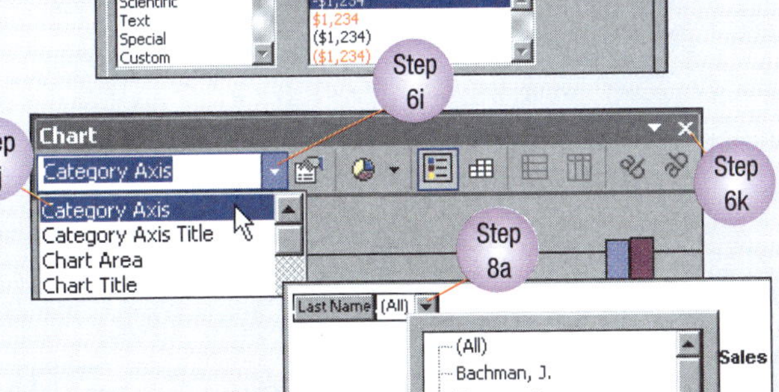

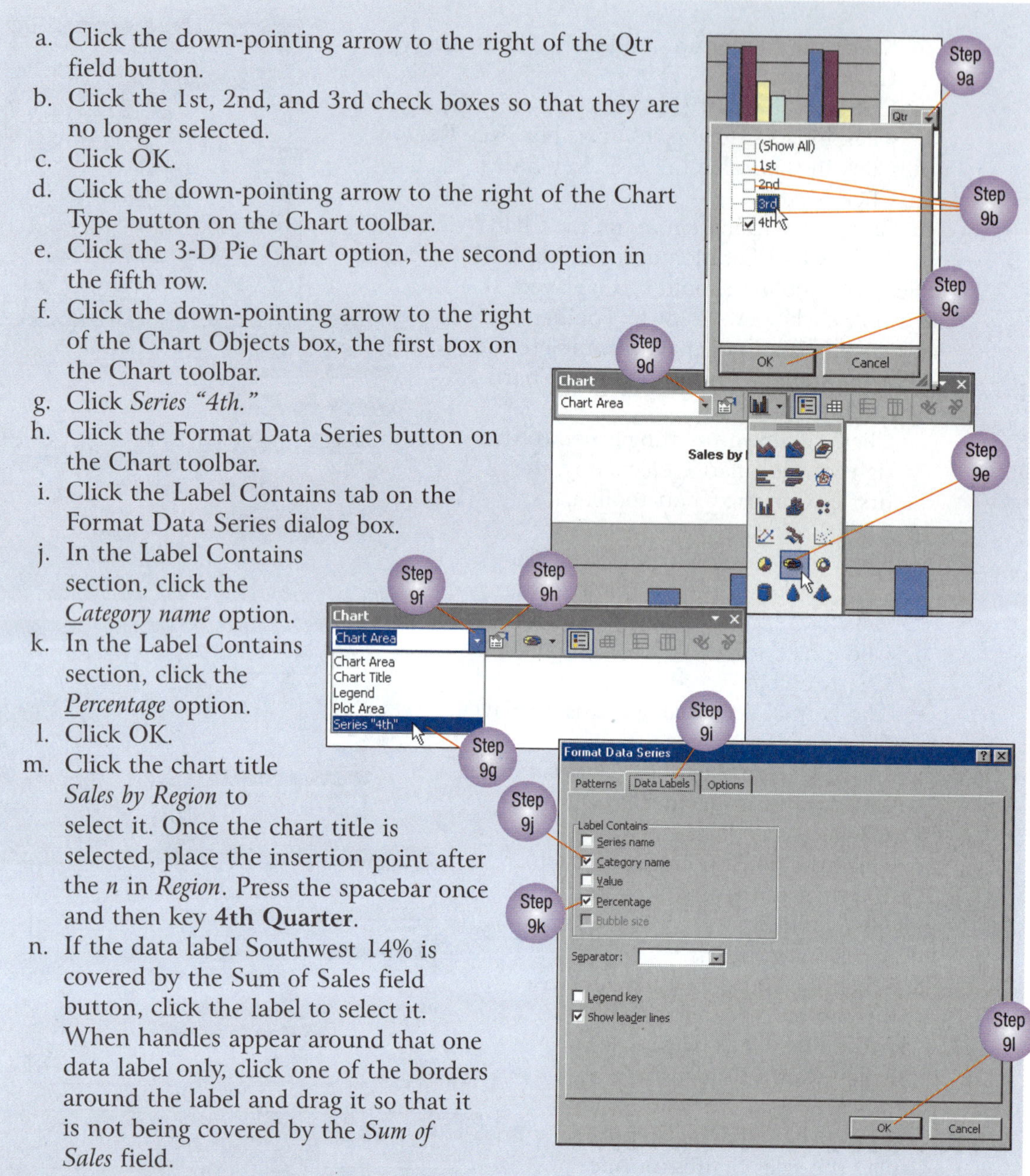

a. Click the down-pointing arrow to the right of the Qtr field button.
b. Click the 1st, 2nd, and 3rd check boxes so that they are no longer selected.
c. Click OK.
d. Click the down-pointing arrow to the right of the Chart Type button on the Chart toolbar.
e. Click the 3-D Pie Chart option, the second option in the fifth row.
f. Click the down-pointing arrow to the right of the Chart Objects box, the first box on the Chart toolbar.
g. Click *Series "4th."*
h. Click the Format Data Series button on the Chart toolbar.
i. Click the Label Contains tab on the Format Data Series dialog box.
j. In the Label Contains section, click the *Category name* option.
k. In the Label Contains section, click the *Percentage* option.
l. Click OK.
m. Click the chart title *Sales by Region* to select it. Once the chart title is selected, place the insertion point after the *n* in *Region*. Press the spacebar once and then key **4th Quarter**.
n. If the data label Southwest 14% is covered by the Sum of Sales field button, click the label to select it. When handles appear around that one data label only, click one of the borders around the label and drag it so that it is not being covered by the *Sum of Sales* field.

10. Print the PivotChart worksheet and save it with the same name (Excel E5, Ex 07).
11. Close the worksheet.

HINT

When you place a PivotTable report on the Web it is called a PivotTable list.

Creating Interactive PivotTables for the Web

A PivotTable report can be saved as a Web page and then published to a public location such as a Web server. Other users who have Microsoft Office Web Components installed can view the PivotTable report using version 4.01 or later of the Microsoft Internet Explorer Web browser. The Microsoft Office Web components are automatically installed when Microsoft Office XP is installed. An interactive PivotTable report that has been published in a public location is called a PivotTable list. Users can interact with a PivotTable list in many of the same ways as PivotTable reports can be manipulated in Excel. A PivotTable list on a Web page includes features and commands similar to an Excel PivotTable report.

One of the ways you can interact with a PivotTable list on a Web page is by adding fields to it or by removing fields from it. Once the PivotTable has been saved as a Web page and is displayed in a Web browser, a toolbar appears above it. As shown in figure 5.13, a list of all the available fields that can be added to the PivotTable is displayed when the Field List button is clicked. To add a field to the PivotTable, click the field name in the list and then click OK. To remove a field from the PivotTable, simply click the field button representing that field and drag it off the PivotTable.

FIGURE 5.13 *Adding Fields to a PivotTable Using a Web Browser*

To add a field to a PivotTable using a Web browser, click the Field List button, click the field to be added from the PivotTable Field List that is displayed, and then click Add to.

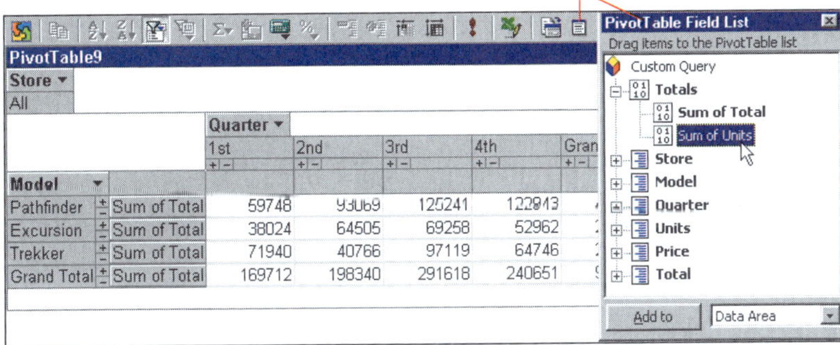

exercise 8 CREATING AN INTERACTIVE PIVOTTABLE FOR THE WEB

1. Open Excel Worksheet E5-04.
2. Save the worksheet using the Save As command and name it Excel E5, Ex 08.
3. If necessary, click the PivotTable worksheet tab.
4. Complete the following steps to save the PivotTable report as a Web page:
   a. Click File and then click Save As Web Page.
   b. The Save As dialog box is displayed. Make sure Entire Workbook is selected.
   c. Click Publish.
   d. The Publish as Web Page dialog box is displayed. If necessary, select *Items on PivotTable* from the drop-down list for the Choose box.

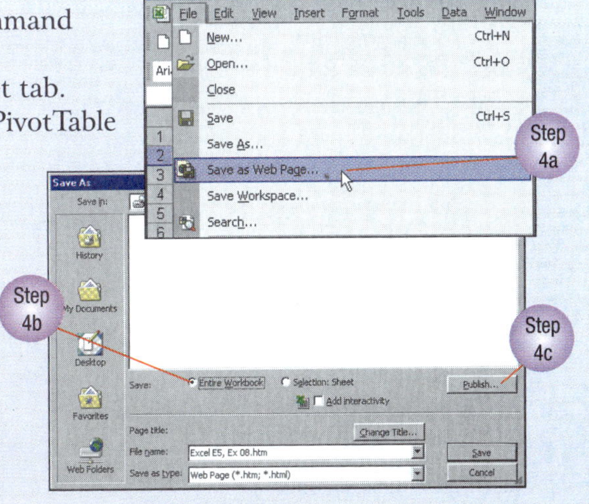

e. Select *PivotTable* from the list under the Choose box.

f. In the Viewing options section, click the Add interactivity with check box to select it.

g. If necessary, choose *PivotTable functionality* from the drop-down list for the Add interactivity with box.

h. Make sure the File name is **Excel E5, Ex 08.htm**.

i. If necessary, click the Open published web page in browser check box to select it.

j. Click Publish.

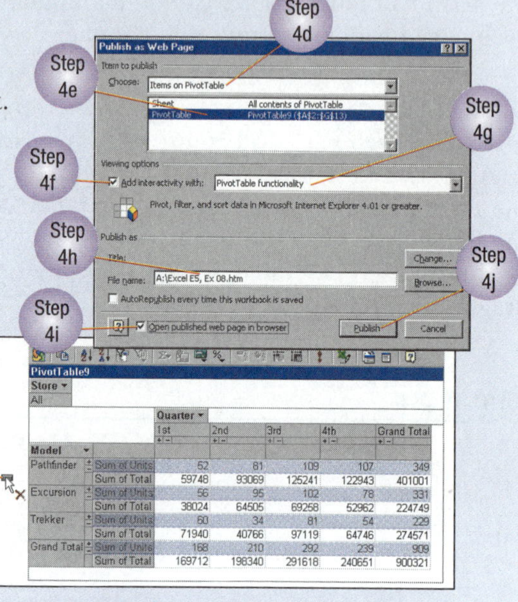

5. The PivotTable is displayed in Microsoft Internet Explorer. Complete the following steps to interact with the PivotTable as a Web page:

Click one of the Sum of Units field buttons and drag it off the PivotTable list to remove it.

a. You do not want to see the figures for the Sum of Units. Click one of the Sum of Units field buttons and drag it off the PivotTable.

b. You want to see the figures for the NorthWest Camping store only. Click the down-pointing arrow to the right of the Store field button.

c. Click the (All) box so that it is no longer selected. Click the NorthWest Camping check box to select it. It should be the only box that is selected.

d. Click OK.

e. Click the Print button.

f. Display all the stores by clicking the down-pointing arrow to the right of the Store field button, clicking the (All) check box to select it, and then clicking OK.

g. You want to display the detail for the Trekker model. Click the plus sign in the box next to Trekker.

h. Click the Print button.

i. Collapse the detail by clicking the minus sign in the box next to Trekker.

j. You want to put the Units back into the PivotTable list. Click the Field List button.

k. The PivotTable Field List dialog box is displayed. Click Sum of Units and drag the item to below the first Sum of Total field button.

l. Close the PivotTable Field List dialog box.

6. Close Microsoft Internet Explorer.

7. Save the worksheet with the same name (Excel E5, Ex 08) and close it.

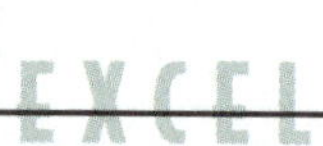

Analyzing Data Using Goal Seek

Excel's Goal Seek is used to calculate a specified result by changing the value of another cell. Goal Seek adjusts the value in a specified cell until a formula dependent on that cell reaches the desired result. For example, suppose a company wanted to buy a machine costing $70,000. The company knows the interest that must be paid on the loan, and they know their payments cannot exceed $4,000. What they need to know is the period of the loan or how many payments it will take to pay the loan off. They know the goal they are seeking—paying off a $70,000 loan at a specific interest rate with monthly payments of $4,000. Goal Seek can tell them what they need to do to reach that goal—that is, how many payments they will need to make.

To use the Goal Seek command, enter the formula and corresponding values in the worksheet. Click Tools and then either wait a few seconds or click the down arrow at the bottom of the menu for the Goal Seek option to be displayed. Click Goal Seek. The Goal Seek dialog box shown in figure 5.14 is displayed. Enter the cell reference to the cell containing the formula in the Set cell box. Enter the goal you are seeking in the To value box. Enter the cell reference to the cell containing the value that can change in the By changing cell box. The Goal Seek Status dialog box is displayed. The value on the worksheet has changed to display the goal being sought after. To enter the goal into the worksheet, click OK. To cancel Goal Seek and return the original value to the worksheet, click Cancel.

FIGURE 5.14 ***The Goal Seek Dialog Box***

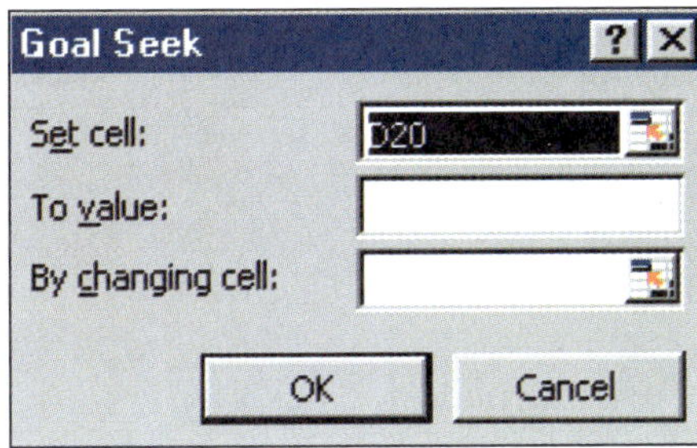

exercise 9 USING GOAL SEEK

1. Open Excel Worksheet E5-05.
2. Save the worksheet using the Save As command and name it Excel E5, Ex 09.
3. Create a custom header that displays your name at the left margin and the file name at the right margin.
4. This worksheet keeps track of the profit the EastWest Crossroads Company makes on each item it sells through its mail-order catalog. View the item in row 16. Right now, item GG-47-1 is only making a $5.00 profit. Complete the following steps to use Goal Seek to find out how much the selling price of the Mosaic Glass Bracelet would have to be to make an $8.00 profit.

a. Click Tools, click the down arrow at the bottom of the menu if necessary and then click Goal Seek.
b. The Goal Seek dialog box appears. The current entry in the Set cell box is already selected. Key **F16**.
c. Click the To value box and key **8.00**.
d. Click the By changing cell box and key **C16**.
e. Click OK.
f. The Goal Seek Status dialog box is displayed. Click OK.

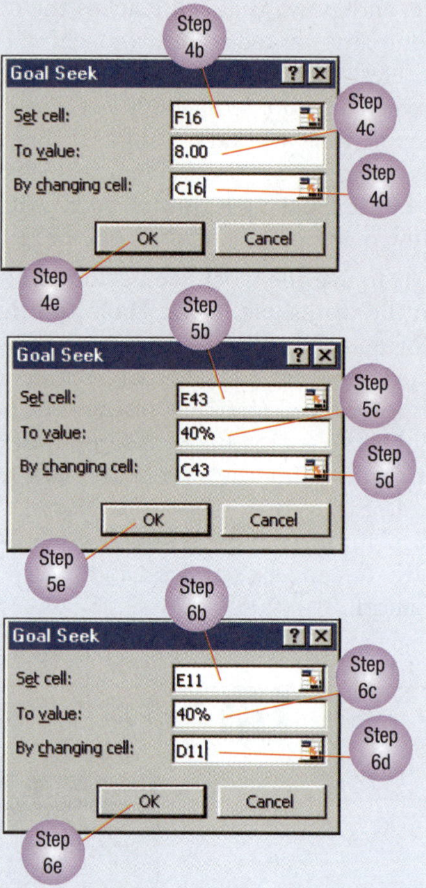

5. Scroll down to view the item in row 43. Right now item GH-82-2, the Stained Glass Lamp, has a 30% markup. Complete the following steps to use Goal Seek to find out how much the selling price would have to be if the markup is 40%:
   a. Click Tools and then click Goal Seek.
   b. The Goal Seek dialog box appears. The current entry in the Set cell box is already selected. Key **E43**.
   c. Click the To value box and key **40%**.
   d. Click the By changing cell box and key **C43**.
   e. Click OK.
   f. The Goal Seek Status dialog box is displayed. Click OK.
6. View the item in row 11. The Unit Cost of the Jakarta Drum is $65.00. Complete the following steps to use Goal Seek to find out how much that unit cost would have to decrease in order for the EastWest Crossroads Company to realize a 40% profit on the drum:
   a. Click Tools and then click Goal Seek.
   b. The Goal Seek dialog box appears. The current entry in the Set cell box is already selected. Key **E11**.
   c. Click the To value box and key **40%**.
   d. Click the By changing cell box and key **D11**.
   e. Click OK.
   f. The Goal Seek Status dialog box is displayed. Click OK.
7. Save the worksheet with the same name (Excel E5, Ex 09) and print it.
8. Close the worksheet.

Analyzing Data Using Solver

Businesses can always meet their objectives in a number of different ways. What businesses must determine is which way is the most efficient way, or the way that will generate the maximum profit, or the way that will optimize the use of plant facilities. The variables involved in meeting the specific objective are subject to restrictions or constraints. For example, a constraint involved in determining the optimal use of plant facilities is that the plant cannot operate more than 24 hours a day. By using Excel's Solver, you can solve problems that have multiple, interdependent variables. Excel's Goal Seek can arrive at a specific result in problems with only one changing variable. With Solver, you can arrive at a specific result in problems that have many changing variables.

Suppose a factory makes two different products using the same machine. The goal is to maximize the total net profit from these two products. The profit for each product is different. The time it takes the machine to produce each product is different. The machine can run only a certain number of hours a week. The products are shipped out at the end of each week, so the products produced in one week cannot exceed the space available for storing them in the warehouse. There is a limit on the weekly demand for one of the products. As you can see, several variables are involved: the net profit for each product, the machine time, the warehouse space, and the demand for one of the products. Each one of these variables has a constraint. The machine can run only a certain number of hours a week. The warehouse is a specific size. There is a limit to the number of one of the products that can be sold in a week. By taking into consideration all the variables and their constraints, Solver finds the optimal solution: the number of each product that should be produced in a week in order to maximize the total net profit.

To use Solver, click Tools and then click Solver. If the Solver command is not on the Tools menu, the Solver add-in needs to be installed. The Solver Parameters dialog box shown in figure 5.15 is displayed. In the Set Target Cell box, enter the cell reference or name for the target cell. The target cell must contain a formula. If the target cell is to be as large as possible, click Max. If it is to be as small as possible, click Min. If it is to be a specific value, click Value of and enter the value in the Value of box. Enter a name or reference for each cell that can be adjusted to meet the target in the By Changing Cells box. Separate nonadjacent references using commas. If you want Solver to automatically propose the cells to be adjusted based on the target cell, click Guess. The cells to be adjusted must not contain formulas, and the target cell must be dependent on them. An adjustment to the value in a cell listed in the By Changing Cells box must affect the value in the target cell. Any constraints to be applied are entered in the Subject to the Constraints box. Once you have defined the problem in the Solver Parameters dialog box, click Solve.

HINT

To install Solver, click Tools and Add-Ins. The Add-Ins dialog box is displayed. Click the Solver Add-in check box and click OK.

HINT

The Target Cell must be a single cell. Only one cell is optimized when using Solver.

FIGURE 5.15 ***The Solver Parameters Dialog Box***

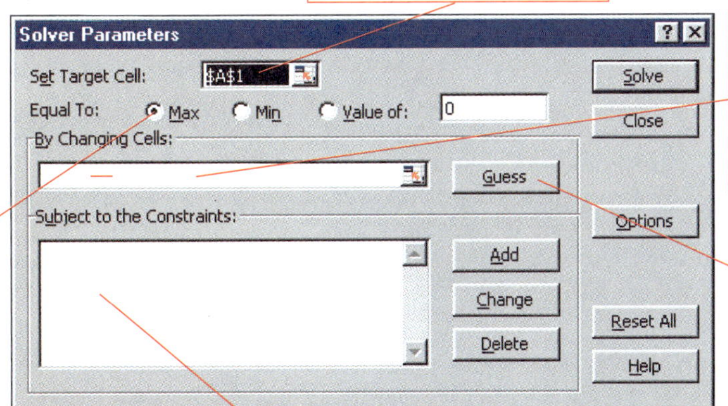

Once you click Solve, the Solver Results dialog box shown in figure 5.16 is displayed. Click Keep Solver Solution to keep the solution values on the worksheet. Click Restore Original Values to restore the original data. The Reports list box allows you to select the type of report you would like to see and places each report on a separate sheet in the workbook. The Answer Report displays the target cell, the changing cells, and the constraints. The Sensitivity Report presents the detailed sensitivity information about the target cell. The Limits Report displays how much the values of the changing cells can be increased or decreased without violating the constraints of the problem.

FIGURE 5.16 ***The Solver Results Dialog Box***

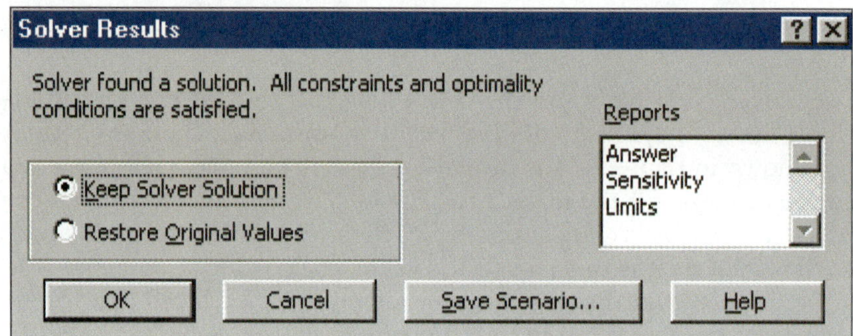

exercise 10 DEFINING AND SOLVING A PROBLEM USING SOLVER

(Note: In order to complete this exercise the Solver add-in needs to be installed. To install Solver see the hint on page E181.)

1. Open Excel Worksheet E5-06.
2. Save the worksheet using the Save As command and name it Excel E5, Ex 10.
3. Create a custom header that displays your name at the left margin and the file name at the right margin.
4. Copper Clad Incorporated makes modem circuit boards for three different modem manufacturers off a single production line. The production line runs 60 hours a week. A weekly production schedule is run where the week is spent producing the three different modem circuit boards and the output is stored in a warehouse during the week. At the end of each week, the modem boards are shipped to each modem manufacturer. It takes three hours to produce 100 boxes of Board A, four hours to produce 100 boxes of Board B, and five hours to produce 100 boxes of Board C. It takes 1.5 cubic feet to store one box of Board A, 2.5 cubic feet to store one box of Board B, and 3 cubic feet to store one box of Board C. The warehouse holds, at most, 2,000 cubic feet. The net profit per box of Board A is $75. The net profit per box of Board B is $100, and the net profit per box of Board C is $150. You can sell as many boxes as you can produce in a week to the companies that buy Board A and Board B. But the company that buys Board C will never purchase more than 250 boxes a week. You want to use Solver to determine a production plan that abides by all the constraints and maximizes the total net profit.

   Look at the worksheet. The target cell, or the total net profit, is surrounded by a blue border. The changing cells, or the number of boxes produced for each modem board, are surrounded by a green border. The constraints on the variables are surrounded by a violet border. First, you are going to name some of the cells in order to make using Solver a little easier to understand. Complete the following steps to name the cells:

a. Name cell F7 **Total_Profit**.
b. Name cell G7 **Total_Space**.
c. Name cell H7 **Total_Hours**.
d. Name cell C11 **Available_Space**.
e. Name cell C12 **Max_Boxes_Board_C**.
f. Name cell C13 **Available_Hours**.

5. Complete the following steps to define the problem using Solver:
   a. Click Tools and then click Solver.
   b. Key **Total_Profit** in the Set Target Cell box.
   c. Make sure Max is selected in the Equal To section.
   d. Key **$E$3:$E$5** in the By Changing Cells box.
   e. Next you must add the constraints. Click Add.
   f. The Add Constraint dialog box is displayed. The first constraint you are going to add is that the total space cannot exceed the space available.
      1) Key **Total_Space** in the Cell Reference box.
      2) Make sure the comparison operator <= is displayed in the middle box.
      3) Key **Available_Space** in the Constraint box.
      4) Click Add.

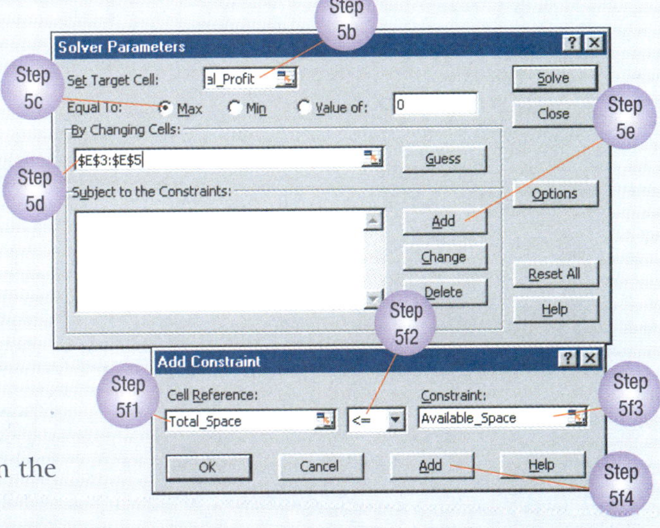

   g. The Add Constraint dialog box is ready for you to enter the second constraint. The second constraint you are going to add is that the maximum boxes produced of Board C can never exceed 250.
      1) Key **$E$5** in the Cell Reference box.
      2) Make sure the comparison operator <= is displayed in the middle box.
      3) Key **Max_Boxes_Board_C** in the Constraint box.
      4) Click Add.
   h. The Add Constraint dialog box is ready for you to enter the third constraint, which is that the total hours can never exceed the available hours.
      1) Key **Total_Hours** in the Cell Reference box.
      2) Make sure the comparison operator <= is displayed in the middle box.
      3) Key **Available_Hours** in the Constraint box.

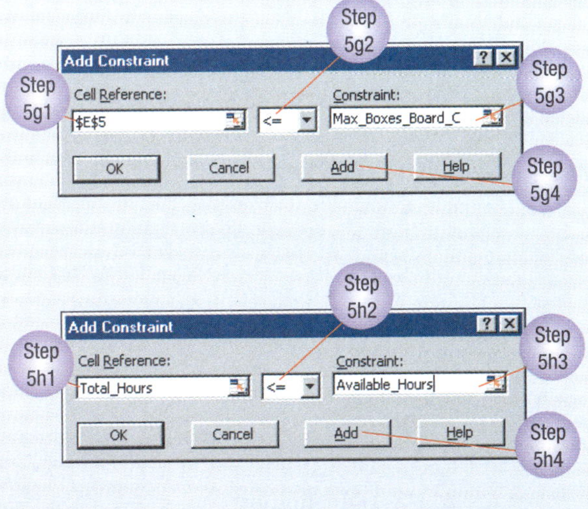

4) Click Add.

i. The Add Constraint dialog box is ready for you to enter the fourth constraint, which is that the number of boxes that are produced of each modem board cannot be a negative number.
   1) Key **$E$3:$E$5** in the Cell Reference box.
   2) Click the down-pointing arrow to the right of the middle box. Click >=.
   3) Key **0** in the Constraint box.
   4) Click Add.

j. The Add Constraint dialog box is ready for you to enter the last constraint, which is that the number of boxes that are produced of each modem board has to be a whole number (an integer).
   1) Key **$E$3:$E$5** in the Cell Reference box.
   2) Click the down-pointing arrow to the right of the middle box. Click *int.*
   3) Click OK.

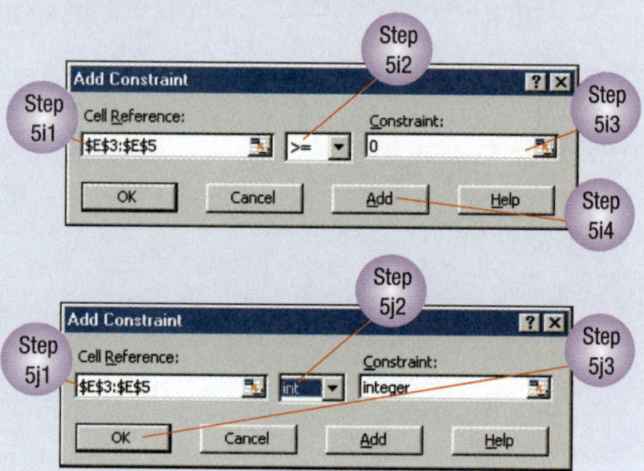

k. The Solver Parameters dialog box is displayed again. The problem has now been defined. Make sure the constraints you have entered are exactly like those on the screen to the right. If you need to edit a constraint, select the constraint to be edited and click Change. Click Solve.

l. The Solver Results dialog box is displayed. Make sure Keep Solver Solution is selected.

m. Click OK.

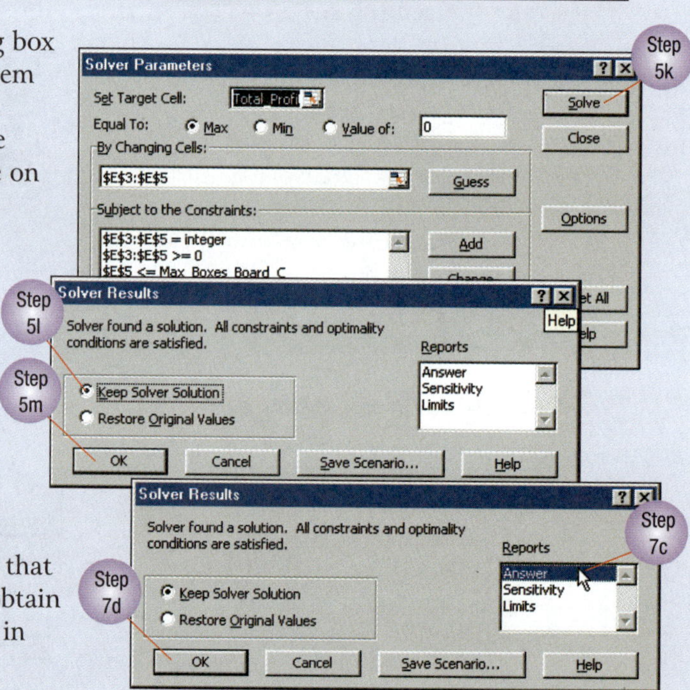

6. The solution is displayed in the worksheet. The number of boxes that should be produced in order to obtain the maximum profit is displayed in cells E3, E4, and E5. Print the Production Plan worksheet.
7. Complete the following steps to generate an Answer Report:
   a. Click Tools and then click Solver.
   b. Click Solve.
   c. Click *Answer* in the Reports list.
   d. Click OK.
   e. Click the Answer Report 1 worksheet tab.
   f. Create a custom header that displays your name at the left margin and the file name at the right margin.
   g. Print the Answer Report 1 worksheet.
8. Save the workbook with the same name (Excel E5, Ex 10) and close it.

Creating Scenarios

Goal Seek and Solver provide one specific answer to a specific question. There are times, however, when examining several different answers to a question would be useful. Scenario Manager allows you to set up several different scenarios. Then you can examine how each scenario affects the final outcome. A company trying to establish a budget for the upcoming year does not know, for example, what the sales for the year will be. The sales figures obviously affect the rest of the budget. With the Scenario Manager you can create a "best case" and a "worst case" scenario. The best case scenario would show what the budget figures would look like if sales for the year were especially good. The worst case scenario would show what the budget figures would look like if sales were especially poor.

To create a scenario, click Tools and then either wait for a few seconds or click the down arrow at the bottom of the menu and click Scenarios. The Scenario Manager dialog box is displayed. Click the Add button. The Add Scenario dialog box is displayed.

HINT

Since creating scenarios changes the original values in cells, you might want to first create a scenario that uses those original values before creating scenarios that will change them. That way you will always be able to go back to the original values.

exercise  CREATING SCENARIOS

1. Open Excel Worksheet E5-07.
2. Save the worksheet using the Save As command and name it Excel E5, Ex 11.
3. Create a custom header that displays your name at the left margin and the file name at the right margin.
4. Case 'N Crate, a company that manufactures wooden boxes and crates, is working on a budget for the upcoming year. Expenses for the year—rent, utilities, and general administrative—are known. What is not known is how much the company will earn in gross revenues and how much the company will spend on the cost of goods sold. Complete the following steps to name the cells with which you will be working:
   a. Name cell B5 **Revenue**.
   b. Name cell B6 **Goods**.
5. Complete the following steps to create a scenario that calculates an outcome for the worst case, which is a low gross revenue and a high cost of goods sold:
   a. Click Tools and then click Scenarios.
   b. The Scenario Manager dialog box is displayed. Click Add.
   c. The Add Scenario dialog box is displayed. Key **Worst Case** in the Scenario name box.
   d. Key **B5:B6** in the Changing cells box.
   e. Click OK.

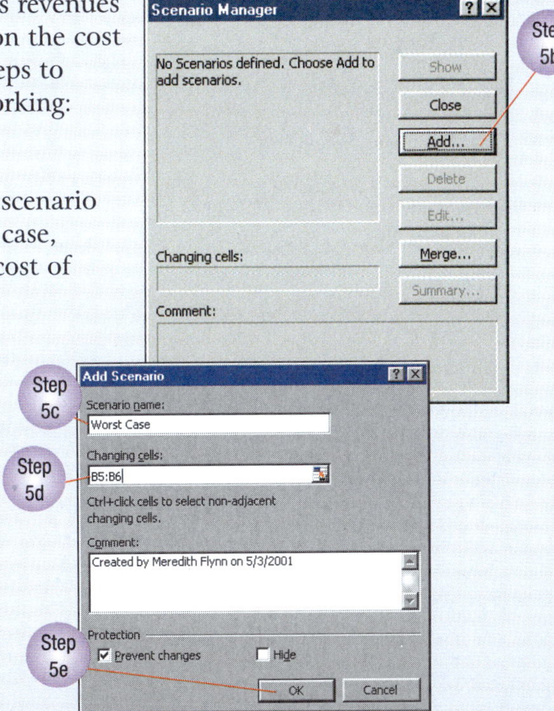

f. The Scenario Values dialog box is displayed. Key **2399128** in the Revenue box.

g. Key **1963610** in the Goods box.

h. Click Add.

6. The Add Scenario dialog box is displayed again. Complete the following steps to create a second scenario that calculates a probable case:
   a. Key **Probable Case** in the Scenario name box.
   b. Make sure B5:B6 is still entered in the Changing cells box.
   c. Click OK.
   d. The Scenario Values dialog box is displayed. Key **3427325** in the Revenue box.
   e. Key **1785100** in the Goods box.
   f. Click Add.
7. The Add Scenario dialog box is displayed again. Complete the following steps to create a third scenario that calculates the best case:
   a. Key **Best Case** in the Scenario name box.
   b. Make sure B5:B6 is still entered in the Changing cells box.
   c. Click OK.
   d. The Scenario Values dialog box is displayed. Key **4284156** in the Revenue box.
   e. Key **1428080** in the Goods box.
   f. Click OK.
8. The Scenario Manager dialog box is displayed again. Complete the following steps to show the worst case scenario:
   a. In the Scenarios list box, click *Worst Case*.
   b. Click Show.
   c. Click Close.
   d. Print the Projected Budget worksheet.
9. Complete the following steps to show the probable case scenario:
   a. Click Tools and then click Scenarios.
   b. In the Scenarios list box, click *Probable Case*.
   c. Click Show.
   d. Click Close.
   e. Print the Projected Budget worksheet.

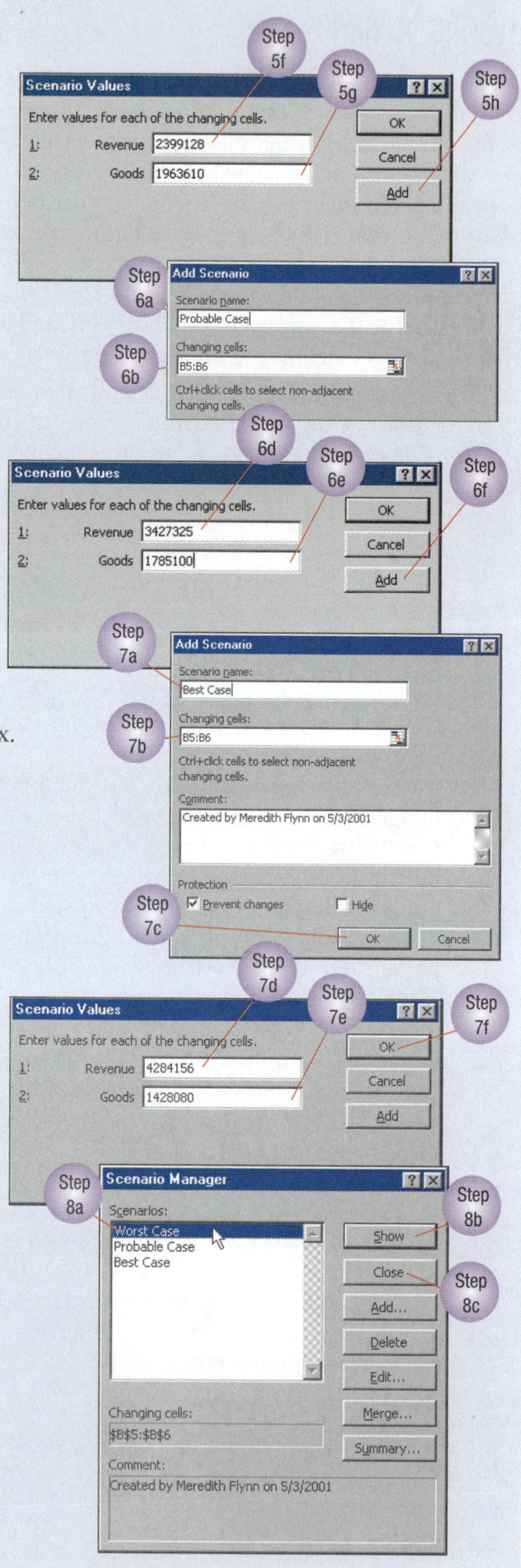

10. Complete the following steps to show the best case scenario:
    a. Click Tools and then click Scenarios.
    b. In the Scenarios list box, click *Best Case*.
    c. Click Show.
    d. Click Close.
    e. Print the Projected Budget worksheet.
11. Complete the following steps to create a scenario summary:
    a. Click Tools and then click Scenarios.
    b. Click Summary.
    c. The Scenario Summary dialog box appears. Make sure the Scenario summary option is selected.
    d. Make sure B15 is entered in the Result cells box.
    e. Click OK.
    f. The scenario summary is created on a new worksheet. Create a custom header for the Scenario Summary worksheet that prints your name at the left margin and the file name at the right margin.
    g. Print the Scenario Summary worksheet.
12. Save the workbook with the same name (Excel E5, Ex 11) and close it.

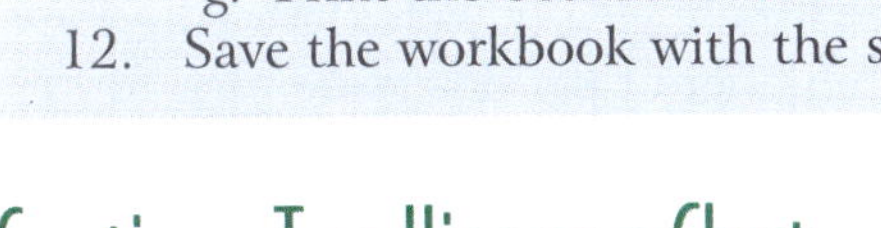

Creating a Trendline on a Chart

Another way you can analyze data in Excel is by using a trendline in a chart in order to make a forecast. A trendline graphically displays trends in data. Based on the given data, a trendline predicts what will happen in the future. A trendline allows you to forecast, for example, what the next five years' population growth will be, based on the past five years' population growth.

To add a trendline to a chart, you must first select the appropriate data series in the chart. Next, click the Chart menu and then click Add Trendline option from the Chart menu. The Add Trendline dialog box shown in figure 5.17 is displayed. This dialog box allows you to select the type of trendline you want. Table 5.1 explains the different types of trendlines. The Order box is used for entering the highest power for the independent variable. The Period box is used for entering the number of periods to be used to calculate the moving average. All the data series in the chart that support trendlines are listed in the Based on series box. To add a trendline to another series, click the name in the box and then select the options you want.

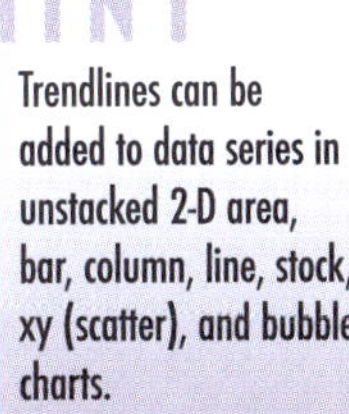

TABLE 5.1 *Types of Trendlines*

Type of Trendline	Description
Linear	A linear trendline is used with linear data sets to represent something that is increasing or decreasing at a steady rate.
Logarithmic	A logarithmic trendline is a curved line that is used to represent data that rises or falls quickly and then levels off.
Polynomial	A polynomial trendline is a curved line that is used to represent data that fluctuates. When Polynomial is selected, enter the highest power for the independent variable in the Order box.
Power	A power trendline is a curved line that is used to represent data that increases at a specific rate.
Exponential	An exponential trendline is a curved line that represents data values that rise or fall at increasingly higher rates.
Moving Average	A moving average trendline is used to smooth out fluctuations in data in order to show a trend more clearly. When Moving Average is selected, enter the number of periods to be used for calculating the moving average in the Period box.

FIGURE 5.17 *The Add Trendline Dialog Box with the Type Tab Selected*

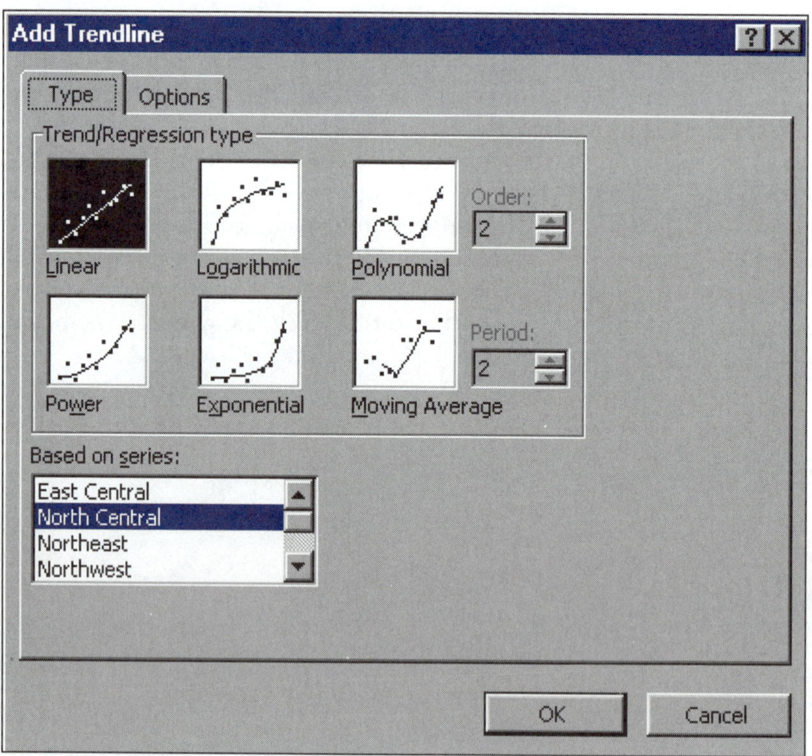

Clicking the Options tab displays the options available for a trendline, as shown in figure 5.18. You can either accept the name given to the trendline automatically or create your own custom name. In the Forecast section you can indicate how many periods you want the trendline to predict into the future or the past.

FIGURE 5.18 ***The Add Trendline Dialog Box With the Options Tab Selected***

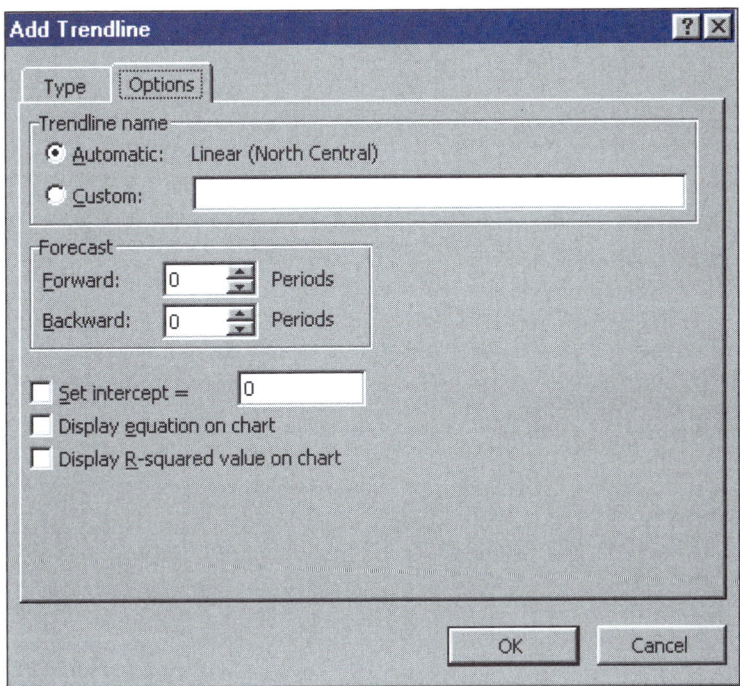

12 CREATING A TRENDLINE

1. Open Excel Worksheet E5-08.
2. Save the worksheet using the Save As command and name it Excel E5, Ex 12.
3. Create a custom header that displays your name at the left margin and the file name at the right margin.
4. This workbook contains sales figures by quarters. You want to create a PivotChart report using this data. Name the list Database.
5. First you need to create a PivotTable report to summarize the data.
   a. Click Data and then click PivotTable and PivotChart Report.
   b. When the PivotTable and PivotChart Wizard – Step 1 of 3 dialog box is displayed, click Next.
   c. The PivotTable and PivotChart Wizard – Step 2 of 3 dialog box is displayed. Database should already be entered in the range box. Click Next.
   d. The PivotTable and PivotChart Wizard – Step 3 of 3 dialog box is displayed. Click Layout.
   e. Drag the Last Name button to the PAGE area.
   f. Drag the Qtr button to the ROW area.

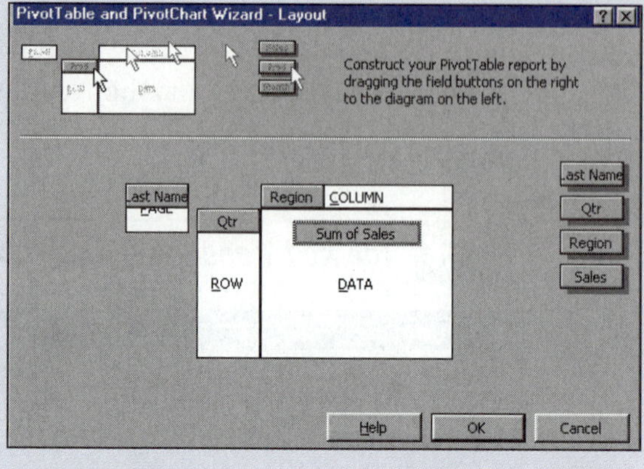

   g. Drag the Region button to the COLUMN area.
   h. Drag the Sales button to the DATA area. The dialog box should now look like the one to the right:
   i. Click OK.
   j. Click Finish.
6. Complete the following steps to remove the grand total from the report:
   a. Right-click in any cell in the PivotTable report.
   b. Click the Table Options on the shortcut menu.
   c. Click the check box next to Grand totals for columns and the check box next to Grand totals for rows so that they are not selected.
   d. Click OK.
7. Complete the following steps to create a PivotChart report:
   a. Click the Chart Wizard button on the PivotTable toolbar.
   b. Excel automatically creates a stacked column chart. Click the Chart Wizard button on the PivotTable toolbar.
   c. Under Chart type, click Line.
   d. Under Chart sub-type, click the first option in the second row.
   e. Click Next.
   f. Enter **Sales by Quarter** in the Chart title box.
   g. Enter **Quarter** in the Category (X) axis box.
   h. Enter Sales in the Value (Y) axis box.
   i. Click Next.
   j. Click Finish.
   k. Click the drop-down arrow to the right of the Chart Objects box on the Chart toolbar. Click the Value Axis option.
   l. Click the Format Axis button on the Chart toolbar.
   m. The Format Axis dialog box is displayed. Click the Number tab.
   n. Under Category, click Currency.
   o. Enter **0** in the Decimal places box.
   p. Press OK.
8. You are now ready to create a trendline. You want to forecast ahead North Central's sales for the next four quarters.
   a. Click the drop-down arrow to the right of the Region button. Click (Show All) and then click North Central. The North Central check box should be the only box that is selected. Click OK.
   b. Click anywhere on the line that is displayed. The North Central data series is now selected.
   c. Click Chart and then click Add Trendline.
   d. The Add Trendline dialog box is displayed. The Type tab should be

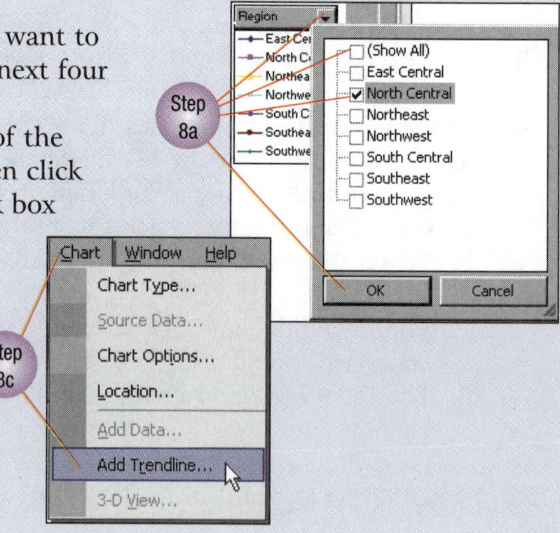

selected. The first option, Linear, should be selected. This is the option you want. Click the Options tab.

e. Under Trendline name, the Automatic option should be selected. The default for the Trendline name, Linear (North Central), is fine. Under Forecast, enter 4 in the Forward box.

f. Click OK.

g. The trendline that is displayed shows what North Central's sales will drop to in another year if they continue their current trend.

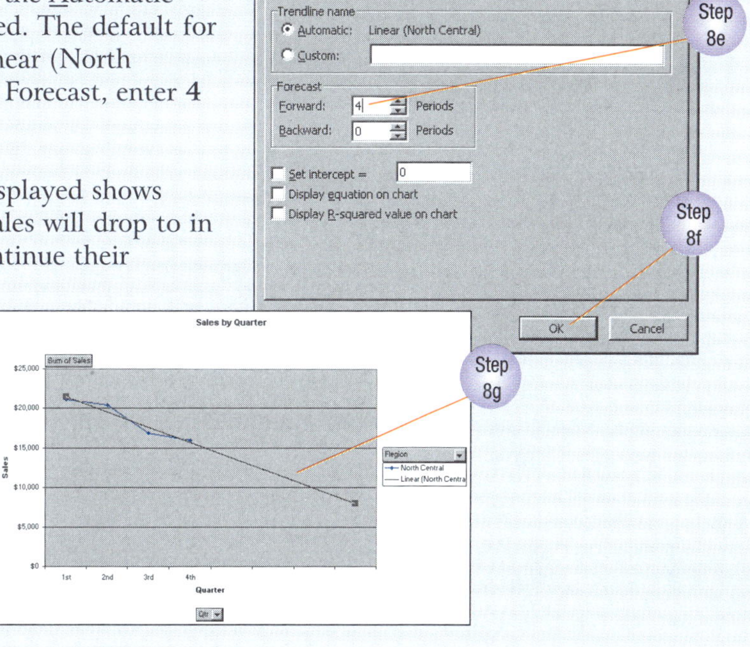

9. Enter a custom header that displays your name at the left margin and the name of the file at the right margin.
10. Print the PivotChart report.
11. Save the workbook with the same name (Excel E5, Ex 12) and close it.

CHAPTER summary

- A PivotTable is an interactive table that summarizes large amounts of data. The rows and columns of a PivotTable can be rotated so that you can see various summaries of the data. The source data is the data upon which a PivotTable report is based. Each field in a PivotTable report corresponds to a column in the source data. The PivotTable Wizard takes you through the steps of creating a PivotTable report.
- A PivotTable report contains fields and items. Fields correspond to columns in the source data. Items are unique values in a field. The fields from the source list containing the data that is summarized in the PivotTable report are the data fields. Data fields can be summarized in a PivotTable report using summary functions such as Sum, Count, or Average.
- Format an entire PivotTable report by clicking the Format Report button on the PivotTable toolbar.
- Items on a PivotTable report can be hidden or filtered. Items are hidden and displayed by clicking the Hide Detail button and Show Detail button on the PivotTable toolbar. Items are filtered by clicking the down-pointing arrow to the right of the field button on the PivotTable report and selecting the fields to be displayed. Hidden items are still a part of the report and are included in the totals. Filtered items are not a part of the report and are not included in the totals.
- The layout of a PivotTable report can be changed by clicking the PivotTable Wizard button on the PivotTable toolbar and then clicking the Layout button on the PivotTable and PivotChart Wizard – Step 3 of 3 dialog box. The PivotTable and PivotChart Wizard

– Layout dialog box containing the PivotTable diagram is displayed. Field buttons can be dragged on to and off the dialog box in order to rearrange the report.

- A PivotChart report is created from a PivotTable report. Row fields in a PivotTable report become category fields in a PivotChart report, and column fields in a PivotTable report become series fields in a PivotChart report. Changes made to the PivotTable report are reflected in the PivotChart report and vice versa.
- An interactive PivotTable that has been saved as a Web page and published to a public location such as a Web server is called a PivotTable list. Users can access a PivotTable list and interact with it in many of the same ways as PivotTable reports can be manipulated in Excel.
- The Goal Seek command calculates a specified result by changing the value of another cell until a formula dependent on that cell reaches the result specified.
- The Solver command calculates a specified result that is based on many changing variables. Solver is used to determine the "best" solution to a problem—that is, the solution that generates the most profit or utilizes resources in the most efficient way, for example. The variables that go into determining the solution can be subject to restrictions or constraints, such as an employee cannot work more than 40 hours a week. By analyzing the variables and their constraints, Solver finds the optimal solution.
- Several different answers, or scenarios, to a specific question can be set up using Excel's Scenario Manager. Each scenario can be examined to see how it affects the final outcome. For example, you can set up one scenario where sales are high and costs are low and a second scenario where sales are low and costs are high and then examine how the two scenarios affect profits.
- A trendline can be added to data series in a chart to display trends in data and to make predictions based on those trends. Trendlines in a chart can be extended beyond the actual data to predict future values based on the data in the selected data series.

COMMANDS review

Command	**Mouse/Keyboard**
Create a PivotTable	Click Data, PivotTable, and PivotChart Report
Sort the items in a field in a PivotTable report	Double-click a field button on the PivotTable and click Advanced
Remove subtotals from a PivotTable report	Double-click a field button on the PivotTable, click None
Remove grand totals from a PivotTable report	Right-click a cell in the PivotTable report, click Table Options
Create a PivotChart report	Click Data, PivotTable, and PivotChart Report
Use Goal Seek	Click Tools, Goal Seek
Use Solver	Click Tools, Solver
Create a Scenario	Click Tools, Scenarios
Create a trendline	Click Chart, Add Trendline

CONCEPTS check

Completion: On a blank sheet of paper, indicate the correct term, symbol, or command for each item.

1. This term refers to a report that is used to quickly summarize and analyze large amounts of data.
2. This term refers to the list upon which a PivotTable report is based.
3. If you name the list this term, Excel will automatically recognize it as the data upon which to base a PivotTable report.
4. To select all the cells belonging to a field in a PivotTable report, the mouse pointer must turn into this symbol when you move it to the top of the data field label in a column.
5. To sort the fields in a PivotTable report, double-click a field button on the PivotTable and click this button.
6. To remove grand totals from a PivotTable report, right-click a cell in the report and click this option from the shortcut menu.
7. To manage the layout of a PivotTable report using the PivotTable Wizard, click the PivotTable and PivotChart Wizard button on the PivotTable toolbar and click this button.
8. This term refers to what you must have in order to create a PivotChart report.
9. This term refers to Excel's analysis tool that calculates a specified result by changing the value of one cell.
10. This term refers to Excel's analysis tool that calculates a specified result by changing several variables.
11. This term refers to Excel's analysis tool that allows you to examine how several different projected plans will affect the final outcome.
12. List the two ways you can filter items on a PivotTable report.
13. List the steps for creating a PivotChart report from scratch and for creating a PivotChart report based on an existing PivotTable.
14. List the steps for saving a PivotTable report as a Web page.

SKILLS check

Assessment 1

1. Open Excel Worksheet E5-09.
2. Save the worksheet using the Save As command and name it Excel E5, SA 01.
3. Case 'N Crate is a company that manufactures wooden boxes, crates, and trays. They sell their products to businesses that use them for packaging fresh fruit and other specialty items. This worksheet keeps track of orders made the first quarter of the year. Name the list Database.

4. Create a PivotTable from the list. Place the PivotTable on a new worksheet. Rename the new worksheet PivotTable.
5. Create a custom header for the PivotTable worksheet with your name displayed at the left margin and the file name displayed at the right margin.
6. Drag the Region button to the Drop Page Fields Here area of the PivotTable diagram. Drag the Month and Sales Representative buttons to the Drop Row Fields Here area. Drag the Product button to the Drop Column Fields Here area. Drag the Total Order button to the Drop Data Items Here area.
7. Format the entire PivotTable report using the Table 8 format from the AutoFormat dialog box.
8. Format all the values for boxes, crates, trays, all the subtotals, and the grand totals as currency with no decimal places.
9. Automatically adjust the width of columns A through F so that each column is at its optimal width.
10. Filter the PivotTable report so that only the orders for the South region are displayed. Print the PivotTable worksheet.
11. Display all the orders. Filter the PivotTable report so that only the orders for March are displayed. Print the PivotTable worksheet.
12. Display all the months. Change the layout of the PivotTable report so that *Product* is displayed as a row field and *Month* is displayed as a column field. Make any necessary adjustments so that the PivotTable report prints on one page. Print the PivotTable worksheet.
13. Adjust the layout of the PivotTable so that both the month and product are displayed as column fields. Hide the detail for the *Month* field. Make sure all the values are formatted as currency with no decimal places. Adjust column width if necessary. Print the PivotTable worksheet.
14. Show the detail for the *Month* field.
15. Edit the layout of the PivotTable by removing the Sales Representative button from the ROW area. Move the *Month* field to the ROW area and the *Product* field to the COLUMN area.
16. Remove the grand totals for columns and the grand totals for rows.
17. Create a PivotChart report. The Chart type should be line and the Chart sub-type should be the first option in the second row.
18. You want to create a trendline. Select the crates data series and create a logarithmic trendline. Forecast ahead for three periods.
19. Print the chart.
20. Save the workbook with the same name (Excel E5, SA 01) and close it.

Assessment 2

1. Open Excel Worksheet E5-10.
2. Save the worksheet using the Save As command and name it Excel E5, SA 02.
3. Nichols Dairy Ice Cream is a company that makes and sells its own ice cream. This list keeps track of ice cream orders. Name the list Database.
4. Create a PivotTable from the list. Place the PivotTable on a new worksheet. Rename the new worksheet PivotTable.
5. Create a custom header for the PivotTable worksheet with your name displayed at the left margin and the file name displayed at the right margin.
6. Drag the Month button to the Drop Page Fields Here area of the PivotTable diagram. Drag the Flavor and Customer buttons to the Drop Row Fields Here area. Drag the Type button to the Drop Column Fields Here area. Drag the Amount button to the Drop Data Items Here area.

7. Format the entire PivotTable report using the Table 4 format from the AutoFormat dialog box.
8. Format the values in the PivotTable report as currency with two decimal places.
9. Display the top two customers according to the total amount of their orders.
10. Adjust the page setup so that rows 1 through 4 repeat at the top as a print title.
11. Print the PivotTable worksheet.
12. Display all the customers.
13. Filter the report by selecting only Low Fat from the Type drop-down list.
14. Remove the grand totals from the report.
15. Print the PivotTable report.
16. Remove the filter from the *Type* field and display the grand totals in the PivotTable report. Print the PivotTable worksheet.
17. Save the workbook with the same name (Excel E5, SA 02) and close it.

Assessment 3

1. Open Excel Worksheet E5-11.
2. Save the worksheet using the Save As command and name it Excel E5, SA 03.
3. Name the list Database.
4. Create a PivotChart using the PivotTable and PivotChart Wizard. Put the PivotTable that will be created on a new worksheet.
5. Drag the Paid button to the Drop Page Fields Here area of the PivotChart diagram. Drag the Vet button to the Drop Series Fields Here area. Drag the Service Rendered button to the Drop Category Fields Here area. Drag the Amount button to the Drop Data Items Here area.
6. Click the Chart Wizard button on the PivotTable toolbar. Select the first option in the first row under Chart sub-type.
7. The chart title should be **Income from Services Rendered**. The title for the Category (X) axis should be **Veterinarian**. The title for the Value (Y) axis should be **Dollars**.
8. Place the chart on a new sheet. Rename the Chart1 worksheet tab PivotChart.
9. Create a custom header for the PivotChart worksheet with your name displayed at the left margin and the name of the file displayed at the right margin.
10. Format the numbers on the value axis as currency with no decimal places.
11. Angle the text on the category axis counterclockwise.
12. Print the PivotChart.
13. Filter the PivotChart so that in the *Paid* field only the No records are displayed and in the *Veterinarian* field only Martin's records are displayed.
14. Click the Chart Wizard button on the PivotTable toolbar. Select the Pie option under Chart type. Select the second option in the second row under Chart sub-type.
15. The chart title should be **Dr. Martin's Unpaid Invoices**.
16. The Data labels should show the percent.
17. Place the chart on a new sheet named PivotChart.
18. Print the PivotChart.
19. Save the workbook with the same name (Excel E5, SA 03) and close it.

Assessment 4

1. Open Excel Worksheet E5-12.
2. Save the worksheet using the Save As command and name it Excel E5, SA 04.
3. If necessary, click the PivotTable worksheet tab.
4. Save the PivotTable as a Web page. Use the same file name (Excel E5, SA 04).

Click the Publish button. Click *PivotTable* from the list under the Choose box. The items you want to publish are the Items on PivotTable. Click the Add interactivity with check box and choose PivotTable functionality from the drop-down list. Make sure the Open published web page in browser check box is selected and then click Publish. In the File name box change the file name to A:\Nichols.htm. Click Publish.

5. You do not want to see the Sum of Amount figures. Drag one of the Sum of Amount field buttons off the PivotTable.
6. Display the figures for the Second Street Market only. Print the PivotTable.
7. Display all the stores.
8. Display the detail for Triple Mocha Madness ice cream by clicking the plus sign next to it. Print the PivotTable.
9. Collapse the detail for Triple Mocha Madness by clicking the minus sign.
10. Put the Sum of Amount button back on the PivotTable as a data item. Print the PivotTable.
11. Close Microsoft Internet Explorer.
12. Save the workbook with the same name (Excel E5, SA 04) and close it.

Assessment 5

1. Open Excel Worksheet E5-13.
2. Save the worksheet using the Save As command and name it Excel E5, SA 05.
3. Create a custom header for the Salary and Commissions worksheet with your name displayed at the left margin and the file name displayed at the right margin.
4. Using Goal Seek, find the total amount Michael Malone's sales would have to increase in order for him to earn a total income of $2,500. Enter that value into the worksheet.
5. Using Goal Seek, find what percentage commission Robert McBride would have to earn in order for his total income to be $3,500. Enter that value into the worksheet.
6. Using Goal Seek, find what Charles Levinson's salary would have to be in order for his total income to be $3,200.
7. Print the Salary and Commissions worksheet.
8. Save the workbook with the same name (Excel E5, SA 05) and close it.

Assessment 6

1. Open Excel Worksheet E5-14.
2. Save the worksheet using the Save As command and name it Excel E5, SA 06.
3. Create a custom header for the worksheet with your name displayed at the left margin and the file name displayed at the right margin.
4. The production manager at Case 'N Crate has to figure out how many gross each of boxes and crates to produce in order to generate the most profit. Look over the worksheet carefully. The worksheet shows how many hours it takes to build and varnish a gross of boxes and a gross of crates. Because of the number of employees available, there is a limit on how many hours a week can be devoted to building and varnishing the boxes and crates.
5. Define the problem using Solver. The target cell is cell E8 and you are trying to find the maximum profit. The cells that can be changed are the number of gross of each to produce (B9 and C9). Add the two constraints. The resources used for carpentry cannot exceed 240 hours. The resources used for varnishing cannot exceed 100 hours.
6. Keep the Solver solution. Print the worksheet.
7. Save the workbook with the same name (Excel E5, SA 06) and close it.

Assessment 7

1. Open Excel Worksheet E5-15.
2. Save the worksheet using the Save As command and name it Excel E5, SA 07.
3. Create a custom header for the Bad Debts worksheet with your name displayed at the left margin and the file name displayed at the right margin.
4. This worksheet is going to be used to project three scenarios. The veterinarians want to know how much money they are going to lose on uncollected accounts and how much this will affect the overall revenue of the company. The total bad debt is a percentage of the total uncollected accounts. Click cell B8. Key **=(B7*B6)+B5**.
5. The anticipated revenue is the gross revenue minus the total bad debt. Click cell B11. Key **=B10-B8**.
6. Name cell B6 *Uncollected*. Name cell B7 *BD_Allowance*.
7. Create a scenario named Worst Case. The changing cells should be B6 and B7. Enter **15500** as the uncollected amount. Enter **.3** as the bad debt allowance.
8. Create a scenario named Probable Case. The changing cells should be B6 and B7. Enter **8500** as the uncollected amount. Enter **.2** as the bad debt allowance.
9. Create a scenario named Best Case. The changing cells should be B6 and B7. Enter **3200** as the uncollected amount. Enter **.1** as the bad debt allowance.
10. Show the Worst Case scenario. Print the Bad Debts worksheet.
11. Show the Probable Case scenario. Print the Bad Debts worksheet.
12. Show the Best Case scenario. Print the Bad Debts worksheet.
13. Save the workbook with the same name (Excel E5, SA 07) and close it.

CHAPTER 6

MANAGING AND AUDITING WORKSHEETS

PERFORMANCE OBJECTIVES

Upon successful completion of chapter 6, you will be able to:

- **Record a macro**
- **Run a macro**
- **Edit a macro using the Microsoft Visual Basic editor**
- **Assign a macro to a command button**
- **Hide and display toolbars**
- **Create a custom toolbar**
- **Create a custom menu**
- **Use the Auditing toolbar**
- **Trace precedents**
- **Trace dependents**
- **Trace errors**
- **Locate and resolve errors in formulas**
- **Identify dependencies in formulas**

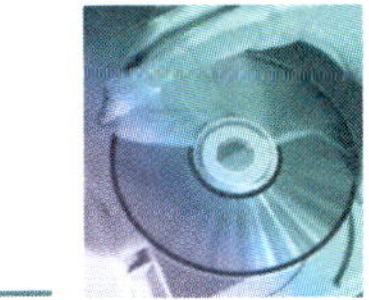

Excel Chapter 06E

Excel includes a number of features that help you manage worksheets. Macros are useful for automating many tasks typically performed on a worksheet. They can save you time by automatically performing tasks that you do repeatedly, or tasks that involve the same sequence of steps. When you assign a macro to a command button, the macro is placed right on the worksheet to give you quick and easy access to it. You can also manage your worksheets by creating custom menus and by creating custom toolbars containing buttons for the commands you routinely use or the macros you have created. Making sure your worksheet is functioning properly is also a part of worksheet management. The auditing features that come with Excel help you trace the cells to which a formula refers and help you trace formulas that refer to a specific cell. If there is an error in the worksheet, Excel's auditing feature will track down the source of the error. The purpose of this chapter is to introduce you to these features in Excel so that you can successfully manage and audit your worksheets.

Introduction to Macros

Macros are used to increase productivity by automating tasks that perform the same sequence of steps or by automating tasks that are performed repeatedly. Instead of performing this same sequence of steps over and over every time you need to perform the task, you can record the steps in a macro. Then, by pressing a key or two, the macro automatically performs the task for you. Once a macro has been created, it can be executed in a number of ways. A macro can be executed by selecting a menu item or by pressing a particular key combination. You can also assign the macro to a toolbar button or to a graphic object on a worksheet.

HINT

The macro recorder does not record any uncompleted tasks. For example, if you open a dialog box, make some changes, and then click Cancel, then the macro recorder will record none of those actions.

Excel's macro recorder makes it easy to record a macro. The macro recorder works much like a tape recorder in that once it is turned on, it records every keystroke and mouse click you make until it is turned off. Macros can be used for very simple tasks such as formatting a worksheet and printing reports. They can also be used for very complex tasks such as automating entire worksheets so that all the user has to do is retrieve the worksheet file and follow the on-screen instructions. Planning each step the macro is to perform before actually recording the macro is very important, as the macro recorder will record every step you perform, including the steps you take to correct any mistakes you make. In order for the macro to run as efficiently as possible, any unnecessary keystrokes, such as those taken to fix a mistake, should not be a part of the macro.

Recording a Macro

Macros recorded in Excel are created automatically in the Visual Basic for Applications programming language, also known as VBA. Excel's Visual Basic toolbar can be quite useful when you are recording a macro. To display the Visual Basic toolbar shown in figure 6.1, right-click a toolbar that is currently displayed and then click Visual Basic.

FIGURE 6.1 *The Visual Basic Toolbar*

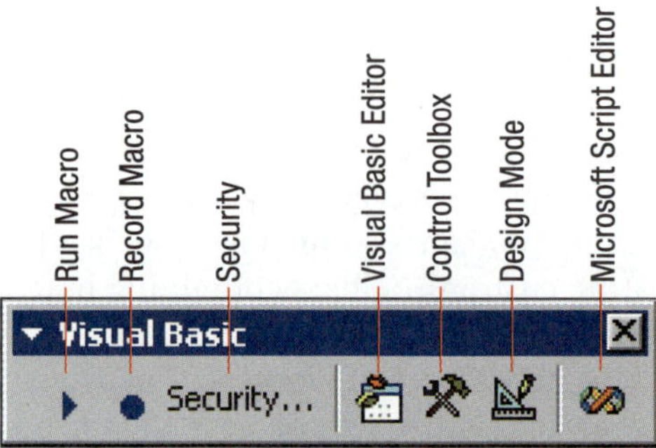

You can display the Record Macro dialog box shown in figure 6.2 by clicking the Record Macro button on the Visual Basic toolbar. You can also display this dialog box using the menus by clicking Tools and then either waiting a couple of seconds or by clicking the down arrow at the bottom of the menu to display the Macro option. Select Macro and then click Record new Macro. A macro name that describes the purpose of the macro is entered in the Macro name box. The first letter of the macro name must be a letter. The other characters in the name can be numbers, letters, or the underscore character. A macro name cannot contain any spaces. A letter that will be pressed together with the Ctrl key to run the macro is entered in the Shortcut key box next to Ctrl. You can use lowercase or uppercase letters. You must use the same case when executing the macro. That is, if you enter a capital *T* in the Shortcut key box, pressing Ctrl and a lowercase *t* will not execute the macro. You can also select where the macro is to be stored. Figure 6.2 shows the drop-down menu that is displayed when the down arrow to the right of the Store macro in box is clicked. If *Personal Macro Workbook* is selected, the macro will be available whenever you use Excel. If either the *New Workbook* or *This Workbook* options are selected, the macro will be available to that workbook only. A description of the macro can be entered in the Description box. When you have finished filling out the dialog box, click OK.

FIGURE 6.2 **The Record Macro Dialog Box (left); The Store Macro in Drop-Down Menu (right)**

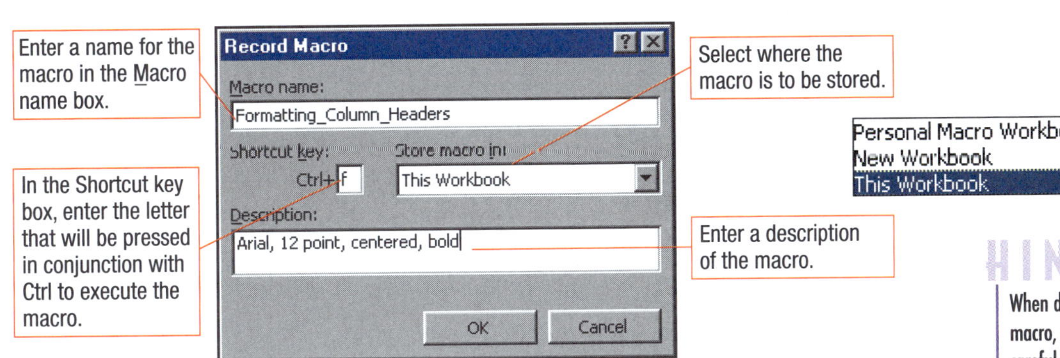

Once you click OK, the Stop Recording toolbar shown in figure 6.3 is displayed. There are two buttons on the toolbar. If part of your macro includes selecting cells, Excel will always select the same cells that were selected when the macro was created because the macro records absolute cell references. If the macro is to select cells no matter where the active cell is located when the macro is run, click the Relative Reference button. Relative references will be recorded until you either click the Stop button or click the Relative Reference button to turn the feature off. When you have finished entering the macro, click the Stop Recording button, which will stop the recording of the macro.

HINT

When designing a macro, you need to be careful about where the cell pointer is located when the macro starts. If the first step in the macro is to select a specific cell, then the macro starts executing in that cell. If the first step in the macro is *not* selecting a specific cell, then the macro is going to start executing in whatever cell happens to be selected when the macro was invoked. If that cell contains data, the data is going to be overwritten by any input that is part of the macro.

FIGURE 6.3 *The Stop Recording Toolbar*

HINT

You should always save your workbook before running a macro. If the macro does not execute exactly as you expected, it could cause serious problems for your workbook. If the macro does cause problems, you can close the workbook without saving it and go back to the version you saved right before running the macro.

Running a Macro

There are several ways to run a macro. One way is to click Tools, select Macro once it is displayed, and then click Macros. The Macro dialog box shown in figure 6.4 is displayed. You can also display this dialog box by clicking the Run Macro button on the Visual Basic toolbar. Select the name of the macro you want to run from the list box and then click Run. The macro you selected is run. If you need to delete a macro, select the name of the macro you want to delete from the list box and then click Delete. Clicking Options displays the Macro Options dialog box, shown in figure 6.5, where you can change the letter assigned to the Shortcut key command and the description.

FIGURE 6.4 *The Macro Dialog Box*

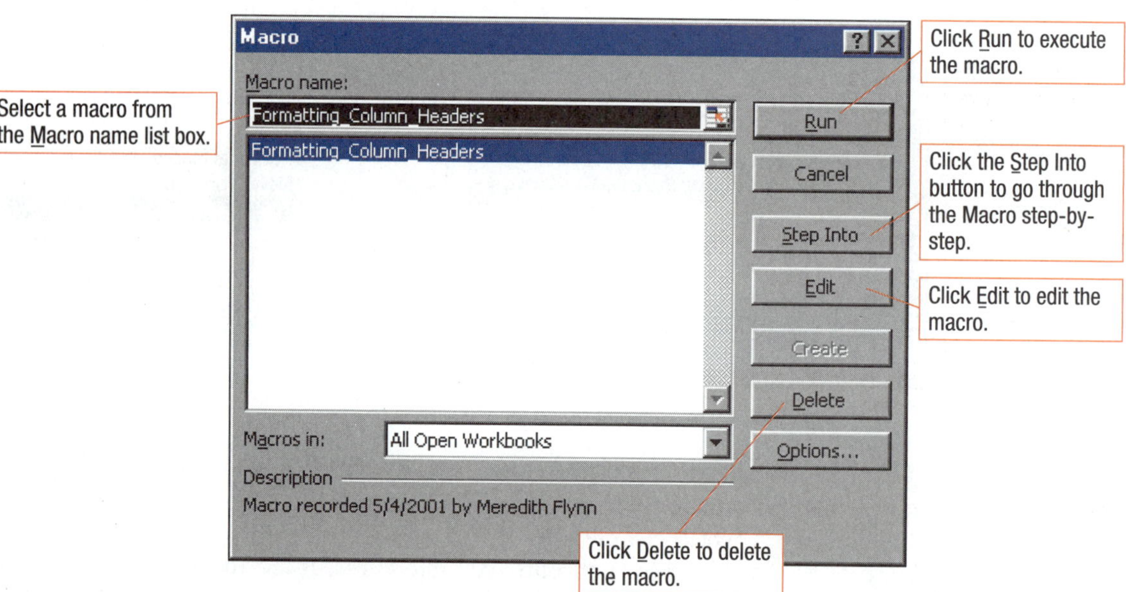

FIGURE

6.5 *The Macro Options Dialog Box*

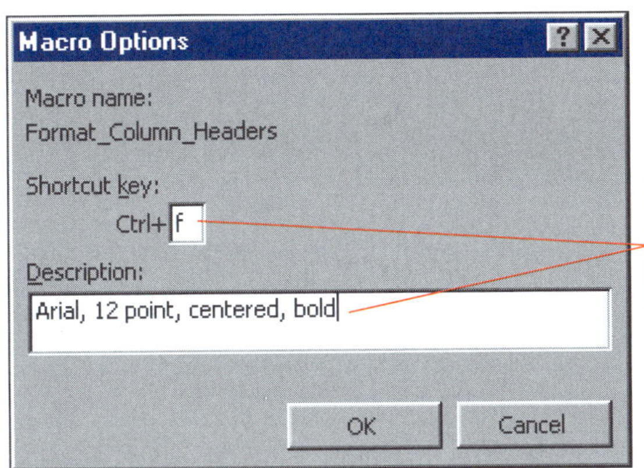

If a keyboard shortcut key has been assigned to the macro either in the Record Macro dialog box when the macro was first recorded or in the Macro Options dialog box after the macro was recorded, the macro can be run by simply pressing the keyboard shortcut key. For example, pressing Ctrl + F might run a macro that formats column headers.

exercise 1 — CREATING AND RUNNING A MACRO

1. Open Excel.
2. Open Excel Worksheet E6-01.
3. Save the worksheet using the Save As command and name it Excel E6, Ex 01.
4. Create a custom header that displays your name at the left margin and the file name at the right margin.
5. Chris Robinson is a freelance PC technician. His company is called Bits Unlimited, and he specializes in offering his PC consulting services to doctors' offices. This worksheet has been created to project his earnings for next year. You are going to create a macro that takes a figure from a cell in the current year and increases it by 5%. Complete the following steps to create the macro:
   a. Click cell H5.
   b. Click View, point to Toolbars, and then click Visual Basic. The Visual Basic toolbar is displayed.
   c. Click the Record Macro button. The Record Macro dialog box is displayed.
   d. Key **Increase** in the Macro name box.
   e. You want to create a shortcut key. Press the Shift key and enter **I** in the Shortcut key box. Notice that it now says "Ctrl+Shift+I" for the shortcut key. Pressing the Ctrl, Shift, and I keys together will execute the macro.
   f. Click OK. The Stop Recording toolbar is displayed.

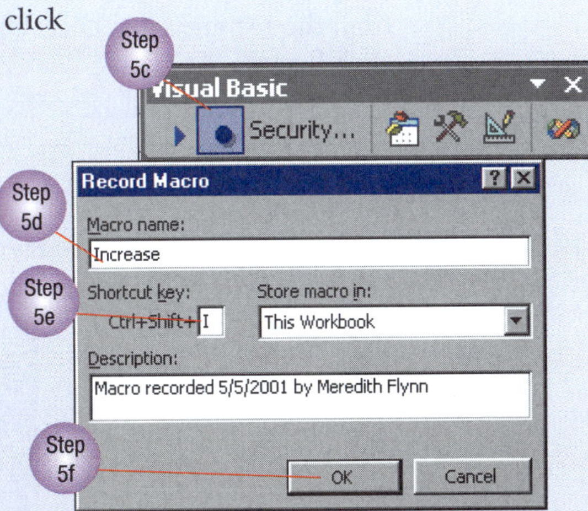

g. Key **=B5*1.05** in the formula bar.
h. Click the Enter button next to the formula bar.
i. Click the Stop Recording button on the Stop Recording toolbar.

6. The macro is created. Complete the following steps to execute the macro:
   a. Click cell H6.
   b. Press Ctrl+Shift+I. The correct formula is automatically entered in cell H6.
   c. Click cell I5.
   d. Click the Run Macro button on the Visual Basic toolbar. The Macro dialog box is displayed.
   e. Make sure the *Increase* macro is selected.
   f. Click Run. The correct formula is automatically entered in cell I5.

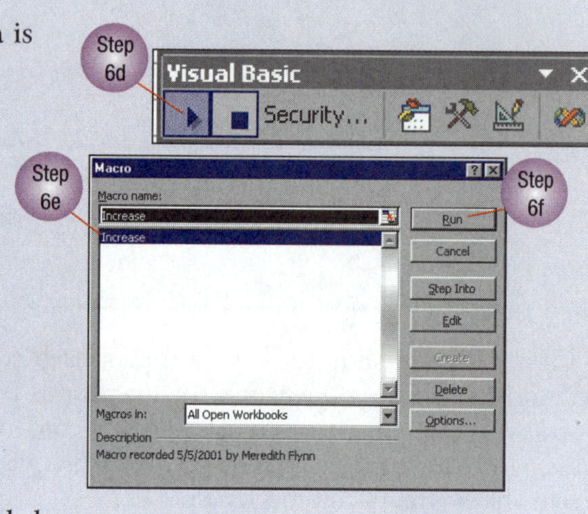

7. Change the orientation of the page to landscape. Print the worksheet.
8. Save the worksheet with the same name (Excel E6, Ex 01). You will use this worksheet in the next exercise. Print the worksheet.
9. Close the worksheet.

Assigning a Macro to a Command Button

You can run an existing macro from a command button placed on the worksheet. To assign a macro to a command button, display the Forms toolbar shown in figure 6.6 and then click the Button button. The mouse pointer turns into a crosshair, and you can drag the control to the size you want. The default name of the button is Button 1, Button 2, and so on. To change the name of the button, select the default name and then key in a new one. To change the format of the button, such as the size of the button or the font and font color used on the button, right-click the button and then click Format Control on the shortcut menu. To assign a macro to the button, right-click the button and then click Assign Macro. The Assign Macro dialog box shown in figure 6.7 is displayed. To assign the button to a macro that has already been created, select the macro name from the list and then click OK. To record a macro to be assigned to the button, click Record.

FIGURE 6.6 ***The Forms Toolbar***

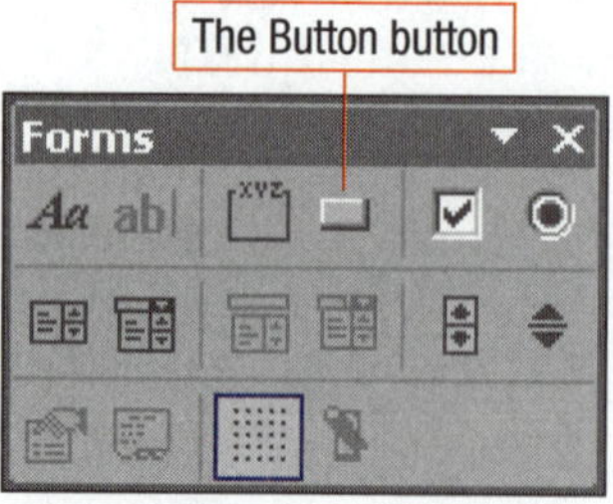

FIGURE 6.7 *The Assign Macro Dialog Box*

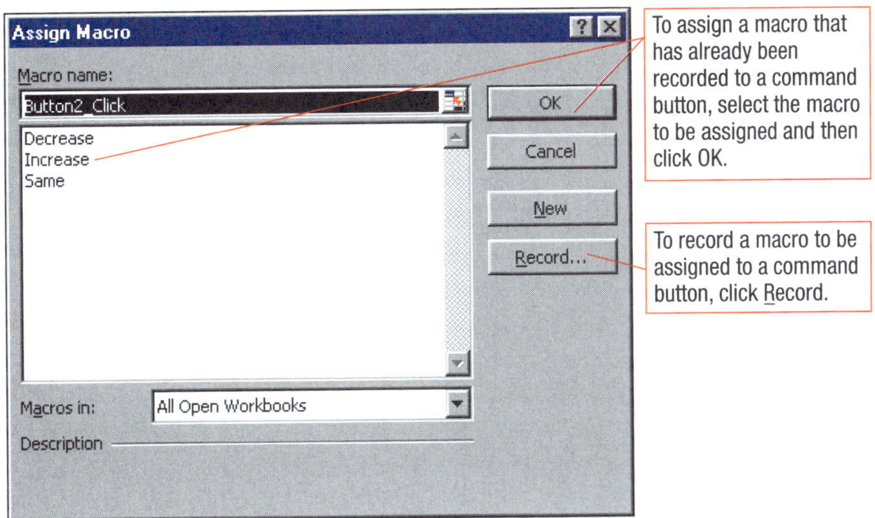

Editing a Macro

To edit a macro, first click the Run Macro button on the Visual Basic toolbar. When the Macro dialog box appears, select the macro to be edited and then click Edit, as shown in figure 6.8. The Visual Basic editor appears as a new application. Macros are edited using the Visual Basic editor.

HINT

In order to do much in the way of editing macros, you need to be familiar with the Visual Basic Editor.

FIGURE 6.8 *Editing a Macro*

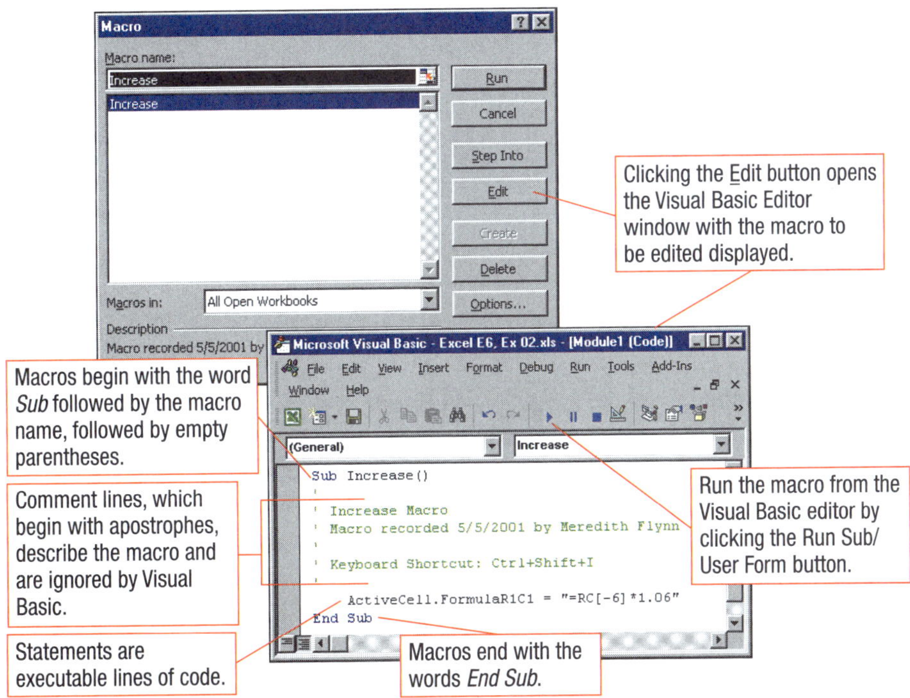

As you can see in figure 6.8, macros begin with the word *Sub,* followed by the macro name, followed by empty parentheses. The next few lines, which begin with apostrophes, are the comment lines. Comment lines describe the macro and are ignored by Visual Basic. After the comment lines is the macro. The executable lines of code in the macro are called statements. In the example in figure 6.8, the statement is made up of two parts that are separated by a period. Everything to the left of the period is the object. The object identifies the part of Excel that is to be affected. In figure 6.8, *ActiveCell* is the object. That is, the currently active cell is the cell that is going to be affected. Everything to the right of the period indicates how the object is to be affected. Edit the statements however necessary. You can run the edited macro right from the Visual Basic editor by clicking the Run Sub/User Form button.

exercise 2

EDITING A MACRO AND ASSIGNING A MACRO TO A COMMAND BUTTON

1. Open worksheet Excel E6, Ex 01. You created this worksheet in exercise 1.
2. Save the worksheet using the Save As command and name it Excel E6, Ex 02.
3. Create a custom header that displays your name at the left margin and the file name at the right margin.
4. Click cell H6. Instead of having a macro that increases the income by 5%, you want it to increase the income by 6%. Complete the following steps to edit and execute the macro:
   a. If necessary, display the Visual Basic toolbar.
   b. Click the Run Macro button on the Visual Basic toolbar.
   c. Make sure the *Increase* macro is selected.
   d. Click Edit.
   e. The Visual Basic editor appears as a new application. Resize the Microsoft Visual Basic window to make it smaller so that you can see the worksheet behind it.
   f. There is one statement line, *ActiveCell.FormulaR1C1 = "=RC[-6]*1.05"*. Edit this line so that the formula is *1.06 instead of *1.05.
   g. Click the Run Sub/User Form button.
   h. Close the Microsoft Visual Basic window.
   i. Click cell I5.
   j. Click the Run Macro button on the Visual Basic toolbar.
   k. The Macro dialog box appears with the macro name *Increase* selected. Click Run.
   l. Click cell H5.
   m. Press Ctrl+Shift+I.

Step 4b

Visual Basic

Security...

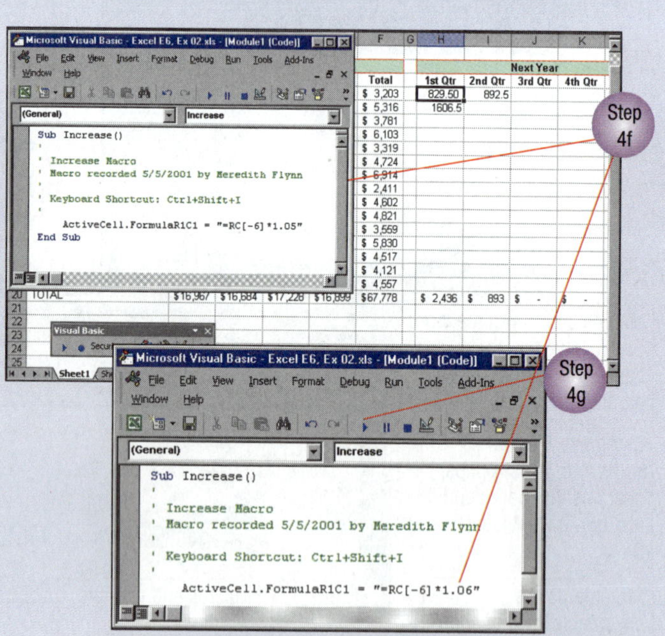

5. Complete the following steps to create and execute two more macros:
   a. Click cell J5.
   b. Click the Record Macro button on the Visual Basic toolbar. The Record Macro dialog box is displayed.
   c. Key **Same** in the Macro name box.
   d. You want to create a shortcut key. Click the Shortcut key box to select it. Press the Shift key and enter **S**. Notice that it now says *Ctrl+Shift+S* for the shortcut key. Pressing the Ctrl, Shift, and S keys together will execute the macro.
   e. Click OK. The Stop Recording toolbar is displayed.
   f. Key **=D5**.
   g. Click the Enter button next to the formula bar.
   h. Click the Stop Recording button on the Stop Recording toolbar.
   i. Click cell J6.
   j. Press Ctrl+Shift+S.
   k. Click cell I6.
   l. Click the Record Macro button. The Record Macro dialog box is displayed.
   m. Key **Decrease** in the Macro name box.
   n. You want to create a shortcut key. Click the Shortcut key box. Press the Shift key and enter **D**.
   o. Click OK. The Stop Recording toolbar is displayed.
   p. Key **=C6-(C6*.04)**.
   q. Click the Enter button next to the formula bar.
   r. Click the Stop Recording button on the Stop Recording toolbar.
   s. Click cell K5.
   t. Press Ctrl+Shift+D.
6. Next you want to assign the Increase macro to a command button. Complete the following steps to assign the macro to a command button:
   a. Click View, point to Toolbars, and then click Forms. The Forms toolbar is displayed.
   b. Click the Button button.
   c. The mouse pointer changes to crosshairs. Underneath and a little to the left of the INCOME FORECAST header, click and drag a rectangle that is approximately 0.25 inches high and 0.75 inches wide. You will set the exact size in a later step.

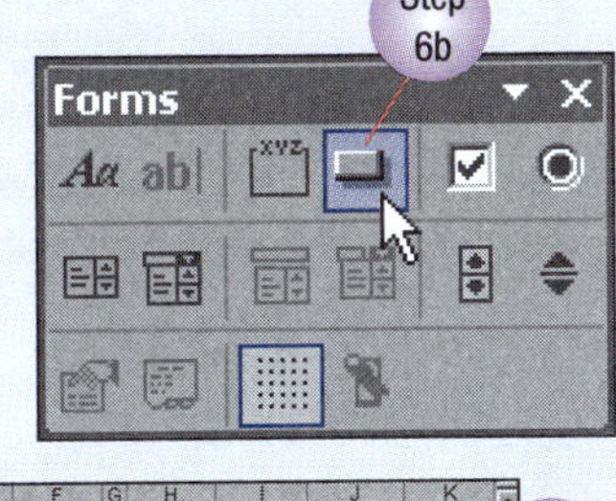

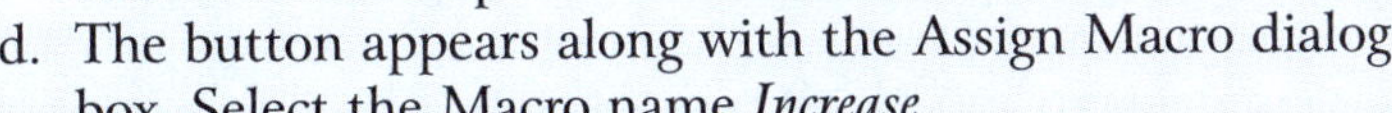

   d. The button appears along with the Assign Macro dialog box. Select the Macro name *Increase*.

   e. Click OK.
   f. Drag across the text currently on the button to select it and then key **Increase**.
   g. Right-click one of the button's edges and click Format Control on the shortcut menu. The Format Control dialog box is displayed.
   h. If necessary, click the Font tab.

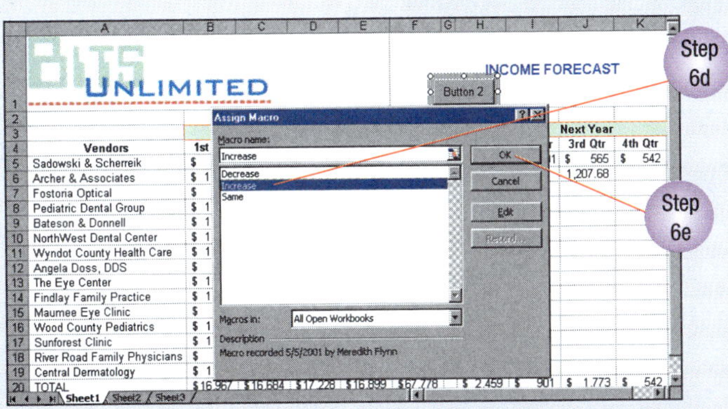

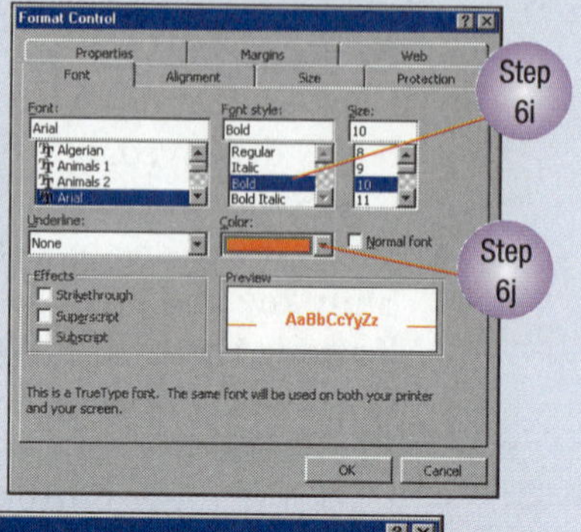

i. Click *Bold* from the Font style list box.

j. Click the down-pointing arrow to the right of the Color box and then click the red button, the first button in the third row.

k. Click the Size tab. Enter **0.25″** in the Height box.

l. Enter **0.75″** in the Width box.

m. Click OK.

7. Complete the following steps to assign the Same macro to a command button:

   a. The Forms toolbar should still be displayed. Click the Button button.

   b. The mouse pointer changes to crosshairs. To the right of the Increase button, click and drag a rectangle that is approximately 0.25 inches high and 0.75 inches wide.

   c. The button appears along with the Assign Macro dialog box. Select the Macro name *Same*.

   d. Click OK.

   e. Drag across the text currently on the button to select it and then key **Same**.

   f. Right-click one of the button's edges and then click Format Control on the shortcut menu. The Format Control dialog box is displayed.

   g. Click the Font tab.

   h. Click Bold from the Font style list box.

   i. Click the down arrow to the right of the Color box and then click the red button, the first button in the third row.

   j. Click the Size tab. Enter **0.25″** in the Height box; enter **0.75″** in the Width box.

   k. Click OK.

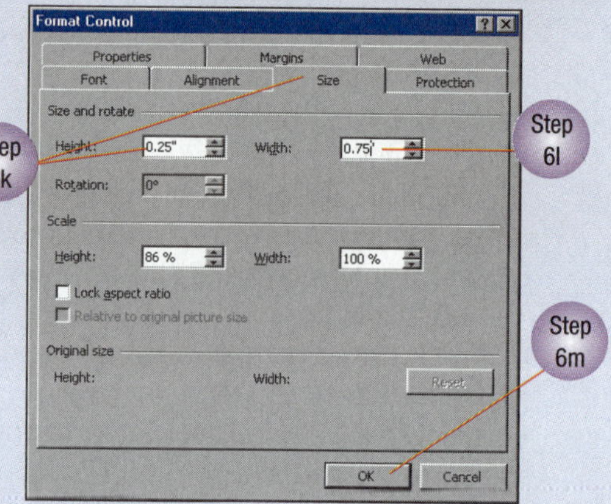

8. Complete the following steps to assign the Decrease macro to a command button:

   a. Click the Button button.

   b. The mouse pointer changes to crosshairs. To the right of the Same button, click and drag a rectangle that is approximately 0.25 inches high and 0.75 inches wide.

   c. The button appears along with the Assign Macro dialog box. Select the Macro name *Decrease*.

   d. Click OK.

   e. Drag across the text currently on the button to select it and then key **Decrease**.

   f. Right-click one of the button's edges and click Format Control on the shortcut menu. The Format Control dialog box is displayed.

   g. Click the Font tab.

   h. Click Bold from the Font style list box.

   i. Click the down arrow to the right of the Color box and then click the red button, the first button in the third row.

   j. Click the Size button. Enter **0.25″** in the Height box; enter **0.75″** in the Width box.

   k. Click OK.

   l. Close the Forms toolbar.

9. Complete the following steps to enter Macros from the command buttons:
   a. Click cell K6.
   b. Click the Decrease button.
   c. Click cell H7.
   d. Click the Same button.
10. To finish filling in the forecast, click the listed command button for each cell in the following list:

Cell	Command Button	Cell	Command Button
H8	Increase	J7	Same
H9	Increase	J8	Same
H10	Same	J9	Increase
H11	Increase	J10	Same
H12	Increase	J11	Increase
H13	Same	J12	Increase
H14	Increase	J13	Decrease
H15	Decrease	J14	Increase
H16	Decrease	J15	Same
H17	Decrease	J16	Increase
H18	Decrease	J17	Increase
H19	Decrease	J18	Increase
I7	Increase	J19	Same
I8	Decrease	K7	Increase
I9	Increase	K8	Decrease
I10	Decrease	K9	Increase
I11	Increase	K10	Same
I12	Increase	K11	Increase
I13	Increase	K12	Increase
I14	Same	K13	Same
I15	Decrease	K14	Increase
I16	Increase	K15	Increase
I17	Same	K16	Same
I18	Same	K17	Increase
I19	Decrease	K18	Increase
		K19	Same

11. Create another macro that uses conditional formatting to display the cells in the Total column that have values under $4,000 as red and those that have values over $6,000 as blue. Complete the following steps to create and execute the macro:
   a. Click cell F5.
   b. Click the Record Macro button on the Visual Basic toolbar.
   c. Key **Format** in the Macro name box.
   d. Click the Shortcut key box. Press the Shift key and then enter **F**.
   e. Click OK. The Stop Recording toolbar is displayed.
   f. You are going to select some cells for the macro, but you want their reference to be relative. Click the Relative Reference button on the Stop Recording toolbar. The button should be outlined.
   g. Select cells F5 through F19.
   h. Click Format and then click Conditional Formatting. The Conditional Formatting dialog box appears.

i. Add a condition that displays any value less than 4000 as bold and in the color red.
j. Add a second condition that displays any value greater than 6000 as bold and in the color blue.
k. Click OK.
l. Click the Stop Recording button on the Stop Recording toolbar.
m. Click cell L5.
n. Press Ctrl+Shift+F.

12. Close the Visual Basic toolbar.
13. Print the worksheet.
14. Save the worksheet using the same name (Excel E6, Ex 02). Close the worksheet.

Working with Toolbars and Menus

The toolbars and menus used in Office 2000 are quite flexible and adaptable. Toolbars can be docked or floating. They can be hidden or displayed. They can be reshaped. You can even make your own customized toolbar by adding and removing buttons and menus.

Floating and Docked Toolbars

Figure 6.9 shows examples of both docked and floating toolbars. A docked toolbar is attached to one of the program window's borders. A docked toolbar can be attached below the program title bar or to the left, right, or bottom border of the program window. A floating toolbar is not attached to the edge of the programming window. Toolbars can be moved to any location on the screen. To move a toolbar that is docked, drag the move handle located at the left side of the docked toolbar. To move a floating toolbar, drag the toolbar's title bar. When a toolbar is dragged to the border of the programming window or close to the edge of another docked toolbar, it becomes a docked toolbar. To undock a toolbar, drag the Move handle at that toolbar's left side.

FIGURE

6.9 ***Docked and Floating Toolbars***

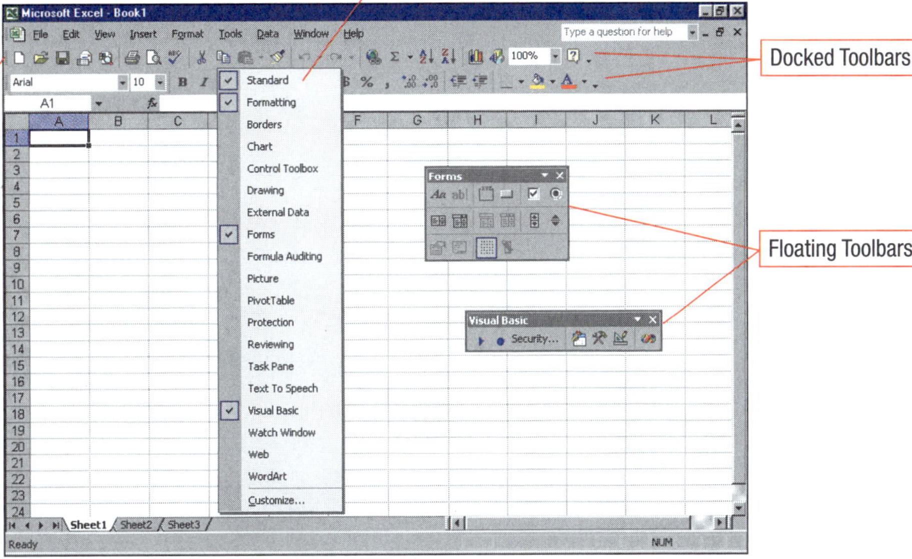

Hiding and Displaying Toolbars

As shown in figure 6.9, you can hide and display toolbars by right-clicking on any displayed toolbar. A menu pops up, listing all the toolbars. Toolbars with a check mark next to them are currently open. Those without check marks are currently hidden. Clicking on a hidden toolbar displays it, and clicking on a displayed toolbar hides it. You can also hide and display toolbars by clicking View and Toolbars. The same menu appears that is displayed when you right-click a toolbar.

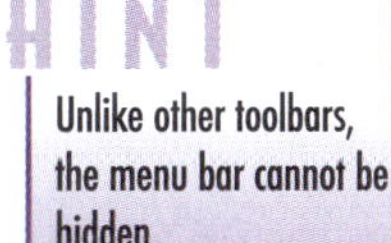
HINT

Unlike other toolbars, the menu bar cannot be hidden.

Customizing Toolbars and Menus

Microsoft Office automatically formats toolbars and menus based on their use. When an Office program is first started, only basic commands are displayed on the menus. As you work in a program, the toolbars and menus are automatically modified to display the menu commands and toolbar buttons that you most often use. You can override these automatic changes by customizing the toolbars and menus yourself.

Toolbars and menus can be customized in a number of ways. The default setting for Excel is to have the Standard and Formatting toolbars share one row. With the two toolbars on one row, there might not be enough room for all the buttons to be displayed. The buttons that are displayed are the ones you have most recently used. To change this default setting so that the Standard and Formatting toolbars appear on two rows, click Tools and then click Customize. The Customize dialog box appears. Click the Options tab. The dialog box will look like figure 6.10. Click the Show Standard and Formatting toolbars on two rows check box so that it is selected.

FIGURE

6.10 ***The Customize Dialog Box with the Options Tab Selected***

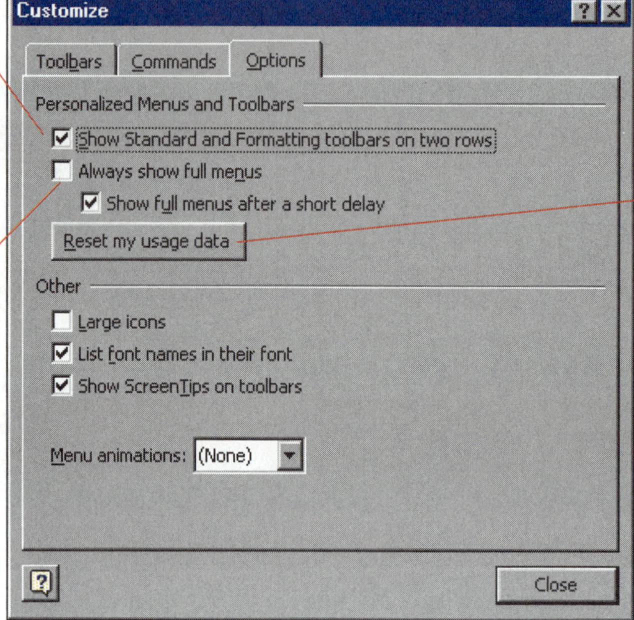

HINT

The Reset my usage data button and the Show Standard and Formatting toolbars on two rows option affect the current application only.

The default setting for menus is for them to display at first only the most basic commands and then to display those commands you use most often. If after using an application for a while you want to go back to displaying the default set of visible commands on the menus and buttons on the toolbars, click the Reset my usage data button. If instead of displaying only the commands you use most often, you want the full menus to be displayed, click the Always show full menus check box.

As shown in figure 6.11, another way to hide or display toolbars is to click the Toolbars tab on the Customize dialog box. To display a toolbar, click the check box next to it. To hide a toolbar, clear the check box next to it. By clicking the New button, you can create a new toolbar. The New Toolbar dialog box is displayed. Enter a name for the toolbar in the Toolbar name box and then click OK. The new toolbar is displayed on the worksheet.

Buttons can be added to a new toolbar a number of different ways. To place one of Excel's existing commands on the new toolbar, click the Commands tab on the Customize dialog box. Click the appropriate category of the command in the Categories list box. Drag the command from the Commands list box to the new toolbar. The appropriate button will appear on the toolbar.

You can place a button that runs a macro on a toolbar by clicking the Commands tab on the Customize dialog box (shown in figure 6.12) and selecting *Macros* in the Categories list box. A custom button appears in the Commands list box. Drag this custom button to the toolbar. To change the name of the button, as well as the image that appears on the button, and to assign the macro to the button, right-click the button on the toolbar.

FIGURE 6.11 The Customize Dialog Box with the Toolbars Tab Selected

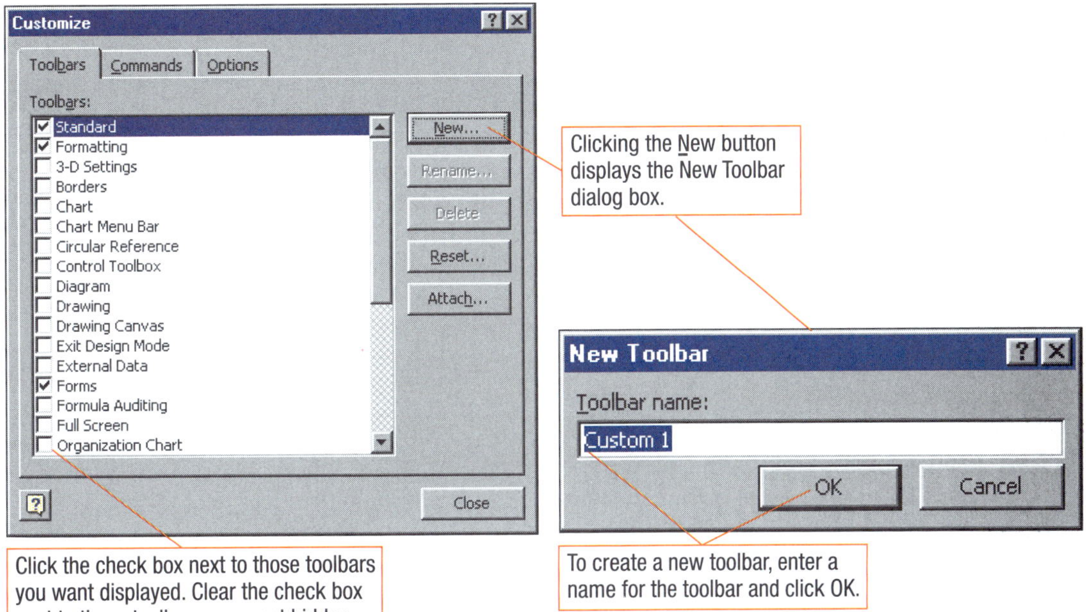

FIGURE 6.12 The Customize Dialog Box with the Commands Tab Selected

To place a button on a new toolbar, select the button's category from the Categories list box. . .

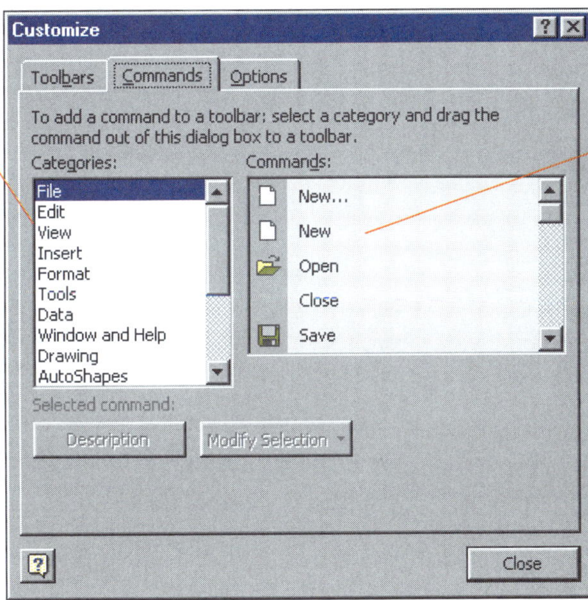

. . . and then drag the command from the Commands list box to the new toolbar.

You can delete a custom toolbar that you have created by clicking the Toolbars tab on the Customize dialog box (shown in figure 6.11). Select the toolbar you want to delete from the Toolbars list box and then click Delete.

exercise 3

CREATING MACROS AND CUSTOMIZING A TOOLBAR AND MENU

1. Open Excel worksheet E6-02.
2. Save the worksheet using the Save As command and name it Excel E6, Ex 03.
3. Click the 7 Percent worksheet tab. Press Shift and click the 8 Percent worksheet tab. All three worksheets should be selected. Create a custom header that displays your name at the left margin and the file name at the right margin. Then de-select the worksheets.
4. When students come into the financial advisor's office at Redwood Community College, they often want to know what kind of payments they can expect on student loans. This worksheet helps students determine what the monthly payments on a student loan would be (depending on how much money they borrow), the interest rate, and the length of the loan. Complete the following steps for creating a macro that will enter the loan amounts:
   a. Click cell A7.
   b. Display the Visual Basic toolbar by right-clicking on a toolbar and then clicking Visual Basic.
   c. Click the Record Macro button on the Visual Basic toolbar. The Record Macro dialog box is displayed.
   d. Key **Amounts** in the Macro name box.
   e. Click the Shortcut key box. Press the Shift key and enter **A**.
   f. Click OK. The Stop Recording toolbar is displayed.
   g. You do not want the cell references to be relative. Make sure the Relative References button on the Stop Recording toolbar is *not* selected. Key the following in the cells indicated:

Cell	Value
A7	**10000**
A8	**15000**
A9	**20000**
A10	**25000**
A11	**30000**
A12	**35000**
A13	**40000**
A14	**45000**
A15	**50000**
A16	**55000**
A17	**60000**

   h. You are going to select some cells, and you want the cell references to be relative. Click the Relative Reference button on the Stop Recording toolbar so that it is selected.
   i. Select cells A7 through A17.
   j. Format cells A7 through A17 as currency with no decimal places.
   k. Click the Stop Recording button on the Stop Recording toolbar.
5. Complete the following steps to create a macro for entering the PMT function:
   a. Click cell B7.
   b. Click the Record Macro button on the Visual Basic toolbar.

c. Key **Payment** in the Macro name box.
d. Press the Shift key and enter **P** in the Shortcut key box. Notice that it now says *Ctrl+Shift+P* for the shortcut key.
e. Click OK. The Stop Recording toolbar is displayed.
f. Make sure the Relative Reference button on the Stop Recording toolbar is selected.
g. Key **=PMT($B$4/12, B$5, -$A7)** in cell B7.
h. Click the Enter button next to the formula bar.
i. Copy the formula in cell B7 down to cell B17 and then across to column F.
j. Click the Stop Recording button on the Stop Recording toolbar.

6. Complete the following steps to create a custom toolbar that will include a button for the Amounts macro and a button for the Payment macro:
   a. Click Tools and then click Customize.
   b. If necessary, click the Toolbars tab.
   c. Click New.
   d. Key **Macros** in the Toolbar name box.
   e. Click OK.
   f. Click the Commands tab.
   g. Select *Macros* from the Categories list box.
   h. Drag the custom Button from the Commands list box to the Macros toolbar twice.

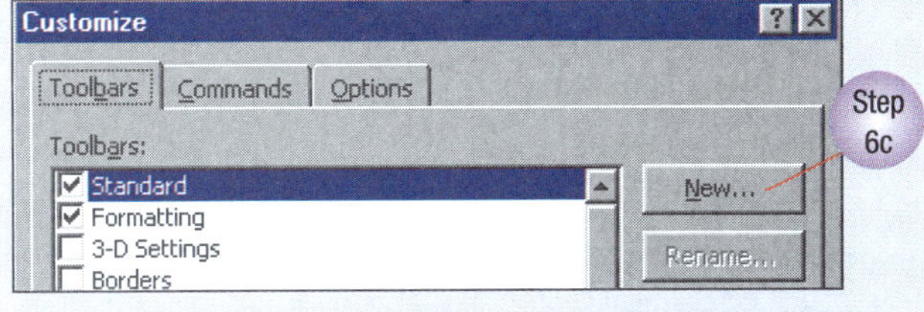

7. Since students often ask for the worksheet to be printed, having the Print and Page setup options available on a custom menu would be convenient. Complete the following steps to add a custom menu to the Macros toolbar:
   a. The Customize dialog box should still be displayed with the Commands tab selected. From the Categories list box, select *New Menu*.
   b. Drag the New Menu button from the Commands list box to the Macros toolbar.
   c. Right-click the New Menu button that is displayed on the Macros toolbar. In the Name box on the shortcut menu, enter **Print**.

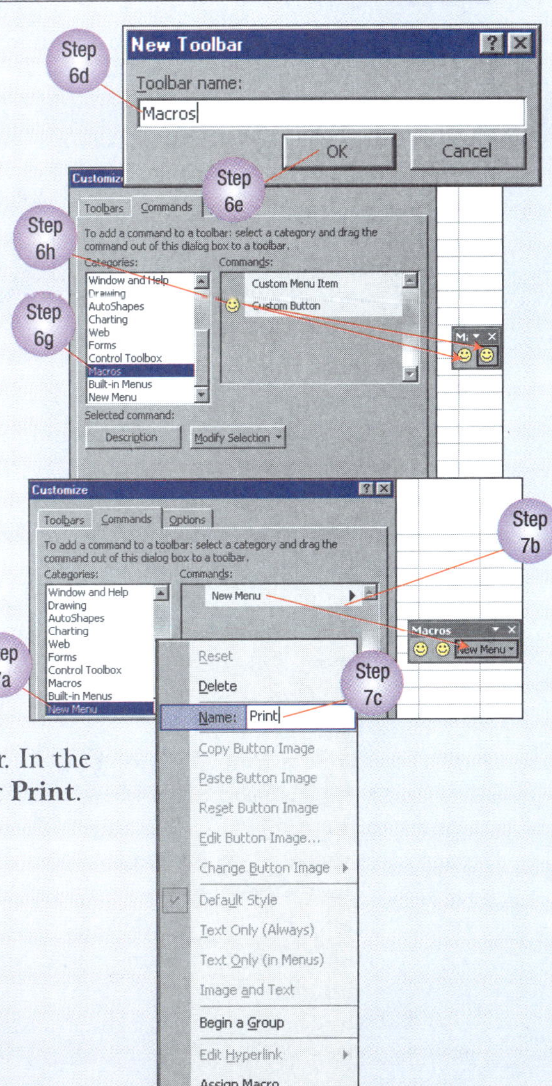

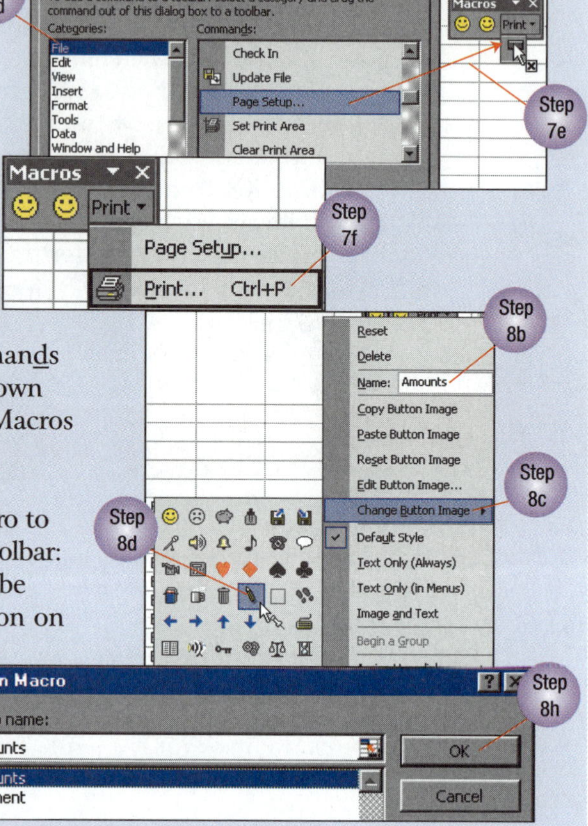

d. Next you want to add the Print command and the Page setup command to your new print menu. Click *File* in the Categories list box.

e. Click the Page Setup button from the Commands list box and then drag it to the Print menu on the Macros toolbar. When it is resting over the menu, the drop-down list box under Print is displayed. Point to the drop-down list box and release the mouse.

f. Click the Print button from the Commands list box and then drag it to the drop-down list box under the Print menu on the Macros toolbar. Place it under the Page Setup command. Release the mouse.

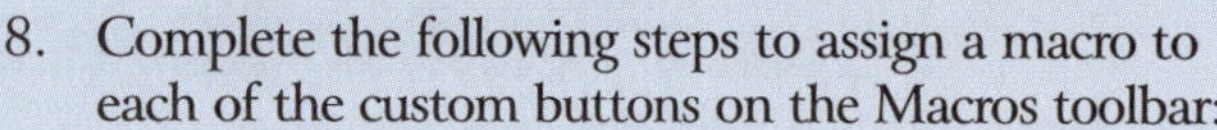

8. Complete the following steps to assign a macro to each of the custom buttons on the Macros toolbar:
   a. The Customize dialog box should still be open. Right-click the first custom button on the Macros toolbar.

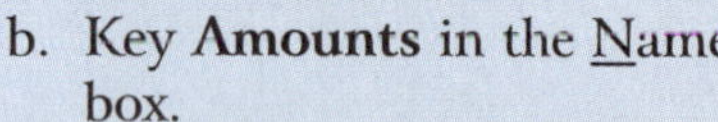

   b. Key **Amounts** in the Name box.
   c. Select Change Button Image.
   d. Click the pencil image, the fourth option in the fourth row.
   e. Right-click the first custom button.
   f. Click Assign Macro.
   g. Select *Amounts* from the Macro name list box.
   h. Click OK.
   i. Right-click the second custom button on the Macros toolbar.
   j. Key **Payment** in the Name box.
   k. Select Change Button Image.
   l. Click the piggy bank button, the third option in row 1.
   m. Right-click the second custom button on the Macros toolbar.
   n. Click Assign Macro.
   o. Select *Payment* from the Macro name list box.
   p. Click OK.
   q. Close the Customize dialog box.
   r. Close the Visual Basic toolbar.

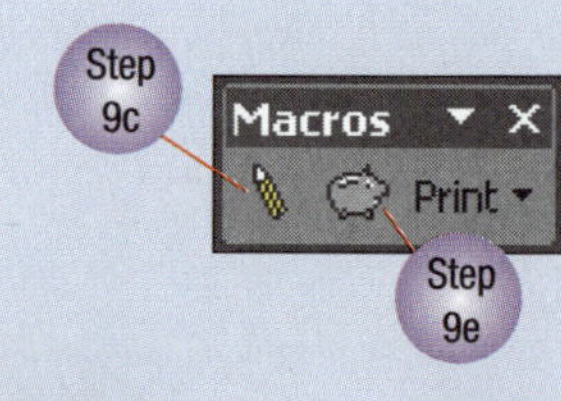

9. Complete the following steps to use the Amounts and Payment macros on the 7.5 Percent worksheet:
   a. Click the 7.5 Percent worksheet tab.
   b. Click cell A7.
   c. Click the Amounts button on the Macros toolbar.
   d. Click cell B7.
   e. Click the Payment button on the Macros toolbar.
   f. Click the Page Setup option on the Print menu.

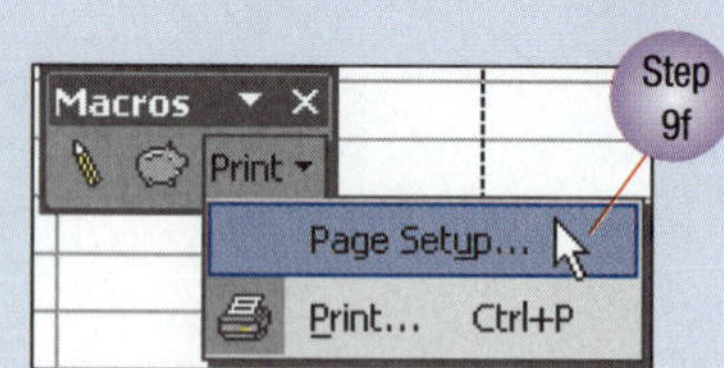

g. On the Page Setup dialog, click the Margins tab. Click the Center on page Horizontally check box. Click OK.
h. Click the Print option on the Print menu. Click OK.

10. Complete the following steps to use the Amounts and Payment macros on the 8 Percent worksheet:
    a. Click the 8 Percent worksheet tab.
    b. Click cell A7.
    c. Click the Amounts button on the Macros toolbar.
    d. Click cell B7.
    e. Click the Payment button on the Macros toolbar.
    f. Click the Page Setup option on the Print menu.
    g. On the Page Setup dialog, click the Margins tab. Click the Center on page Horizontally check box. Click OK.
11. Complete the following steps to delete the Macros toolbar:
    a. Right-click the Macros toolbar.
    b. Click Customize, the last option in the list.
    c. Click the Toolbars tab.
    d. Select *Macros* from the Toolbars list box.
    e. Click Delete.
    f. Click OK.
    g. Close the Customize dialog box.
12. Save the workbook using the same name (Excel E6, Ex 03) and close it.

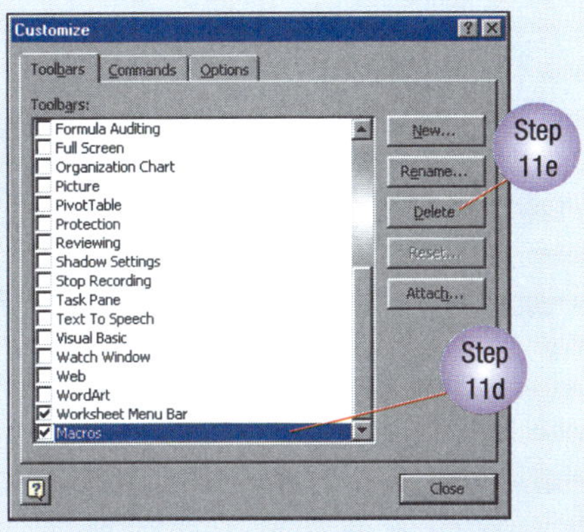

Auditing Workbooks

Making sure a large and complex worksheet is functioning accurately could be a difficult chore. Excel's built-in auditing features help simplify that task. Excel's auditing features allow you to locate dependencies in formulas—that is, cells on which the formula is dependent or cells that are dependent on the formula. You can display tracer arrows to find precedents—the cells on which the formula is dependent because they provide data for the formula. Tracer arrows are also used to find dependents, or cells that depend on the value provided by the formula.

Displaying the Auditing Toolbar

To display the Auditing toolbar, right-click a toolbar and then click Customize. Click the Toolbars tab and then select *Formula Auditing* from the Toolbars list box. The Formula Auditing toolbar shown in figure 6.13 is displayed. You can also display the Formula Auditing toolbar by clicking Tools, selecting Formula Auditing, and then clicking Show Formula Auditing Toolbar. Table 6.1 describes the buttons found on the Formula Auditing toolbar.

FIGURE

6.13 Displaying the Auditing Toolbar

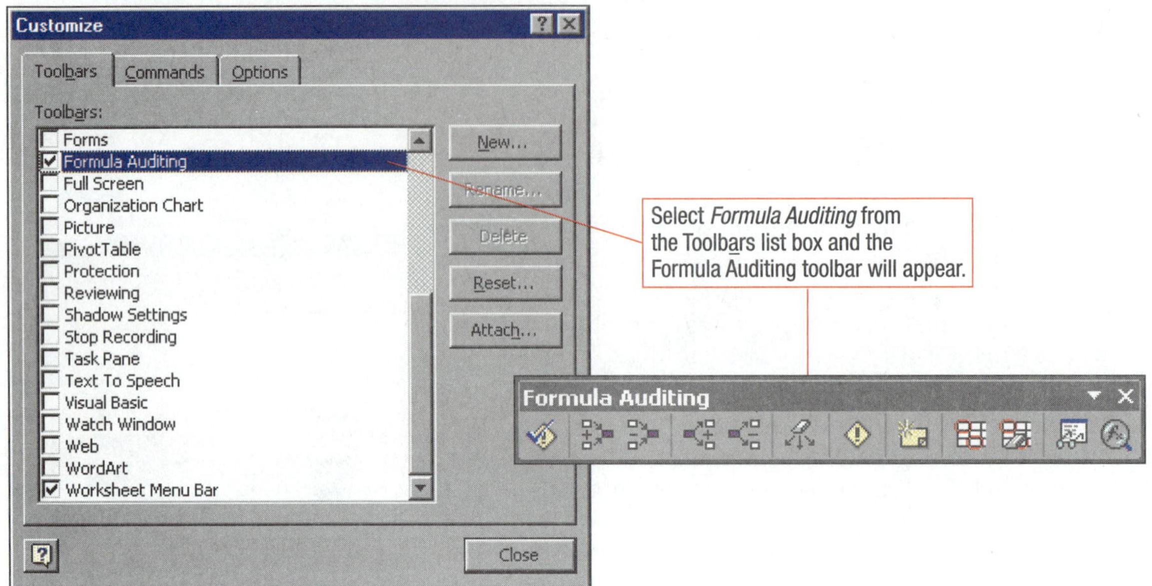

TABLE

6.1 The Formula Auditing Toolbar

The Error Checking button checks the active worksheet for errors.

The Trace Precedents button displays tracer arrows that indicate the cells on which the formula in the active cell is dependent.

The Remove Precedent Arrows button removes tracer arrows generated by the Trace Precedents button.

The Trace Dependents button displays tracer arrows that indicate cells containing formulas that depend on the value in the active cell.

The Remove Dependent Arrows button removes tracer arrows generated by the Trace Dependents button.

The Remove All Arrows button removes all precedent tracer arrows and dependent tracer arrows.

The Trace Error button finds cells contributing to an error in a cell.

The New Comment button allows you to write a comment that is attached to a cell.

The Circle Invalid Data button circles cells containing data outside the valid range defined with the Validation feature.

The Clear Validation Circles button removes circles generated by the Circle Invalid Data button.

The Show Watch Window button displays or hides a watch window to keep track of the results of cells in the spreadsheet when it recalculates.

The Evaluate Formula button evaluates the formula one step at a time.

Tracing Dependents and Precedents

A precedent cell is a cell that is referred to by a formula in another cell. For example, if cell G5 contains the formula =F5*1.05, F5 is a precedent to G5. A dependent cell is a cell containing a formula that refers to another cell. In the preceding example, G5 is a dependent of F5. To trace the precedents or dependents of a cell, select the appropriate cell and then click either the Trace Precedents or Trace Dependents button. Blue tracer arrows are displayed indicating cells with a direct relationship to the selected cell's result. If you click the button again, additional arrows that indicate the next level of cells with a relationship to the selected cell's result are drawn. You can keep clicking the button until Excel beeps, which means there are no more relationships to be found. The tracer arrows can be removed by clicking the Remove Precedent button, Remove Dependent button, or the Remove All Arrows button.

> **HINT**
> Pressing F2 displays the color-coded precedents for the argument in the formula in the active cell.

> **HINT**
> Double-clicking a tracer arrow selects the cell at the other end of the arrow.

Tracing Errors

If an error result such as #DIV/0! is being displayed in a cell, clicking the cell containing the error and then clicking the Trace Error button draws red tracer arrows to the cells that are causing the error. To remove the tracer arrows, click the Remove All Arrows button.

exercise 4 AUDITING A WORKSHEET

1. Open Excel Worksheet E6-03.
2. Save the worksheet using the Save As command and name it Excel E6, Ex 04.
3. Create a custom header that displays your name at the left margin and the file name at the right margin.
4. There are cells divided by zero error messages in this worksheet. Complete the following steps to find the cells causing this error:
   a. Right-click the Formatting toolbar and then click Customize.
   b. Click the Toolbars tab.
   c. Click the *Formula Auditing* check box in the Toolbars list box to select it. The Auditing toolbar is displayed.
   d. Click the Close button.
   e. Click cell C5.
   f. Click the Trace Error button on the Auditing toolbar. A red tracer arrow is drawn to cell D27.

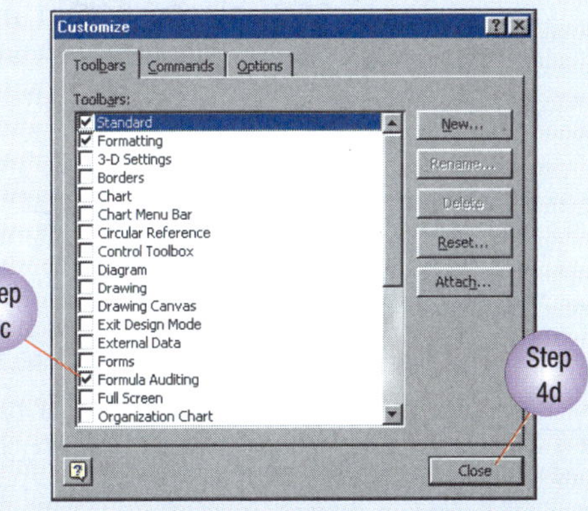

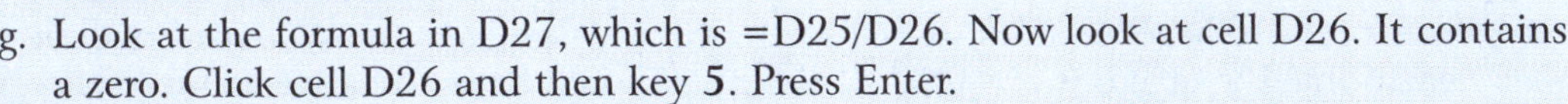

   g. Look at the formula in D27, which is =D25/D26. Now look at cell D26. It contains a zero. Click cell D26 and then key **5**. Press Enter.
   h. The red tracer line changes to a blue tracer line because the error was fixed.
   i. Click cell D11.
   j. Click the Trace Precedents button on the Formula Auditing toolbar.
   k. Click the Trace Precedents button a second time. You can now see that cells D4, D5, D7, D9, and D10 are all precedents to the contents of cell D11. The first level

precedents are cells D9 and D10. The next level of precedents are cells D4, D5, and D7.

   l. You can follow a trace by double-clicking one of the dots on the tracer line. The active cell immediately becomes the cell at the other end of the arrow. Double-click the blue dot in cell D4. Cell D9 is now the active cell.
   m. Double-click the blue dot in cell D4 again to move the active cell back to cell D4.
   n. Click cell G11.
   o. Click the Trace Dependents button. The tracer arrow that is drawn shows you that cell G16 contains a formula that refers to cell G11.
5. Print the worksheet.
6. Click the Remove All Arrows button on the Auditing toolbar.
7. Complete the following steps to enter a new comment for cell A5:
   a. Click cell A5.
   b. Click the New Comment button on the Auditing toolbar.
   c. Key the following:
      Figures for calculating the depreciation on new machine are found in cells C21 through D27.
8. Close the Formula Auditing toolbar.
9. Save the workbook using the same name (Excel E6, Ex 04) and close it.

CHAPTER summary

- Macros automate tasks that perform the same sequence of steps or tasks that are performed repeatedly. Excel's macro recorder records every keystroke and mouse click so that they can be played back at a later time.
- Excel macros are automatically created in the Visual Basic for Applications programming language.
- Record a macro by clicking Tools, selecting Macro, and then clicking Record new Macro. In the Record Macro dialog box, enter a macro name and, if desired, a shortcut key and description. A macro name must begin with a letter but can contain numbers, letters, and the underscore character. A shortcut key is a letter that is pressed together with Ctrl or Ctrl+Shift in order to execute the macro.
- Planning the exact steps of a macro before recording it is important because everything that is entered, including mistakes and the keystrokes taken to fix the mistakes, is recorded and executed every time the macro is run.
- When selecting cells is a step to be included in a macro, you must know whether the selected cells should have an absolute cell reference or a relative cell reference. The default is for cells to have an absolute cell reference, which means the same cells will be selected each time the macro is executed. If the cells should have a relative cell reference, click the Relative Reference button on the Stop Recording toolbar. If the Relative Reference button appears to be pressed in when the cells are selected, the selected cells will have a relative reference. If the button is not pressed in, then the cells will have an absolute reference.
- Run a macro by pressing the shortcut key, pressing the Run Macro button on the Visual Basic toolbar, or clicking Tools, selecting Macro, and clicking Macros.

- Macros can be run from a command button placed on the worksheet. Assign a macro to a command button by clicking the Button button on the Forms toolbar. The mouse pointer turns into a crosshair, and you can click and drag to make the command button the size you want. Once the button has been placed on the worksheet, you can change its name and format and assign a macro to it.
- Edit a macro by accessing the Macro dialog box, selecting the macro to be edited, and then clicking Edit. The macro is displayed in the Microsoft Visual Basic editor.
- Docked toolbars are attached to one of the program window's borders or to another toolbar. Floating toolbars are not attached to anything. Move a docked toolbar by dragging the move handle located at the left side of the docked toolbar. Move a floating toolbar by dragging the toolbar's title bar.
- Change the default setting so that Excel's Standard and Formatting toolbars are on two rows instead of one by clicking Tools and then Customize. Click the Options tab on the Customize dialog box. The Standard Formatting toolbars share one row check box should not be selected.
- Precedents are cells that provide data to a formula. Dependents are cells containing formulas that refer to other cells.

COMMANDS review

Command	Mouse/Keyboard
Display or hide toolbars	Click View, Toolbars
Record a macro	Click Tools, Macro, Record new Macro
Run a macro	Click Tools, Macro, Run
Delete a macro	Click Tools, Macro, Delete
Edit a macro's shortcut key command	Click Tools, Macro, Options
Change the format of a command button	Right-click the button, Format Control
Assign a macro to a command button	Right-click the button, Assign Macro
Change the default setting for toolbars	Click Tools, Customize, Options tab
Create a new toolbar	Click Tools, Customize, Toolbars tab, New
Place a button that runs an Excel command	Click Tools, Customize, Commands
Place a menu	Click Tools, Customize, Commands
Delete a custom toolbar	Click Tools, Customize, Toolbars tab, Delete
Display the Auditing toolbar	Click Tools, Customize, Toolbars tab

CONCEPTS check

Completion: On a blank sheet of paper, indicate the correct term, symbol, or command for each item.

1. This term refers to the programming language in which Excel macros are created.
2. This is the toolbar that needs to be displayed in order to place a command button on a worksheet.
3. This term refers to the editor used to edit Excel macros.
4. Display this box to edit a macro.
5. This is the term used to refer to the executable lines in a macro.
6. This is the button you click on the Forms toolbar if you want to place a command button on a worksheet.
7. When editing a macro, the comment lines describing the macro begin with this character.
8. This term describes a toolbar that is attached to the border of a program window.
9. If you right-click a toolbar, this is what appears.
10. This term refers to a cell that is referred to by a formula in another cell.
11. This is the term that refers to a cell containing a formula that refers to another cell.
12. If red tracer arrows appear on a worksheet, you know that this button was pressed.
13. Explain why it is so important to carefully plan the steps of a macro before recording it.
14. Explain the rules that must be followed for naming a macro.
15. List the steps you would take to place a button that runs a macro on a toolbar.

SKILLS check

Assessment 1

1. Open Excel worksheet E6-04.
2. Save the worksheet using the Save As command and name it Excel E6, SA 01.
3. This workbook is used by Chris Robinson to keep track of the software installed at all the offices where he works as a freelance PC technician. There are 10 worksheets in the workbook. Each worksheet contains the records for a different office. Scroll through the worksheet tabs at the bottom of the window to see the 10 tabs that are there.
4. Click on the Archer worksheet tab. Scroll to the end of the worksheet tabs. Press the Shift key. Click the River Road worksheet tab. All the worksheet tabs should be selected. Create a custom header that displays your name at the left margin and the file name at the right margin. Be sure to use the file name button for entering the file name in the header. The header will now appear on all the selected worksheets.
5. The applications installed on the various PCs and the NT server at each office can be either served or local. If an application is local, it resides on the hard drive of that computer. If an application is served, it resides on a different computer on the

network. A served application can be either an image or a copy. A served image is a unique installation. A served copy is a copy of a served image. Chris needs to keep track of the number of each kind of installation there is at each office. Click the Archer worksheet tab. Record a macro called Count. You should be able to execute the macro with the shortcut key combination Ctrl+Shift+C. The macro should use absolute cell referencing and should include these steps:

- In cell H4, enter a COUNTIF function that counts the number of times the letter *I* occurs in cells B4 through G4. *(Hint: Since the macro uses absolute cell referencing, make sure that selecting cell H4 is part of the macro.)*
- Copy the function in cell H4 down through cell H8.
- In cell I4, enter a COUNTIF function that counts the number of times the letter *S* occurs in cells B4 through G4.
- Copy the function in cell I4 down through cell I8.
- In cell J4, enter a COUNTIF function that counts the number of times the letter *L* appears in cells B4 through G4.
- Copy the function in cell J4 down through cell J8.
- Enter a SUM function in cell H9 that totals cells H4 through H8.
- Copy the function in cell H9 to cells I9 and J9.
- Enter a formula in cell H11 that adds together the values in cells H9 and J9.

6. Once the Count macro has been recorded, click on the Bateson worksheet tab.
7. Run the macro using the shortcut key combination Ctrl+Shift+C.
8. Print the Archer and Bateson worksheets.
9. Save the workbook using the same name (Excel E6, SA 01). This worksheet is used in the assessment 2 exercise. Close the workbook.

Assessment 2

1. Open workbook Excel E6, SA 01. You created this workbook in the assessment 1 exercise.
2. Save the worksheet using the Save As command and name it Excel E6, SA 02.
3. Click the Central worksheet tab.
4. Create a custom toolbar. Name the toolbar My Commands.
5. Place a button on the My Commands toolbar for the Count macro. The name of the button for the Count macro should be Count. Choose a different graphic image for the button other than the default. Assign the Count macro to the button.
6. Place a button for the print command on the My Commands toolbar.
7. Add a custom menu to the My Commands toolbar. Name the menu Locate. Place the Find and the Go To options found in the Edit menu on the new Locate menu.
8. Use the Find menu to find all occurrences of *Hosta*.
9. Run the Count macro using the Count button on the My Commands toolbar.
10. Print the Central worksheet using the Print button on the My Commands toolbar.
11. Click the Doss worksheet tab.
12. Run the Count macro using the Count button on the My Commands toolbar.
13. Print the Doss worksheet using the Print button on the My Commands toolbar.
14. Click the Findlay worksheet tab.
15. Run the Count macro using the Count button on the My Commands toolbar.
16. Print the Findlay worksheet using the Print button on the My Commands toolbar.
17. Close the My Commands toolbar.
18. Save the workbook using the same name (Excel E6, SA 02). Close the workbook.

Assessment 3

1. Open Excel worksheet E6-05.
2. Save the worksheet using the Save As command and name it Excel E6, SA 03.
3. Create a custom header for the worksheet that displays your name at the left margin and the file name at the right margin.
4. Create a macro that uses AutoFilter to display only the shade plants. Name the macro Shade.
5. Create a macro that uses AutoFilter to display all the plants. Name the macro All.
6. Create a macro that uses AutoFilter to display all the sun plants. Name the macro Sun.
7. Create a custom button on the worksheet. The button should be toward the top and to the right of the list. Assign the Shade macro to the button. Rename the button Shade. The letters on the button should be bold and the color sea green. The size of the button should be .25 inches high and .75 inches wide. On the Properties tab in the Format Control dialog box, the option Don't move or size with cells should be selected.
8. Create another custom button that is underneath the Shade custom button. Assign the Sun macro to the button. Rename the button Sun. The letters on the button should be bold and the color sea green. The size of the button should be .25 inches high and .75 inches wide. On the Properties tab in the Format Control dialog box, the option Don't move or size with cells should be selected.
9. Create another custom button that is underneath the Sun custom button. Assign the All macro to the button. Rename the button All. The letters on the button should be bold and the color sea green. The size of the button should be .25 inches high and .75 inches wide. On the Properties tab in the Format Control dialog box, the option Don't move or size with cells should be selected.
10. Click the Shade button. Print the worksheet.
11. Click the All button. *(Hint: You must click the All button before clicking either the Shade button or the Sun button.)* Print the worksheet.
12. Click the Sun button. Print the worksheet.
13. Click the All button.
14. Save the worksheet using the same name (Excel E6, SA 03) and close it.

Assessment 4

1. Open Excel worksheet E6-06.
2. Save the worksheet using the Save As command and name it Excel E6, SA 04.
3. Create a custom header for the worksheet that displays your name at the left margin and the file name at the right margin.
4. Display the Formula Auditing toolbar.
5. There is an error somewhere in this worksheet. Click cell F12. Click the Trace Error button. The tracer arrows indicate that the formula in cell E12 references cells J13 through K16, which are empty. Remove the tracer arrows. In the VLOOKUP function, the references to the cells that make up the lookup table should be absolute. Click cell E3. Edit the formula so that the references to the lookup table are absolute. Copy the formula to cells E4 through E22.
6. Click cell E3. Click the Trace Precedents button.
7. Click cell E6. Click the Trace Dependents button. Click the Trace Dependents button again.
8. Print the worksheet.
9. Remove all the tracer arrows.
10. Close the Auditing toolbar.
11. Save the worksheet using the same name (Excel E6, SA 04) and close it.

CHAPTER 7

COLLABORATING WITH WORKGROUPS

PERFORMANCE OBJECTIVES

Upon successful completion of chapter 7, you will be able to:

- **Apply and remove passwords**
- **Apply and remove workbook protection**
- **Apply and remove worksheet protection**
- **Add cell protection**
- **Track changes in a shared workbook**
- **Accept and reject tracked changes**
- **Create, edit, and remove a comment**
- **Merge workbooks**
- **View multiple worksheets**
- **Print multiple worksheets**

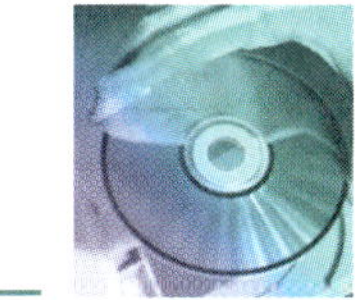

Excel Chapter 07E

In chapter 2 you were introduced to sharing workbooks. In this chapter, you will learn more about sharing workbooks and the concept of workgroup computing. One of the goals of computer networks is to make it easy and efficient for people to work together in groups. The term *workgroup computing* refers to a group of people working on a common project using computer resources to share ideas, software, and data. Typically, a workgroup is made up of a small number of people who work at the same location.

Excel includes two groups of features that help promote workgroup computing: workgroup sharing features and workgroup security features. As you already know, several users, or members of a workgroup, can share a workbook. Each workgroup member can edit the workbook simultaneously. These workgroup sharing features help stimulate workgroup collaboration. Excel's security features allow you to prevent certain types of access to a shared workbook. All the features that help facilitate workgroup collaboration will be discussed in this chapter.

Benefits and Limitations of Sharing Workbooks

Typically, in any kind of a business project, several people are involved. Those people directly involved in the project make up a workgroup. Often each individual in the workgroup is responsible for a certain aspect of the project. The manager of the project has to gather information from the workgroup members and consolidate that information in one place. One way for the manager to do this would be to collect hard copies of the data from individual workgroup members and then key all of the collected data into one workbook. But this method would be extremely inefficient. Instead, the workgroup members could all share the workbook, and each member could key in his or her own data. Sharing workbooks increases productivity, saves time, and increases the likelihood that the data will be accurate.

Some limitations are involved when you work with shared workbooks. Security is an issue, because anyone who has access to the network location where the shared workbook is stored has access to that shared workbook. You have to use workbook or worksheet protection (or both) to ensure the information in the workbook is available only to those who should have access to it. In addition, some features are not available in shared workbooks. These features include deleting worksheets; merging cells; using conditional formatting; using drawing tools; inserting or deleting blocks of cells; inserting or editing charts, pictures, objects, or hyperlinks; using the drawing tools, creating or editing PivotTables; creating or editing macros; and assigning passwords to individual worksheets or to the whole workbook.

Protecting Workbooks

Workbooks often contain sensitive information. Sometimes a workbook should be accessible only to certain people within the organization. At other times, people within an organization should be able to access a workbook but not make any changes to it. Or perhaps only specific users are allowed to make changes to certain cells. You may want to prohibit users from removing a workbook from shared use. Several different levels of protection can be placed on a worksheet or workbook.

Applying and Removing Passwords

HINT

Typically, a good password combines uppercase and lowercase letters, numbers, and special symbols such as !, @, or *. Do not use names or easily identifiable dates, such as your birth date, for a password.

Password protection for an entire workbook is the highest level of protection a workbook can have. If a password has been assigned to a workbook, the workbook cannot be opened by anyone who does not know the password. When a password has been assigned to a workbook, that workbook cannot be shared.

To apply a password to a workbook, click File and then click Save As. Click the Tools button on the Save As dialog box and click General Options. The Save Options dialog box is displayed. Enter the password in the Password to open box. If a workbook is to be generally accessible but only certain people should be able to make changes to it, enter a password in the Password to modify box. Anyone will be able to open the workbook, but only those who know the password will be able to add changes.

As can be seen in figure 7.1, when the password is entered, asterisks are displayed in the box. Passwords can be up to 15 characters long. They are case sensitive, which means that uppercase and lowercase does matter. If a password contains a capital letter, that letter must be capitalized when entering the password or the workbook will not open. The same is true with lowercase letters.

FIGURE 7.1 *The Save Options Dialog Box*

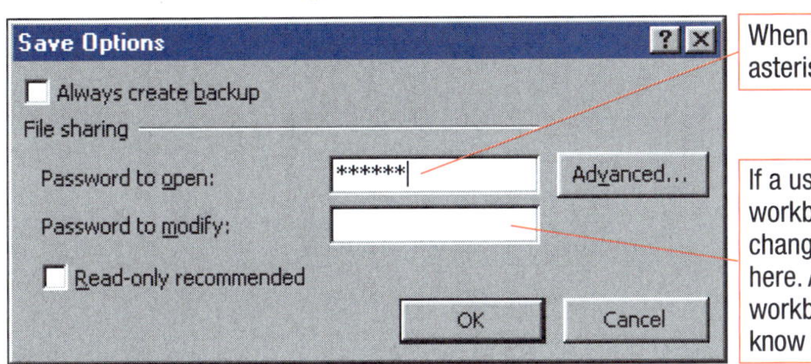

Once the password has been entered, click OK. The Confirm Password dialog box shown in figure 7.2 is displayed. Enter the password again in the Reenter password to proceed box. Again, the password is displayed in asterisks. A message appears in this dialog box, warning you that if the password is lost or forgotten, there is no way to recover it and the workbook cannot be opened. If the warning box appears, asking if you want to replace the existing workbook with the open workbook, click Yes.

FIGURE 7.2 *Confirm Password Dialog Box*

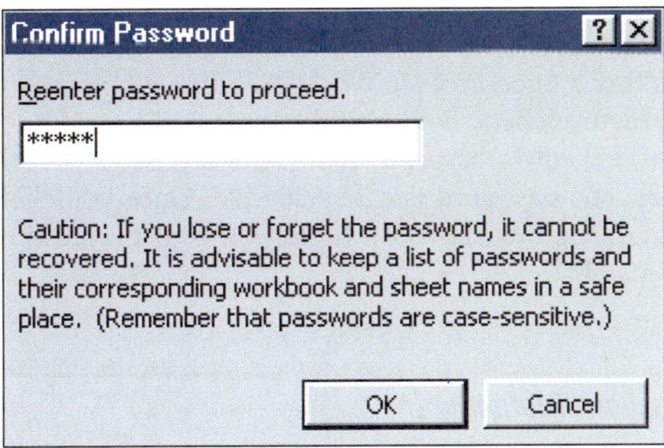

When you try to open a password-protected workbook, the dialog box shown in figure 7.3 is displayed. As you enter the password, asterisks are once again displayed. After entering the password, click OK. If the password was entered correctly, the workbook is opened.

HINT

If you think you have entered the password correctly but Excel will not open the workbook, make sure the CAPS LOCK key is not on.

FIGURE

7.3 ***The Password Dialog Box***

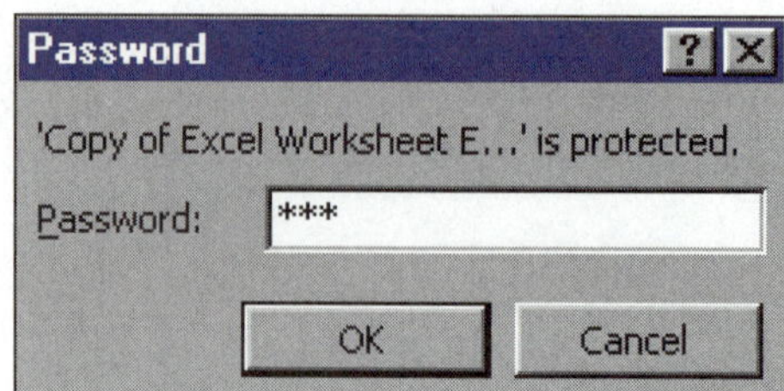

To remove a password from a workbook, click File and then click Save As. Click the Tools button on the Save As dialog box and then click General Options. Delete the asterisks from the Password to open box and click OK. When you click Save and a warning box appears, asking if you want to replace the existing file, click Yes.

Applying and Removing Cell, Worksheet, and Workbook Protection

HINT

Shared workbooks also can be protected. To protect a shared workbook, click Tools, point to Protection, and click Protect and Share Workbook. The Protect Shared Workbook dialog box is displayed. Click the Sharing with track changes check box to select it. Enter a password if desired, and click OK.

You can protect a worksheet by hiding it from view or by locking its cells so that changes cannot be made to them. To hide an entire worksheet from view, click the worksheet to be hidden and then click Format, select Sheet, and click Hide. The worksheet that was selected is no longer displayed.

Once a worksheet is hidden, the workbook must be protected in order to prevent other users from redisplaying it. When a workbook is protected, other users cannot insert, delete, hide, move, or rename worksheets unless they know the password. To protect the workbook, click Tools, point to Protection, and then click Protect Workbook. The Protect Workbook dialog box shown in figure 7.4 is displayed. The Structure check box should be selected in order for the underlying structure of the worksheet to be protected. Enter a password in the Password box and then click OK. The password is case sensitive. Once you click OK, the Confirm Password dialog box shown in figure 7.2 is displayed. Enter the password again and then click OK.

FIGURE

7.4 ***The Protect Workbook Dialog Box***

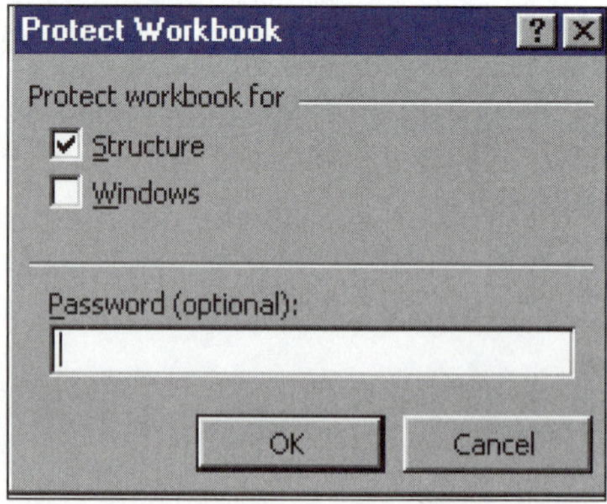

If you want to display a worksheet that has been hidden, you must first remove the workbook protection. To remove workbook protection, click Tools, point to Protection, and then click Unprotect Workbook. The Unprotect Workbook dialog box is displayed. Enter the password in the Password box and then click OK. You can then unhide the worksheet by clicking Format, pointing to Sheet, and then clicking Unhide. The Unhide dialog box is displayed. Click the worksheet to be unhidden and then click OK. The worksheet is once again displayed.

You also can protect individual cells from being changed. This feature is useful for protecting formulas that you want to make sure do not get overwritten with other data. When you use this feature to protect cells, all the cells on the worksheet are protected. You then have to indicate those cells that can be changed. Select the cells in the worksheet that can be changed and then click Format and Cells. Click the Protection tab on the Format Cells dialog box. As shown in figure 7.5, there are two options in the dialog box: Locked and Hidden.

FIGURE 7.5 *Format Cells Dialog Box with Protection Tab Selected*

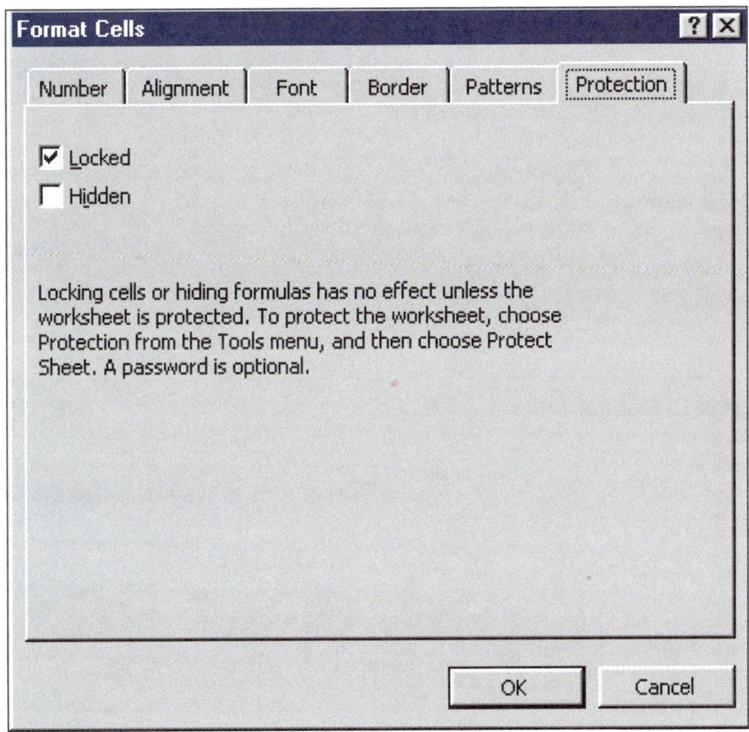

Click the Locked check box so that it is no longer selected. This will unlock the selected cells so that changes can be made to them. Click OK to close the Format Cells dialog box. Click Tools, select Protection, and then click Protect Sheet. The Protect Sheet dialog box shown in figure 7.6 is displayed. The default is for Excel to protect everything in the worksheet except for the cells that you unlocked. An optional password can be entered in the Password box. The password is case sensitive. If you enter a password, you will have to reenter it in the Confirm Password dialog box. The Allow all users of this worksheet to list box enables you to select specific formatting commands that users will be able to perform even on a protected worksheet.

HINT

The password to protect a sheet is optional. However, if you do not provide a password, anyone will be able to unprotect the sheet and change the protected elements.

FIGURE 7.6 *The Protect Sheet Dialog Box*

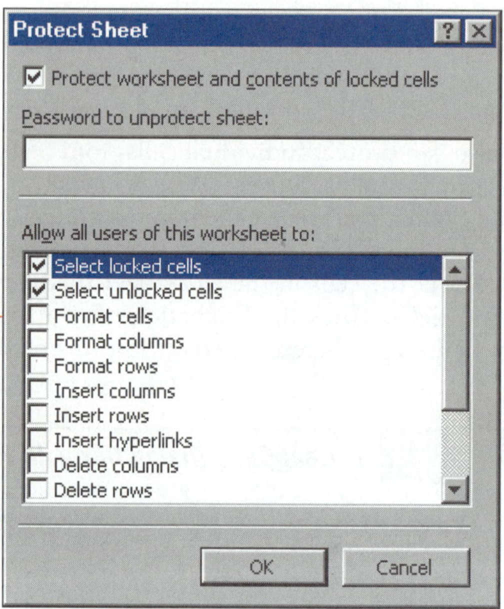

The Protect Sheet dialog box enables you to protect cell values and formulas while allowing cells to be formatted. Users will be able to perform any of the formatting commands that are selected.

Once the cells have been protected, the warning box shown in figure 7.7 is displayed. To remove cell protection, click Tools, point to Protection, and then click Unprotect Sheet. If the worksheet is password protected, you will have to enter the password in the Password box on the Unprotect Sheet dialog box and then click OK.

FIGURE 7.7 *Protect Sheet Warning Box*

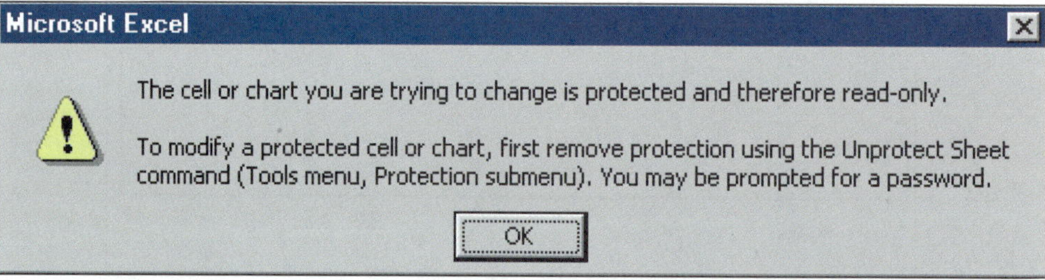

You can give specific users access to cells that have been protected by clicking Tools, pointing to Protection, and then clicking Allow Users to Edit Ranges. In order to use this command, the worksheet cannot be protected. The Allow Users to Edit Ranges dialog box is displayed. Click the New button. As shown in the dialog box in figure 7.8, you need to enter a title for the range to which you are granting access in the Title box. In the Refers to cells box, enter or select the range of cells to which you are granting access. This entry must always begin with an equal sign (=). In the Range password box, enter the password needed to access the range. If you do not enter a password, any user will be able to edit the cells. Click OK. The Allow Users to Edit Ranges dialog box shown in figure 7.9 is

HINT

The Allow Users to Edit Ranges command is available only when the worksheet is not protected.

displayed. Click the Protect Sheet button. The Protect Sheet Dialog Box, shown in figure 7.6 is displayed. Make the necessary selections and click OK. If you entered a password for the worksheet, you will need to reenter the password to confirm it.

HINT

You must have Windows 2000 to give specific users access to ranges.

FIGURE 7.8 *The New Range Dialog Box*

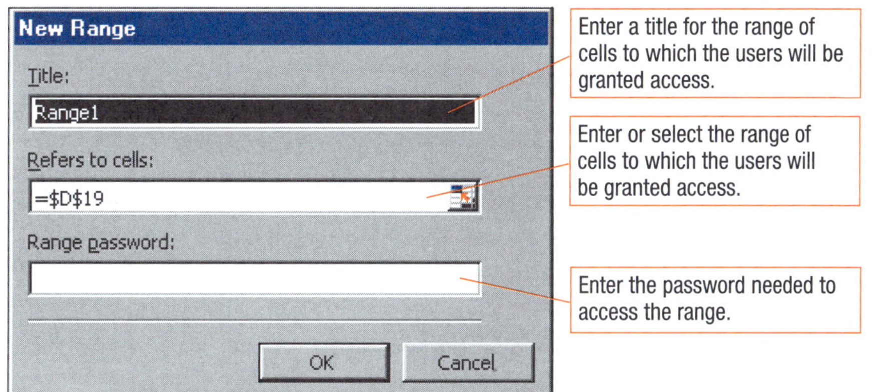

FIGURE 7.9 *The Allow Users to Edit Ranges Dialog box*

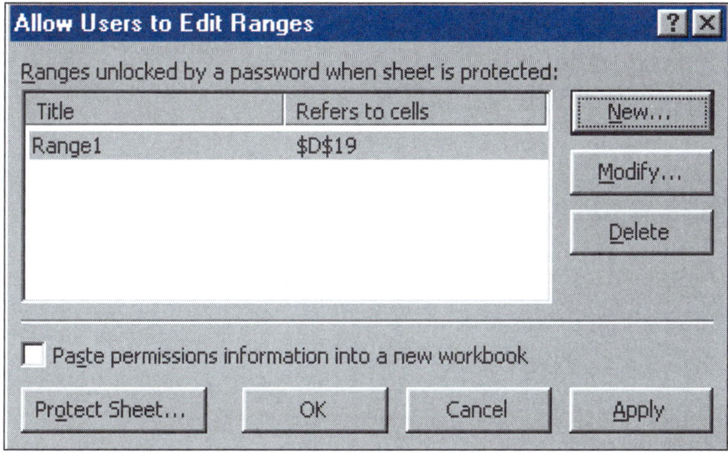

exercise 1 ASSIGNING A WORKBOOK PASSWORD AND PROTECTING CELLS, WORKSHEETS, AND WORKBOOKS

1. Open Excel.
2. Open Excel Worksheet E7-01.
3. Save the workbook using the Save As command and name it Excel E7, Ex 01.
4. Create a custom header for the Income Statement worksheet that displays your name at the left margin and the file name at the right margin.
5. Complete the following steps to assign a password to the workbook:
   a. Click File and then click Save As.

b. Click the Tools button on the Save As dialog box and click General Options.
c. Key **C1401C** in the Password to open box on the Save Options dialog box. Only asterisks are displayed.
d. Click OK.
e. Key **C1401C** in the Reenter password to proceed box on the Confirm Password dialog box. Only asterisks are displayed.
f. Click OK.
g. Click Save.
h. The warning is displayed, asking if you want to replace the existing file. Click Yes.

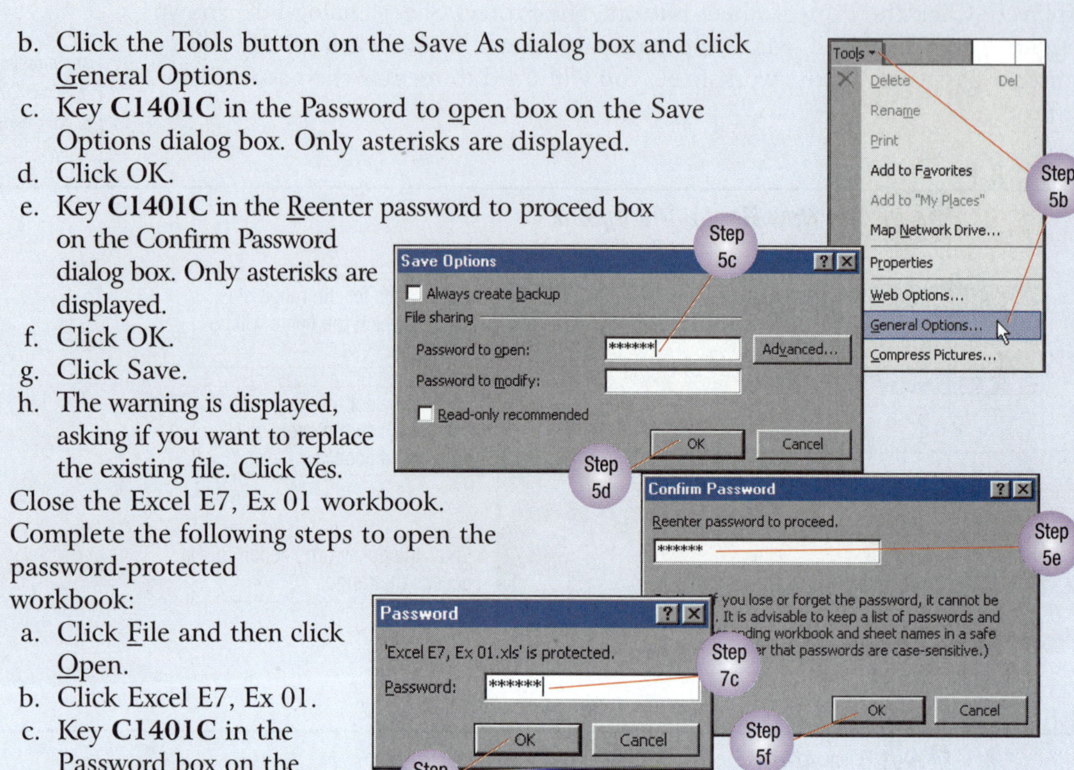

6. Close the Excel E7, Ex 01 workbook.
7. Complete the following steps to open the password-protected workbook:
   a. Click File and then click Open.
   b. Click Excel E7, Ex 01.
   c. Key **C1401C** in the Password box on the Password dialog box.
   d. Click OK.
8. Make sure the Income Statement worksheet is selected. Click cell C8. This cell is linked to a cell on the Cost of Goods Sold worksheet. The figures on this worksheet are confidential, so you want to hide this worksheet. Complete the following steps to hide the Cost of Goods Sold worksheet:
   a. Click the Cost of Goods Sold worksheet tab.
   b. Click Format, point to Sheet, and then click Hide.
   c. Click Tools, point to Protection, and then click Protect Workbook. The Protect Workbook dialog box is displayed.
   d. Make sure the Structure option is selected.
   e. Key **cg0128** in the Password box.
   f. Click OK.
   g. Key **cg0128** in the Reenter password to proceed box on the Confirm Password dialog box.
   h. Click OK.
9. Click the Income Statement worksheet tab. Cells C7, C8, C9, C12, C16, C18, and C20 on the worksheet contain formulas. You want to make sure these formulas cannot be changed. Complete the following steps to protect the cells containing formulas:
   a. Click cell B4. Press Ctrl and then click the following cells in order to select them all: B5, B6, B7, B11, B12, C13, C14, C15, C17, and C19.

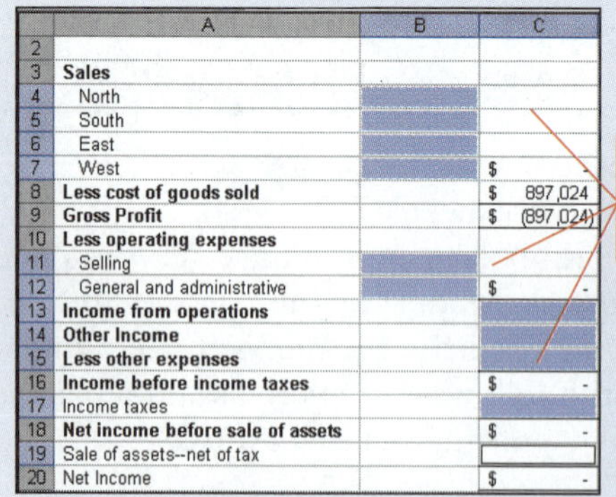

b. Click Format and then click Cells.
c. Click the Protection tab on the Format Cells dialog box.
d. Click the Locked check box so that it is no longer selected.
e. Click OK.
f. Click Tools, point to Protection, and then click Protect Sheet.
g. Key **IFY05ws** in the Password to unprotect sheet box on the Protect Sheet dialog box.
h. Click the Format cells check box to select it.
i. Click OK.
j. Key **IFY05ws** in the Reenter password to proceed box on the confirm Password dialog box.
k. Click OK.
l. Click cell C12 and try to delete it. A warning box appears, saying that the cell is protected. Click OK. If a warning box does not appear, click Edit and Undo. Repeat steps a through j to protect the cells on the worksheet.

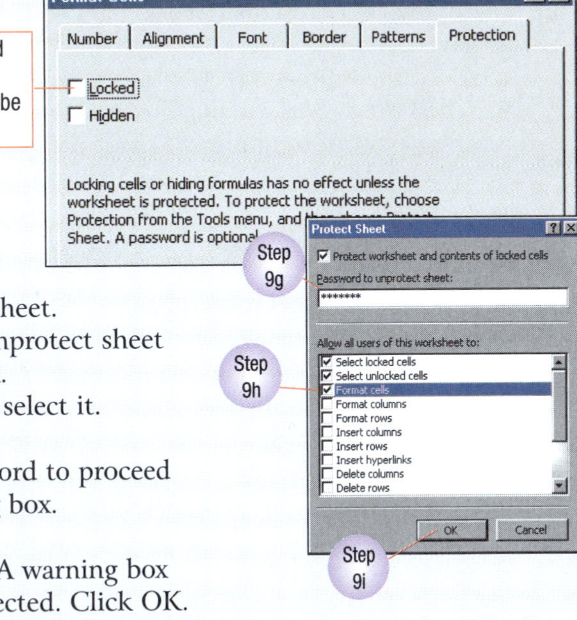

10. Save the workbook using the same name (Excel E7, Ex 01). You will be using this workbook in exercise 3. Close the workbook.

exercise 2 GIVING SPECIFIC USERS ACCESS TO PROTECTED RANGES

(Note: You must be using Windows 2000 in order to complete this exercise.)

1. Open Excel Worksheet E7-02.
2. Save the workbook using the Save As command and name it Excel E7, Ex 02.
3. Create a custom header for the Loan Payments worksheet that displays your name at the left margin and the file name at the right margin.
4. The owners of the company Bits Unlimited are considering purchasing some vans for their business. This worksheet allows them to compare different loan payment options. You are going to password-protect a range of cells in this worksheet.
   a. Click Tools, point to Protection, and then click Allow Users to Edit Ranges.
   b. The Allow Users to Edit Ranges dialog box is displayed. Click New.
   c. The New Range dialog box is displayed. In the Title box, key **Loan Variables**.
   d. Click in the Refers to cells box. Select cells B5 through B9.
   e. In the Range password box, key **02lpBU**.
   f. Click OK.

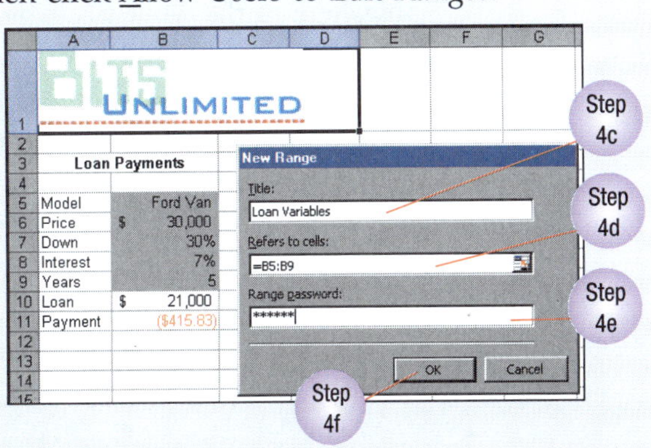

g. In the Confirm Password dialog box, enter **02lpBU**.

5. The Allow Users to Edit Ranges dialog box is displayed.
   a. Click the Protect Sheet button.
   b. The Protect Sheet dialog box is displayed. In the Password to unprotect sheet box, enter **lB*Upv01**.
   c. Click OK.
   d. In the Confirm Password dialog box, enter **lB*Upv01**.

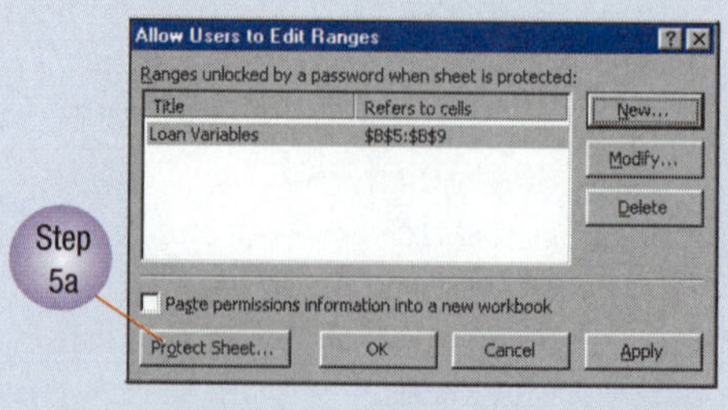

6. Only those who know the password can now make changes to cells B5 through B9.
   a. Click cell B7.
   b. Key **2**.
   c. The Unlock Range dialog box is displayed. Enter **02lpBU.**
   d. Click OK.
   e. Enter **20** in cell B7.
   f. Enter **3** in cell B9.

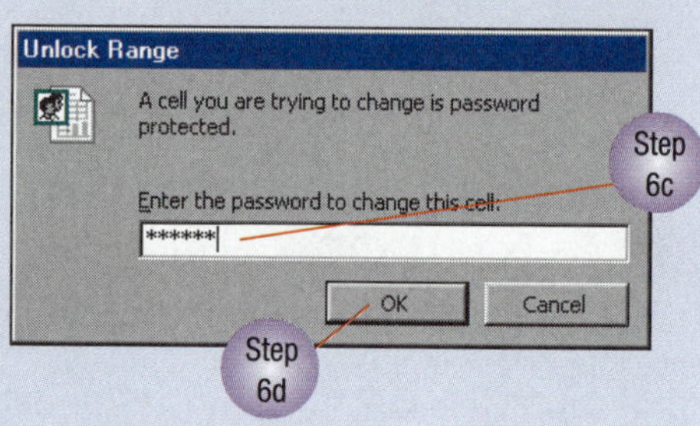

7. Save the worksheet using the same file name and print it.
8. Save the workbook using the same name (Excel E7, Ex 02) and print it.
9. Close the workbook.

Tracking Changes

Excel can make it easy to track changes made to the contents of a cell by highlighting those changes. If a workbook is not already set up to be shared, when you use the Highlight Changes command, the workbook sharing feature is automatically turned on. Each user's changes are highlighted in a different color.

To track the changes, click Tools and then either wait for a few moments or click the down arrow at the bottom of the menu to display more options. Point to Track changes and then click Highlight Changes. Click the Track changes while editing check box, as shown in figure 7.10. If you want to make specific limitations on the tracking feature, you can do so in the Highlight which changes area in the dialog box. You can select what to track according to when the changes were made, by whom they were made, or specifically where on the worksheet they were made. If none of these options are selected, Excel tracks changes made anywhere in the worksheet, by any user, at any time. Excel can track the changes either by highlighting them on the screen or by listing them on a new worksheet.

When any changes are made to the contents of a cell, a border appears around the cell and a revision triangle appears in the upper left corner of the cell. When the mouse pointer is moved over the revision triangle, a box is displayed that lists who made the change, when the change was made, and what the change was.

FIGURE 7.10 *Highlight Changes Dialog Box*

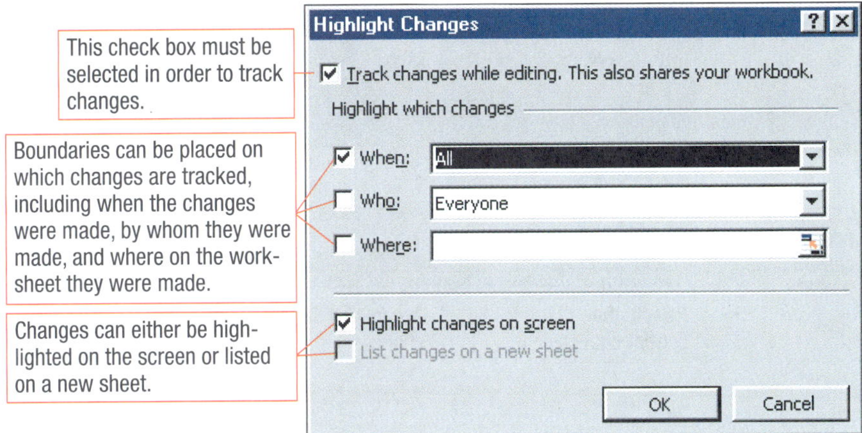

Accepting and Rejecting Tracked Changes

Tracked changes can be either accepted or rejected. They can be accepted or rejected all at one time, or you can go through each change individually and decide whether to accept or reject it. To accept or reject tracked changes, click Tools, point to Track Changes, and then click Accept or Reject Changes. The Select Changes to Accept or Reject dialog box as shown in figure 7.11 is displayed. The changes to be viewed can be limited by when they were made, by whom they were made, or where on the worksheet they were made. Click OK and the Accept or Reject Changes dialog box shown in figure 7.12 is displayed. To accept just the one change that is displayed, click Accept. To reject just the one change that is displayed, click Reject. To accept all of the changes that were made, click Accept All. To reject all the changes that were made, click Reject all.

FIGURE 7.11 *Select Changes to Accept or Reject Dialog Box*

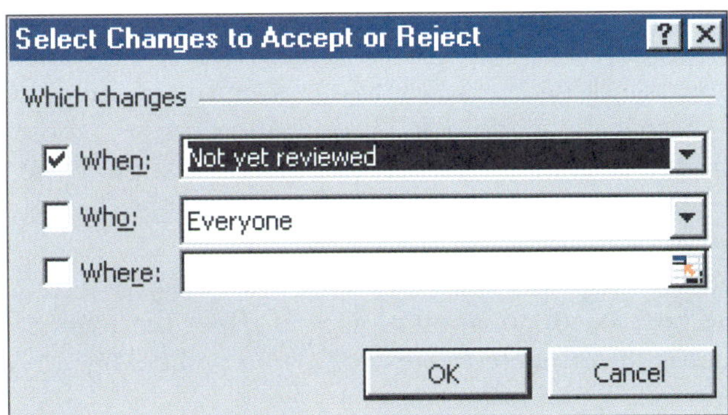

FIGURE

7.12 ***Accept or Reject Changes Dialog Box***

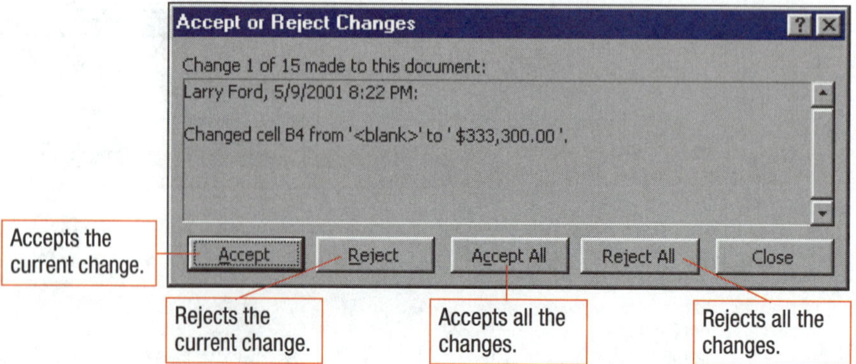

exercise 3

TRACKING CHANGES AND ACCEPTING OR REJECTING CHANGES TO A WORKBOOK

1. Open Excel E7, Ex 01. You created this worksheet in exercise 1. The password to open the workbook is C1401C.
2. Save the workbook using the Save As command and name it Excel E7, Ex 03.
3. If necessary, edit the custom header for the Income Statement worksheet so that the current file name is displayed at the right margin.
4. You are going to be sharing this workbook, and you cannot share a workbook that is password protected. Complete the following steps to remove the password protection from the workbook:
   a. Click Tools, point to Protection, and then click Unprotect Workbook. The Unprotect Workbook dialog box is displayed.
   b. Key **cg0128** in the Password box.
   c. Click OK.
   d. Click File and then click Save As.
   e. Click the Tools button on the Save As dialog box and then click General Options.
   f. Delete all the asterisks from the Password to open box.
   g. Click OK.
   h. Click Save.
   i. When the warning appears, asking if you want to replace the existing file, click Yes.
5. Since you are going to be sharing the workbook, you need to change the user name so that you can keep track of who is using the shared workbook. Complete the following steps to change the user name:
   a. Click Tools and then Options.
   b. Click the General tab on the Options dialog box.
   c. Look in the User name box. Write down on a piece of paper the name that is currently entered. When you complete this exercise, you will change the name back to what is currently entered.
   d. Enter your name in the User name box.
   e. Click OK.
   f. Click the Save button on the Standard toolbar.
6. Complete the following steps to turn on the tracking feature:
   a. Click Tools and then point to Track Changes. You may need to expand the menu in order to see the Track Changes option.

b. Click Highlight Changes. The Highlight Changes dialog box is displayed.
c. Click the Track changes while editing check box to select it.
d. Click OK.
e. Click OK to save the workbook.

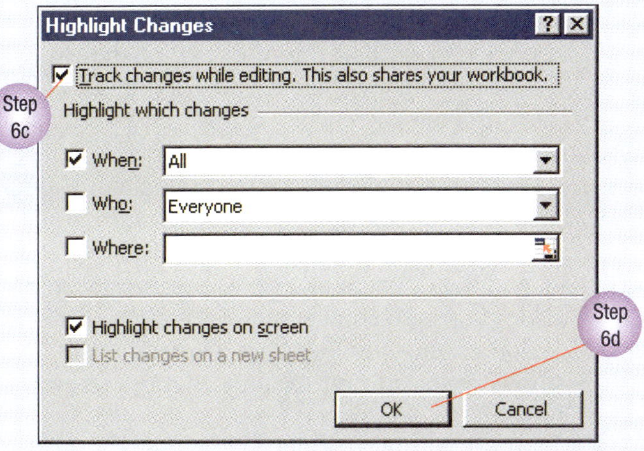

7. Look in the title bar. The word *[Shared]* should now be in the title bar after the workbook name. Complete the following steps to set up a second copy of the workbook:
   a. Click the Start button.
   b. Select Programs and open another copy of Excel.
   c. Right-click the task bar and then click Tile Windows Vertically. Larry's copy should be on the right and your copy on the left. If necessary, rearrange the windows so your copy of the file is on the left.
   d. Click Tools and Options in the second copy of Excel.
   e. Click the General tab on the Options dialog box.
   f. In the User name box, key **Larry Ford**.
   g. Click OK.
   h. Open the Excel E7, Ex 03 workbook in the second copy of Excel.
8. Larry Ford is the vice president of finance, and he has some estimates you need to complete this income statement. Key the following values in the cells indicated in Larry's copy of Excel (the copy on the right):

Cell	Value
B4	**333,300**
B5	**250,996**
B6	**345,023**
B7	**242,024**
B11	**94,039**
B12	**124,178**

   Save the workbook.
9. Click your copy of Excel (the one on the left). Save the workbook so that you can see the changes made by Larry Ford. Click OK when the information box appears, notifying you that the workbook has been updated. Enter the remaining values into the worksheet.

Cell	Value
C13	**86,101**
C14	**22,828**
C15	**21,765**
C17	**23,369**
C19	**24,349**

   Save the workbook.
10. Select Larry's copy of Excel (the one on the right) and save the workbook so that the changes you just made are displayed. Click OK when the information box is displayed, notifying you that the workbook has been updated.

11. Notice that the changes you made are highlighted in one color on Larry Ford's copy of the worksheet and Larry's changes are highlighted in a different color on your copy. Click cell B4 on your copy of Excel (the one on the left). Position the mouse pointer on top of the revision triangle in the upper left corner of cell B4. The box explaining the change that was made should be displayed.
12. As you and Larry look over the figures each other made, you agree that some of the figures the other person entered are incorrect. Complete the following steps to make some changes to each worksheet:
    a. Click Larry's copy of Excel (the one on the right) to select it.
    b. Click cell C17 and key **24,287**.
    c. Click cell C19 and key **26,024**.
    d. Save the workbook.
    e. Click your copy of Excel (the one on the left) to select it.
    f. Click cell B11 and key **96,102**.
    g. Click cell B12 and key **122,189**.
    h. Save the workbook.
    i. Click OK when the box displays telling you the workbook has been updated.
    j. Click Larry's copy of Excel (the one on the right) to select it.
    k. Save the workbook.
    l. Click OK when the box displays telling you the workbook has been updated.
13. Complete the following steps to accept or reject the tracked changes:
    a. Click your copy of Excel (the one on the left) to select it.
    b. Click Tools, point to Track Changes, and then click Accept or Reject Changes. The Select Changes to Accept or Reject dialog box is displayed.
    c. Click OK. The Accept or Reject Changes dialog box is displayed.
    d. The first change made is for cell B4. Notice that cell B4 has a moving border to indicate which cell is currently under consideration. Click Accept.
    e. Accept all the changes until you get to the change for cell B11. After further investigation, you have decided Larry Ford's figure is correct. Click the option for *$94,039*, the figure Larry entered, to select it.
    f. Click Accept.
    g. You need to select which value to accept for cell B12. This time you think your figure is the correct one. Click the option for *$122,189* to select it.
    h. Click Accept.
    i. You want to accept all the rest of the changes, so click Accept All.
    j. Print a copy of the worksheet.

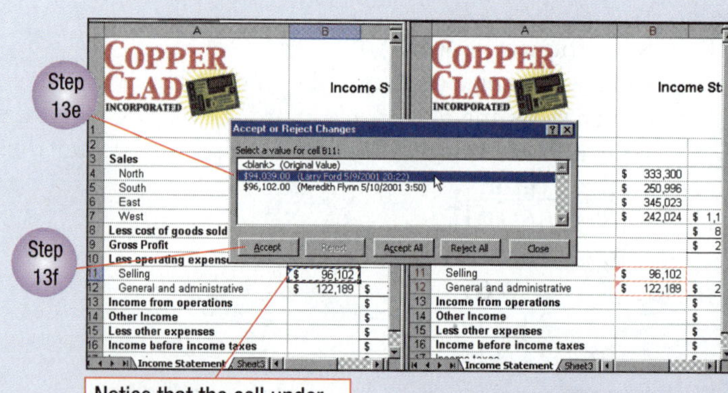

Notice that the cell under consideration has a special border around it.

14. Click Larry's copy of Excel (the one on the right). Complete the following steps to change the user name back to the original entry and exit Larry's copy of Excel:
    a. Click Tools and then click Options.
    b. Click the General tab.
    c. In the User name box, key the name that was originally displayed when you started the exercise.
    d. Click OK.
    e. Save the file. Click File and then click Exit.
15. Maximize the window of your copy of Excel. Complete the following steps to turn off the Track Changes option:
    a. Click Tools, point to Track Changes, and then click Highlight Changes. The Highlight Changes dialog box is displayed.
    b. Click the Track changes while editing check box so that it is no longer selected.
    c. Click OK.
    d. An information box is displayed, asking if you want to remove the workbook from shared use. Click Yes.
16. Complete the following steps to change the user name back to the original entry:
    a. Click Tools and then click Options.
    b. Click the General tab.
    c. In the User name box, key the name that was originally displayed when you started the exercise.
    d. Click OK.
17. Complete the following steps to unhide the hidden worksheet:
    a. Click Format, point to Sheet, and then click Unhide.
    b. Select *Cost of Goods Sold*.
    c. Click OK.
18. Save the workbook with the same name (Excel E7, Ex 03) and close it.

Creating, Editing, and Removing a Comment

Comments can be added to any cell on a worksheet. Comments can be used to explain or clarify the contents of a cell. Comments are not printed when the worksheet is printed. If a cell has a comment attached to it, a small red triangle appears in the upper right corner of the cell. Passing the mouse pointer over this triangle displays the comment. To add a comment, right-click the cell to which the comment is to be added. Click Insert Comment from the shortcut menu. As shown in figure 7.13, the comment box appears with the name of the user who is entered on the General tab of the Options menu. Enter the comment and then click anywhere outside the comment box. To edit a comment, right-click the cell containing the comment to be edited and then click Edit Comment from the shortcut menu. Make the necessary changes and click anywhere outside the comment. To delete a comment, right-click the cell containing the comment to be deleted and then click Delete Comment.

HINT

You can review the comments in a workbook by clicking View and Comments. The reviewing toolbar is displayed. Click the Next Comment button or the Previous Comments button.

FIGURE 7.13 *Creating Comments*

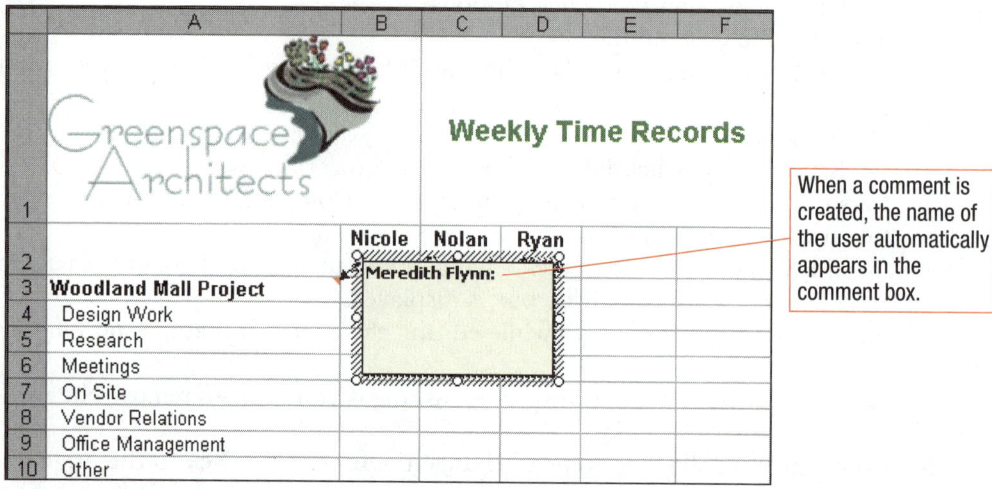

Merging Workbooks

Another way to share workbooks is to send a copy of the shared workbook to different users. Each user can then make his or her own changes to the workbook. All those changes can then be merged into one workbook. The first step in merging workbooks is to open the shared workbook that will be used as the copy into which all the other copies will be merged. Next, click Tools and Compare and Merge Workbooks. If you are prompted to save the workbook, click OK. The Select Files to Merge Into Current Workbook dialog box is displayed. Choose the workbooks to be merged and click OK. As many workbooks as needed can be merged.

exercise 4 CREATING, EDITING, AND REMOVING COMMENTS, AND MERGING WORKBOOKS

1. Open Excel Worksheet E7-03.
2. Save the workbook using the Save As command and name it Excel E7, Ex 04.
3. Create a custom header for the Time Sheet worksheet that displays your name at the left margin and the file name at the right margin.
4. This worksheet is used to keep track of the weekly project time spent by three of the employees at Greenspace Architects, a company that provides landscaping services.
5. Complete the following steps to add a comment to cell A3:
   a. Right-click cell A3.
   b. Click Insert Comment on the shortcut menu.
   c. Key the following in the comment box: **This project is nearing completion and therefore very few hours need to be devoted to it.**

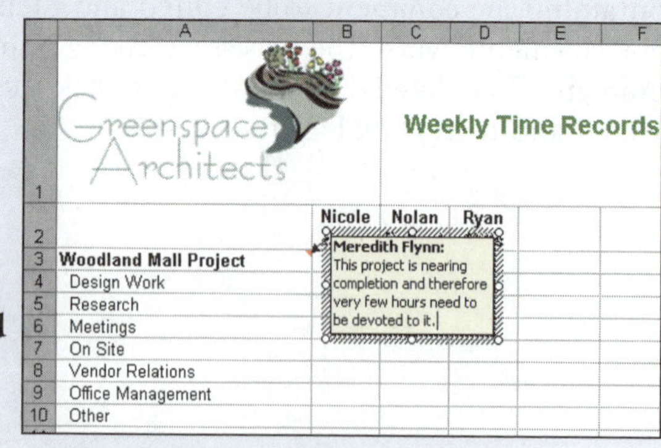

d. Click anywhere outside the comment box.

6. Nicole, Nolan, and Ryan each need to enter their hours in this worksheet. Before they can do that, you need to set up the workbook as a shared workbook. Complete the following steps to designate Excel E7, Ex 04 as a shared workbook.
   a. Click Tools and then click Share Workbook.
   b. If necessary, click the Editing tab.
   c. Click the Allow changes by more than one user at the same time check box to select it.
   d. Click OK.
   e. Click OK to save the workbook.
   f. Close the Excel E7, Ex 04 workbook.

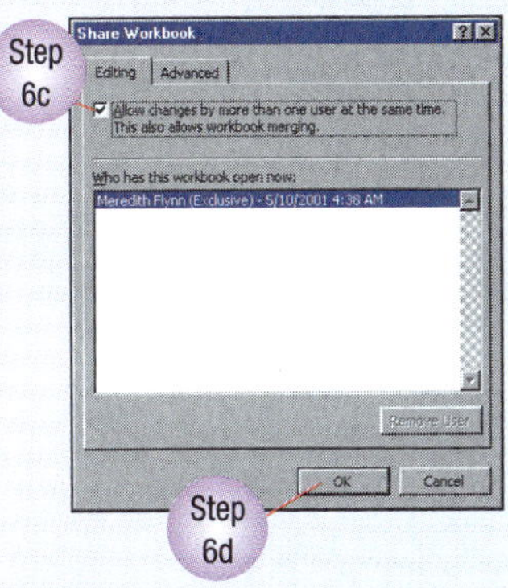

7. In order to simulate this shared workbook being sent to three different employees, you will have to open the file three times. Each employee would open up his or her copy of the shared workbook to enter the requested figures. Nicole is now ready to enter her hours in the weekly time sheet. Open Excel E7, Ex 04. It should say *[Shared]* in the title bar. Save the workbook using the Save As command and name it Nicole 9-18.
8. Key the following values in the cells indicated:

Cell	Value
B7	1
B9	2
B14	3
B15	5
B16	10
B17	4
B18	8
B19	4.5
B23	2
B25	4

9. Save the workbook using the same name (Nicole 9-18) and close it.
10. Nolan is now ready to enter his hours in the weekly time sheet. Open Excel E7, Ex 04. It should say *[Shared]* in the title bar. Save the workbook using the Save As command and name it Nolan 9-18.
11. Key the following values in the cells indicated:

Cell	Value
C6	1
C8	2
C9	1
C13	10
C14	2
C16	5
C18	1
C22	15
C23	3
C24	2
C25	6

12. Save the workbook using the same name (Nolan 9-18) and close it.
13. Ryan is now ready to enter his hours in the weekly time sheet. Open Excel E7, Ex 04. It should say *[Shared]* in the title bar. Save the workbook using the Save As command and name it Ryan 9-18.

14. Key the following values in the cells indicated:

Cell	Value
D13	4
D14	2
D15	3
D16	5
D17	1
D18	2
D19	2
D22	3
D23	2
D24	4
D25	6
D26	3
D27	2
D28	3

15. Save the workbook using the same name (Ryan 9-18) and close it.
16. You are now ready to merge the three workbooks into one workbook. Open Excel E7, Ex 04. Complete the following steps to merge the workbooks:
    a. Click Tools and then click Compare and Merge Workbooks. You may have to expand the menu to see the Compare and Merge Workbooks option.
    b. Click OK to save the workbook. The Select Files to Merge Into Current Workbook dialog box is displayed.
    c. Select the Nicole 9-18, Nolan 9-18, and Ryan 9-18 files.
    d. Click OK. The values from the three workbooks are merged into the one workbook.

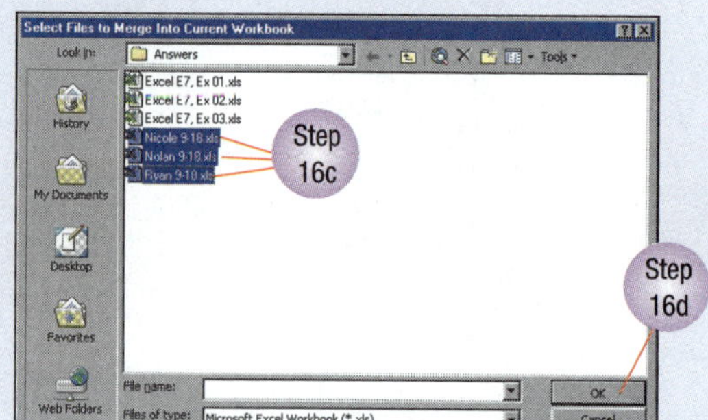

17. You no longer want this to be a shared workbook. Click Tools and Share Workbook. Click the Allow changes by more than one user at the same time check box so that it is no longer selected. Click OK and then click Yes.
18. Complete the following steps to edit the comment box:
    a. Right-click cell A3.
    b. Click Edit Comment from the shortcut menu.
    c. In the comment box delete the phrase *is nearing completion* and key the following to take its place: **will be completed on 9/25**
19. Save the workbook using the same name (Excel E7, Ex 04) and print it.
20. Close the workbook.

Working with Multiple Worksheets

When there is more than one worksheet in a workbook, you often want to perform the same command on two or more, or perhaps even on all, of the worksheets in the workbook. For example, you might want to place the same header on all the worksheets. Or you might want to print two of the four worksheets. In order to perform a command on more than one worksheet at a time, you first need to select the worksheets. If more than one worksheet is selected, the command executed on the active worksheet will be made on all the selected worksheets.

To select two or more adjacent worksheets in a workbook, click the worksheet tab for the first worksheet, hold down the Shift key, and then click the worksheet tab for the last worksheet you want selected. To select two or more worksheets that are not adjacent, click the worksheet tab for the first worksheet, hold down the Ctrl key, and then click the worksheet tab for each worksheet you want selected. To select all the worksheets in a workbook, right-click a worksheet tab and then click Select All Sheets on the shortcut menu.

If you wanted to view more than one worksheet at a time, for example, you would select all the worksheets to be viewed and then click the Print Preview button on the Standard toolbar. The first worksheet would be displayed. Clicking the Next button would display the next worksheet and so on. If you want to print more than one worksheet at a time, select the worksheets to be printed before issuing the Print command. All of the selected worksheets will print.

exercise 5 WORKING WITH MULTIPLE WORKSHEETS

1. Open Excel Worksheet E7-04.
2. Save the workbook using the Save As command and name it Excel E7, Ex 05.
3. You want the custom header you create to appear on all the worksheets in this workbook. Complete the following steps to create a header that appears on all the worksheets:
   a. Right-click the North worksheet tab.
   b. Click Select All Sheets from the shortcut menu. Notice that the word *[Group]* now appears in the title bar to the right of the file name.
   c. Create a custom header for the North worksheet that displays your name at the left margin and the file name at the right margin.
4. You want to preview all the worksheets to make sure the header appears on all of them. All the worksheets should still be selected. Click the Print Preview button on the Standard toolbar. The first worksheet is displayed. Click the Next button. The next worksheet is displayed and the header appears at the top of it. Keep clicking Next until you have viewed all the worksheets. Click Close.
5. Click the North worksheet tab. Only the North worksheet is selected.
6. You want to print the South and West worksheet. Click the South worksheet tab. Press the Ctrl key and then click the West worksheet tab. The two worksheets are now selected. Click the Print button on the Standard toolbar. The two worksheets should print.
7. Click the North worksheet tab. Only the North worksheet is selected.
8. Save the workbook using the same name (Excel E7, Ex 05) and close it.

CHAPTER summary

- A workgroup is made up of individuals who are working together on the same project.
- Being able to share a workbook enables workgroup members to work together more efficiently.
- Security is an issue when sharing a workbook because whoever has access to the network location where the shared workbook is located has access to that shared workbook.
- A workbook can be completely protected by assigning a password to it. Only those who know the password are able to open it. A workbook can also be protected so that anyone can view the workbook but only those who know the password can make changes to it.
- Worksheets can be hidden from view. Hidden worksheets can be assigned a password so that only those knowing the password can unhide the worksheet.
- Individual cells on a worksheet can be protected. If a cell is protected, the contents of the cell cannot be changed or deleted. This feature is useful for protecting formulas.
- Use the Highlight Changes command to track the changes made by each person using a shared workbook. A cell that has been changed is displayed with a border around it and a revision triangle in the upper right corner. When the mouse pointer is passed over the revision triangle, a box is displayed that lists who made the change, when the change was made, and what the change was.
- Tracked changes can be accepted or rejected all at one time, or each change can be accepted or rejected individually.
- A comment is useful for explaining or clarifying the contents of a cell. Cells with comments attached to them have red comment triangles in the upper right corner of the cell. When the mouse pointer is passed over the comment triangle, a comment box is displayed.
- Each member in a workgroup can make changes to his or her own copy of a shared workbook. All those copies of the shared workbook then can be merged into one workbook.
- To select multiple worksheets that are adjacent to one another, click the first worksheet tab, press the Shift key, and then click the last worksheet tab. To select multiple copies of nonadjacent worksheets, press the Ctrl key and then click the worksheet tab for each worksheet to be selected. Once multiple worksheets are selected, commands carried out on the active worksheet affect all the selected worksheets. For example, if several worksheets are selected and the print command is issued, all the selected worksheets will be printed.

COMMANDS review

Command	Mouse/Keyboard
Apply or remove a password to a workbook	Click File, Save As, Tools button, General Options
Hide a worksheet	Click Format, Sheet, Hide
Protect a workbook	Click Tools, Protection, Protect Workbook
Remove workbook protection	Click Tools, Protection, Unprotect Workbook
Unhide a worksheet	Click Format, Sheet, Unhide
Protect individual cells	Click Format, Cells, Protection tab
Protect a worksheet	Click Tools, Protection, Protect Sheet
Remove worksheet protection	Click Tools, Protection, Unprotect Sheet
Give specific users access to protected cells	Click Tools, Protection, Allow Users to Edit Ranges
Track changes in a shared workbook	Click Tools, Track Changes, Highlight Changes
Accept or reject tracked changes	Click Tools, Track Changes, Accept or Reject Changes
Add a comment	Right-click the cell, click Insert Comment
Edit a comment	Right-click the cell, click Edit Comment
Delete a comment	Right-click the cell, click Delete Comment
Merge shared workbooks	Click Tools, Merge Workbooks

CONCEPTS check

Completion: On a blank sheet of paper, indicate the correct term, symbol, or command for each item.

1. This term refers to all the people working together on the same project.
2. The commands for protecting a workbook and worksheet are found on this menu.
3. This is what appears in the box when you enter a password.
4. When creating a password to be used for password protection, the password is always entered this many times.
5. If a worksheet is hidden, this is what must be protected in order to prevent other users from unhiding it.
6. When individual cells have been protected on a worksheet so that changes cannot be made to them, you also have to protect this.
7. The Highlight Changes command automatically turns this feature on.
8. The option for tracking changes is found on this menu.

9. This term refers to boxes attached to individual cells which contain information regarding the specific cell to which they are attached.
10. Press this key to select multiple worksheets that are adjacent to one another.
11. Press this key to select multiple worksheets that are not adjacent to one another.
12. The command for merging shared workbooks is found on this menu.
13. List the benefits of sharing workbooks.
14. Explain what security issues you must consider when sharing a workbook.
15. List the Excel features that are not available in a shared workbook.

SKILLS check

Assessment 1

1. Open Excel Worksheet E7-05.
2. Save the worksheet using the Save As command and name it Excel E7, SA 01.
3. This workbook is the cash flow schedule for a ski shop that sells downhill and cross-country ski supplies.
4. Click File and then click Save As. Click the Tools button on the Save As dialog box and then click General Options. Assign the following password to the workbook: **CM5!78sts**.
5. Close Excel E7, SA 01. You will be using this file in assessment 2.

Assessment 2

1. Open Excel E7, SA 01. The password to open the file is CM5!78sts.
2. Save the worksheet using the Save As command and name it Excel E7, SA 02.
3. Select both worksheets. Create a custom header with your name displayed at the left margin and the file name displayed at the right margin.
4. The values in cells B9, C9, and D9 are linked to the Commissions worksheet, which is confidential. Hide the Commissions worksheet.
5. Protect the workbook by using the following password: 131!63C. Allow users to format cells.
6. All the cells that currently have something entered in them contain formulas, which you want to protect, so these cells should remain locked. Select the cells that are empty, which would be cells B3 through D5, B10 through D13, and B19. Format these cells so that they are no longer locked.
7. Protect the worksheet using the following password: W89**25s.
8. Save the workbook using the same name (Excel E7, SA 02) and close it. You will be using this file in assessment 3.

Assessment 3

1. Open Excel E7, SA 02. The password to open the file is CM5!78sts.
2. Save the worksheet using the Save As command and name it Excel E7, SA 03.
3. If necessary, edit the custom header so that the current name of the file (Excel E7, SA 03) is displayed at the right margin.
4. Click Tools, point to Protection, and then click Unprotect workbook to remove the workbook protection. The password for the workbook protection is 131!63C.
5. Click File and then click Save As. Click the Tools button and then click General Options. Delete all the asterisks from the Password to Open box. Save the file, replacing the existing Excel E7, SA 03 file.

6. Change the user name to your name. Make sure you jot down the current user name so that you can change it back at the end of the exercise.
7. Use the Highlight Changes command to turn the tracking feature on. You want to track all the changes made by everyone. The word *[Shared]* should appear in the title bar.
8. Resize the Excel window so that it appears on the left half of the desktop.
9. Open a second copy of the Excel program. Resize the second copy so that it is displayed on the right half of the desktop. Change the user name for this copy of Excel to **Megan Bassett**.
10. Open Excel E7, SA 03 in the second copy of Excel. Both you and Megan have some of the figures that go into this worksheet. Key the following figures in the cells indicated on Megan's copy of Excel (the one on the right):

Cell	Value
B3	**36,540**
B4	**6,000**
B5	**2,658.50**
C3	**43,960**
C5	**5,110**
D3	**33,271**
D5	**16,506**

    Save the workbook.
11. Click your copy of Excel (the one on the left). Save it so that you can see the changes made by Megan.
12. Key the following figures in the cells indicated on your copy of Excel (the one on the left):

Cell	Value
B10	**24,500**
B11	**10,720**
B12	**6,280**
C10	**24,500**
C11	**13,584**
C12	**6,589**
D10	**24,500**
D11	**13,072**
D12	**6,432**
D13	**2,000**

    Save the workbook.
13. Click Megan's copy of Excel (the one on the right). Save it so that you can see the changes that were made. Megan knows the loan/interest repayment in March is supposed to be $2,200. Change the value in cell D13 to **2,200**. She also knows that the beginning cash balance in January was $750. Enter **750** in cell B19. Save the worksheet.
14. Change the user name back to the original entry. Save and exit Megan's copy of Excel.
15. Click your copy of Excel (the one on the left). Maximize the window. Save the worksheet to see the changes. Accept all the changes that were made to the worksheet.
16. Turn off the Track Changes option.
17. Unhide the Commissions worksheet.
18. Preview and print both the Cash Flow and the Commissions worksheets.
19. Change the user name back to what it was originally.
20. Save the workbook using the same file name (Excel E7, SA 03) and close it.

Assessment 4

1. Open Excel Worksheet E7-06.
2. Save the worksheet using the Save As command and name it Excel E7, SA 04.
3. Create a custom header with your name displayed at the left margin and the name of the file displayed at the right margin.
4. Attach a comment to cell A5. The comment should read as follows: **This inventory reflects stock on hand as of December 15.**
5. Designate this workbook as a shared workbook.
6. Close the workbook.
7. Open the workbook and rename it New York Inventory.
8. Key the following values in the cells indicated:

Cell	Value
B8	**5**
B9	**6**
B10	**10**
B11	**2**
B12	**1**
B13	**4**
B14	**7**
B15	**20**
B16	**15**
B17	**35**
B18	**12**
B19	**8**
B20	**5**
B21	**14**
B22	**2**
B23	**19**
B24	**30**
B25	**18**
B26	**0**
B27	**28**
B28	**25**
B29	**6**

9. Save the workbook using the same name (New York Inventory) and close it.
10. Open Excel E7, SA 04. Open the workbook and rename it Los Angeles Inventory.
11. Key the following values in the cells indicated:

Cell	Value
E8	**5**
E9	**10**
E10	**3**
E11	**18**
E12	**12**
E13	**10**
E14	**8**
E15	**36**
E16	**25**
E17	**28**
E18	**35**

Cell	Value
E19	**4**
E20	**6**
E21	**0**
E22	**13**
E23	**18**
E24	**22**
E25	**8**
E26	**5**
E27	**31**
E28	**24**
E29	**22**

12. Save the workbook using the same name (Los Angeles Inventory) and close it.
13. Open Excel E7, SA 04. Merge the New York Inventory workbook and the Los Angeles Inventory workbook into the Excel E7, SA 04 workbook.
14. Remove the workbook from shared use.
15. Edit the comment attached to cell A5 so the date is December 31 rather than December 15. Save the workbook using the same name (Excel E7, SA 04).
16. Print and then close the workbook.

Assessment 5

1. Open Excel Worksheet E7-07.
2. Save the worksheet using the Save As command and name it Excel E7, SA 05.
3. Create a custom header with your name displayed at the left margin and the name of the file displayed at the right margin.
4. You want to password protect cells B4 and B5 so that only specific users can have access to them. Use Microsoft Excel Help to learn more about worksheet protection. Key **How do I password protect a cell?** in the Ask a Question box. Select *Password protect a worksheet or workbook* from the topics that are returned. Read about giving specific users access to protected ranges. Using the information provided, password protect cells B4 and B5 with the password **ST45**. Use the password **B02fy** to protect the worksheet.
5. Enter the following values in the cells indicated:

Cell	Value
B4	**1,199,564**
B5	**681,805**

6. Save and print the worksheet.
7. Enter the following values in the cells indicated:

Cell	Value
B4	**1,713,660**
B5	**892,550**

8. Save and print the worksheet.
9. Save the workbook using the same name (Excel E7, SA 05) and close it.

CHAPTER 8

USING DATA FROM THE INTERNET AND OTHER SOURCES

PERFORMANCE OBJECTIVES

Upon successful completion of chapter 8, you will be able to:

- **Import data from text files**
- **Export data to text files**
- **Place a noninteractive worksheet on the Web**
- **Place an interactive worksheet on the Web**
- **Take an Excel workbook on a "round trip"**
- **Place an interactive chart on the Web**
- **Import data from a Web page into Excel**
- **Query a database using Microsoft Query**
- **Retrieve data from a Web page using Web Query on XML Query**
- **Use XML to share Excel data on the Web**
- **Link an object in an Excel worksheet**
- **Embed an object in an Excel worksheet**

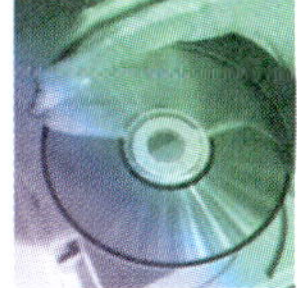

Excel Chapter 08E

In chapter 7, you were introduced to the concept of workgroup computing. People working together in a workgroup on a particular project often share not only data found in Excel workbooks, but data from other applications as well. Data in an Excel workbook may need to be accessed by another application, or you may need to have the data from another application in an Excel workbook. When data from Excel is sent to another application, such as Word, the data is said to be exported from Excel. When data from another application, such as a Web browser, is sent to Excel, the data is said to be imported into Excel. Knowing how to import and export data to and from Excel enables you to share your Excel data across applications. One of the ways to accomplish this, which is covered in this chapter, is by linking or embedding objects.

Microsoft Excel 2002 includes many Web features. You can easily place worksheets and workbooks on the Web as well as import the data from a Web page into Excel. With the increasing popularity of intranets, which are described in this chapter, Excel data is frequently imported from and exported to Web pages as an easy way for people to share data.

Importing from and Exporting to Text Files

A text file is a file that contains only printable letters, numbers, and symbols, usually from the ASCII character set. There are no formatting codes in a text file. The strength of text files is that they are easily shared. The text file format is supported by nearly every application on every machine. The weakness of text files is that they cannot contain any formatting codes. If you need to share data with others, however, using text files can be a good solution.

Importing Data from Text Files

There are a number of reasons why you might have to import a text file. The source of the data might be a mainframe computer report, which has been saved as a text file so that it can be used on a personal computer. The data might come from an older application program, and the only way you might be able to open it in Excel is by saving the data from the older program as a text file. Data sent to you in e-mail messages might be in a text file format.

Excel provides automatic help when importing text files. There are two common formats for data that is arranged in rows and columns in a text file: a delimited text file and a fixed width text file. A delimited text file uses a special character or delimiter, which is often a comma or a tab, to separate one column from the next. In figure 8.1a, the delimiter is a comma. As shown in figure 8.1b, the number of characters or spaces (or both) in each column in a fixed width text file is set.

FIGURE 8.1 *Two Common Text File Formats*

a. Delimited Text

```
Last Name, First Name, SS Number, Position, Hourly Wage
Dillard, Nancy, 555-90-2121, President, $75.00
Chung, Robert, 777-56-7654, Vice President, $55.00
Campbell, Norman, 444-78-7658, Designer, $38.00
Kimsey, C.J., 999-52-1014, Sales, $18.00
Simpson, Katie, 555-68-3564, $29.00
```

b. Fixed-Width Text

```
Last Name   First Name   SS Number     Position         Hourly Wage
Dillard     Nancy        555-90-2121   President        $75.00
Chung       Robert       777-56-7654   Vice President   $55.00
Campbell    Norman       444-78-7658   Designer         $38.00
Kimsey      C.J.         999-52-1014   Sales            $18.00
Simpson     Katie        555-68-3564   Designer         $29.00
```

To import a text file, click File and then click Open. The Open dialog box appears. Click the down-pointing arrow to the right of the Files of type box and then select *Text Files*. All the files with the extension .txt will be displayed. Usually text files end with the extension .txt. If the text file you are trying to open has a different extension, select *All Files* from the Files of type list box. Locate the file to open and then click Open. The Text Import Wizard - Step 1 of 3 dialog box, shown in figure 8.2, is displayed. You can select whether the file is Delimited or Fixed width, although Excel will probably make the proper selection for you automatically. You can also enter a value in the Start import at row box if you want the first row of the data to be a row other than 1.

HINT

Text files can be imported into Excel so that they are refreshable, which means they can be updated to the most recent version of the original data. To import text so that it is refreshable, click Data, point to Get External Data, and click Import Text File. Locate and double-click the text file to be imported. Follow the directions in the Text Import Wizard. To refresh the data when the original text changes, click the Refresh Data button on the External Data toolbar.

FIGURE

8.2 *The Text Import Wizard – Step 1 of 3 Dialog Box*

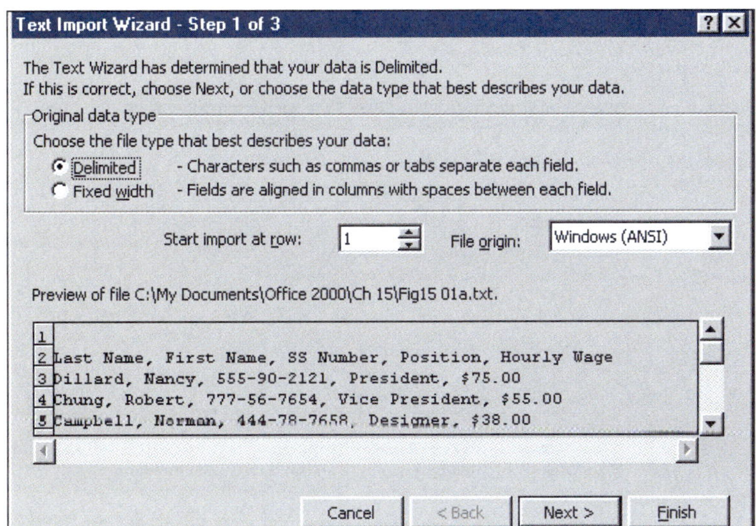

Click Next. The Text Import Wizard - Step 2 of 3 dialog box is displayed. As shown in figure 8.3, the dialog box that is displayed depends on whether the file is delimited or fixed width. If the file is delimited, the Step 2 dialog box allows you to set what character should be used as the delimiter. You also can select the Text qualifier, which typically is the quotation mark. Any text entered between text qualifiers would be placed in one column. For example "Vice President" indicates that the words *Vice President* make up the contents of a column. If the file is fixed width, the Step 2 dialog box allows you to set the column breaks.

FIGURE

8.3 *The Text Import Wizard – Step 2 of 3 Dialog Box*

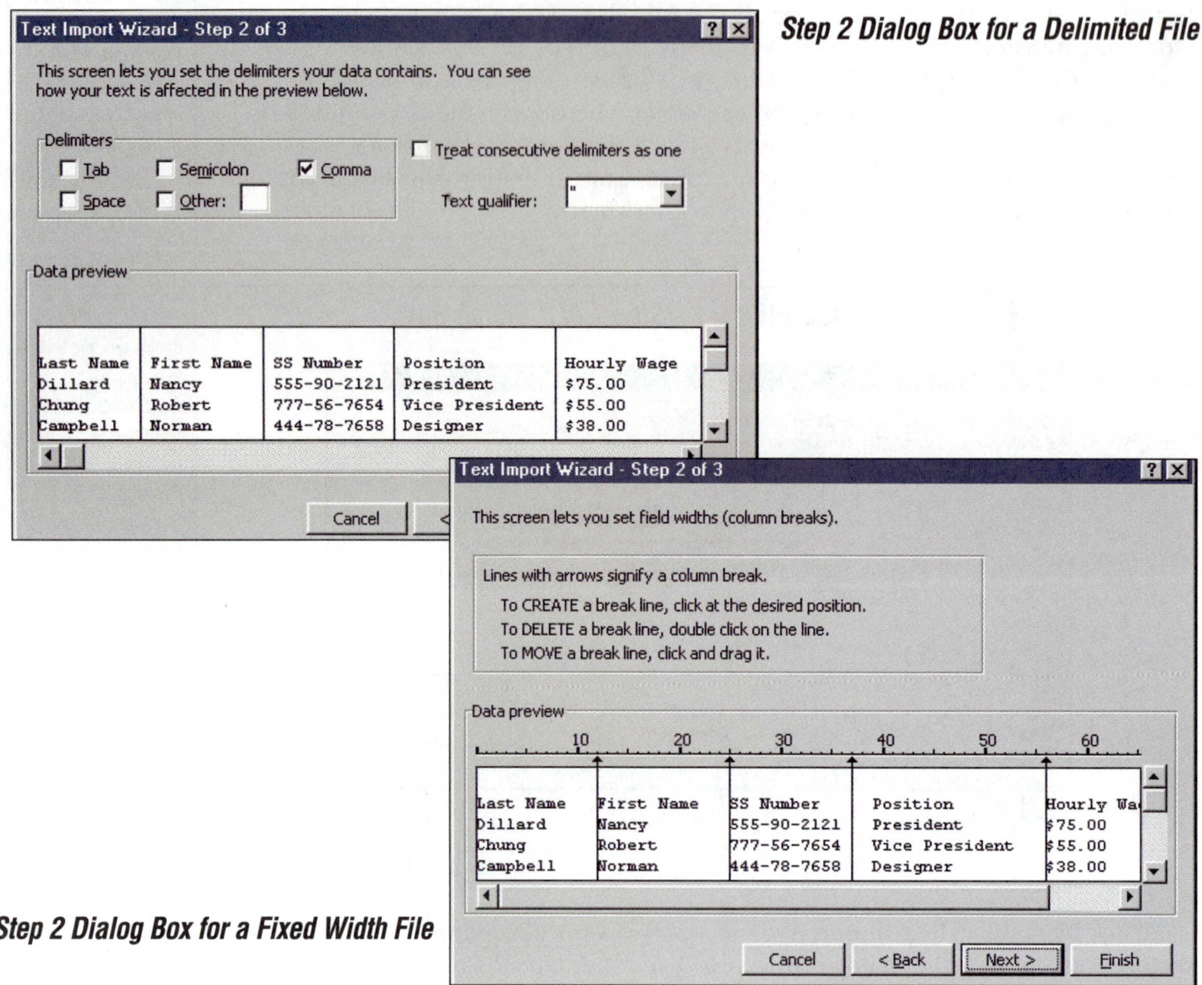

Click Next. The Text Import Wizard - Step 3 of 3 dialog box allows you to set the Data Format for each column. You can also select the Do not import column (skip) option if you do not want to import the data from a particular column or columns. Click Finish. The data is imported into an Excel worksheet.

Importing Data from Word Using Drag and Drop

Text from a Word document can be imported into an Excel workbook using drag and drop. To drag and drop between Word and Excel, arrange the windows so that you can see both applications. Select the text to be imported from the Word document. If you click on the selected text using the left mouse button and then drag it to a cell in an Excel worksheet, the text will be moved from the Word document to the Excel workbook. If you click on the selected text using the right mouse button and then drag it to a cell in an Excel worksheet, a shortcut menu appears, giving you the option of moving the text, copying the text, linking the document, creating a hyperlink, or creating a shortcut.

1. Open Excel.
2. Taylor Made, a company owned and operated by Linda Taylor, designs and makes custom clothing. Sales representatives for Taylor Made call on owners or managers of clothing stores and boutiques who might be interested in carrying Taylor Made clothes. These sales representatives e-mail information on new contacts back to the main office. The e-mail messages are saved as text files, which are then imported into an Excel worksheet. You are going to import one of these text files into an Excel worksheet. Complete the following steps to open the file:
   a. Click File and then click Open.
   b. Click the down-pointing arrow to the right of the Files of type box and select *Text Files*.
   c. Open the Contacts.txt file from your data disk.
3. The Text Import Wizard - Step 1 of 3 dialog box is displayed. This is a delimited file, and the data can be imported starting at row 1, so click Next to accept the default setting on this dialog box.
4. The Text Import Wizard - Step 2 of 3 dialog box is displayed. Complete the following steps:
   a. Click the Tab check box so that it is no longer selected.
   b. Click the Comma check box to select it.
   c. Click Next.

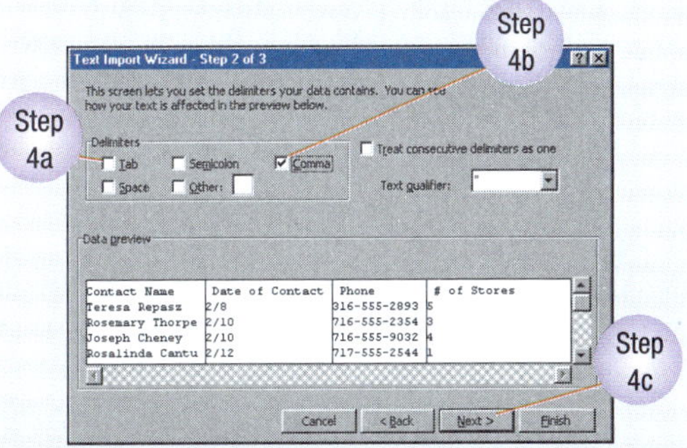

5. The Text Import Wizard - Step 3 of 3 dialog box is displayed. Complete the following steps:
   a. The first column in the Data preview area is selected. Under Column data format, click the Text option.
   b. Click the second column, *Date of Contact*, to select it.
   c. Click the Date option.
   d. Click the third column, *Phone*, to select it.
   e. Click the Text option.
   f. The last column, *# of Stores*, is already set as a General data format, which is what it should be. Click Finish.

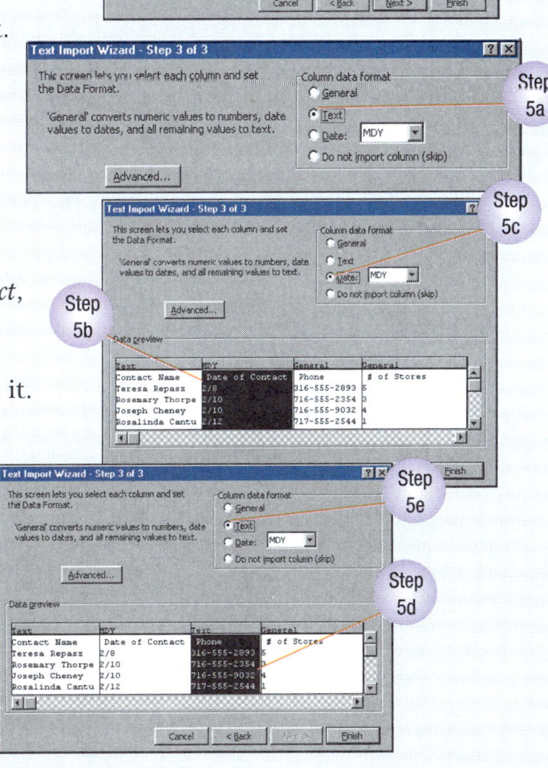

6. Adjust the width of the columns so that all the data can be seen.
7. Click File and then click Save As. Click the down-pointing arrow to the right of the Save as type box and select *Microsoft Excel Workbook*. Change the file name to Excel E8, Ex 01. Click Save.
8. Create a custom header for the worksheet that displays your name at the left margin and the file name at the right margin.

9. Start Word and open the Memo.doc file on your data disk. Arrange the windows for Word and Excel so that you can see both applications. To drag and drop data from the Memo.doc file in Word to the Excel E8, Ex 01.xls file in Excel, complete the following steps:
   a. Select the name *Jane Mercereau* in the Memo.doc file.
   b. Right-click on the name *Jane Mercereau* and drag it to cell A13 in the Excel E8, Ex 01 file.
   c. From the shortcut menu that appears, select Copy Here. 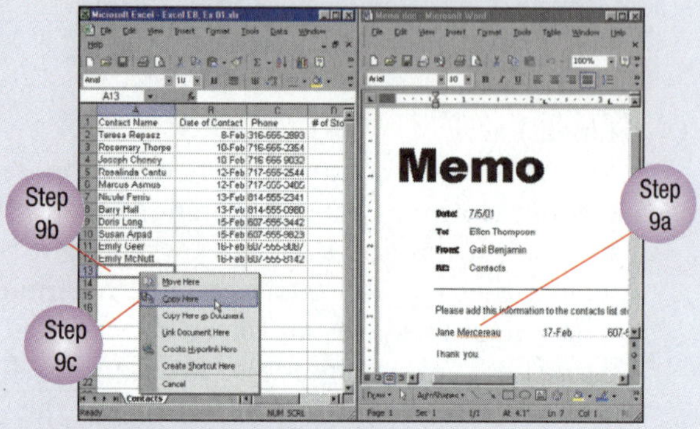
10. Repeat steps 9a through 9c to drag and drop the date *17-Feb* to cell B13, the phone number *607-555-0303* to cell C13, and the number *5* to cell D13. Exit Word.
11. Save the workbook again using the same file name (Excel E8, Ex 01) and print it.
12. Close the workbook.

Exporting Data to Text Files

There may be times when you want to share data with someone who does not have the Excel program. To do so, you can export the data in an Excel worksheet to a text file. To export a worksheet, open the worksheet, click File and then click Save As. Enter a name for the file in the file name box. Click the down-pointing arrow to the right of the Save as type box. The option you select from this list depends on the application that is going to use the file. Table 8.1 explains some of the text file options found in this list. Once you have made your selection, click Save.

TABLE 8.1 ***Text File Formats from the Save as Type List Box***

Option	Description
Text (Tab delimited)	Columns are separated by tabs
CSV (Comma delimited)	Columns are separated by commas
Formatted Text (Space delimited)	Columns are a fixed width

1. Open Excel Worksheet E8-01.
2. Complete the following steps to save the file as a text file:
   a. Click File and then click Save As.
   b. Change the file name to Sales.
   c. Click the down-pointing arrow to the right of the Save as type dialog box. Select *Text (Tab delimited).*
   d. Click Save.
   e. A dialog box is displayed, warning you that the file may contain features that are not compatible with Text (Tab delimited). Click Yes.
   f. Close the Sales.txt file. If a dialog box appears, asking if you want to save the changes you made, click No.
3. Start Microsoft Word and open the Sales.txt file. You may have to select *All Files (*.*)* from the Files of type selection box in order to display the Sales.txt file in the Open dialog box.
4. Select all the text in the document.
5. Set left tab stops at 1.5″ and 2.75″.
6. Save the file as a Word document using the file name Excel E8, Ex 02. You will have to select *Word Document (*.doc)* from the Save as type selection box on the Save As dialog box.
7. Enter a header that prints your name at the left margin and the file name Excel E8, Ex 02 at the right margin.
8. Save the Word file again using the same file name (Excel E8, Ex 02) and print it.
9. Exit Microsoft Word.

Accessing and Placing Data on the Web

Shortly after the World Wide Web appeared on the scene in the late 1980s, businesses began to take advantage of the capability to develop company intranets. An intranet is a local area or wide area network that provides an organization or business with services similar to those provided by the Internet without necessarily being connected to the Internet. Since about 1995, intranets have become increasingly popular in corporate computing because of the availability of inexpensive or, in some cases, free commercial browser and Web server software. An intranet is an excellent way to distribute information within a company. Employees find the graphical user interface of the Web easy to use. Intranets allow employees to easily access and share information. The HTML markup language used to create Web pages can be used on every desktop system. Therefore, even if some employees are using a Windows environment, some Macintosh, and others UNIX, all can access the company's intranet.

Excel 2002 incorporates many Web capabilities. You can export a workbook, worksheet, chart, or graph to HTML and then make it available on an HTTP site, on an FTP site, in a Web server, or on a network server. Users can then access the file using a Web browser. One of the advantages of putting Excel data on the Web is that people do not have to have Excel installed in order to interact with the data. All they need is a Web browser.

HINT

Worksheets you place on the Web should be no more than six columns wide. If the worksheet contains more than six columns, it may be too wide to fit in the browser window or the columns will be so narrow they will be hard to read. If possible, the worksheet should be no more than about twelve rows long. The larger the worksheet, the longer it will take to download.

Publishing Excel Worksheets as HTML

HINT

If you get a message saying the file name cannot be accessed when you try to publish Excel data as a Web page, the amount of data you are trying to save might be too large, especially if the data is to be interactive. Break the worksheet up into two or more worksheets so that you can save a smaller amount of data.

The data that you export to the Web can be either interactive or noninteractive. If the Excel data on the Web is interactive, users can enter, format, calculate, analyze, sort, and filter the data. If it is noninteractive, users will be able to view the data, but they will not be able to make any changes to it.

To publish Excel data on the Web, select the worksheet to be put on a Web page. Click File. You may have to expand the menu to see the Save as Web Page option. When the Save as Web Page option is displayed, select it. The Save As dialog box is displayed. Click Publish. The Publish As Web Page dialog box is displayed. In the Choose list box, you can select to publish a range of cells, all the items on an entire sheet, or previously published items. If the data is to be interactive, click the Add interactivity with check box. You can choose to have either spreadsheet functionality or PivotTable functionality. Clicking Change displays the Set Title dialog box. Anything you enter here will be centered over the published data. In the File name box, you must select the drive, folder, Web folder, Web server, or FTP location where the Web page should be published or saved. Click the Browse button to help you find the proper location. To view the published Web page as it will appear on the Web, make sure the Open published web page in browser check box is selected. When all the selections have been made, click Publish.

exercise 3

PLACING A NONINTERACTIVE WORKSHEET ON THE WEB

1. Open Excel Worksheet E8-03.
2. Save the workbook using the Save As command and name it Excel E8, Ex 03.
3. Complete the following steps to save noninteractive data on the Web:
   a. Select cells A1 through D7.
   b. Click File. If necessary, either wait a few moments or click the down arrow at the bottom of the menu. Click Save as Web Page.
   c. The Save As dialog box appears. Click Publish.
   d. The default range of cells under Item to publish should be A1 through D7 on Sheet 1.
   e. Click Change.
   f. The Set Title dialog box is displayed. Key **Sales Report** in the Title box.
   g. Click OK.
   h. Change the name in the File name box to **CNCSales.htm**.
   i. Make sure the Open published web page in browser check box is selected.
   j. Click Publish.

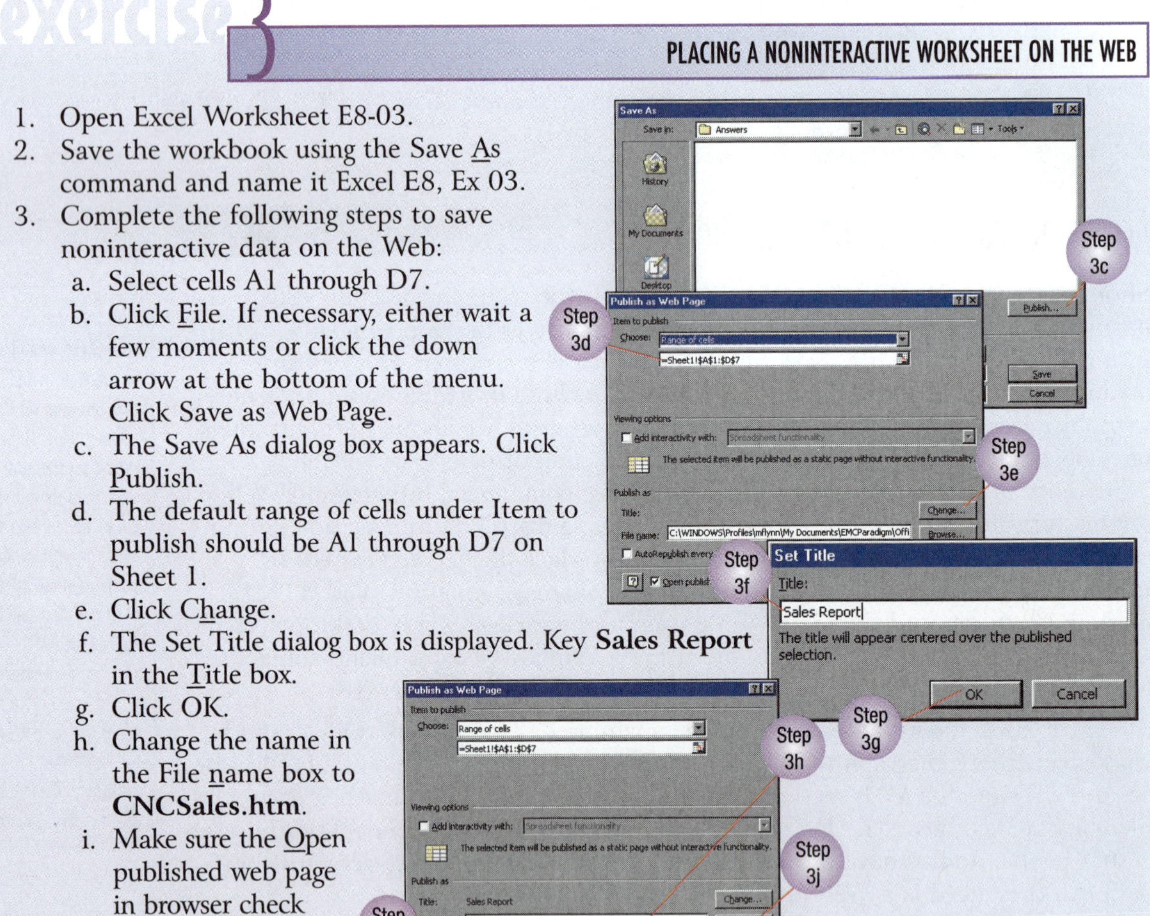

4. The Web page is displayed in Internet Explorer. Click the Print button to print the Web page.
5. Close Internet Explorer.
6. Save the workbook using the same file name (Excel E8, Ex 03) and close it.

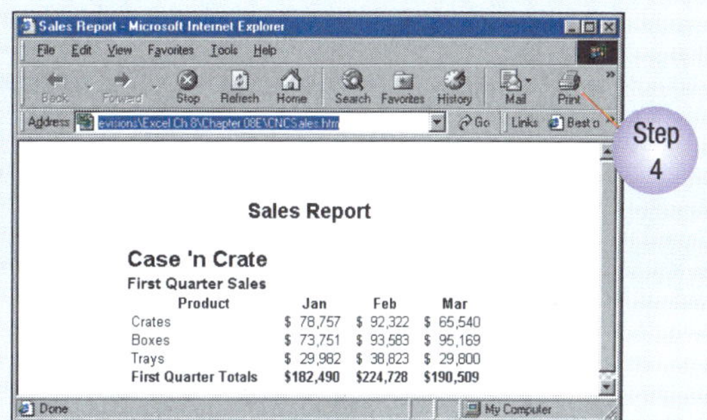

exercise 

PUBLISHING AN INTERACTIVE WORKSHEET ON THE WEB

1. Open Excel Worksheet E8-04.
2. Save the workbook using the Save As command and name it Excel E8, Ex 04.
3. Managers at Case 'n Crate need to compute sales representatives' earnings on a weekly basis. The sales representatives earn a commission based on their sales for the week. Those sales representatives who are a category 1 also receive a flat weekly salary of $200. This worksheet automatically calculates the earnings. The managers want it published on the company's intranet so they can use it to make the weekly calculations. Complete the following steps to save this worksheet as interactive data on the Web:
   a. Click File and then click Save as Web Page.
   b. The Save As dialog box appears. Click Publish.
   c. Make sure *Items on Sheet1* is selected in the Choose box.
   d. Click the Add interactivity with check box.
   e. Make sure *Spreadsheet functionality* is selected in the Add interactivity with list box.
   f. Click Change.
   g. The Set Title dialog box is displayed. Key **Managers' Worksheet for Calculating Earnings** in the Title box.
   h. Click OK.
   i. Change the name in the File name box to **CNCEarnings.htm**.
   j. Make sure the Open published web page in browser check box is selected.
   k. Click Publish.

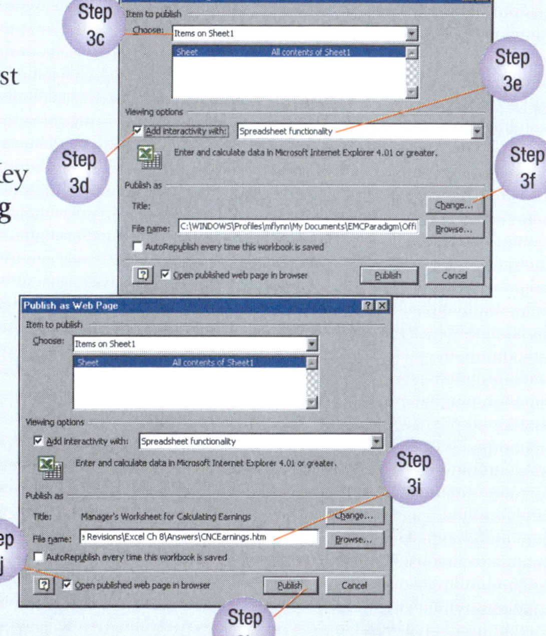

4. The Web page is displayed in Internet Explorer as an interactive data file. Complete the following steps to make changes to the worksheet:
   a. Click cell A5.

b. To sort the worksheet by sales representatives, click the drop-down arrow to the right of the Sort Ascending button and then click *Sales Rep* from the drop-down list.
c. Key the following values in the cells indicated:

Cell	Value
C5	18,252
C6	31,350
C7	17,652
C8	33,467
C9	22,406
C10	28,309
C11	24,892
C12	13,902
C13	27,346

d. Change the value in cell B6 to 1.
e. Click the AutoFilter button.
f. Click the down-pointing arrow to the right of the Salary column.
g. Click the check box next to the *$* - option so that it is no longer selected.
h. Click OK. Only the sales representatives who earn the $200 salary are displayed.
i. Click the Print button to print the worksheet.
j. Click the down-pointing arrow to the right of the Salary label.
k. Click the check box next to (Show All) to select it.
l. Click OK.

5. Close Internet Explorer.
6. Save the workbook using the same file name (Excel E8, Ex 04) and close it.

5 PLACING AN INTERACTIVE CHART ON THE WEB

1. Open Excel Worksheet E8-05.
2. Save the workbook using the Save As command and name it Excel E8, Ex 05.
3. This chart can be used by the sales representatives at Case 'N Crate to track their first-quarter sales. Management at Case 'N Crate would like this chart put on the company intranet so the sales representatives can chart their own sales. Complete these steps to save the chart on a Web page:
   a. Click File and then click Save as Web Page.
   b. The Save As dialog box appears. Click Publish.
   c. Select *Chart* from the Choose list box.
   d. Click the Add interactivity with check box.
   e. Make sure *Chart functionality* is selected in the Add interactivity with list box.

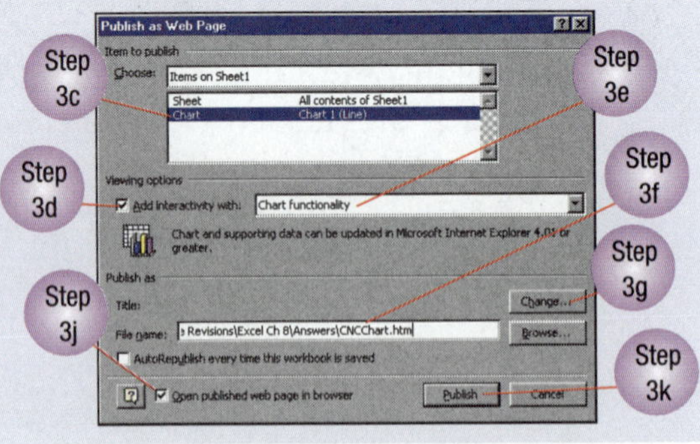

f. Change the name in the File name box to **CNCChart.htm.**

g. Click Change.

h. The Set Title dialog box is displayed. Key **Chart Your First Quarter Sales** in the Title box.

i. Click OK.

j. Make sure the Open published web page in browser check box is selected.

k. Click Publish.

4. The Web page is displayed in Internet Explorer. The chart is interactive. Key the following values in the cells indicated to make changes to the chart:

Cell	Value	Cell	Value	Cell	Value
B2	**1,895**	C2	**3,926**	D2	**4,053**
B3	**2,058**	C3	**8,502**	D3	**5,021**
B4	**7,358**	C4	**4,987**	D4	**7,932**

5. Click the Print button to print the worksheet.
6. Close Internet Explorer.
7. Save the workbook using the same file name (Excel E8, Ex 05) and close it.

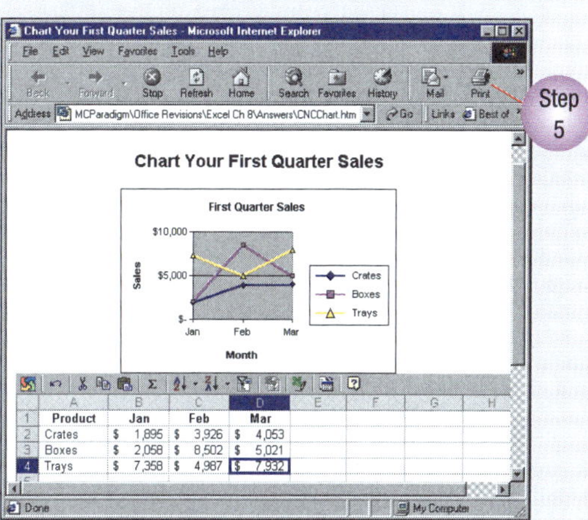

Importing Data from a Web Page into Excel

There are many ways to import data from a Web page into Excel. Depending on which method you choose, some of the data might display differently in Excel than it does on the Web page.

Simply copying and pasting is one way to import data from a Web page into Excel. Select the data you want to import and right-click on any of the cells. From the shortcut menu that appears, click Copy. Click an appropriate cell on the worksheet into which you want to import the copied data and then click the Paste button on the Standard toolbar. The data from the Web page is copied into the worksheet.

Data from a Web page can be imported into Excel using drag and drop. First select the data to be imported from the Web page and then click the selected data and drag it to the desired cell in Excel.

The Object command from the Insert menu enables you to insert a Web page in an Excel worksheet. When the object is inserted, an icon for the Web page is displayed. Double-clicking the icon opens the Web page in Internet Explorer.

You can import data from a Web page into Excel from the Web browser by clicking the Export to Excel toolbar button. When you click the Export to Excel button, a read-only copy of the data immediately appears in Excel. Using the Save As command and giving the file a new name allows you to save the data permanently as an Excel worksheet.

Export to Excel

Finally, you can open any .html file in Excel by using the Open command on the File menu. This method imports the entire Web page, although some content, such as .gif image files, might be lost.

exercise 6

IMPORTING DATA FROM A WEB PAGE INTO EXCEL

1. Complete the following steps to use the copy and paste method to import data from a Web page into Excel:
   a. Open Internet Explorer (or Netscape). You do not have to be online.
   b. Click the File menu in Internet Explorer and then click Open.
   c. The Open dialog box appears. Locate the sales_reps.html file on your data disk and open it.
   d. Open a new workbook in Excel. Arrange the windows so that you can see both the entire width of the table in the Web browser and at least cell A1 in Excel.
   e. The Web page lists the phone numbers of the sales representatives for Case 'N Crate. Click the First Name box in the upper left corner of the table and drag to the last telephone number in order to select the entire table.
   f. Click on the selected table in the Web browser and drag the mouse pointer to cell A1 in the Excel worksheet.
   g. Click the Minimize button to place Internet Explorer on the taskbar.
   h. Switch to the Excel worksheet and maximize it.
   i. Widen columns C and D so that the data in these columns is displayed on one line.
   j. Save the worksheet using the file name Excel E8, Ex 06a.
   k. Create a custom header for the worksheet that displays your name at the left margin and the file name at the right margin.
   l. Print the worksheet and then close it.
2. Complete the following steps to use the Open command to import data from a Web page into Excel:
   a. Click File and then click Open.
   b. Locate the sales_reps.html file and open it.
   c. If the Case 'N Crate logo is covering the title *Sales Representatives*, click the logo to select it and drag it to the right so that it is no longer covering the title.
   d. Save the worksheet as an Excel workbook using the file name Excel E8, Ex 06b.
   e. Create a custom header for the worksheet that displays your name at the left margin and the file name at the right margin.
   f. Save the worksheet using the same file name.
   g. Print the worksheet and then close it.

Using Database and Web Queries

Another way to retrieve external data into Excel is by using the New Web Query or the New Database Query command. The New Database Query command enables you to access databases, such as Microsoft Access, in order to retrieve data into a worksheet where it can then be analyzed in Excel. Whenever the database is updated with new information, Excel reports or summaries based on that data are automatically updated. The New Web based Query command enables you to retrieve data on a Web page and analyze it in Excel.

In order to retrieve data from a database into Excel, you create a query or question based on the data. For example, you might want to know last year's sales figures for a particular product. When creating the query, you select only the specific data you want to retrieve. There are three steps to using Query to retrieve data. First, you establish the data source of the data to be retrieved; second, you use the Query Wizard to select the specific data to be retrieved; and third, you return the data to Excel where it can be formatted, summarized, and used for creating reports.

To create a Database Query, click the cell on the Excel worksheet where the external data range is to start. Click Data, point to Import External Data, and then click New Database Query. If Query has not already been installed on your computer, you will be prompted to install Query. Once Query is installed, the Choose Data Source dialog box shown in figure 8.4 is displayed. This dialog box is used for establishing the data source. On the Databases tab, make sure the Use the Query Wizard to create/edit queries check box is selected. Double-click the database from which the data is to be retrieved. The Select Database dialog box is displayed. Double-click the database file where the data is located. From this point you can follow the directions provided by the Query Wizard. The Query Wizard enables you to select the tables and fields to be included, sort the data, and do simple filtering before the data is returned to an Excel worksheet.

FIGURE 8.4 ***The Choose Data Source Dialog Box***

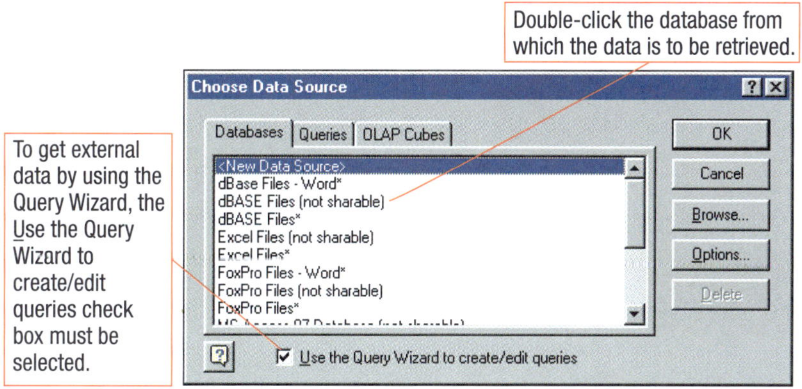

Web queries, or XML queries, are particularly useful for retrieving data that is in tables. You will learn more about XML in the following section. You can create a Web query by starting either in Excel or in the browser. If you start in Excel, click Data, select Import External Data, and then click New Web Query. In the New Web Query dialog box, enter the URL for the Web page from which you want to get data. Click Go. If you start in a browser, browse to the Web page containing the data you want to retrieve. Click the arrow next to the Edit with button and click Edit with Microsoft Excel.

When the Web page is displayed in the browser, yellow arrow buttons appear next to each table on the page, as shown in figure 8.5. Click the arrow button next to the table you want to import. Click Import. The data can be returned either to the existing worksheet or to a new worksheet. Once the data is imported, it can be refreshed either by the clicking of a button, automatically whenever the workbook is opened, or at timed intervals.

FIGURE 8.5 *The New Web Query Dialog Box*

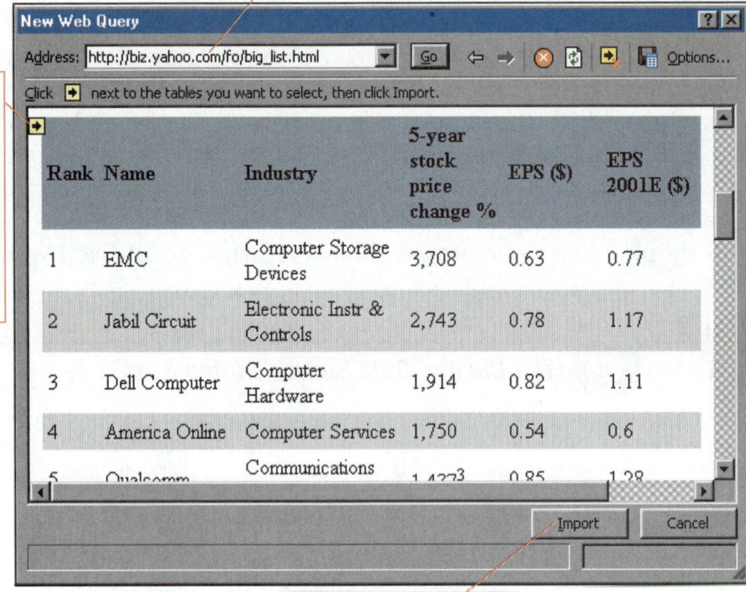

exercise 7

RUNNING A WEB QUERY

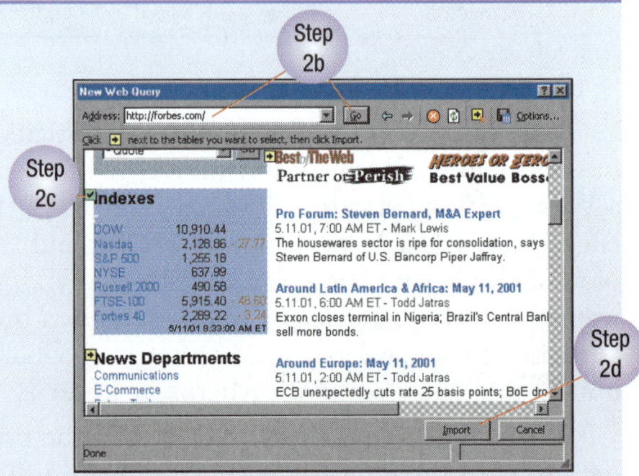

(Note: In order to complete the following exercise you must be online.)

1. If necessary, open a new workbook in Excel and click cell A1.
2. Complete the following steps to run a Web Query:
   a. Click Data, select Import External Data, and then click New Web Query.
   b. The New Web Query dialog box is displayed. Enter the following URL: **forbes.com**
   Click Go.
   c. Find the Indexes on the home page and click the yellow arrow button next to them. When you click the button, the plus sign turns into a check mark.
   d. Click Import.

3. The Import Data dialog box is displayed. You want to put the data on the existing worksheet in cell A1. Click Properties.

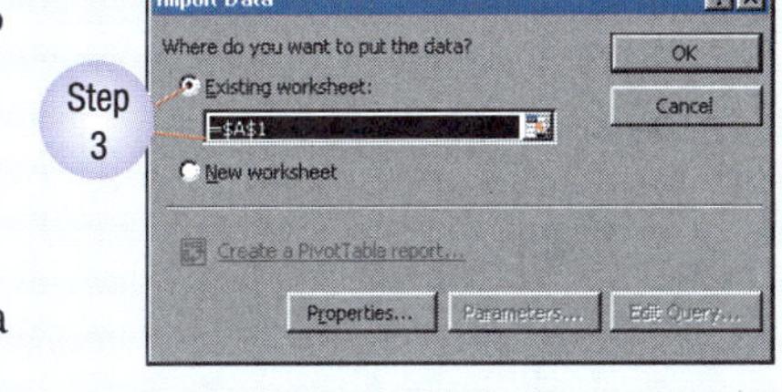

4. The External Data Range Properties dialog box is displayed. This dialog box enables you to adjust refresh times for the live data. Check the Refresh data on file open option. Click OK. Click OK again to import the data.
5. Save the file using the file name Excel E8, Ex 07.
6. Enter a custom header that prints your name at the left margin and the name of the file at the right margin.
7. Print the worksheet.
8. Save the file and close Excel.
9. If necessary, disconnect from your Internet Service Provider.

USING MICROSOFT QUERY TO QUERY A DATABASE

1. If necessary, open a new workbook in Excel and click cell A1. Make sure the CD-ROM that accompanies this book is in the CD-ROM drive.
2. The CD-ROM has a Microsoft Access database file called Payroll.mdb. Retrieve data from this database from the *Excel Expert Student Files* folder using Microsoft Query by completing the following steps:
   a. Click Data, point to Import External Data, and then click New Database Query.
   b. If necessary, click the Databases tab.
   c. Make sure the Use the Query Wizard to create/edit queries check box is selected.
   d. Double-click the *MS Access Database** option.
   e. The Select Database dialog box is displayed. From the drop-down menu for the Drives box, select the CD-ROM drive. Usually, this is drive E. If your CD-ROM drive is a drive other than E, ask your instructor for help.
   f. Double-click the *payroll.mdb* option from the Database Name list.
   g. The Query Wizard – Choose Columns dialog box is displayed. Click the plus sign next to *Employee Information*.

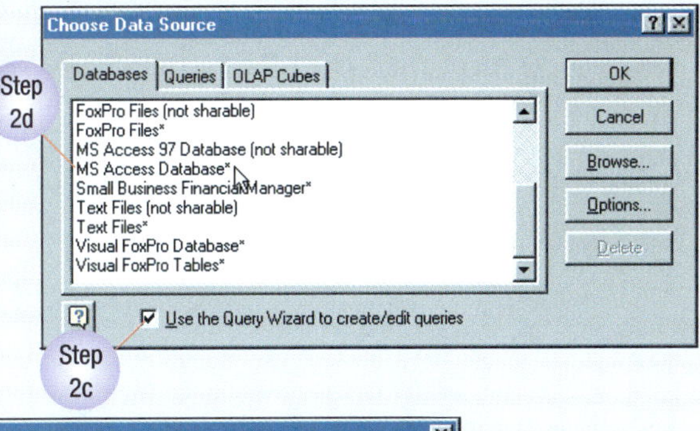

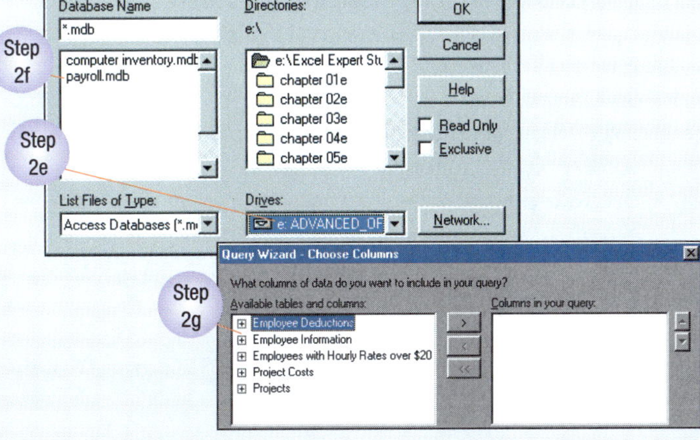

h. A list of all the fields in the Employee Information table is displayed. Click the *Firstname* option in the Available tables and columns list.

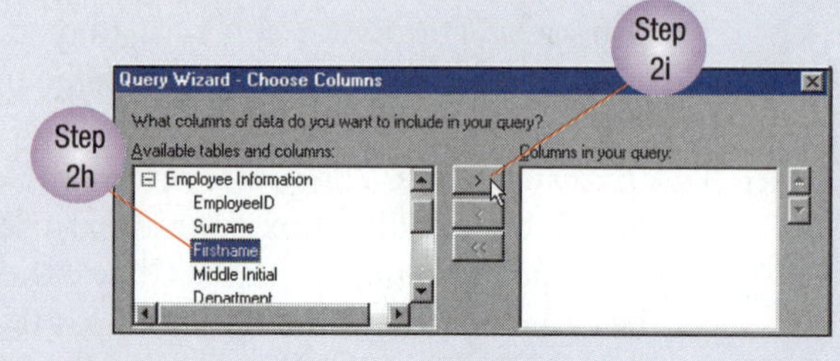

i. Click the top arrow button. The *Firstname* option has now moved from the Available tables and columns list to the Columns in your query list.

j. Click the *Surname* option in the Available tables and columns list. Click the top arrow button.

k. Click the *HourlyRate* option in the Available tables and columns list. Click the top arrow button. *Firstname*, *Surname*, and *HourlyRate* should all be listed in the Columns in your query list.

l. Click Next.

m. The Query – Wizard Filter Data dialog box is displayed. You want to retrieve only those records of employees who earn more than $20.00 an hour. In the Column to filter box, click *HourlyRate*.

n. In the first box in the Only include rows where section, select *is greater than*.

o. Key **20** in the second box in the Only include rows where section.

p. Click Next.

q. The Query Wizard – Sort Order dialog box is displayed. You want to sort the rows by Surname. Click the down-pointing arrow to the right of the Sort by box and click *Surname*.

r. Click Next.

s. The Query Wizard – Finish dialog box is displayed. Make sure the Return Data to Microsoft Excel option is selected.

t. Click Finish.

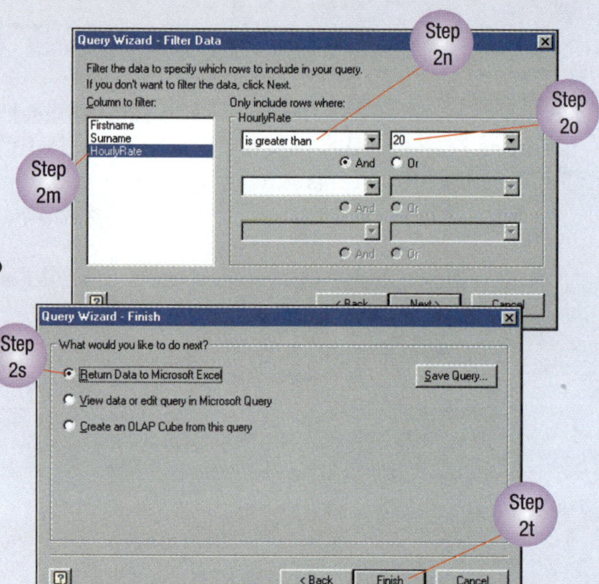

3. The Import Data dialog box is displayed. Make sure that the Existing worksheet is selected and cell A1 is entered in the box. Click OK.

4. The appropriate data is retrieved into Excel. Format the figures in column C to display as currency with two decimal places.

5. Save the worksheet using the file name Excel E8, Ex 08.

6. Create a custom header for the worksheet that displays your name at the left margin and the file name at the right margin.

7. Print the worksheet.

8. Save the workbook using the same file name (Excel E8, Ex 08) and close it.

Using XML to Share Excel Data on the Web

XML, or Extensible Markup Language, is designed to improve the functionality of the Web by providing a more flexible way to identify information. XML is based on SGML, the same language on which HTML is based. Businesses are finding that HTML, currently the language most commonly used for documents on the Web, is limited in terms of the ways it can describe information. HTML focuses on the presentation of information, or on the way the information is formatted. XML focuses on the information itself. With an XML document, it is much easier to work with or manipulate data than it is with an HTML document. With XML, data from different applications are given a standardized format, making XML the data-exchange format of choice for many business applications. Since XML allows for much more flexibility in manipulating data and since it allows for easy data exchange, it is becoming an essential tool for business transactions.

With Excel 2002 you can create and analyze XML data. Excel 2002 can recognize and open any XML document. With the XML Spreadsheet file format included with Excel 2002, you also can save an Excel spreadsheet as an XML file. Any XML document can be loaded into Excel by clicking File and Open. Click the down-pointing arrow to the right of the files of type box and click *XML Files (*.xml).* Select the file to be opened and click Open. To save an Excel spreadsheet as an XML file, click File and Save As. Click the down-pointing arrow to the right of the Save as type box and click *XML Spreadsheet (*.xml).*

exercise  OPENING AN XML FILE IN EXCEL

1. Your *Chapter 08E* folder contains an XML file named Phone Numbers.XML. Complete the following steps to open the Phone Numbers.XML file in Excel.
   a. Click File and Open.
   b. Click the down-pointing arrow to the right of the Files of type box and click *XML Files (*.xml).*
   c. Click *Phone Numbers.XML* and click Open.
2. The Phone Numbers. XML file is opened in Excel. Save the file as an Excel worksheet. Name the worksheet file Excel E8, Ex 09.
3. Print and close the Excel E8, Ex 09 worksheet file.

Linking and Embedding Objects

Another way of sharing Excel data with other applications is by copying the information as either a linked object or an embedded object. The information that is being copied is called the object. The file from which the object comes is called the source file. The file into which the object is being copied is called the destination file.

A linked object is stored with the source file. Any changes made to the object in the source file are automatically reflected in the destination file. An embedded object is stored with the destination file. If an object is embedded, there is no link to the source file. Therefore, any changes made to the object in the source file are not reflected in the destination file. Since an embedded object is stored with the destination file, it can be edited only in the destination file.

An important difference between linking and embedding objects is the size of the destination file. The size of the destination file is much larger if the object is embedded. Linking an object requires much less disk space for the destination file than embedding an object.

There is more than one way to link or embed an object in Excel. Using the Insert Object command provides you with the most control over the process. To insert a linked or embedded object, access the destination file, which is the worksheet where the object is to be placed. Click Insert and then click Object. The Object dialog box appears. To create a new object, click the Create New tab as shown in figure 8.6. To insert an object from an existing file, click the Create from File tab shown in figure 8.7.

FIGURE 8.6 ***Object Dialog Box with the Create New Tab Selected***

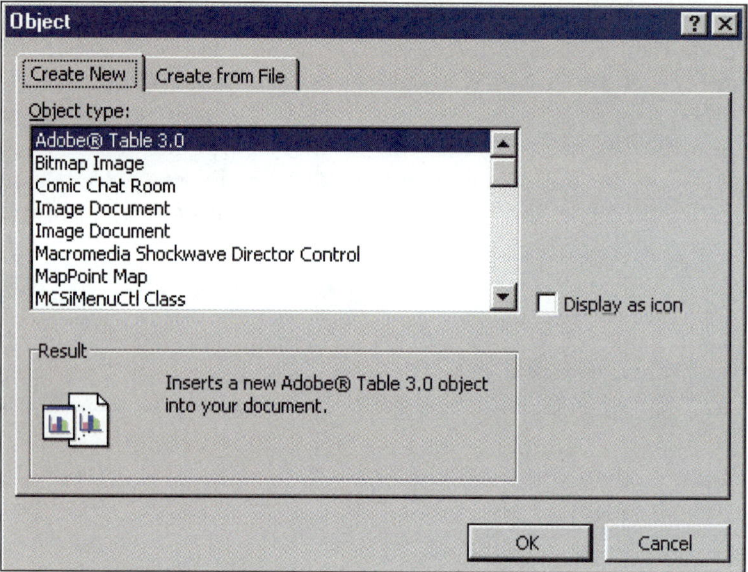

FIGURE 8.7 ***Object Dialog Box with the Create from File Tab Selected***

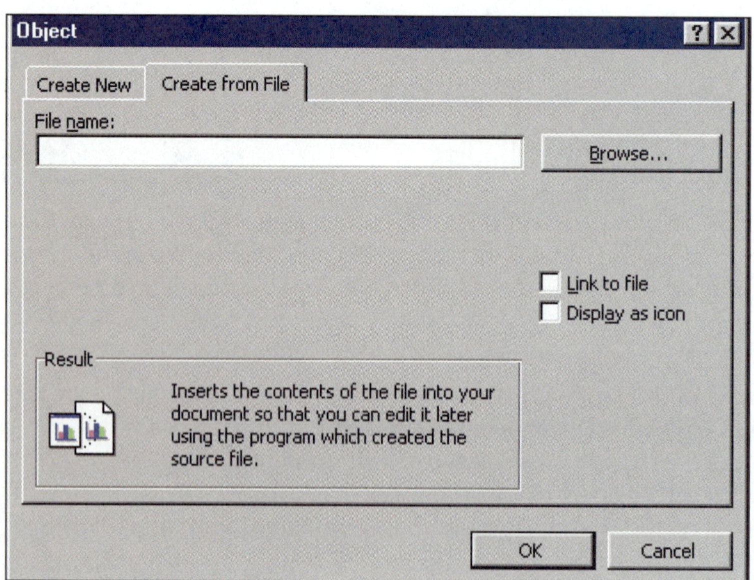

If you are creating a new embedded object, select the type of object you want to create from the Object type box. If you plan to put the workbook online, clicking the Display as icon check box will display the object as an icon that viewers can double-click to display the object. If you are inserting a linked or embedded object from an existing file, enter the name of the file in the File name box. If the Link to file check box is not selected, the object will be embedded. If it is selected, the object will be linked. Clicking the Display as icon check box will display the object as an icon to those viewing the workbook online.

In addition to inserting a linked object or embedded object from an existing file, you can copy information from an existing file as a linked or embedded object. First, select the information to be copied. Right-click the selected information and then click Copy on the shortcut menu. Switch to the worksheet that is to be the destination file. Click Edit and then click Paste Special. The Paste Special dialog box shown in figure 8.8 is displayed. Selecting the Paste option from this dialog box copies the information as an embedded object. Selecting the Paste link option copies the information as a linked object. In the As box, make sure the option that has the word Object in its name is selected.

HINT

When data that has been copied as a linked or embedded object is pasted into the destination file, make sure that no data in the destination file is overwritten.

FIGURE 8.8 ***Paste Special Dialog Box***

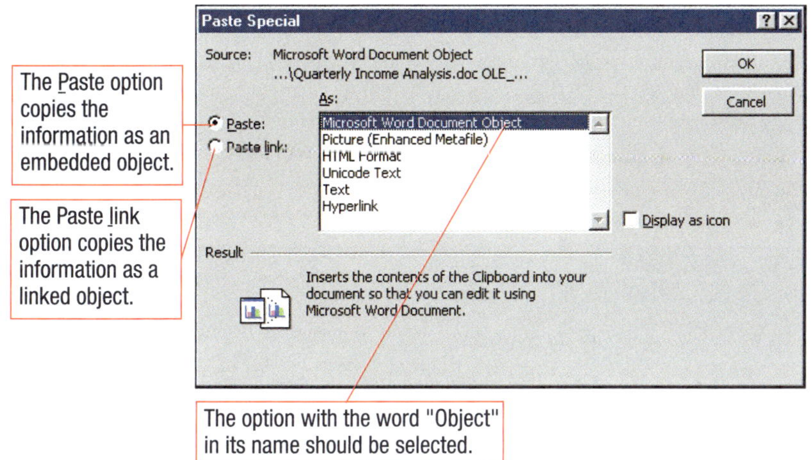

exercise 10

LINKING OBJECTS

1. Open Excel Worksheet E8-06.
2. Save the worksheet using the Save As command and name it Excel E8, Ex 10.
3. Create a custom header that displays your name at the left margin and the file name at the right margin.
4. The figure for the proposed budget increase that needs to be entered into cell B10 can be found in the Budget.doc file. To insert text from the Budget.doc file into the Excel E8, Ex 10 file, complete the following steps:
   a. Click cell A19.
   b. Click Insert and then click Object.
   c. The Object dialog box is displayed. Click the Create from file tab.
   d. Click the Browse button.
   e. From the Browse dialog box, select Budget.doc from your data disk.
   f. Click Insert.
   g. Click the Link to file check box to select it.
   h. Click OK.
5. The linked object is inserted in the worksheet. Read the information that is displayed. Key **10** in cell B10. Save the workbook using the same file name (Excel E8, Ex 10) and print it.
6. Double-click the linked object. Word opens automatically and Budget.doc is the active file. Delete *10* and in its place key **08**. Save the file. Exit from Word.
7. If necessary, switch to the Excel E8, Ex 10 workbook in Excel. The text in the linked object automatically changed from *10* to *.08*. Key **.08** in cell B10. Save the workbook using the same file name (Excel E8, Ex 10) and print it.
8. Close the workbook.

exercise 11

EMBEDDING AN OBJECT

1. Open Excel Worksheet E8-07.
2. Save the worksheet using the Save As command and name it Excel E8, Ex 11.
3. The logo for Linda Taylor's custom-made clothing store, Taylor Made, is stored on your data disk. Complete the following steps to insert the logo as an embedded object:
   a. Click cell A1.
   b. Click Insert and then click Object.
   c. The Object dialog box is displayed. Click the Create from file tab.
   d. Click the Browse button.
   e. From the Browse dialog box, select Taylor.bmp from your data disk.
   f. Click Insert.
   g. Make sure that the Link to file check box is clear.
   h. Click OK.
4. The object is embedded in the worksheet. Double-click the object to access it in the Paint program. Make a change to the image and save it. Close the Paint program. Your change will automatically take effect in the Excel worksheet.
5. Create a custom header that displays your name at the left margin and the file name at the right margin.
6. Save the workbook using the same file name (Excel E8, Ex 11) and print it.
7. Close the workbook.

CHAPTER summary

- Importing data to Excel refers to sending data from another application to an Excel workbook. Exporting data from Excel refers to sending Excel data to another application.
- A text file contains only printable letters, numbers, and symbols, usually from the ASCII character set. A text file contains no formatting codes. A text file is supported by practically every application on every computer platform.
- There are two common formats for data that is arranged in rows and columns in a text file. A delimited text file uses a special character called a delimiter to separate one column from the next. Commas and tabs are often used as delimiters. Each column has a set number of characters or spaces (or both) in a fixed width text file.
- An intranet provides the services similar to those provided by the Internet within a business or an organization. An intranet is not necessarily connected to the Internet. Intranets use the same Web browser and Web server software as the Internet.
- Excel data placed on a Web page can be either interactive or noninteractive. If it is interactive, users can enter, format, calculate, analyze, sort, and filter the data. If it is noninteractive, users will be able to view the data only. They cannot make any changes to it.
- Place Excel data on a Web page by clicking File and Save as Web page and then clicking the Publish button on the Save As dialog box.
- You can import data from a Web page into Excel by copying and pasting, by using the Export to Excel button in the Web browser, by using a Web Query, or by using the Open command on the File menu in Excel.
- During the linking and embedding process, the information being copied is called the object. The file from which the object originates is called the source file. The file into which the object will be placed is called the destination file.
- A linked object is stored with the source file. Changes made to the object in the source file are automatically reflected in the destination file.
- An embedded object is stored with the destination file. Any changes made to the source file are not reflected in the destination file. Changes can be made to an embedded object in the destination file only.
- If an object is embedded in the destination file, the destination file will be significantly larger than if the object is linked to the destination file.
- Objects can be linked or embedded by using the Copy and Paste Special commands.

COMMANDS review

Command	Mouse/Keyboard
Import from a text file	Click File, Open, select *Text Files* from the Files of type list box
Export to a text file	Click File, Save As
Export Excel data to a Web page	Click File, Save As Web Page, Publish
Import Excel data from a Web page	Right-click the data to be imported, click Copy, click a cell on the worksheet, click the Paste button
Run a Web Query	Click Data, Import External Data, New Web Query
Query a database	Click Data, Import External Data, New Database Query
Open an .html file in Excel	Click File, Open
Open an XML file in Excel	Click File, Open, select *XML Files* from the files of type list box
Save an Excel worksheet as an XML file	Click File, Save As, select *XML Spreadsheet* from the Save as type box
Insert a linked or embedded object	Click Insert, Object
Copy a linked or embedded object	In the source file, right-click the object to be copied, click Copy. In the destination file, click Edit, Paste Special

CONCEPTS check

Completion: On a blank sheet of paper, indicate the correct term, symbol, or command for each item.

1. This term refers to sending data from Excel to another application.
2. The characters from a text file usually come from this character set.
3. This term refers to a text file that uses commas or another special character to separate the columns.
4. Text files usually end with this extension.
5. This term refers to a local area or wide area network that provides a business or organization with services similar to those provided by the Internet without necessarily being connected to the Internet.
6. This is the name of the markup language used to create Web pages.
7. This is the only software users need to access Excel data that has been placed on the Web.
8. This term describes Excel data on the Web that can be entered, formatted, calculated, analyzed, sorted, and filtered.
9. One way to import data from a Web page into Excel is to click this button from the Web page displaying the data to be imported.

10. This type of object is stored with the source file.
11. This type of object has to be edited in the destination file.
12. If you are linking an object by copying it, you have to click this option from the Edit menu in the destination file.
13. List the reasons why you might need to import a text file to Excel.
14. List the advantages of using a company intranet for distributing information.
15. You need to share Excel data with other applications, but the available storage space is limited. Explain whether you would choose to link or embed the data and why.

SKILLS check

Assessment 1

1. Someone has sent you some advertising figures as a text file. You need to import them into Excel. Open the Advertising.txt file. Advertising.txt is a fixed width file. The data in the first column is text. The remaining columns should be formatted as General.
2. Save the workbook as a Microsoft Excel workbook file using the Save As command. Name the file Excel E8, SA 01.
3. Create a custom header that displays your name at the left margin and the file name at the right margin.
4. Print the worksheet.
5. Save the workbook using the same file name (Excel E8, SA 01) and close it.

Assessment 2

1. Open Excel Worksheet E8-08.
2. This worksheet contains pricing information on some fabrics. Save this file as a text (tab delimited) file. Name the saved file Excel E8, SA 02.txt.
3. Close the Excel E8, SA 02.txt file.
4. Start Word and open the Excel E8, SA 02.txt file.
5. Select all the text in the document and, using the ruler, set left tab stops at 2.25″, 3″, 3.75″, 4.75″, and 5.75″.
6. Save the file as a Word document using the file name Excel E8, SA 02.doc.
7. Create a custom header for the Word document that prints your name at the left margin and the file name at the right margin.
8. Save the document again using the same file name (Excel E8, SA 02) and close it.

Assessment 3

1. Open Excel Worksheet E8-09.
2. Save the workbook using the Save As command and name it Excel E8, SA 03.
3. Save cells A5 through E24 as a noninteractive Web page. The data should be published using the file name Addresses.
4. Print the Web page from Internet Explorer (or Netscape Navigator).
5. Close Internet Explorer.
6. Save the workbook again using the same file name (Excel E8, SA 03) and close it.

Assessment 4

1. Open Excel Worksheet E8-10.
2. Save the workbook using the Save As command and name it Excel E8, SA 04a.
3. Designers who help design clothes for Linda Taylor's company, Taylor Made, often need to calculate how much the fabric for their designs will cost. Linda Taylor wants this worksheet published on the company intranet so the designers can use it when needed. Select cells A3 through E15. Save this worksheet as interactive data on the Web. When the Save As dialog box displays, click the option for saving only the selected range of cells. Set the title for the published data as Fabric Cost Calculations. The data should be published using the file name Fabric Cost.
4. When the Web page is displayed in Internet Explorer, delete the values in cells D2, D5, D9, and D10.
5. Key the following values in the cells indicated:

Cell	Value
D3	**35**
D5	**18**
D9	**42**
D11	**20**

6. Print the Web page.
7. Delete the values in cells D3, D5, D9, and D11.
8. Sort the data in the 01-24 yards column from the most expensive fabric to the least expensive fabric.
9. Filter the data so that only the fabrics that cost less than $100 a yard for 24 or fewer yards is displayed.
10. Key the following values in the cells indicated:

Cell	Value
D3	**12**
D7	**26**
D11	**8**

11. Print the Web page.
12. Change the filter so that all the fabrics are displayed.
13. Click the Export to Excel button.
14. The worksheet is displayed in Excel. Save the workbook on your data disk. Change the file type to Microsoft Excel workbook. Use the file name Excel E8, SA 04b. Print the worksheet and close it. Close worksheet Excel E8, SA 04a.
15. Close Internet Explorer.

Assessment 5

1. Open Excel Worksheet E8-11.
2. Save the workbook using the Save As command and name it Excel E8, SA 05.
3. This file can be used by designers and the office management at Taylor Made to break down the design costs of individual designs. Linda Taylor would like it placed on the company's intranet. Save this chart as interactive data on the Web. Set the title for the published data as Calculating Design Costs. The data should be published using the file name Design Cost.
4. When the Web page is displayed in Internet Explorer, key the following values in the cells indicated:

Cell	Value
B1	**300**
B2	**175**

B3 **2560**
B4 **782**
B5 **679**

5. Print the Web page.
6. Close Internet Explorer.
7. Save the Excel workbook using the same file name (Excel E8, SA 05) and close it.

Assessment 6

1. Open Internet Explorer (or Netscape). You do not have to be online.
2. Open the Employees.html file. This is a list of the employees who work at Whitewater Canoe and Kayak Corporation, along with their titles and the number of years they have been employed there.
3. Open a new workbook in Excel. Arrange the windows so that you can see both the entire width of the table in Internet Explorer and at least cell A1 in Excel.
4. Select the entire table in Internet Explorer. Click on the selected table and drag it to cell A1 in Excel.
5. Close Internet Explorer. Maximize the Excel window.
6. Widen the columns as necessary so that all the data is displayed.
7. Adjust the row height of all the rows in the table to 12.75. Save the worksheet using the file name Excel E8, SA 06a.
8. Create a custom header for the worksheet that displays your name at the left margin and the name of the file at the right margin.
9. Print the worksheet. Save and close it.
10. From Excel, open the employees.html file.
11. Adjust the height of row 1 so the company logo fits in it.
12. Save the worksheet as an Excel Workbook using the file name Excel E8, SA 06b.
13. Create a custom header for the worksheet that displays your name at the left margin and the name of the file at the right margin.
14. Print the worksheet. Save and close it.
15. Open Internet Explorer.
16. Open the Vacation.htm file in Internet Explorer.
17. This interactive worksheet calculates the number of vacation days for which employees are eligible. Key **15** in cell B3 to see how it works.
18. Export the table to Excel using the Export to Excel button.
19. Save the data on your data disk as an Excel workbook using the file name Excel E8, SA 06c.
20. Create a custom header for the worksheet that displays your name at the left margin and the name of the file at the right margin.
21. Print the worksheet. Save and close it.
22. Close Internet Explorer.

Assessment 7

1. The CD-ROM has a Microsoft Access database file called Computer Inventory.mdb. Retrieve data from this database using the New Database Query command. From the Product List table include the *PartName, SupplierNo,* and *ListPrice* columns. From the Suppliers Table include the *SupplierName* column.
2. Filter the data that is retrieved so that only those records are retrieved where the supplier name equals ComputerWay or Jorge Computers.
3. Sort the data by SupplierName and then by PartName.
4. Return the data to Microsoft Excel.
5. Format the figures in column C as currency with two decimal places.

6. Save the worksheet using the file name Excel E8, SA 07.
7. Create a custom header for the worksheet that displays your name at the left margin and the name of the file at the right margin.
8. Save the worksheet again using the same file name (Excel E8, SA 07) and print it.
9. Close the worksheet.

Assessment 8

1. Start Windows' Paint application.
2. In Paint, open the Copper.bmp file.
3. You want to embed the logo in a worksheet. Copy the logo and use the Paste Special to paste it into the Excel Worksheet E8-12.
4. Save the worksheet using the Save As command and name it Excel E8, SA 08.
5. Adjust the size of the logo so that it fits in rows 1 through 7.
6. Double-click the logo to edit it.
7. Click Image and then click Invert Colors.
8. Click anywhere outside the logo.
9. Create a custom header that displays your name at the left margin and the file name at the right margin.
10. Save the file using the same file name (Excel E8, SA 08) and print it.
11. Close the workbook.

Assessment 9

1. Open the XML document Employee Training Hours.
2. Save the Employee Training Hours file as an Excel workbook. Name the workbook file Excel E8, SA 09. Print the file.
3. Close the workbook.

Interpreting and Integrating Data

ASSESSING proficiency

In this unit, you have learned how to use PivotTables, PivotCharts, Goal Seek, Solver, and Scenario Manager. You learned how to record, run, and edit macros; assign macros to command buttons; create custom toolbars; and use the auditing toolbar. You learned how to share workbooks; change workbook properties; apply and remove passwords, workbook protection, and worksheet protection; merge workbooks; import and export data from text files; place a noninteractive and an interactive worksheet on the Web; import data from an Access database and a Web page; use Web Query; and link and embed objects.

Assessment 1

1. Open Excel Worksheet 07.
2. Save the workbook using the Save As command and name it Excel, EPA 01.
3. Create a PivotTable report that uses the data in cells A3 through G30. Place the PivotTable on a new worksheet. Rename the new worksheet PivotTable Report.
4. Create a custom header for the PivotTable Report worksheet that has your name left aligned and the file name right aligned.
5. Drag the Country button into the Drop Row Fields Here area.
6. Drag the Item button to the Drop Row Fields Here area, under the Country button. When the PivotTable is displayed, the *Item* field should be to the right of the *Country* field.
7. Drag the Profit button to the Drop Data Items Here area.
8. Format the values in the Total column as currency with no decimal places.
9. Display only China and Saudi Arabia. Print the PivotTable Report worksheet.
10. Display all the countries. Print the PivotTable Report worksheet.
11. Save the workbook using the same name (Excel, EPA 01) and close it.

Assessment 2

1. Open Excel Worksheet 08.
2. Save the workbook using the Save As command and name it Excel, EPA 02.
3. There are three different work schedules for the employees of the Books Galore bookstore. Each employee gets two days off in a row. At the top of the Employee Schedule worksheet are the three schedules. The zeros

represent the days off for that schedule and the ones represent the days worked. Cells C7 through I7 display the total staff needed for that day. Cells C8 through I8 display the average number of customers who come into the store on a particular day. Cells C9 through I9 display the number of employees needed for each day based on a staff to customer ratio of 1 employee for every 80 customers who come into the store in a day. Cell B11 displays that ratio. The owner of the bookstore wants a comparison of two staff to customer ratios. Her goal is to find the lowest total payroll cost while adequately staffing the bookstore. Click cell B13 and enter the daily salary amount for one employee, which would be the average hourly salary times the average hours worked in a day. The average hourly salary is $10, and the average hours worked in a day is eight.

4. Click cell A16. Enter the total payroll amount. The total payroll amount would be the total staff needed, which is found in cell B7, times the daily salary, which is found in cell B13.
5. Use Solver to find the minimum payroll amount. The target cell is the total payroll, which is found in cell A16. You want the target cell to be equal to the minimum value. The cells that can be changed are cells B3 through B5. The following constraints must be applied:
   - The cells that can change (B3:B5) must be an integer.
   - The cells that can change (B3:B5) must be greater than or equal to zero.
   - The total staff (C7:I7) must be greater than or equal to the staffing demand (C9:I9).

   When Solver finds a solution, save it as a scenario. Name the scenario Staff/Customer Ratio of 1 to 80. Be sure to click the Restore Original Values option before leaving the Solver Results dialog box.
6. Change the staff/customer ratio to 1 to 100.
7. Use Solver to find the schedule that finds the minimum payroll amount at this new higher ratio. The constraints all stay the same from step 6. Save the results as a scenario. Name this scenario Staff/Customer Ratio of 1 to 100. Be sure to click the Restore Original Values option before leaving the Solver Results dialog box.
8. Use the Scenarios command to print a summary of each saved scenario. In the Scenario Manager dialog box, click *Staff/Customer Ratio of 1 to 80* and then click Summary. The report type you want is scenario summary, and the result cell is A16.
9. Create a custom header that has your name left aligned and the file name right aligned for the Scenario Summary worksheet. Change the orientation of the page to landscape.
10. Save the workbook using the same name (Excel, EPA 02) and print it.
11. Close the Excel, EPA 02 workbook.

Assessment 3

1. Open Excel Worksheet 09.
2. Save the workbook using the Save As command and name it Excel, EPA 03.

3. Create a custom header that has your name left aligned and the file name right aligned.
4. This worksheet lists some basic information on many of the cruises offered by the travel agency Travel Advantage. You want to create two filters for the list, save them as macros, and create a third macro that displays all the records. Then you will customize a toolbar by creating three buttons to run each of the macros. Click anywhere in the list. Display the Visual Basic toolbar and then click the Record Macro button. When the Record Macro dialog box is displayed, name the macro Under_1500. Enter the letter **u** in the Shortcut key box. Click OK.
5. Use AutoFilter to display cruises on which the average price is less than $1,500.
6. Click the Stop Recording button.
7. Follow steps 4 through 6 to create a second macro that turns off the AutoFilter feature. Name the macro Display_all and enter **d** as a shortcut key.
8. Follow steps 4 through 6 to create a third macro that displays all the cruises that provide children's activities. Name the macro Children and enter **c** as a shortcut key.
9. Press Ctrl+d to display all the records.
10. Display the Forms toolbar. Click the Button button on the toolbar. When the mouse pointer turns into a crosshair, click and drag in the shaded blue area at the top of the worksheet to place the button. Assign the Under_1500 macro to this button. The button should be .40 inches high and .85 inches wide. Change the name on the button to Cruises Under $1500.
11. Create a second button and place it in the blue shaded area next to the first button. Assign the Children macro to this button. The button should be .40 inches high and .85 inches wide. Change the name on the button to Activities for Children.
12. Create a third button and place it in the blue shaded area next to the second button. Assign the Display_all macro to this button. The button should be .40 inches high and .85 inches wide. Change the name on the button to Display All.
13. Click the Activities for Children button. Print the Cruises worksheet.
14. Click the Display All button.
15. Click the Cruises Under $1500 button. Print the Cruises worksheet.
16. Click the Display All button.
17. Save the workbook using the same name (Excel, EPA 03) and close it.

Assessment 4

1. Open Excel Worksheet 10.
2. Save the workbook using the Save As command and name it Excel, EPA 04.
3. Create a custom header that has your name left aligned and the file name right aligned.
4. Redwood Community College offers some computer classes at two extensions. The head of the Computer Science Department on the main

campus wants the enrollment figures for both extensions. Two different instructors are in charge of each extension. You want to set up this worksheet as a shared worksheet so that each instructor can enter the appropriate enrollment figures. Then you will merge the two worksheets. Before you do that, however, you want to enter a comment. Attach the following comment to cell C10:

Since this is the first semester this course is being offered at the extensions, enrollment figures are expected to be low.

Resize the comment box so that all the text is displayed.

5. Set up the Excel, EPA 12 workbook as a shared workbook.
6. Start a second copy of Excel and open the Excel, EPA 04 workbook. Save this copy of the workbook using the Save As command and name it North Branch.
7. Key the following values in the cells indicated:

Cell	Value
B5	**185**
B6	**78**
B7	**123**
B8	**118**
B9	**69**
B10	**35**

8. Save the workbook using the same name (North Branch). Exit from the second copy of Excel.
9. Switch to the Excel, EPA 04 workbook.
10. Save this copy of the workbook using the Save As command and name it West Branch.
11. Key the following values in the cells indicated:

Cell	Value
C5	**210**
C6	**96**
C7	**162**
C8	**149**
C9	**112**
C10	**58**

12. Save the workbook using the same name (West Branch) and close it.
13. Open Excel, EPA 04. Merge the North Branch and West Branch workbooks into the Excel, EPA 04 workbook.
14. Remove the workbook from shared use.
15. Save the workbook using the same name (Excel, EPA 04) and print it.
16. Close the workbook.

WRITING activities

The following activities give you the opportunity to practice your writing skills along with demonstrating an understanding of some of the important Word and Excel features you have mastered in this and previous units. Use correct grammar, appropriate word choices, and clear sentence constructions.

Activity 1

The owner of the Waterfront Café wants to be able to project the amount of money the restaurant might make on any one night, depending on how many people are seated during the night and the average price each person spends on a meal. Prepare a worksheet that includes an appropriate title and a header with your name at the left margin and the file name at the right margin. Save the workbook using the file name Excel, Act E1. Use the Scenarios command to set up a scenario for holidays (which is when the restaurant tends to do very well), average nights, and slow nights. Use the following information for setting up the scenarios:

- The operating expense is $2,800, which is what it costs per evening to operate the restaurant.
- On holidays, the restaurant typically seats 725 people in an evening, and the average cost of each meal is $14.
- On an average night, the restaurant typically seats 600 people, and the average cost of each meal is $10.
- On a slow night, the restaurant typically seats 475 people, and the average cost of each meal is $8.

Each scenario should include the income for the evening, which would be the total amount of money taken in (the cost of each meal times the number of people seated) minus the operating expense for the evening.

Display and print each one of the scenarios (holidays, average nights, and slow nights). Create a scenario summary. On the Scenario Summary worksheet, create a custom header that prints your name at the left margin and the file name at the right margin. Print the Scenario Summary worksheet. Save the workbook again using the same file name (Excel, Act E1) and close it.

Activity 2

Import the text file Sheet Music.txt into an Excel worksheet starting in cell A1. The data in the Sheet Music.txt file is delimited. Tabs were used as the delimiters. The data format for all of the columns is text, except for the last column, *Price*, which is general. Save the file as an Excel workbook using the file name Excel, Act E2. This is a partial list of the Little Music Shop's sheet music inventory. Format the headings *Song Title*, *Artist*, *Instrument*, *Level*, and *Price* as bold. Sheet music by the Beatles has become quite popular. Adjust the width of the columns as needed. Use conditional formatting so that every "Beatles" entry is displayed as bold and red. Since you will be adding more records to this list, make sure the conditional formatting applies to the entire worksheet.

Create three drop-down lists for entering data into the list. One drop-down list is for the Instrument column, one for the Level column, and one for the Price column. There should be two items on the drop-down list for the Instrument column: *Piano* and *Guitar*. There should be three items on the drop-down list for the Level column: *Easy*, *Intermediate*, and *Hard*. There should be four items on the drop-down list for the Price column: *$1.95*, *$2.50*, *$3.25*, and *$3.95*. Include appropriate input and error messages for each drop-down list.

Add the following records to the list:

Song Title	Artist	Instrument	Level	Price
Can You Feel the Love Tonight?	**John, Elton**	**Piano**	**Easy**	**$1.95**
Can You Feel the Love Tonight?	**John, Elton**	**Piano**	**Intermediate**	**$2.50**
Can You Feel the Love Tonight?	**John, Elton**	**Guitar**	**Easy**	**$2.50**
Can You Feel the Love Tonight?	**John, Elton**	**Guitar**	**Intermediate**	**$3.25**
Can't Buy Me Love	**Beatles**	**Guitar**	**Intermediate**	**$2.50**
Can't Buy Me Love	**Beatles**	**Piano**	**Intermediate**	**$2.50**

Sort this list first by song title, next by instrument, and finally by level. Create a custom header that includes your name at the left margin and the file name at the right margin. Save the workbook again using the same file name (Excel, Act E2) and print it. Close the workbook.

Activity 3

Open workbook Excel, Act E2. Using the Save As command, name the workbook Excel, Act E3. Insert four rows above the list for a criteria range. Copy the labels for the list to the first blank row. Name the range of cells that includes the labels and the first blank row under them (A1:E2) *Criteria.* Create a macro that uses Advanced Filter to filter the list to a new location, starting in G5. Extract from the records all the songs by the Beatles written for the guitar. Include as part of the macro optimizing the column widths for the extracted records and deleting the words *Beatles* and *Guitar* from the criteria range. Create a second macro that deletes anything entered in the range of cells G5 through K100. Create a third macro that uses Advanced Filter to filter the list to a new location, starting in G5. Extract from the records all the songs written for the piano that are easy. Include as part of the macro optimizing the column widths for the extracted records and deleting the words *Piano* and *Easy* from the criteria range.

Create a command button on the worksheet for each macro. Give each button an appropriate name. Filter the list using the command button that displays all the songs by the Beatles for the guitar. Print the list. Delete the extracted records using the appropriate command button. Filter the list using the command button that displays all the songs for the piano that are easy. Print the list. Delete the extracted records using the appropriate command button.

A music teacher has requested a list of sheet music that is for guitar and by the Beatles. Filter the list again using the appropriate command button. Start Word. Write a business letter to the instructor thanking him for his inquiry. The address for The Little Music Shop is 459 Sundance Square, Boulder, Colorado 80301. If you want, you can use The Little Music Shop's logo, which is the file Lilmusic.tif, as part of the letterhead. The name and address of the teacher requesting the information is Rodman Bates, 2285 10th Street, Boulder, Colorado 80301. Copy the filtered list from Excel into the business letter. Save the completed letter and name it Word, Act E3. Print and then close Word, Act E3. Display all the records in Excel using the appropriate command button. Save the list again using the same file name (Excel, Act E3) and close it.

INTERNET project

The Books Galore bookstore is starting a special reading group for mothers and their daughters who are ages 9 to 12. Make sure you are connected to the Internet and then explore the following two sites:

- www.amazon.com
- www.barnesandnoble.com

Each of these sites provides a special section for "Kids." In each of these sections, you can search for books that are of particular interest to children ages 9 to 12. The reading group is going to focus on historical adventure books. Use the keywords **adventure and history** to search these Web sites for books that would appeal to girls ages 9 to 12. Select at least five books you think the mothers and daughters would enjoy reading. Take notes on the name of the book, the author, a brief description of what the book is about, and the price.

In Word prepare an announcement for the reading group. The announcement should include the name of each book and a brief description of what the book is about. If you want, you can use the Books Galore logo, which is the file Booksgal.tif, as part of the announcement. The reading group is going to meet from 7:00 P.M. to 8:30 P.M. the first Monday of the month from October through February and is open to mothers and their daughters ages 9 to 12. The reading group will meet at Books Galore. The address of Books Galore is 138 Waterhouse Street, Cambridge, Massachusetts. The telephone number is (607) 555-1221. Print the announcement.

In Excel prepare a worksheet that lists each book's title, author, and price. Books Galore wants to put this worksheet on their Web site. Publish this worksheet on the Web as a noninteractive worksheet. Provide it with an appropriate title. Print the Web page.

JOB study

You have been asked to review the first quarter report for Thaxton Industries, and to prepare a revised report presentation to company management. Open FURNITURE from Unit 1. Click the *Qtr 1* worksheet tab. Trace precedents to determine if there are errors in the formulas or functions. Turn off Trace Precedents. Create a macro, called Thaxton, which will select the print area for the Year-End worksheet as all the cells containing data; change the page layout to landscape; and change the number of copies to 2. Save the file as THAXTON. Assign a macro button to be placed on the top right corner of the Year-End worksheet tab—next to Thaxton Industries. Assign this macro to a command button to be placed on the Standard toolbar. Edit the macro to change the background color of the title, Thaxton Industries, to green with white lettering. Save the file and print your copies.

INDEX